IMMIGRATION LAW A
SOCIAL JUSTICE

2020 Case and Statutory Supplement

IMMIGRATION LAW AND SOCIAL JUSTICE

2020 Case and Statutory Supplement

Bill Ong Hing

Professor of Law and Migration Studies
Director of the Immigration and Deportation
Defense Clinic
University of San Francisco, School of Law

Jennifer M. Chacón

Professor of Law
University of California, Los Angeles School of Law

Kevin R. Johnson

Dean and Mabie-Apallas Professor of Public Interest Law
and Chicana/o Studies
University of California, Davis School of Law

Wolters Kluwer

Published by Wolters Kluwer in New York.

Wolters Kluwer Legal & Regulatory U.S. serves customers worldwide with CCH, Aspen Publishers, and Kluwer Law International products. (www.WKLegaledu.com)

To contact Customer Service, e-mail customer.service@wolterskluwer.com, call 1-800-234-1660, fax 1-800-901-9075, or mail correspondence to:

Wolters Kluwer
Attn: Order Department
PO Box 990
Frederick, MD 21705

Printed in the United States of America.

1 2 3 4 5 6 7 8 9 0

ISBN 978-1-5438-1575-7

About Wolters Kluwer Legal & Regulatory U.S.

Wolters Kluwer Legal & Regulatory U.S. delivers expert content and solutions in the areas of law, corporate compliance, health compliance, reimbursement, and legal education. Its practical solutions help customers successfully navigate the demands of a changing environment to drive their daily activities, enhance decision quality and inspire confident outcomes.

Serving customers worldwide, its legal and regulatory portfolio includes products under the Aspen Publishers, CCH Incorporated, Kluwer Law International, ftwilliam.com and MediRegs names. They are regarded as exceptional and trusted resources for general legal and practice-specific knowledge, compliance and risk management, dynamic workflow solutions, and expert commentary.

CONTENTS

Contents

Contents

PREFACE

From its beginning, the Trump administration has maintained a relentless onslaught of new immigration enforcement policies and procedures in its effort to resist the changing demographics of the nation and the nature of who gains entry into our borders. Our text was able to include early analysis of such things as the Muslim ban, attacks on family immigration categories, the rescission of prosecutorial discretion memoranda, and the attack on sanctuary jurisdictions. However, since the publication of the text, the assault has intensified and the Supreme Court has provided traction to many of the administration's actions. The third iteration of the Muslim ban was upheld by the Court, as was a maneuver to reallocate Defense Department funding toward efforts to build "The Wall." The rescission of the Deferred Action for Childhood Arrivals (DACA) program has been ordered and Temporary Protected Status (TPS) has been terminated for more than 200,000 recipients. Regulations have been promulgated to deny lawful residence status to those who are "likely to become a public charge" due to food stamp use or housing assistance. Expedited removal without an immigration court hearing can now be imposed on undocumented immigrants who have resided anywhere in the country for less than two years. And attorneys general Jeff Sessions and William Barr overturned BIA precedent to make it harder for applicants to qualify for asylam based on domestic violence or threats against family members.

Many of the most high profile changes have been imposed at the border. A so-called Migrant Protection Protocol, aka Remain in Mexico Policy, has required thousands of would-be asylum seekers to remain in dangerous Mexican cities across the border. Those who attempt to enter without inspection are deemed ineligible to apply for asylum. Asylum will be denied if the applicant did not first apply for asylum in any third country through which they first crossed. Regulations have been proposed that would allow indefinite detention of migrant families with children. For many months beginning at the end of 2017, migrant children were separated from their parents; the excuse was a zero-tolerance policy of criminally prosecuting their parents for illegal entry and the argument that the children had to be taken away because they could not be in criminal custody with their parents.

Virtually all of the administration's efforts have met with legal and social resistance. This has led to scores of judicial decisions and scholarly analyses from us to choose from to include in this supplement. We are living in unprecedented times that challenge the commitment, strength, and creativity of social justice advocates. No matter what the outcome of legal challenges (e.g., this term the Supreme Court will decided the fate of DACA recipients) and the 2020 election, much damage has been done to our institutions and the psyche of immigrant communities that will take years from which to recover. Today's students of immigration law will be leading those efforts of recovery.

Bill Ong Hing
Jennifer M. Chacón
Kevin R. Johnson

October 2019

Chapter 1

AN INTRODUCTION TO IMMIGRATION LAW THROUGH A SOCIAL JUSTICE LENS

II. Background and Brief History on Immigration Flows and Policies

At page 20, after the Notes and Questions, add:

For a summary timeline of some U.S. immigration laws and events, *see* U.S. Immigration Timeline, History.Com, May 14, 2019, at https://www. history.com/topics/immigration/immigration-united-states-timeline and Major U.S. Immigration Laws, 1790 – Present, Migration Policy Institute, Mar. 2013, at https://www.migrationpolicy.org/research/timeline-1790

VII. Morality of Immigration Restrictions

At page 91, prior to the Notes and Questions.

A great deal of "moral outrage" has been expressed over the separation of migrant children from their parents, highlighted over the summer of 2018. *See, e.g.*, Ashly Fetters, *The Moral Failure of Family Separation, To separate children from their parents is an offense against nature and civilized society*, THE ATLANTIC, Jan. 13, 2019. That led to greater indignation over the terrible conditions that children have been detained. For example, New York Re. Alexandria Ocasio-Cortez labeled the facilities "dehumanizing" where a "violent culture" inside CBP existed. *See* Ciara Nugent, *Democratic Lawmakers Outraged by 'Dehumanizing' Conditions at Migrant Detention Centers*, TIME MAGAZINE, July 2, 2019.

QUESTIONS

What effect have these expressions of moral outrage had?

Chapter 2

THE IMMIGRATION SOCIAL JUSTICE LAWYER

Add the following at the end of the chapter at page 151:

IV. Race and Race-Conscious Lawyering

Adequately studying and practicing immigration law requires us to mindful of race and race-conscious lawyering. In Chapter 1, part III, we reviewed how racism has been institutionalized and implemented in the immigration laws. Also, who can deny that racism plays a big role in Donald Trump's views on immigration policy and enforcement.

We should also be mindful of cross-racial and cross-cultural issues in practicing immigration law and relationships with our clients and immigrant communities. Consider these views:

Bill Ong Hing, *Raising Personal Identification Issues of Class, Race, Ethnicity, Gender, Sexual Orientation, Physical Disability, and Age in Lawyering Courses,* 45 STAN. L. REV. 1401 (1993).

. . .

I. WHY AN EFFECTIVE COMMUNITY LAWYER MUST BE CONSCIOUS OF AND SENSITIVE TO THE CLASS, RACE, ETHNICITY, GENDER, SEXUAL ORIENTATION, PHYSICAL DISABILITY, AND AGE OF THE VARIOUS PLAYERS IN THE LEGAL ENVIRONMENT

As I stated above, an effective community lawyer must be aware of the personal identification differences of the various players involved in a case. Imagine the following situation: I am a twenty-seven-year-old male, Chinese American lawyer who is hired as the housing attorney for the East Palo Alto Community Law Project, located in East Palo Alto, California. East Palo Alto is a poor, small, incorporated community located adjacent to several affluent communities. In 1950 East Palo Alto had fewer than 2,000 residents and almost no African Americans. The population grew to 15,000 by 1960, with about 3,300 African Americans. By 1980, the city of 18,850 was about 64 percent African American and 13 percent Latino. Today, almost a third of the population is Latino. The Law Project is a community poverty law office which handles housing, public benefits, and education related cases. Suppose that one of my first clients is Ms. Pierce, a 30 year old, single, African American woman who has two children. She has sought my help because her apartment is in terrible shape. There are plumbing problems and roach infestation, not all the burners on the stove work, and plaster is falling away in certain parts of the unit, and she cannot get the manager of the building to fumigate and make necessary repairs. In addition to the manager, there are an array of possible players in this case. Other tenants, the building owner, the health inspector, tenant rights advocates, rent board officials, Ms. Pierce's children, and media reporters come to mind.

In order to be sensitive to personal identification differences in the case, I must consider several factors while representing Ms. Pierce. The class, race, and gender differences between Ms. Pierce and me have a definite impact on our rapport. Certainly, most clients experience some difficulty in confiding in a stranger- lawyer, but here, that difficulty may be exaggerated, as I am of a different class than Ms. Pierce, a low income client. This class difference is likely to be apparent even if I were from a poor background myself, because my poor background would likely be different from that of Ms. Pierce's and, in reality, my education has changed me, especially in the eyes of Ms. Pierce. I must be conscious of my manner of speech and the setting in which the interview is conducted. In attempting to develop a rapport with Ms. Pierce, I must be aware of the subject matter of any small talk. The difference in our racial and ethnic backgrounds may also make it more or less likely for her to open up to me. Our gender difference is a variable in our rapport as well. However, by knowing more about her race and culture and by being cognizant of our differences, I may avoid making inappropriate assumptions and establishing false expectations and thereby improve my ability to communicate with her.

This attorney-client hypothetical illustrates why training in dealing with personal identification differences is important to the success the community lawyer. Every client is unique, and the effect of identification differences will vary from client to client. However, I am convinced of the need to be conscious of and sensitive to these differences in the development of all attorney-client relationships.

An attorney who differs from a client in personal identification terms can be effective, but must be conscious of these differences and work towards developing the necessary rapport. This rapport can be critical to the success of the relationship and the outcome of the case. An attorney who is out of touch on these issues may be able to get by and even achieve good results for clients. However, learning about identification differences and understanding their potential significance can only enhance the attorney-client relationship and the attorney's effectiveness. Even if one is skeptical of their significance, most people will recognize the value of being tactful when confronting at least one of the following issues: class, race, ethnicity/culture, gender, sexual orientation, disability, or age difference. For example, most attorneys realize that sensitivity to gender difference with the client can help the relationship. Practicing and learning how to deal with that difference is the honing of a skill helpful to the practice of law. Similarly, developing an approach in the case of racial or cultural differences is also useful, especially when the client may have strong separatist feelings and the attorney would benefit from understanding the source of that sentiment.

Some individuals may view all this as a matter of common sense. But the truth is that most young community lawyers need training on how to respond to personal identification issues. We all have opinions on these matters, but we have had little opportunity to review these issues in the critical format of the classroom. Common sense, without training, is dangerously fashioned by our own class, race, ethnicity/culture, gender, and sexual background. What we think of as common sense may make little sense or even be offensive to someone of a different identification background. Thus, the opportunity to learn and discuss different approaches with the help of different perspectives from readings, the opinions of others, and self-critique is unique.

Continuing the hypothetical example of the Chinese American attorney and the African American client, one can imagine that personal identification differences with other players will impact the case as well. In the interaction of lawyer and/or client with the manager, the apartment owner, the health inspector, other tenants, tenants' rights advocates, and rent board officials, these differences will affect the cooperation, ability to communicate, and receptivity to unique perspectives. For example, if one strategy which Ms. Pierce and I conclude is worth pursuing involves contacting other tenants in the building in order to form a tenants group, the fact that some tenants are Spanish speaking, undocumented immigrants will be quite important to the success of such organizing. Communication problems have to be solved if those tenants don't speak English and neither Ms. Pierce nor I speak Spanish. Ms. Pierce and I will have to deal with the fact that some tenants may be biased against undocumented workers or non-English speakers. All tenants who are asked to organize may fear retaliatory eviction by the owner, but undocumented tenants might also fear being reported to immigration officials. In addition, suppose that two tenants supportive of a tenants' organization are a lesbian couple who has been ostracized by many other tenants in the building. Ms. Pierce and I would need to sensitize other tenants to accept homosexual lifestyles.

In short, understanding personal identification differences and how to manage them is integral to my vision of good community lawyering and my approach to the Lawyering for Social Change curriculum at Stanford. Similar to training in alternative approaches to legal problems, training on identification issues, working in partnership with the client, working with community allies, and respecting the client's own talents contributes to establishing an attorney-client relationship that is not simply another subordinating experience for the client, but is productive.

. . .

Tammi Wong, *Race-Conscious Community Lawyering-Practicing Outside the Box*, Clearinghouse Rev. J. of Pov. & Law (2008)

The growing cultural diversity throughout the country is leading to the forced integration of cultural, social, and political mores between people and systems in the United States. Over time the interaction of cultural differences will result, I hope, in a more tolerant and aware society. However, the newly emerging multiracial communities in states other than California and New York lead to a tension between cultural isolation and acculturation and assimilation. This tension comes from adjustment by new population groups to the structure of American society and is found not only between ethnic and racial population groups but also within ethnic population groups themselves. Nonnative arrivals struggle in adapting to a sudden upheaval of norms: structural, cultural, social, and political. Public interest advocates can decrease the burden placed on newly arrived population groups to adapt to American society. We can also create awareness about our society's obligation to incorporate values and practices of diverse population groups into our own systems and decision making. Here I describe community lawyering as a strategy to develop cultural competence between our client population and the systems with which our clients interact by providing them with the tools and resources necessary to establish a presence in their communities. Citing the Sacramento Hmong Mediation Council as an example, I discuss some community-lawyering principles that can apply to any racial or ethnic population for whom we provide advocacy.

Background

Historically, Hmong people experienced persecution by the Chinese, French, and Communist government of Laos. They most recently became refugees after serving for the U.S. Central Intelligence Agency in the Vietnam War and were forced to flee their native country of Laos to avoid persecution by the Vietnamese and Laotian governments. The migration from Laos, to Thai refugee camps, to life in the United States since 1975 has been traumatic for many Hmong. The multistage resettlement and geographic shift to the United States created tension between young and old, between men and women, and among clans. The trauma is compounded by the forced interaction among Hmong people, law enforcement, social services, and the American courts. The Hmong community gains its strength from culture, but the community began to break down in America as the Hmong were no longer isolated from other population groups and systems as they were in Laos or Thailand.

One method the Hmong community concluded could help acculturate its members to American structures, but simultaneously maintain its culture, was to incorporate Western legal and cultural principles into their cultural dispute resolution system. The traditional model of Hmong dispute resolution is embedded in the clan-based structure of the community. The system includes family elders, clan elders, and council elders. Family and clan elders function as negotiators who listen and attempt to resolve a variety of intra- and interclan disputes. For more complex disputes or interclan disputes, a council representing each of the clans gathers to determine how to resolve the problem. Much like the role of the judge in American courts, the elders hear evidence and ask questions in an endeavor to seek the truth, allocate fault, and determine the resolution or punishment. As more Hmong people had contact with the American court system, they realized that they were not legally bound by the elders' decisions. The strength of the community began to break down as conflicts arose between a system that recognized cultural values but whose decisions were not legally binding and a system whose decisions were legally enforceable but not culturally competent.

Principles of Community Lawyering

Community lawyering, as a skill, is not the natural instinct of the new public interest lawyer. With the limited practical experience we gain in law school, our expectations are often to use the traditional model of lawyering to seek justice for our clients. This model describes our roles as litigators, negotiators of claims, and counselors to clients in their transactional or dispute resolution decision making. In a practice that emphasizes one-on one attorney-client relationships, the traditional direct service strategy alone creates a dependence on the attorney as the holder of the knowledge necessary to solve the problem. The traditional methods can benefit our clients and their legal needs but may not lead to the fulfillment of many of our legal aid goals such as empowering our clients to identify and defeat the causes of poverty.

The concept behind community lawyering is to develop inside the client population a sustainable knowledge base that allows the population to build foundations for opportunity from within. The attorney is a tool people can choose to use in creating their own resources for achieving equality or negotiating the systems with which poor people come into contact on a regular basis. Community lawyering has many names: collaborative lawyering, community development, client empowerment, and lay lawyering. The common thread among them is that the clients, not the attorneys, play a central role in resolving the issues that have an impact on their opportunities to succeed.

Another critical component of community lawyering is creating cultural competence—a set of beliefs, values, and skills built into a structure that enables one to negotiate cross-cultural situations in a manner that does not force one to assimilate to the other. Without this competence, the systems with which our clients interact will continue to exclude them from an equal opportunity to utilize the systems as they were designed to serve people in America. A lack of cultural competence is to ignore that diversity in beliefs, values, and attitudes influences how people determine their self-worth and abilities to interact within American society. Legal aid programs are no exception to institutions that need to be culturally competent and must examine how we are providing service to communities of color. So that groups understand how to adapt to their surroundings, cultural competence about American structures and values must be developed within our client communities. In the case of the Hmong dispute resolution program, we would aim for the court to be cognizant of the values of the Hmong refugee community and consider them both in their personal interactions as well as their decision making. Similarly we would want the refugee community to be aware of how the law determines value and fault so that its members can access the courts for their purposes.

Entrance into the Community

By definition, a community lawyer is part of the community. The traditional model of lawyering places the burden on the client to seek out the attorney. If the client does not make it to the attorney, the attorney does not know, or must seek out, the client. Alternatively, under the community-lawyering model, the attorney would leave the office and attempt to integrate herself into the communities served. In doing so, she is in a position of keeping her finger on the pulse of community issues as they affect particular sectors of the population. By building a relationship with people, before her services are needed, she becomes accessible to people who otherwise would not have a legal advocate as part of their repertoire.

Often the attorney does not belong to the community she is attempting to serve. She must become conscious of her own biases and instinct to take the lead in the situation. In what is termed as "mindful lawyering," the attorney can better approach the community by understanding the need to develop adequate attorney client communication to prevent divisiveness. She must then train herself in the skills of listening without judgment and speaking without offending the community's sensibilities.

Advocates must recognize that we, too, are guided by our own stereotypes. We are not consciously activating our stereotypes to influence our work, but our subconscious application of them can have an impact on our effectiveness as community lawyers. Social cognition theory posits that the brain takes shortcuts in order to be more efficient. Based on our previous experiences, exposure, and information gathering, the brain creates categories of characteristics which, when activated by certain stimuli, help us draw conclusions about what it is we see.18 One of the first exercises in community lawyering is taking the time to become aware of the stereotypes we hold about our clients and how they are activated. By becoming aware, we can be less inhibited by our need to assert the "attorney" in us and listen to how people articulate their needs.

As part of its Race Equity Project, our program, Legal Services of Northern California (LSNC), decided to explore why Asian and Pacific Islanders were underutilizing their services despite a quarter of the population living in poverty. Not native to Sacramento, advocates began their inquiry by visiting the community based organizations that provide social services to the Asian and Pacific Islander community. The legal services advocates used previous connections, word of mouth, and the phone book to make appointments with community-based organizations in the county to survey the needs of low-income Asian and Pacific Islanders. Some organizations welcomed the advocates, and others were suspicious of contacts from unfamiliar people. The advocates investigated the legal needs and maintained contact with the community-based organizations to create ways for the advocates to become an as-needed resource to the service population.

The range of needs was great: language competence, public benefits, immigration, and accessible legal services. The advocates worked to integrate themselves into some community-based organizations to build a bond with the organizations. By having a physical presence, getting to know staff, and maintaining regular communication, the advocates began to gain trust. Here the advocates and service providers developed cultural competence, one about the other, to understand how to articulate the community's needs. By becoming conscious of the differences among ethnic Asian population groups, the ethnic background of advocates themselves, and the legal culture, the advocates and community-based organizations could better express the role of a legal advocate and how the advocates and community-based organizations could work together. Mindful of asserting their privilege of class, education, and notions of justice, the advocates let go of their instinct to tell the community what the community needed.

From this outreach, one LSNC attorney developed a close working relationship with the Hmong community in Sacramento to create a culturally appropriate dispute resolution program. The dynamics among the normally highly isolated Hmong community in Sacramento were changing as people became more settled in America and the Office for Refugee Resettlement funded their resettlement. Faced with a lot of negative press, Hmong leaders were grappling with how to adjust to systems of justice that did not correspond with cultural practices. The timely legal services outreach allowed Hmong leaders to develop an understanding of the American legal system and LSNC to develop a greater awareness of one of its client groups.

Building a Fundamental Knowledge Base Within the Community

Community lawyering involves working with clients to assist them in navigating the ways about immediate problems. One goal is to leave behind a knowledge base in the community so that people can take their seat at the table when political, social, and economic decisions are being made. A community lawyer recognizes that the needs of the community may not be legal in the traditional sense: that litigation or related advocacy may not always be the solution. The lawyer recognizes that her time with any particular client population is finite and that she will eventually leave or be taken away. Part of the solution then becomes working with community members to create awareness of methods to develop and implement resources that enable people to interact with political systems and government agencies.

Through community town hall meetings, LSNC learned that one of the challenges in the Hmong community was interacting with the court system. Primarily in family court, Hmong people did not understand—because of language and cultural barriers—court processes, proceedings, and decision making. Through the traditional legal model, we assessed the potential for a language access lawsuit under federal and state civil rights laws. The Hmong community resisted adversarial measures and requested instead that we assist them in bettering their cultural dispute resolution process so that it could be endorsed by the California court system and laws.

Our program conducted extensive training about Western mediation, California law, and court systems for many Hmong community members and elders. Language, age, and gender were challenges faced. How could an English-speaking person describe the principles of mediation, concepts of justice, and fairness to primarily elder Hmong men whose perception of justice and fairness differed? How could a young non-Hmong female earn the trust of a community where she was an outsider? Through months of trial and error, the community and the advocate patiently worked together to teach each other about dispute resolution processes and value-motivated outcomes. The advocate learned about Hmong systems and how to analogize Western systems so that they made sense to Hmong people.

A small delegation of Hmong community members and attorneys working with them traveled to St. Paul, Minnesota, to learn about the Hmong mediation program there. The idea behind the trip was for both the community members and the attorneys to interact and learn from Minnesota Hmong people, lawyers, and judges about how to create a program. By maintaining the client-lawyer dynamic, the Hmong delegates were able to inform, translate for, and gain acceptance by, the Hmong community in St. Paul. The attorney delegates were able similarly to inform, translate for, and gain acceptance by, the judicial and legal community—all were players in developing the Minnesota program. Together the team could bring back information to Sacramento to develop a local model.

Equipped with the history and knowledge from Minnesota, the Sacramento delegation returned ready to build a program. The seemingly slow progress of the program development thus far had been purposeful. We hoped that, by involving the Hmong leaders in developing a community resource, training about principles of Western mediation and creating a knowledge base about program development, Hmong people could increase their skill sets and create a meaningful service in their community.

In essence, for the attorney to develop a knowledge base in the community, she acted as a translator. By first developing her own foundation of knowledge about Hmong culture, she was able to translate the legal terms and concepts into terms and concepts that created a better understanding among the Hmong community about how to maintain its cultural practices and incorporate California law and dispute resolution processes. By learning about the Hmong language and culture from Hmong people, she could understand better how the community described its practices and she could then try to make the American system of justice more comprehensible.

2. The Immigration Social Justice Lawyer

Developing Community Relations

Sometimes the role of the advocate is to negotiate relationships, or to guide discussion using her unique role as an outsider. LSNC and the Hmong group could not be the only players in the development of the cultural mediation program. What the Hmong leaders sought was an established relationship with the judicial system to legitimize their decisions. However, they did not have the connections to the judicial systems, resources to develop a viable nonprofit incorporation, and finances. What they also lacked was perspective on how to maintain their own cultural practices while interacting with Western ones. One service we could provide was to broker relationships and discussion between the Hmong group and our resources as well as facilitating discussion within the Hmong community regarding acculturation.

Knowing that partnership with the state superior court for Sacramento County was crucial, we set out to determine what the court's requirements would be to adopt a Hmong mediation program as one of its alternate dispute resolution resources. Using the long-standing relationship between LSNC and the bench, we surveyed judicial officers to find out how the court understood Hmong culture, where culture could serve a role in judicial rulings, and what principles of equity the court would refuse to accept as a cultural norm. We learned that, based on the press or their limited interaction with Hmong people through the court system, some judges had misperceptions about Hmong values. Many indicated that they believed partnering with the Hmong community to raise awareness among the bench about this community would assist them in making the court more accessible and in making more culturally competent decisions. One judge with close ties to Hmong people committed to adopting the mediation program as one of her community-focused projects.

The first community relationship we brokered was between Hmong men and Hmong women. Traditionally women are very well respected within Hmong families. However, when a family decision is presented, the male presents the decision on behalf of the family. The court refused to consider the Hmong mediation program if women were not equally allowed to speak as men. LSNC and the Hmong mediation team met to discuss gender roles, to consider if women mediators would decrease the acceptance of the program within the community, and to identify women mediators. We were cautious to facilitate the discussion by sharing American concepts of gender roles without disrespecting those of Hmong people and without imposing or influencing the committee's decision to include women for the sole reason of obtaining the court's blessing. The planning team ultimately determined that women mediators would not fundamentally change the culture and successfully recruited women to the team.

The second community relationship we brokered was between Hmong elders and younger generation Hmong. Traditionally Hmong clan elders are the arbiters of dispute between people. Our work with both Hmong elders and Hmong youth made clear that a major source of tension throughout the transition to life in the

11

United States was between generations. The younger generation, after learning in school, realized that some of the Hmong ways conflicted with American values of family, freedom, and fairness. As the younger generation struggled with negotiating traditional Hmong family and American ways, the elder generation struggled to maintain cultural methods and values. This generational strain led to conflicts—the type of dispute that a culturally appropriate dispute resolution model could resolve if it were cognizant of both Hmong culture and American culture. Again, the advocate's role was to walk the fine line between observing as an outsider to offer context and avoiding undue influence during community decision making. The planning team determined that a multigenerational team would benefit the program and be diversified by age.

LSNC brokered relationships between other community organizations and the Hmong community. Asian Legal Services Outreach is partnered with the mediation planning committee to provide financial support and legal advice and consultation. Asian Resources Incorporated is a partner incubating the mediation program and providing infrastructure for meetings and fund-raising. The Superior Court, County of Sacramento, Community Focused Court Planning Committee works with the mediation program to conduct training about court rules and processes within particular jurisdictions, currently in the family law court.

The uniqueness of doing community lawyering is that we serve in roles we are not used to playing. We must take crash courses in language and culture to be more cognizant of community politics, values, and systems. However, by sharing an outsider perspective and brokering new relationships, community lawyers can open otherwise closed channels of communication and enable people and systems to coexist.

Framing Outcomes and Letting Go

The Sacramento Hmong mediation planning committee recently filed its articles of incorporation and is now a legal entity known as Sacramento Hmong Mediation Council. Drafting the bylaws, we trained the board of directors in establishing the foundations of a business. After years of training, planning, and meeting, Hmong community members and their partners created what, we hope, will be a culturally appropriate alternative dispute resolution program. The council is fund-raising, consulting with the court about cultural interpretations of events, and selecting and training its mediators. The partnerships with other legal and nonprofit service agencies are well developed and will continue until the council is a fully functioning not-for-profit organization.

So where does the attorney go now? For the past four years one advocate worked in one community and generated direct service cases, outreach, community economic development projects, and a mediation program. Does she still have a role? Can her energy be placed elsewhere to share a knowledge base with another community seeking to create its own resources to serve its needs? Will her old community let her go, or has she become so entrenched in its operation that she is now a community member? And if she is so entrenched, has she then defeated the goal of serving as a tool to build a foundation rather than a box that keeps the pieces together?

The difficulty—and the challenge—that the community lawyer faces is to let go. There comes a time when the community can and should be able to achieve its goals without her. When is that point reached? When the attorney and the clients are comfortable with the mutual relationship they have built, the attorney can go in one or the other direction. She can continue focusing her energy on a particular community, on their particular cases, and seeing to it that the community understands the multifaceted use of legal aid. Or she can begin to extract herself and redirect her energy to a new community where once again she places herself in the position of an outsider, uncomfortable with her presence, but making available her skills in an effort to empower another community to seek justice or equality. Either is a worthwhile goal. Both achieve the mission of empowering low-income people of color to identify their needs and develop and sustain resources to meet those needs.

* * *

Community lawyering at heart is the advocate being able to realize that before she is an attorney, she is a human being: perhaps poor herself once, an immigrant, of color, or simply seeking justice through her chosen career. We need to expose our ignorance about the people we serve, our inability to know the solutions to all problems, and our own class, social, and ethnic biases. Like any human relationship, community lawyering is reciprocal trust building that does not always need to be outcome-driven. In recognizing the humanness of our work, we can better develop relationships with our clients such that exposing their needs and knowledge gap is not an uncomfortable and invasive. Instead our awareness can equip our clients with strategies to bolster their voices for the opportunities they seek.

NOTES AND QUESTIONS

1. How are the concepts and ideas in these two readings relevant to immigration lawyers?

2. How do you prepare to represent a client who is of a different race or culture?

3. How do you prepare to represent a client with whom you need to use an interpreter?

Chapter 3

THE ADMINISTRATION OF IMMIGRATION LAW

IV. Immigration-Related Federal Agencies

A. Department of Homeland Security

At the top of page 159, after the first bullet, add the following:

ICE actually has two components: Homeland Security Investigations (HSI) and Enforcement and Removal Operations (ERO).[1] ERO generally carries out the immigration enforcement responsibilities of ICE, while HSI agents usually focus on human rights violations, human smuggling, trafficking, transnational gangs, counterfeit identity documents, and ev+en child pornography via the internet.[2] However, under the Trump administration, HSI is now mandated to make collateral immigration arrests of non-targeted individuals found at the scene of criminal violations.[3] *See also* the Immigrant Legal Resource Center's backgrounder on HSI at https://www.ilrc.org/sites/default/files/resources/hsi-backgrounder-2019_0.pdf

VI. Federalism and State Roles

B. Pro-Immigrant Laws

At the end of the chapter at page 246, insert the following:

Federal courts have upheld sanctuary ordinances enacted by San Francisco, Santa Clara County, and Philadelphia as well as California's state law, as you see in the next case. In this case, three California laws were attacked by the Trump administration's Department of Justice: AB 450, which requires employers to alert employees before federal immigration inspections; AB 103, which imposes

---

1. *Who We Are*, U.S. ICE, https://www.ice.gov/about.
2. *Id.*
3. Hamed Aleaziz, *Police alliance strained by raids*, SAN FRANCISCO CHRON., Apr. 30, 2017.

inspection requirements on facilities that house civil immigration detainees; and SB 54 (the state "sanctuary law"), which limits the cooperation between state and local law enforcement and federal immigration authorities.

UNITED STATES v. CALIFORNIA, et al.

921 F. 3d 865 (2019)

Before: MILAN D. SMITH, JR., PAUL J. WATFORD, and ANDREW D. HURWITZ, Circuit Judges.

OPINION

M. SMITH, Circuit Judge:

Defendant-Appellee State of California (California) enacted three laws expressly designed to protect its residents from federal immigration enforcement: AB 450, which requires employers to alert employees before federal immigration inspections; AB 103, which imposes inspection requirements on facilities that house civil immigration detainees; and SB 54, which limits the cooperation between state and local law enforcement and federal immigration authorities. Plaintiff-Appellant United States of America (the United States) challenged these enactments under the Supremacy Clause and moved to enjoin their enforcement. The district court concluded that the United States was unlikely to succeed on the merits of many of its claims, and so denied in large part the motion for a preliminary injunction.

The district court did not abuse its discretion when it concluded that AB 450's employee-notice provisions neither burden the federal government nor conflict with federal activities, and that any obstruction caused by SB 54 is consistent with California's prerogatives under the Tenth Amendment and the anticommandeering rule. We therefore affirm the district court's denial of a preliminary injunction as to these laws. We also affirm the denial of a preliminary injunction as to those provisions of AB 103 that duplicate inspection requirements otherwise mandated under California law. But we conclude that one subsection of AB 103—codified at California Government Code section 12532(b)(1)(C)—discriminates against and impermissibly burdens the federal government, and so is unlawful under the doctrine of intergovernmental immunity. . .

. . .

ANALYSIS

. . .

The doctrine of intergovernmental immunity is derived from the Supremacy Clause, U.S. Const., art. VI, which mandates that "the activities of the Federal Government are free from regulation by any state." *Boeing Co. v. Movassaghi*, 768 F.3d 832, 839 (9th Cir. 2014) (quoting *Mayo v. United States*, 319 U.S. 441, 445, 63 S.Ct. 1137, 87 L.Ed. 1504 (1943)). "Accordingly, state laws are invalid if they 'regulate[] the United States directly or discriminate[] against the Federal

3. The Administration of Immigration Law

Government or those with whom it deals.'" *Id.* (alterations in original) (quoting *North Dakota v. United States*, 495 U.S. 423, 435, 110 S.Ct. 1986, 109 L.Ed.2d 420 (1990) (plurality opinion)).

Under the doctrine of conflict preemption, "state laws are preempted when they conflict with federal law. This includes cases where 'compliance with both federal and state regulations is a physical impossibility,' and those instances where the challenged state law 'stands as an obstacle to the accomplishment and execution of the full purposes and objectives of Congress.'" *Arizona v. United States* (*Arizona II*), 567 U.S. 387, 399 (2012), 132 S.Ct. 2492 (citations omitted) (first quoting *Fla. Lime & Avocado Growers, Inc. v. Paul*, 373 U.S. 132, 142–43, 83 S.Ct. 1210, 10 L.Ed.2d 248 (1963); and then quoting *Hines v. Davidowitz*, 312 U.S. 52, 67, 61 S.Ct. 399, 85 L.Ed. 581 (1941)). The latter instances constitute so-called "obstacle preemption," and "[t]o determine whether obstacle preemption exists, the Supreme Court has instructed that we employ our 'judgment, to be informed by examining the federal statute as a whole and identifying its purpose and intended effects.'" *United States v. Arizona* (*Arizona I*), 641 F.3d 339, 345 (9th Cir. 2011). . . . The Court has emphasized that "[i]mplied preemption analysis does not justify a 'freewheeling judicial inquiry into whether a state statute is in tension with federal objectives'; such an endeavor 'would undercut the principle that it is Congress rather than the courts that preempts state law.' . . . [A] high threshold must be met if a state law is to be preempted for conflicting with the purposes of a federal Act." *Chamber of Commerce of U.S. v. Whiting*, 563 U.S. 582, 607, 131 S.Ct. 1968, 179 L.Ed.2d 1031 (2011). . .

I. AB 450

. . .

A. Intergovernmental Immunity

The United States contends that "AB 450's provisions impermissibly target and discriminate against federal immigration enforcement operations." It reasons that "[i]f any other entity—such as a state or federal regulator, or a private entity—inspects an employer's records, the employer would have no obligation under AB 450 to notify its employees," and thus that AB 450 impermissibly imposes a "unique regime" on the federal government.

This argument, however, extends intergovernmental immunity beyond its defined scope. The doctrine has been invoked, to give a few examples, to prevent a state from imposing more onerous clean-up standards on a federal hazardous waste site than a non-federal project, *Boeing*, 768 F.3d at 842–43; to preclude cities from banning only the U.S. military and its agents from recruiting minors, *United States v. City of Arcata*, 629 F.3d 986, 988, 990–92 (9th Cir. 2010); and to foreclose a state from taxing the lessees of federal property while exempting from the tax lessees of state property, *Phillips Chem. Co. v. Dumas Indep. Sch. Dist.*, 361 U.S.

376, 381–82, 387, 80 S.Ct. 474, 4 L.Ed.2d 384 (1960). Those cases dealt with laws that directly or indirectly affected the operation of a federal program or contract. The situation here is distinguishable—AB 450 is directed at the conduct of *employers*, not the United States or its agents, and no federal activity is regulated. We agree with California: "The mere fact that those notices contain information about federal inspections does not convert them into a burden on those inspections." Similarly, the mere fact that the actions of the federal government are incidentally *targeted* by AB 450 does not mean that they are incidentally *burdened*, and while the latter scenario might implicate intergovernmental immunity, the former does not. As the district court correctly recognized, to rule otherwise "would stretch the doctrine beyond its borders." *California I*, 314 F.Supp.3d at 1097.

. . .

B. Preemption

The United States also contends that AB 450's employee-notice provisions are preempted because they seek "to alter the manner in which the federal government conducts inspections, by imposing requirements that neither Congress nor the implementing agency saw fit to impose." We disagree. The cases to which the United States cites concerned either the disruption of a federal relationship or the undermining of a federal operation. Here, there is indisputably a federal relationship, but it is between federal immigration authorities and the employers they regulate[6]—*not* between employers and their employees. AB 450 impacts the latter relationship, not the former, and imposes no additional or contrary obligations that undermine or disrupt the activities of federal immigration authorities. In *Arizona II*, the Supreme Court observed that a "[c]onflict in technique can be fully as disruptive to the system Congress erected as conflict in overt policy." 567 U.S. at 406, 132 S.Ct. 2492 (alteration in original) (quoting *Amalgamated Ass'n of St., Elec. Ry. & Motor Coach Emps. of Am. v. Lockridge*, 403 U.S. 274, 287, 91 S.Ct. 1909, 29 L.Ed.2d 473 (1971)); *see also Crosby*, 530 U.S. at 376–77, 120 S.Ct. 2288 (finding preempted a state law "imposing a different, state system" that "undermines the President's intended statutory authority"). Here, by contrast, there is no "conflict in technique," because federal activity is not regulated.

AB 450's employee-notice provisions do not permit employers to hire individuals without federally defined authorization, or impose sanctions inconsistent with federal law, either of which *would* impermissibly "frustrate[] the purpose of the national legislation or impair[] the efficiency of those agencies of the Federal government." *Nash v. Fla. Indus. Comm'n*, 389 U.S. 235, 240, 88 S.Ct. 362, 19 L.Ed.2d 438 (1967). . .

II. AB 103

AB 103 authorizes the California Attorney General to inspect detention facilities that house civil immigration detainees. The United States contends that the law "impermissibly seeks to require facilities housing federal immigration detainees to cooperate with broad investigations that examine the due process provided to detainees and the circumstances surrounding the detainee's apprehension and transfer to the facility." Again, it invokes intergovernmental immunity and obstacle preemption.

A.   Intergovernmental Immunity

Like AB 450, AB 103 relates exclusively to federal conduct, as it applies only to "facilities in which noncitizens are being housed or detained for purposes of civil immigration proceedings in California." Cal. Gov't Code § 12532(a).[7] Unlike AB 450, AB 103 imposes a specialized burden on federal activity, as the district court recognized. *See California I*, 314 F.Supp.3d at 1093. That vital distinction renders the burdensome provisions of AB 103 unlawful under the doctrine of intergovernmental immunity.

Prior to the enactment of AB 103, California law already required periodic inspections of prisons and detainment facilities. *See* Cal. Penal Code § 6031.1 (mandating biennial inspections of "[h]ealth and safety," "[f]ire suppression preplanning," "[s]ecurity, rehabilitation programs, recreation, treatment of persons confined in the facilities, and personnel training," and visitation conditions, as well as the completion of subsequent reports). AB 103, however, does not merely replicate this inspection scheme; in addition to requiring "[a] review of the conditions of confinement," the enactment also calls for reviews of the "standard of care and due process provided to" detainees, and "the circumstances around their apprehension and transfer to the facility." Cal. Gov't Code § 12532(b)(1). These additional requirements burden federal operations, and *only* federal operations.[8]

. . .

That is not to say, however, that the United States is likely to succeed on the merits as to the *entirety* of AB 103. Only those provisions that impose an additional economic burden exclusively on the federal government are invalid under the doctrine of intergovernmental immunity.

California maintains that all of AB 103's requirements duplicate preexisting inspection demands imposed on state and local detention facilities. It points to regulations requiring its Board of State and Community Corrections (the Board) to inspect not only compliance with general health and safety standards—which are included in AB 103. . .

In the context of this appeal from the denial of a preliminary injunction, we accept California's limited construction. We therefore conclude that AB 103's due process provision likely does not violate the doctrine of intergovernmental immunity, and that the district court's denial of a preliminary injunction as to this provision should be affirmed. We note, however, that a broader reading of the term "due process" might empower the California Attorney General to scrutinize, say, an immigration judge's analysis, the results of the Board of Immigration Appeals, or other related court proceedings—all of which are well outside the purview of a state attorney general, and not duplicative of the inspection requirements otherwise imposed on California's state and local detention facilities.

That is not the end of our inquiry, for as the United States observes, California "does not even attempt to identify any provision of the pre-existing inspection scheme analogous to the unique requirement for immigration detainees that inspectors must examine the circumstances surrounding their apprehension and transfer to the facility." *See* Cal. Gov't Code § 12532(b)(1)(C). This is a novel requirement, apparently distinct from any other inspection requirements imposed by California law. The district court was therefore incorrect when it concluded that "the review appears no more burdensome than reviews required under California Penal Code §§ 6030, 6031.1." *California I*, 314 F.Supp.3d at 1093.

In light of this apparent factual error, and the district court's erroneous reliance on a de minimis exception to the doctrine of intergovernmental immunity, we reverse the district court's denial of a preliminary injunction as to California Government Code section 12532(b)(1)(C)—the provision of AB 103 requiring examination of the circumstances surrounding the apprehension and transfer of immigration detainees.

B. Preemption

The United States further argues that "even if AB 103's inspection regime had not discriminatorily targeted facilities holding federal immigration detainees, it still would be preempted by federal law." We disagree.

The cases on which the United States relies involved a far clearer interference with federal activity than AB 103 creates. . . .

The district court was correct when it concluded, "Given the Attorney General's power to conduct investigations related to state law enforcement—a power which [the United States] concedes—the Court does not find this directive in any way constitutes an obstacle to the federal government's enforcement of its immigration laws or detention scheme."...

III. SB 54

. . .

A. Preemption

The United States argues that SB 54 unlawfully obstructs the enforcement of federal immigration laws. It focuses on a provision of the law that prohibits California law enforcement agencies from "[t]ransfer[ring] an individual to immigration authorities unless authorized by a judicial warrant or judicial probable cause determination." . . .

We have no doubt that SB 54 makes the jobs of federal immigration authorities more difficult. The question, though, is whether that constitutes a "[c]onflict in technique" that is impermissible under the doctrine of obstacle preemption. . . .

3. The Administration of Immigration Law

The United States relies in part on our opinion in *Oregon Prescription Drug Monitoring Program v. DEA*, 860 F.3d 1228 (9th Cir. 2017), but that case is easily distinguished. There, a federal agency issued statutorily authorized subpoenas to a state agency, and the latter sought a declaration that it need not respond because of a state statute requiring "a valid court order" in all cases in which a subpoena is issued. *Id.* at 1231–32, 1236. We concluded that the state statute "stands as an obstacle to the full implementation of the [federal statute] because it 'interferes with the methods by which the federal statute was designed to reach [its] goal.'" *Id.* at 1236 (second alteration in original) (quoting *Gade*, 505 U.S. at 103, 112 S.Ct. 2374 (plurality opinion)). Here, by contrast, neither an administrative warrant issued by federal authorities nor any other provision of law identified by the United States *compels* any action by a state or local official. With the exception of § 1373(a), discussed below, the various statutory provisions to which the United States points direct *federal* activities, not those of state or local governments. *See* 8 U.S.C. §§ 1226, 1231.

. . .

In short, SB 54 does not directly conflict with any obligations that the INA or other federal statutes impose on state or local governments, because federal law does not actually mandate any state action (again, with the exception of § 1373, discussed below).

But that does not resolve the lingering issue of obstacle preemption. The United States notes that SB 54 requires federal officers to, "in effect, stake out a jail and seek to make a public arrest.... Arrests of aliens in public settings generally require five officers and present risks to the arresting officer and the general public." It contends that "Congress did not contemplate that, as a consequence of letting state detention proceed first, federal officers who sought to detain an alien for immigration purposes would need to race to the front of a local detention facility and seek to effectuate an arrest before the alien manages to escape." Compounding the problem, the United States further claims, are provisions of SB 54 that preclude agencies from providing personal information and release dates to immigration authorities. *See* Cal. Gov't Code § 7284.6(a)(1)(C)–(D). "So not only would California require DHS to stake out jails to detain aliens upon their release," the United States continues, "but California would require DHS to do so indefinitely because the agency would not otherwise know if and when any given alien would be released."

The district court concluded that this frustration does not constitute obstacle preemption:

> California's decision not to assist federal immigration enforcement in its endeavors is not an "obstacle" to that enforcement effort. [The United States'] argument that SB 54 makes immigration enforcement far more burdensome begs the question: more burdensome than what? The laws make enforcement more burdensome than it would be if state and local law enforcement provided immigration officers with their assistance. But refusing to help is not the same as impeding. If such

were the rule, obstacle preemption could be used to commandeer state resources and subvert Tenth Amendment principles.

. . . We agree. Even if SB 54 obstructs federal immigration enforcement, the United States' position that such obstruction is unlawful runs directly afoul of the Tenth Amendment and the anticommandeering rule.

B.   The Tenth Amendment and Anticommandeering Rule

. . .

Ultimately, we conclude that the specter of the anticommandeering rule distinguishes the case before us from the preemption cases on which the United States relies. Those cases concerned state laws that affirmatively disrupted federal operations by mandating action (or inaction) contrary to the status quo. In each, a state statute affirmatively instituted a regulatory scheme that conflicted with federal law, either by commission (for example, by applying differing standards or mandating affirmative action irreconcilable with federal law) or omission (by demanding inaction that directly conflicted with federal requirements). The solution to avoid conflict preemption was the same: invalidate the state enactment. In each case, the status quo would return — either no future conflicting action would be taken, or active compliance with federal law would recommence — and federal activity would no longer be obstructed.

Here, by contrast, invalidating SB 54 would *not* prevent obstruction of the federal government's activities, because the INA does not require any particular action on the part of California or its political subdivisions. Federal law provides states and localities the *option*, not the *requirement*, of assisting federal immigration authorities. SB 54 simply makes that choice for California law enforcement agencies.

. . .

Federal schemes are inevitably frustrated when states opt not to participate in federal programs or enforcement efforts. But the choice of a state to refrain from participation cannot be invalid under the doctrine of obstacle preemption where, as here, it retains the right of refusal. Extending conflict or obstacle preemption to SB 54 would, in effect, "dictate[] what a state legislature may and may not do," *Murphy*, 138 S.Ct. at 1478, because it would imply that a state's otherwise lawful decision *not* to assist federal authorities is made unlawful when it is codified as state law.

. . .

SB 54 may well frustrate the federal government's immigration enforcement efforts. However, whatever the wisdom of the underlying policy adopted by California, that frustration is permissible, because California has the right, pursuant to the anticommandeering rule, to refrain from assisting with federal efforts. The United States stresses that, in crafting the INA, Congress expected cooperation between states and federal immigration authorities. That is likely the case. But when questions of federalism are involved, we must distinguish between expectations and requirements. In this context, the federal government was free to *expect* as much as it wanted, but it could not *require* California's cooperation without running afoul of the Tenth Amendment.

3. The Administration of Immigration Law

. . .

C.   Intergovernmental Immunity
. . .

A finding that SB 54 violates the doctrine of intergovernmental immunity would imply that California *cannot* choose to discriminate against federal immigration authorities by refusing to assist their enforcement efforts—a result that would be inconsistent with the Tenth Amendment and the anticommandeering rule.

D.   Section 1373

Lastly, the United States contends that 8 U.S.C. § 1373 directly prohibits SB 54's information-sharing restrictions.

Section 1373 provides that "a Federal, State, or local government entity or official may not prohibit, or in any way restrict, any government entity or official from sending to, or receiving from, [DHS] information regarding the citizenship or immigration status, lawful or unlawful, of any individual." 8 U.S.C. § 1373(a). SB 54, in turn, expressly *permits* the sharing of such information, and so does not appear to conflict with § 1373. *See* Cal. Gov't Code § 7284.6(e) ("This section does not prohibit or restrict any government entity or official from sending to, or receiving from, federal immigration authorities, information regarding the citizenship or immigration status, lawful or unlawful, of an individual . . . pursuant to Section[] 1373."). But the United States argues that § 1373 actually applies to more information than just immigration status, and hence that SB 54's prohibition on sharing *other* information creates a direct conflict.

We disagree. Although the United States contends that "whether a given alien may actually be removed or detained by federal immigration authorities is, at a minimum, information regarding that alien's immigration status," the phrase "information regarding the citizenship or immigration status, lawful or unlawful, of any individual" is naturally understood as a reference to a person's legal classification under federal law, as the district court concluded.

. . .

In summation, the district court correctly concluded that "Section 1373 and the information sharing provisions of SB 54 do not directly conflict." . . .

NOTES AND QUESTIONS

1. How did the Ninth Circuit address the preemption and intergovernmental immunity challenges?

2. What role did the Tenth Amendment have in the decision?

Terminology.

Is there a problem with the term "sanctuary" ordinance or law? Michael Kagan thinks so.

. . . When immigrant rights advocates ask their local, state and university leaders to become "sanctuary cities," "sanctuary states," "sanctuary campuses," and so on, they carelessly hurt immigrants in places like Nevada, Texas, and Arizona. And there are a lot of immigrants in those states. People who mean to help immigrants are hurting them.

. . . When I say that advocates of "sanctuary" are hurting immigrants, I am criticizing myself as much as anyone else. In particular, I signed a letter to my own university asking that it declare itself to be a "sanctuary campus." Moreover, I am personally likely to support most of the specific policies associated with immigrant sanctuary campaigns. My criticism is not about specific policies. It is about the rhetoric and the labeling.

My central point is that calls for official "sanctuary" are rhetorical malpractice by immigrant advocates. These calls mislead both supporters and opponents, and ultimately reduce the political support for pro-immigrant policies at the local and state level. On the one hand, pro-sanctuary movements are rhetorically misleading because the label fails to accurately describe the actual policies that are usually included under the sanctuary umbrella. On the other hand, the sanctuary label is counterproductive because it turns off potentially persuadable voters, and makes a ripe target for demagoguery that is hostile to immigrants' interests.

These issues are critically important now, as I write this Essay in January 2018, because the Republican Party made fighting "sanctuary cities" a central part of its anti-immigrant policies in the first year of the Trump Administration. In 2017, Republican candidates loosely aligned with Trump echoed this line of attack in off-year elections.[3] Despite disappointing electoral results for Republicans, all signs indicate that "sanctuary" policies will be a prominent issue in 2018 congressional elections. This is certainly the case in my home state of Nevada, where leading Republican candidates for governor, lieutenant governor, attorney general, and U.S. Senate made opposition to "sanctuary" a central issue in their campaigns. Nevada Republicans have also used purported efforts to make Nevada a "sanctuary state" a justification for seeking special recall elections against several Democratic state senators. I take it as a given that these are forms of "dog-whistle politics," in which appeals to voters' racial anxieties are coded within a less overtly offensive argument. However, my central point is that sanctuary campaigns have also been a form of coded political rhetoric on the left, in that they tend to signify more than they deliver, which facilitates mobilization and enthusiasm from immigrant supporters. But this comes at a cost, precisely because it makes the dog-whistle on the right much louder. In effect, the political left validates the rhetoric of the political right.

. . . Despite the problematic terminology, some polling indicates that majorities will support sanctuary policies if they are framed in a certain way. An online poll of Floridians tested this, using the "sanctuary city" label explicitly. But rather than focus on people who have been arrested, or on ignoring federal requests, this poll framed questions around how localities should respond to pressure from the Trump

Administration. The answers were overwhelming. One question asked, "Should the federal government cut off funds to cities that provide sanctuary for illegal immigrants?" The majority said "no," by a fifty-two to thirty-six percent margin. Another asked, "Do you agree or disagree with Tampa becoming a Sanctuary City?" The answer was supportive of Tampa being a sanctuary, by a sixty-one to thirty-nine percent margin. The poll defined "sanctuary city" as a place that "offers safe harbor for undocumented immigrants." Not that these questions focused on the practical impact ("might otherwise be deported"), and did not imply defiance to federal laws. Instead, it focused on the federal government's efforts to pressure localities ("cut off funds").

The key is for immigrant advocates to be aware of the downside of the sanctuary label, even when the label cannot be avoided. The label is not an insurmountable obstacle, but it is a challenge which makes careful framing of issues all the more important. Most important, any strategy that hopes to win over the largest number of allies for immigrants in an electoral contest must be aware that some voters are confused about why illegal immigration happens, and do not inherently think that strict enforcement of the law is a bad thing. Such voters are potential allies for immigrants, but they are also potential allies for their opponents.

See Michael Kagan, *What We Talk About When We Talk About Sanctuary Cities*, 52 U.C. Davis L. Rev. 391, 391-93, 405-06 (2018).

Is there better terminology? Is "non-cooperation" any better?

Chapter 4

CITIZENSHIP

IV. Acquisition and Derivation

A. Acquisition of U.S. Citizenship By a Child Born Abroad

At page 296, after part 5, insert the following:

In the next case, the Supreme Court addressed the question of whether the acquisition of citizenship requirements unconstitutionally discriminated against unwed father.

Sessions v. Morales-Santana

137 S.Ct. 1678 (2017)

GINSBURG, J., delivered the opinion of the Court, in which ROBERTS, C.J., and KENNEDY, BREYER, SOTOMAYOR, and KAGAN, JJ., joined. THOMAS, J., filed an opinion concurring in the judgment in part, in which ALITO, J., joined. GORSUCH, J., took no part in the consideration or decision of the case.

Justice GINSBURG delivered the opinion of the Court.

I.

This case concerns a gender-based differential in the law governing acquisition of U.S. citizenship by a child born abroad, when one parent is a U.S. citizen, the other, a citizen of another nation. The main rule appears in 8 U.S.C. § 1401(a)(7) (1958 ed.), now § 1401(g) (2012 ed.). Applicable to married couples, § 1401(a)(7) requires a period of physical presence in the United States for the U.S.-citizen parent. The requirement, as initially prescribed, was ten years' physical presence prior to the child's birth, § 601(g) (1940 ed.); currently, the requirement is five years pre-birth, § 1401(g) (2012 ed.). That main rule is rendered applicable to unwed U.S.-citizen fathers by § 1409(a). Congress ordered an exception, however, for unwed U.S.-citizen mothers. Contained in § 1409(c), the exception allows an unwed mother to transmit her citizenship to a child born abroad if she has lived in the United States for just one year prior to the child's birth.

The respondent in this case, Luis Ramón **Morales–Santana**, was born in the Dominican Republic when his father was just 20 days short of meeting § 1401(a)(7)'s physical-presence requirement. Opposing removal to the Dominican Republic,

Morales–Santana asserts that the equal protection principle implicit in the Fifth Amendment entitles him to citizenship stature. We hold that the gender line Congress drew is incompatible with the requirement that the Government accord to all persons "the equal protection of the laws." Nevertheless, we cannot convert § 1409(c)'s exception for unwed mothers into the main rule displacing § 1401(a)(7) (covering married couples) and § 1409(a) (covering unwed fathers). We must therefore leave it to Congress to select, going forward, a physical-presence requirement (ten years, one year, or some other period) uniformly applicable to all children born abroad with one U.S.-citizen and one alien parent, wed or unwed. In the interim, the Government must ensure that the laws in question are administered in a manner free from gender-based discrimination.

A

We first describe in greater detail the regime Congress constructed. The general rules for acquiring U.S. citizenship are found in 8 U.S.C. § 1401, the first section in Chapter 1 of Title III of the Immigration and Nationality Act (1952 Act or INA), § 301, 66 Stat. 235–236. Section 1401 sets forth the INA's rules for determining who "shall be nationals and citizens of the United States at birth" by establishing a range of residency and physical-presence requirements calibrated primarily to the parents' nationality and the child's place of birth. § 1401(a) (1958 ed.); § 1401 (2012 ed.). The primacy of § 1401 in the statutory scheme is evident. Comprehensive in coverage, § 1401 provides the general framework for the acquisition of citizenship at birth. In particular, at the time relevant here, § 1401(a)(7) provided for the U.S. citizenship of

> "a person born outside the geographical limits of the United States and its outlying possessions of parents one of whom is an alien, and the other a citizen of the United States who, prior to the birth of such person, was physically present in the United States or its outlying possessions for a period or periods totaling not less than ten years, at least five of which were after attaining the age of fourteen years: *Provided*, That any periods of honorable service in the Armed Forces of the United States by such citizen parent may be included in computing the physical presence requirements of this paragraph."

Congress has since reduced the duration requirement to five years, two after age 14. § 1401(g) (2012 ed.).

Section 1409 pertains specifically to children with unmarried parents. Its first subsection, § 1409(a), incorporates by reference the physical-presence requirements of § 1401, thereby allowing an acknowledged unwed citizen parent to transmit U.S. citizenship to a foreign-born child under the same terms as a married citizen parent. Section 1409(c)—a provision applicable only to unwed U.S.-citizen mothers—states an exception to the physical-presence requirements of §§ 1401 and 1409(a). Under § 1409(c)'s exception, only one year of continuous physical presence is required before unwed mothers may pass citizenship to their children born abroad.

4. Citizenship

B

Respondent Luis Ramón **Morales–Santana** moved to the United States at age 13, and has resided in this country most of his life. Now facing deportation, he asserts U.S. citizenship at birth based on the citizenship of his biological father, José **Morales**, who accepted parental responsibility and included **Morales–Santana** in his household.

José **Morales** was born in Guánica, Puerto Rico, on March 19, 1900. Record 55–56. Puerto Rico was then, as it is now, part of the United States, see *Puerto Rico v. Sanchez Valle*, 579 U.S. _____, _____, 136 S.Ct. 1863, 1868–1869, 195 L.Ed.2d 179 (2016); 8 U.S.C. § 1101(a)(38) (1958 ed.) ("The term United States . . . means the continental United States, Alaska, Hawaii, Puerto Rico, Guam, and the [U.S.] Virgin Islands." (internal quotation marks omitted)); § 1101(a)(38) (2012 ed.) (similar), and José became a U.S. citizen under the Organic Act of Puerto Rico, ch. 145, § 5, 39 Stat. 953 (a predecessor to 8 U.S.C. § 1402). After living in Puerto Rico for nearly two decades, José left his childhood home on February 27, 1919, 20 days short of his 19th birthday, therefore failing to satisfy § 1401(a)(7)'s requirement of five years' physical presence after age 14. Record 57, 66. He did so to take up employment as a builder-mechanic for a U.S. company in the then-U.S.-occupied Dominican Republic. *Ibid.*

By 1959, José attested in a June 21, 1971 affidavit presented to the U.S. Embassy in the Dominican Republic, he was living with Yrma **Santana** Montilla, a Dominican woman he would eventually marry. *Id.*, at 57. In 1962, Yrma gave birth to their child, respondent Luis **Morales–Santana**. *Id.*, at 166–167. While the record before us reveals little about **Morales–Santana's** childhood, the Dominican archives disclose that Yrma and José married in 1970, and that José was then added to **Morales–Santana's** birth certificate as his father. *Id.*, at 163–164, 167. José also related in the same affidavit that he was then saving money "for the susten[ance] of [his] family" in anticipation of undergoing surgery in Puerto Rico, where members of his family still resided. *Id.*, at 57. In 1975, when **Morales–Santana** was 13, he moved to Puerto Rico, *id.*, at 368, and by 1976, the year his father died, he was attending public school in the Bronx, a New York City borough, *id.*, at 140, 369.

C

In 2000, the Government placed **Morales–Santana** in removal proceedings based on several convictions for offenses under New York State Penal Law, all of them rendered on May 17, 1995. *Id.*, at 426. **Morales–Santana** ranked as an alien despite the many years he lived in the United States, because, at the time of his birth, his father did not satisfy the requirement of five years' physical presence after age 14. See *supra*, at 1686 – 1687, and n. 3. An immigration judge rejected **Morales–Santana's** claim to citizenship derived from the U.S. citizenship of his father, and ordered **Morales–Santana's** removal to the Dominican Republic. . .

. . .

II.

Because § 1409 treats sons and daughters alike, **Morales–Santana** does not suffer discrimination on the basis of *his* gender. He complains, instead, of gender-based discrimination against his father, who was unwed at the time of **Morales–Santana's** birth and was not accorded the right an unwed U.S.-citizen mother would have to transmit citizenship to her child.

. . .

Sections 1401 and 1409, we note, date from an era when the lawbooks of our Nation were rife with overbroad generalizations about the way men and women are. See, *e.g., Hoyt v. Florida,* 368 U.S. 57, 62, 82 S.Ct. 159, 7 L.Ed.2d 118 (1961) (women are the "center of home and family life," therefore they can be "relieved from the civic duty of jury service"); *Goesaert v. Cleary,* 335 U.S. 464, 466, 69 S.Ct. 198, 93 L.Ed. 163 (1948) (States may draw "a sharp line between the sexes"). Today, laws of this kind are subject to review under the heightened scrutiny that now attends "all gender-based classifications." *J.E.B. v. Alabama ex rel. T. B.,* 511 U.S. 127, 136, 114 S.Ct. 1419, 128 L.Ed.2d 89 (1994); see, *e.g., United States v. Virginia,* 518 U.S. 515, 555–556, 116 S.Ct. 2264, 135 L.Ed.2d 735 (1996) (state-maintained military academy may not deny admission to qualified women).

. . .

Prescribing one rule for mothers, another for fathers, § 1409 is of the same genre as the classifications we declared unconstitutional in *Reed, Frontiero, Wiesenfeld, Goldfarb,* and *Westcott.* As in those cases, heightened scrutiny is in order. Successful defense of legislation that differentiates on the basis of gender, we have reiterated, requires an "exceedingly persuasive justification." *Virginia,* 518 U.S., at 531, 116 S.Ct. 2264 (internal quotation marks omitted); *Kirchberg v. Feenstra,* 450 U.S. 455, 461, 101 S.Ct. 1195, 67 L.Ed.2d 428 (1981) (internal quotation marks omitted).

A

The defender of legislation that differentiates on the basis of gender must show "at least that the [challenged] classification serves important governmental objectives and that the discriminatory means employed are substantially related to the achievement of those objectives." *Virginia,* 518 U.S., at 533, 116 S.Ct. 2264 (quoting *Mississippi Univ. for Women v. Hogan,* 458 U.S. 718, 724, 102 S.Ct. 3331, 73 L.Ed.2d 1090 (1982); alteration in original); see *Tuan Anh Nguyen v. INS,* 533 U.S. 53, 60, 70, 121 S.Ct. 2053, 150 L.Ed.2d 115 (2001). Moreover, the classification must substantially serve an important governmental interest *today,* for "in interpreting the [e]qual [p]rotection [guarantee], [we have] recognized that new insights and societal understandings can reveal unjustified inequality . . . that once passed unnoticed and unchallenged." *Obergefell v. Hodges,* 576 U.S. ____, ____, 135 S.Ct. 2584, 2603, 192 L.Ed.2d 609 (2015). Here, the Government has supplied no "exceedingly persuasive justification," *Virginia,* 518 U.S., at 531,

4. Citizenship

116 S.Ct. 2264 (internal quotation marks omitted), for § 1409(a) and (c)'s "gender-based" and "gender-biased" disparity, *Westcott*, 443 U.S., at 84, 99 S.Ct. 2655 (internal quotation marks omitted).

. . .

In the 1940 Act, Congress discarded the father-controls assumption concerning married parents, but codified the mother-as-sole-guardian perception regarding unmarried parents. The Roosevelt administration, which proposed § 1409, explained: "[T]he mother [of a nonmarital child] stands in the place of the father . . . [,] has a right to the custody and control of such a child as against the putative father, and is bound to maintain it as its natural guardian." 1940 Hearings 431 (internal quotation marks omitted).

This unwed-mother-as-natural-guardian notion renders § 1409's gender-based residency rules understandable. Fearing that a foreign-born child could turn out "more alien than American in character," the administration believed that a citizen parent with lengthy ties to the United States would counteract the influence of the alien parent. *Id.*, at 426–427. Concern about the attachment of foreign-born children to the United States explains the treatment of unwed citizen fathers, who, according to the familiar stereotype, would care little about, and have scant contact with, their nonmarital children. For unwed citizen mothers, however, there was no need for a prolonged residency prophylactic: The alien father, who might transmit foreign ways, was presumptively out of the picture. See *id.*, at 431; Collins 2203 (in "nearly uniform view" of U.S. officials, "almost invariably," the mother alone "concern[ed] herself with [a nonmarital] child" (internal quotation marks omitted)).

. . .

In accord with this eventual understanding, the Court has held that no "important [governmental] interest" is served by laws grounded, as § 1409(a) and (c) are, in the obsolescing view that "unwed fathers [are] invariably less qualified and entitled than mothers" to take responsibility for nonmarital children. *Caban v. Mohammed*, 441 U.S. 380, 382, 394, 99 S.Ct. 1760, 60 L.Ed.2d 297 (1979).[12] Overbroad generalizations of that order, the Court has come to comprehend, have a constraining impact, descriptive though they may be of the way many people still order their lives.[13] Laws according or denying benefits in reliance on "[s]tereotypes about women's domestic roles," the Court has observed, may "creat[e] a self-fulfilling cycle of discrimination that force[s] women to continue to assume the role of primary family caregiver." *Nevada Dept. of Human Resources v. Hibbs*, 538 U.S. 721, 736, 123 S.Ct. 1972, 155 L.Ed.2d 953 (2003). Correspondingly, such laws may disserve men who exercise responsibility for raising their children. See *ibid.* In light of the equal protection jurisprudence this Court has developed since 1971, see *Virginia*, 518 U.S., at 531–534, 116 S.Ct. 2264, § 1409(a) and (c)'s discrete duration-of-residence requirements for unwed mothers and fathers who have accepted parental responsibility is stunningly anachronistic.

B

In urging this Court nevertheless to reject **Morales–Santana's** equal protection plea, the Government cites three decisions of this Court: *Fiallo v. Bell*, 430 U.S. 787, 97 S.Ct. 1473, 52 L.Ed.2d 50 (1977); *Miller v. Albright*, 523 U.S. 420, 118 S.Ct. 1428, 140 L.Ed.2d 575; and *Nguyen v. INS*, 533 U.S. 53, 121 S.Ct. 2053, 150 L.Ed.2d 115. None controls this case.

The 1952 Act provision at issue in *Fiallo* gave special immigration preferences to alien children of citizen (or lawful-permanent-resident) mothers, and to alien unwed mothers of citizen (or lawful-permanent-resident) children. 430 U.S., at 788–789, and n. 1, 97 S.Ct. 1473. Unwed fathers and their children, asserting their right to equal protection, sought the same preferences. *Id.*, at 791, 97 S.Ct. 1473. Applying minimal scrutiny (rational-basis review), the Court upheld the provision, relying on Congress' "exceptionally broad power" to admit or exclude aliens. *Id.*, at 792, 794, 97 S.Ct. 1473. This case, however, involves no entry preference for aliens. **Morales–Santana** claims he is, and since birth has been, a U.S. citizen. Examining a claim of that order, the Court has not disclaimed, as it did in *Fiallo*, the application of an exacting standard of review. See *Nguyen*, 533 U.S., at 60–61, 70, 121 S.Ct. 2053; *Miller*, 523 U.S., at 434–435, n. 11, 118 S.Ct. 1428 (opinion of Stevens, J.).

The provision challenged in *Miller* and *Nguyen* as violative of equal protection requires unwed U.S.-citizen fathers, but not mothers, to formally acknowledge parenthood of their foreign-born children in order to transmit their U.S. citizenship to those children. See § 1409(a)(4) (2012 ed.).[15] After *Miller* produced no opinion for the Court, see 523 U.S., at 423, 118 S.Ct. 1428 we took up the issue anew in *Nguyen*. There, the Court held that imposing a paternal-acknowledgment requirement on fathers was a justifiable, easily met means of ensuring the existence of a biological parent-child relationship, which the mother establishes by giving birth. See 533 U.S., at 62–63, 121 S.Ct. 2053. **Morales–Santana's** challenge does not renew the contest over § 1409's paternal-acknowledgment requirement (whether the current version or that in effect in 1970), and the Government does not dispute that **Morales–Santana's** father, by marrying **Morales–Santana's** mother, satisfied that requirement.

Unlike the paternal-acknowledgment requirement at issue in *Nguyen* and *Miller*, the physical-presence requirements now before us relate solely to the duration of the parent's prebirth residency in the United States, not to the parent's filial tie to the child. As the Court of Appeals observed in this case, a man needs no more time in the United States than a woman "in order to have assimilated citizenship-related values to transmit to [his] child." 804 F.3d, at 531. And unlike *Nguyen* 's parental-acknowledgment requirement, § 1409(a)'s age-calibrated physical-presence requirements cannot fairly be described as "minimal." 533 U.S., at 70, 121 S.Ct. 2053.

C

Notwithstanding § 1409(a) and (c)'s provenance in traditional notions of the way women and men are, the Government maintains that the statute serves two important objectives: (1) ensuring a connection between the child to become a citizen and the United States and (2) preventing "statelessness," *i.e.*, a child's possession of no citizenship at all. Even indulging the assumption that Congress intended § 1409 to serve these interests, but see *supra*, at 1683–1693, neither rationale survives heightened scrutiny.

1

We take up first the Government's assertion that § 1409(a) and (c)'s gender-based differential ensures that a child born abroad has a connection to the United States of sufficient strength to warrant conferral of citizenship at birth. The Government does not contend, nor could it, that unmarried men take more time to absorb U.S. values than unmarried women do. See *supra*, at 1694. Instead, it presents a novel argument, one it did not advance in *Flores–Villar*.

An unwed mother, the Government urges, is the child's only "legally recognized" parent at the time of childbirth. Brief for Petitioner 9–10, 28–32. An unwed citizen father enters the scene later, as a second parent. A longer physical connection to the United States is warranted for the unwed father, the Government maintains, because of the "competing national influence" of the alien mother. *Id.*, at 9–10. Congress, the Government suggests, designed the statute to bracket an unwed U.S.-citizen mother with a married couple in which both parents are U.S. citizens, and to align an unwed U.S.-citizen father with a married couple, one spouse a citizen, the other, an alien.

Underlying this apparent design is the assumption that the alien father of a nonmarital child born abroad to a U.S.-citizen mother will not accept parental responsibility. For an actual affiliation between alien father and nonmarital child would create the "competing national influence" that, according to the Government, justifies imposing on unwed U.S.-citizen fathers, but not unwed U.S.-citizen mothers, lengthy physical-presence requirements. Hardly gender neutral, see *id.*, at 9, that assumption conforms to the long-held view that unwed fathers care little about, indeed are strangers to, their children. See *supra*, at 1690–1693. Lump characterization of that kind, however, no longer passes equal protection inspection. See *supra*, at 1692–1693, and n. 13.

Accepting, *arguendo*, that Congress intended the diverse physical-presence prescriptions to serve an interest in ensuring a connection between the foreign-born nonmarital child and the United States, the gender-based means scarcely serve the posited end. The scheme permits the transmission of citizenship to children who have no tie to the United States so long as their mother was a U.S. citizen continuously present in the United States for one year at any point in her life *prior* to the child's birth. The transmission holds even if the mother marries the child's alien father immediately after the child's birth and never returns with the child to the United States. At the same time, the legislation precludes citizenship transmission by a U.S.-citizen father who falls a few days short of meeting § 1401(a)(7)'s longer physical-presence requirements, even if the father acknowledges paternity on the day of the child's birth and raises the child in the United

States. One cannot see in this driven-by-gender scheme the close means-end fit required to survive heightened scrutiny. See, *e.g.*, *Wengler v. Druggists Mut. Ins. Co.*, 446 U.S. 142, 151–152, 100 S.Ct. 1540, 64 L.Ed.2d 107 (1980) (holding unconstitutional state workers' compensation death-benefits statute presuming widows' but not widowers' dependence on their spouse's earnings); *Westcott*, 443 U.S., at 88–89, 99 S.Ct. 2655.

2

The Government maintains that Congress established the gender-based residency differential in § 1409(a) and (c) to reduce the risk that a foreign-born child of a U.S. citizen would be born stateless. Brief for Petitioner 33. This risk, according to the Government, was substantially greater for the foreign-born child of an unwed U.S.-citizen mother than it was for the foreign-born child of an unwed U.S.-citizen father. *Ibid.* But there is little reason to believe that a stateless-ness concern prompted the diverse physical-presence requirements. Nor has the Government shown that the risk of statelessness disproportionately endangered the children of unwed mothers.

As the Court of Appeals pointed out, with one exception,[20] nothing in the congressional hearings and reports on the 1940 and 1952 Acts "refer[s] to the problem of statelessness for children born abroad." 804 F.3d, at 532–533. See Collins 2205, n. 283 (author examined "many hundreds of pre–1940 adminis-trative memos . . . defend[ing] or explain[ing] recognition of the nonmarital for-eign-born children of American mothers as citizens"; of the hundreds, "exactly one memo by a U.S. official . . . mentions the risk of statelessness for the for-eign-born nonmarital children of American mothers as a concern"). Reducing the incidence of statelessness was the express goal of *other* sections of the 1940 Act. See 1940 Hearings 430 ("stateless[ness]" is "object" of section on found-lings). The justification for § 1409's gender-based dichotomy, however, was not the child's plight, it was the mother's role as the "natural guardian" of a nonmar-ital child. See *supra*, at 1690 – 1693; Collins 2205 ("[T]he pronounced gender asymmetry of the Nationality Act's treatment of nonmarital foreign-born children of American mothers and fathers was shaped by contemporary maternalist norms regarding the mother's relationship with her nonmarital child—and the father's lack of such a relationship."). It will not do to "hypothesiz[e] or inven[t]" gov-ernmental purposes for gender classifications "*post hoc* in response to litigation." *Virginia*, 518 U.S., at 533, 535–536, 116 S.Ct. 2264.

Infecting the Government's risk-of-statelessness argument is an assumption without foundation. "[F]oreign laws that would put the child of the U.S.-citizen mother at risk of statelessness (by not providing for the child to acquire the father's citizenship at birth)," the Government asserts, "would *protect* the child of the U.S.-citizen father against statelessness by providing that the child would take his mother's citizenship." Brief for Petitioner 35. The Government, however, neglected to expose this supposed "protection" to a reality check. Had it done so, it would have recognized the formidable impediments placed by foreign laws on an unwed mother's transmission of citizenship to her child. See Brief for Scholars on Statelessness as *Amici Curiae* 13–22, A1–A15.

. . .

In 2014, the United Nations High Commissioner for Refugees (UNHCR) undertook a ten-year project to eliminate statelessness by 2024. See generally UNHCR, Ending Statelessness Within 10 Years, online at http://www.unhcr.org/en-us/protection/statelessness/546217229/special–report–ending–statelessness–10–years.html (all Internet materials as last visited June 9, 2017). Cognizant that discrimination against either mothers or fathers in citizenship and nationality laws is a major cause of statelessness, the Commissioner has made a key component of its project the elimination of gender discrimination in such laws. UNHCR, The Campaign To End Statelessness: April 2016 Update 1 (referring to speech of UNHCR "highlight[ing] the issue of gender discrimination in the nationality laws of 27 countries—a major cause of statelessness globally"), online at http://www.unhcr.org/ibelong/wp-content/uploads/Campaign–Update–April–2016.pdf; UNHCR, Background Note on Gender Equality, Nationality Laws and Statelessness 2016, p. 1 ("Ensuring gender equality in nationality laws can mitigate the risks of statelessness."), online at http://www.refworld.org/docid/56de83ca4.html. In this light, we cannot countenance risk of statelessness as a reason to uphold, rather than strike out, differential treatment of unmarried women and men with regard to transmission of citizenship to their children.

In sum, the Government has advanced no "exceedingly persuasive" justification for § 1409(a) and (c)'s gender-specific residency and age criteria. Those disparate criteria, we hold, cannot withstand inspection under a Constitution that requires the Government to respect the equal dignity and stature of its male and female citizens.

IV

While the equal protection infirmity in retaining a longer physical-presence requirement for unwed fathers than for unwed mothers is clear, this Court is not equipped to grant the relief **Morales–Santana** seeks, *i.e.*, extending to his father (and, derivatively, to him) the benefit of the one-year physical-presence term § 1409(c) reserves for unwed mothers.

There are "two remedial alternatives," our decisions instruct, *Westcott*, 443 U.S., at 89, 99 S.Ct. 2655 (quoting *Welsh v. United States*, 398 U.S. 333, 361, 90 S.Ct. 1792, 26 L.Ed.2d 308 (1970) (Harlan, J., concurring in result)), when a statute benefits one class (in this case, unwed mothers and their children), as § 1409(c) does, and excludes another from the benefit (here, unwed fathers and their children). "[A] court may either declare [the statute] a nullity and order that its benefits not extend to the class that the legislature intended to benefit, or it may extend the coverage of the statute to include those who are aggrieved by exclusion." *Westcott*, 443 U.S., at 89, 99 S.Ct. 2655 (quoting *Welsh*, 398 U.S., at 361, 90 S.Ct. 1792 (opinion of Harlan, J.)). "[W]hen the 'right invoked is that to equal treatment,' the appropriate remedy is a mandate of equal treatment, a result that can be accomplished by withdrawal of benefits from the favored class as well as by extension of benefits to the excluded class." *Heckler v. Mathews*, 465 U.S. 728, 740, 104 S.Ct. 1387, 79 L.Ed.2d 646 (1984) (quoting *Iowa–Des Moines Nat. Bank v. Bennett*, 284 U.S. 239, 247, 52 S.Ct. 133, 76 L.Ed. 265 (1931); emphasis deleted). "How equality is accomplished . . . is a matter on which the Constitution is silent." *Levin v. Commerce Energy, Inc.*, 560 U.S. 413, 426–427, 130 S.Ct. 2323, 176 L.Ed.2d 1131 (2010).

The choice between these outcomes is governed by the legislature's intent, as revealed by the statute at hand. See *id.*, at 427, 130 S.Ct. 2323 ("On finding unlawful discrimination, . . . courts may attempt, within the bounds of their institutional competence, to implement what the legislature would have willed had it been apprised of the constitutional infirmity."). See also *Ayotte v. Planned Parenthood of Northern New Eng.*, 546 U.S. 320, 330, 126 S.Ct. 961, 163 L.Ed.2d 812 (2006) ("the touchstone for any decision about remedy is legislative intent").

Ordinarily, we have reiterated, "extension, rather than nullification, is the proper course." *Westcott*, 443 U.S., at 89, 99 S.Ct. 2655. Illustratively, in a series of cases involving federal financial assistance benefits, the Court struck discriminatory exceptions denying benefits to discrete groups, which meant benefits previously denied were extended. See, *e.g.*, *Goldfarb*, 430 U.S., at 202–204, 213–217, 97 S.Ct. 1021 (plurality opinion) (survivors' benefits), aff'g 396 F.Supp. 308, 309 (E.D.N.Y.1975) (*per curiam*); *Jimenez v. Weinberger*, 417 U.S. 628, 630–631, and n. 2, 637–638, 94 S.Ct. 2496, 41 L.Ed.2d 363 (1974) (disability benefits); *Department of Agriculture v. Moreno*, 413 U.S. 528, 529–530, 538, 93 S.Ct. 2821, 37 L.Ed.2d 782 (1973) (food stamps); *Frontiero*, 411 U.S., at 678–679, and n. 2, 691, and n. 25 (plurality opinion) (military spousal benefits). Here, however, the discriminatory exception consists of *favorable* treatment for a discrete group (a shorter physical-presence requirement for unwed U.S.-citizen mothers giving birth abroad). Following the same approach as in those benefits cases—striking the discriminatory exception—leads here to extending the general rule of longer physical-presence requirements to cover the previously favored group.

The Court has looked to Justice Harlan's concurring opinion in *Welsh v. United States*, 398 U.S., at 361–367, 90 S.Ct. 1792 in considering whether the legislature would have struck an exception and applied the general rule equally to all, or instead, would have broadened the exception to cure the equal protection violation. In making this assessment, a court should " 'measure the intensity of commitment to the residual policy' "—the main rule, not the exception— " 'and consider the degree of potential disruption of the statutory scheme that would occur by extension as opposed to abrogation.' " *Heckler*, 465 U.S., at 739, n. 5, 104 S.Ct. 1387 (quoting *Welsh*, 398 U.S., at 365, 90 S.Ct. 1792 (opinion of Harlan, J.)).

The residual policy here, the longer physical-presence requirement stated in §§ 1401(a)(7) and 1409, evidences Congress' recognition of "the importance of residence in this country as the talisman of dedicated attachment." *Rogers v.*

Bellei, 401 U.S. 815, 834, 91 S.Ct. 1060, 28 L.Ed.2d 499 (1971); see *Weedin v. Chin Bow*, 274 U.S. 657, 665–666, 47 S.Ct. 772, 71 L.Ed. 1284 (1927) (Congress "attached more importance to actual residence in the United States as indicating a basis for citizenship than it did to descent. . . . [T]he heritable blood of citizenship was thus associated unmistakeably with residence within the country which was thus recognized as essential to full citizenship." (internal quotation marks omitted)). And the potential for "disruption of the statutory scheme" is large. For if § 1409(c)'s one-year dispensation were extended to unwed citizen fathers, would it not be irrational to retain the longer term when the U.S.-citizen parent is married? Disadvantageous treatment of marital children in comparison to nonmarital children is scarcely a purpose one can sensibly attribute to Congress.

Although extension of benefits is customary in federal benefit cases, see *supra*, at 1698 – 1699, n. 22, 25, all indicators in this case point in the opposite direction. Put to the choice, Congress, we believe, would have abrogated § 1409(c)'s exception, preferring preservation of the general rule.

V

The gender-based distinction infecting §§ 1401(a)(7) and 1409(a) and (c), we hold, violates the equal protection principle, as the Court of Appeals correctly ruled. For the reasons stated, however, we must adopt the remedial course Congress likely would have chosen "had it been apprised of the constitutional infirmity." *Levin*, 560 U.S., at 427, 130 S.Ct. 2323. Although the preferred rule in the typical case is to extend favorable treatment, see *Westcott*, 443 U.S., at 89–90, 99 S.Ct. 2655 this is hardly the typical case. Extension here would render the special treatment Congress prescribed in § 1409(c), the one-year physical-presence requirement for U.S.-citizen mothers, the general rule, no longer an exception. Section 1401(a)(7)'s longer physical-presence requirement, applicable to a substantial majority of children born abroad to one U.S.-citizen parent and one foreign-citizen parent, therefore, must hold sway. Going forward, Congress may address the issue and settle on a uniform prescription that neither favors nor disadvantages any person on the basis of gender. In the interim, as the Government suggests, § 1401(a)(7)'s now-five-year requirement should apply, prospectively, to children born to unwed U.S.-citizen mothers. . . .

The judgment of the Court of Appeals for the Second Circuit is affirmed in part and reversed in part, and the case is remanded for further proceedings consistent with this opinion.

It is so ordered.

NOTES AND QUESTIONS

What do you think of the actual outcome, namely, that instead of allowing an exception to the longer residency requirement of Mr. Morales-Santana (i.e., men), women would now be subject to the general residency requirement? Does this leave to Congress whether it wants to change the general rule.

Child Born to Surrogate: Out of Wedlock?

The "out of wedlock" requirements for acquisition have been imposed on married same-sex couples who use a surrogate abroad and a donated egg from an unknown woman. Although litigation is pending, the State Department policy on "assisted reproductive technology" provides that "a child born abroad to a surrogate, whose genetic parents are a U.S. citizen father and anonymous egg donor, is considered for citizenship purposes to be a person born out of wedlock." *See* Jennifer Hansler, CNN, *Trump admin is denying citizenship to some children of same-sex couples*, May 18, 2018.

V.   Loss of U.S. Citizenship

At page 311, after the Notes and Questions, add the following:

Operation Janus and Operation Second Look.

The Obama administration uncovered a flaw in the naturalization process in 2016. The USCIS Office of Inspector General reported that almost 900 individuals had been granted citizenship based on incomplete fingerprint records—older paper records had not been uploaded into FBI digital databases. In fact, close to 150,000 records had not been properly digitized, and more than 300,000 cases were being investigated. So an investigation (Operation Janus) ensued turning up individuals who should not have been granted naturalization. One such person was Baljinder Singh who had changed identities after having been ordered deported in absentia and later married a U.S. citizen through whom he obtained status. When the truth was revealed, Singh's citizenship was revoked. *See Feds revoke citizenship of New Jersey man who used alias to enter U.S.*, CBS NEWS, Jan. 11, 2018.

The denaturalization of such individuals has continued under the Trump administration as "Operation Second Look." For example, Odette Dureland, who had fled Haiti in the early 1990s, alleged had been denied asylum and ordered deported under a different name. Eventually she obtained status and citizenship through her husband. After Trump officials felt they had sufficient evidence, they brought criminal denaturalization proceedings against Dureland. A jury found her guilty of criminal naturalization fraud and faced removal.

See Seth Freed Wessler, Is Denaturalization the Next Front in the Trump Administration's War on Immigration?, NY Times Magazine, Dec. 19, 2018.

4. Citizenship

NOTES AND QUESTIONS

1. What is gained by the revocation of citizenship of Dureland and Singh? The integrity of the system?

2. Dureland's citizenship was revoked through criminal proceedings. Consider the next example in the text.

Chapter 5

NONIMMIGRANTS

Section I.   Introduction

Addendum: At the very beginning of the chapter, add the following:

Unlike the immigrant visas covered in the last chapter, nonimmigrant visas are issued to foreign nationals for a defined period of time, and generally are restricted to those foreign nationals who do not have an intent to remain permanently in the United States. (The complex issue of intent is taken up later in this chapter.) The following stories illustrate some of the many ways that people use nonimmigrant visas in the U.S., as well as some of the problems that they may encounter in the process.

Story #1

In 2011, Preeta moved with her husband from India to the United States. Her husband entered the country with an H-1B visa. Preeta had an H-4 visa. H-4 visas cover the spouses and children of the primary visa holder – in his case, Preeta's husband. When Preeta arrived in the U.S., she was not able to work, nothwithstanding the fact that she was highly educated. At the time, regulations did not allow for work authorization for H-4 visa holders. This changed on May 26, 2015, when the Obama administration put into place a new rule amending immigration regulations so as to allow the spouses of H-1B visa holders present on H-4 visas to work. (A copy of the changed rule can be found here: https://www.federalregister.gov/documents/2015/02/25/2015-04042/employment-authorization-for-certain-h-4-dependent-spouses?utm_campaign=pi+subscription+mailing+list&utm_medium=email&utm_source=federalregister.gov).

Preeta was thrilled with the rule change. Under the new rule, she was able to obtain a social security number and work authorization, and in short order she was able to find a fulfilling job. The Trump administration is currently considering rescinding work authorization for H-4 visa holders. Preeta is concerned that she will have to stop working.

Story #2

Bob is a 60 year old African American engineer who works in information technology at a major public research university. Recently, the state imposed a series of budget cuts on the university. In order to continue to operate on its reduced budget, the university has decided to replace some of its workers with less expensive workers from abroad. Bob is told that he will be laid off in 60 days and that, during his last two months of work, he will be expected to train his replacement from India. The worker from India will enter the country on an H-1B visa. He will have the same job responsibilities as Bob but will be paid substantially less and will have a less generous package of benefits.

Story #3

Mershad is a U.S. citizen who lives in Southern California. He petitioned for a K-1 fiancee visa for the Iranian woman to whom he was engaged in March of 2016. The petition was approved in September 2016. Mershad's fiancée completed her interview abroad in November 2016, but the U.S.government did not issue a visa at that time. Several month's later, the travel ban went into effect, barring most citizens from Iran from entering the country, subject to special waivers. To date, the number of waivers issued by the Trump administration has been quite small. The status of Mershad's fiancee's visa in "administrative processing" — has remained unchanged for over two years. The couple has had to make short trips to third countries to see one another, but it is difficult for them. The mental health of Mershad's fiancée has taken a toll.

These stories offer a window into different aspects of immigration policy as it affects nonimmigrant visa petitioners and those who are affected by their presence.

* * *

Errata: At page 342, in the last sentence of the second full paragraph, strike the word "designs" from the sentence. It should read "But the process for obtaining these visas…"

Section II.   An Introduction to Nonimmigrant Visas

For those reading the book in 2019, here are a few updates to textbook pages 343-344:

1) Page 343 contains the NIV admission numbers for 2015. In 2017, that number was 181 million. (See https://www.dhs.gov/sites/default/files/ publications/Nonimmigrant_Admissions_2017.pdf)

2) Page 343 contains Immigrant Visa figures for 2015. The comparison figure for Immigrant Visas in 2017 was 1,127,67, 49% of whom were already in

the country when the immigrant visa issued. (See https://www.dhs.gov/
sites/default/files/publications/Lawful_Permanent_Residents_2017.pdf)

3) Page 343 provides the percentage of Mexican and Canadian visitors as a
percentage of NIV admissions. In 2017, that number was 103 million, or
almost 57% of the total number of admissions. (See https://www.dhs.gov/
sites/default/files/publications/Nonimmigrant_Admissions_2017.pdf)

4) Page 344 provides a list of the 36 visa waiver countries and Taiwan. In
2014, Chile was added to that list. Source: https://travel.state.gov/content/
travel/en/us-visas/tourism-visit/visa-waiver-program.html. Taiwan is also
on the list. Id.

5) Page 344 footnote 4 could be updated to cite to Table 25 of the 2017
DHS Yearbook of Immigration Statistics. (See https://www.dhs.gov/
immigration-statistics/yearbook/2017)

Section III. Student Visas

For those reading the book in 2019, here are a couple of updates to page 344:

1) Page 344 provides the number of student visa holders in 2015. In 2017,
that number (including accompanying family members) was 1,940,171.
(See https://www.dhs.gov/sites/default/files/publications/Nonimmigrant_
Admissions_2017.pdf)

2) The number of exchange visitors in 2016 was 594,185.

Addendum: After page 344 add:

Student visa numbers have declined over the past few years. Although the
number of student visa admissions recorded by DHS show a slight decrease (about
2.5% between 2017 and 2018), the State Department reported that it issued 8%
fewer student visas in fiscal year 2017-2018 than in the previous fiscal year. The
number of Indian students receiving a student visa declined by a dramatic 31 percent. In an interview with National Public Radio, Stuart Anderson of the National
Foundation for American Policy hypothesized that: "Indian students have decided
that America may not be the best place to make their career. They've seen an
increase in the number of denials for H-1B visas to work after graduation. And
also, there is very long wait times for employment-based green cards for Indians."
(https://www.npr.org/2019/03/10/701987091/why-u-s-visa-numbers-are-down).

This interview highlights the ways that demand for student visas are driven
in part by the likelihood that a student will be able to convert that visa into a temporary employment visa (the H-1B) and, ultimately, lawful permanent residence
through an employment-based visa. Each of these visa types will be explored in

greater detail later in the chapter. Other factors that have been cited to explain the decline in student visa numbers include the anti-immigrant climate created by the Trump administration, the rise in hate crimes against certain immigrant groups, the ban on travel from countries covered by President Trump's 2017 executive order and the rising cost of education at U.S. institutions.

The decline is problematic for U.S. institutions of higher education, which have become increasingly reliant on international student to fill their programs.

Addendum: After page 345 add:

Thousands of students with F-3 and M-3 visas cross the U.S. border daily to attend U.S. institutions of higher education. For individuals crossing the U.S.-Mexico border that journey has become increasingly difficult in recent years. In 2017, Alana Semuels followed one student, Valeria Padilla, a U.S. citizen who lives in Ciudad Juárez, Mexico, with her family, but who daily commutes to El Paso, Texas, to attend the University of Texas, El Paso. Semuels writes:

> Wait-times to get into Mexico have become longer after U.S. Customs and Border Protection began requiring Mexican agents to check cars entering Mexico for guns and money, according to Tony Payan, the director of the Mexico Institute at Rice University. . . . [A]s Padilla and I cross the border after about an hour of waiting, crawling slowly down El Paso streets and then past gun-toting Mexican agents whose faces are covered, supposedly so they won't be identified for bribery, our car is flagged and a Mexican agent asks Valeria to pull over and open her trunk. This is typical, and it's the reason that it can take Padilla an hour or two to travel the three miles from campus to Juarez on any given day.

Alana Semuels, Crossing the Mexican-American Border, Every Day, The Atlantic, Jan. 25, 2016 (https://www.theatlantic.com/business/archive/2016/01/crossing-the-mexican-american-border-every-day/426678/).

Section IV.   Nonimmigrant Visas Designed for Workers: Bs, Hs, Ls, Os, and Ps

Erratum: Page 354 of the textbook summarizes litigation over the Obama Administration's extenstion of the OPT period. First, an important correction to a typographical error: OPT stands for Optional Practical Training (not Optional Professional Training).

Addendum: Second, an update to insert before the first full paragraph on page 355: the case discussed in these pages has been resolved. Subsequent developments were summarized in the government's briefing in a fee dispute on which the Supreme Court denied cert on March 5, 2018. As the government's brief in opposition to cert stated at pages 3-4:

> The district court largely rejected petitioner's claims. The court dismissed petitioner's challenge to the OPT program as a whole, holding that petitioner lacked

5. Nonimmigrants

Article III standing to challenge the original 12-month OPT program and, alternatively, that any challenge to the relevant 1992 regulations was barred by the statute of limitations. The court also entered summary judgment for the government on petitioner's statutory claim challenging the 17-month STEM extension, holding that the 2008 rule was within DHS's substantive authority because it was consistent with the provisions of the Immigration and Nationality Act, 8 U.S.C. 1101 et seq.

The district court concluded, however, that DHS had not sufficiently justified its invocation of the APA's good-cause exception based on an "economic crisis." The court nevertheless determined that immediate vacatur of the 17-month STEM extension rule would "caus[e] substantial hard-ship for foreign students and a major labor disruption for the technology sector." The court accordingly ordered that "the 17-month STEM extension" be vacated but that the vacatur order would be stayed until February 12, 2016. The district court subsequently extended that stay, over petitioner's opposition, to May 10, 2016. 153 F. Supp. 3d 93, 101 (2016).

While petitioner's appeal was pending, DHS initiated notice-and-comment rulemaking to revise its STEM OPT rules. 80 Fed. Reg. 63,376 (Oct. 19, 2015). DHS proposed, inter alia, to adopt a "24-month extension" that would "replace the 17-month STEM OPT extension" that petitioner had challenged, but that was still "available" to students because of the district court's stay. Ibid.

In early 2016, DHS adopted a final rule that, as relevant here, adopted the longer 24-month STEM extension. 81 Fed. Reg. 13,040, 13,041, 13,117 (Mar. 11, 2016) (promulgating 8 C.F.R. 214.2(f)(10)(ii)(C) (2017)). The rule also provided that students who had obtained a 17-month STEM extension before the rule's effective date would obtain (or retain) work authorization for the 17-month period and could apply for "an additional 7-month period of OPT" (for a total 24-month extension). Id. at 13,121 (promulgating 8 C.F.R. 214.16(b), (c)(1) and (2) (2017)). The final rule became effective on May 10, 2016, id. at 13,040, the same date on which the district court's stay ultimately expired.

The new rule discussed in the government's briefs remains in place and can be found at 8 C.F.R. § 214.2(f)(10)(ii)(C) (2017).

* * *

Section IV.C.   Category Problems: B or H?

Addedum: At page 370, before **Notes and Questions**, add:

On April 18, 2017, President Trump signed the Presidential Executive Order on Buy American and Hire American. Section 5 of the Order reads as follows:

Sec. 5. Ensuring the Integrity of the Immigration System in Order to "Hire American." (a) In order to advance the policy outlined in section 2(b) of this order, the Secretary of State, the Attorney General, the Secretary of Labor, and the Secretary of Homeland Security shall, as soon as practicable, and consistent with applicable law, propose new rules and issue new guidance, to supersede or revise previous rules and guidance if appropriate, to protect the interests of United States workers in the administration of our immigration system, including through the prevention of fraud or abuse.

(b) In order to promote the proper functioning of the H-1B visa program, the Secretary of State, the Attorney General, the Secretary of Labor, and the Secretary of Homeland Security shall, as soon as practicable, suggest reforms to help ensure that H-1B visas are awarded to the most-skilled or highest-paid petition beneficiaries.

To date, the Order has not resulted in any significant changes to the H-1B system. However, the Order suggests that at least some members of the Trump Administration share the concerns of some experts that the H-1B system operates to the disadvantage of American workers. In no industry has this issue been more hotly debated than in the technology sector. On February 5, 2017, the New York Times reported that a "research report by Goldman Sachs estimates that 900,000 to a million H-1B visa holders now reside in the United States, and that they account for up to 13 percent of American technology jobs." Daisuke Wakabayashi and Nelson D. Schwartz, Not Everyone in Tech Cheers Visa Program for Foreign Workers, N.Y. Times, February 5, 2017 at B1. Some industry insiders and experts believe that the H-1B program displaces U.S. workers and lowers industry wages. A study by Ronil Hira, a professor of public policy at Howard University, finds that nearly 1/3 of H-1B visas actually go to IT services firms, many based in India, that specialize in consulting or outsourcing. Hiro argues that, far from simply supplementing the supply of U.S. workers, H-1B visas are being used in ways that favor the outsourcing of good jobs and the importation of workers to perform relatively low-skill, low wage jobs in the tech industry. He concludes that the program keeps U.S. workers out of jobs and also results in downward pressure on wages.

Many others, including Giovanni Peri, an economist at U.C. Davis, maintain that the H-1B program is necessary because there are not enough qualified U.S. workers to fill these positions. These industry insiders and experts also argue that the program allows the U.S. to compete for the world's most qualified workers. They suggest that the result of shrinking the H-1B program will me more outsourcing, not more jobs for U.S. citizens. Some studies have even found that the program is responsible for a modest increase in U.S. wages. For more citations to studies finding the H-1B visa beneficial to U.S. workers, see The American Immigration Counsel, The H-1B Visa Program: A Primer on the Program and Its Impact on Jobs, Wages, and the Economy, April 16, 2019 (https://www.americanimmigrationcouncil.org/sites/default/files/research/the_h-1b_visa_program_a_primer_on_the_program_and_its_impact_on_jobs_wages_and_the_economy.pdf).

Chapter 6

IMMIGRANTS

I. Introduction (p. 385)

Chapter 6 covers immigrant visas.

Update: Page 385 - Updated statistic: in 2017, the number of NIV admissions was 181,100,000. The number of immigrant visas was 1,127,167, 49% of whom were already present in the country.

II. Worldwide Quota and Preference Categories (p. 386)

This section describes how visas are allocated between regions and countries, as well as between categories. Visa categories are summarized at page 388.

Errata: There is a correction needed near the bottom of page 387. In the second to the last paragraph, first sentence, the words "family-based" should be inserted before "visa admissions" so that the phrase reads: "The formula for total annual worldwide family-based visa admissions is:" And at the end of that paragraph, the following sentence should be added:

"The formula for total annual worldwide employment-based visas is: 140,000 plus the family-based visas not used in the previous fiscal year."

Addendum: Page 389

The updated link for footnote 1 is: https://travel.state.gov/content/travel/en/legal/visa-law0/visa-bulletin/2019/visa-bulletin-for-july-2019.html

Some more updated data for 2019 to replace the information in the fourth paragraph of section B, page 389:

Coming from most countries, the visa petition filed on behalf of someone who could apply for her visa in July 2019 as the first preference unmarried daughter to a U.S. citizen was filed in March 2012 - a wait time of over 7 years. But if that daughter was from Mexico, the wait would be almost 23 years. A third preference, married daughter generally would face a wait of 12 years, but one from the Philippines would wait more than 22 years.

III.   Family-based visas (p. 390)

Section III.A.2. "Children" In the Family-Based Visa Process

Addendum: After the discussion of the definition of "child" at page 408, add the following:

As noted in Chapter 4, however, the Court more recently rejected distinctions in the INA's definition of "child" that turned on sex-based distinctions. In *Sessions v. Morales Santana*, 582 U.S. ___ (2016), the Court held that the statutory distinction between the physical presence requirements for transferral of derivative citizenship for unwed citizen mothers and unwed citizen fathers of foreign-born children violates the Equal Protection Clause of the Fifth Amendment. Unfortunately for the Petitioner in that case, the Court also determined that Congress, not the Court would have to create an appropriate statutory solution that did not rely on impermissible sex-based discrimination, and that in the interim, the more stringent standards applicable to fathers would also apply to mothers.

The complexity and formalism of the definition of "child" in the INA have been highlighted by Recent media accounts exploring the effects of a State Department policy denying passports to children of same-sex couples when the child cannot establish genetic or gestational ties to the U.S. citizen parent. In the Department's view, these children do not meet the statutory definition of "child." The State Department website reads:

The U.S. Department of State determines whether a child born abroad to a U.S. citizen parent acquired U.S. citizenship at birth

A child born abroad may acquire U.S. citizenship at birth if the parent/parents of the child meet the conditions prescribed in the Immigration and Nationality Act (INA).

The U.S. Department of State interprets the INA to mean that a child born abroad must be biologically related to a U.S. citizen parent who meets the following statutory transmission requirements of INA 301 or 309 in order for the child to acquire U.S. citizenship at birth:

- *A U.S. citizen father must be the genetic parent of the child and meet all other statutory requirements in order to transmit U.S. citizenship to the child at birth.*
- *A U.S. citizen mother must be the genetic and/or the gestational* and legal mother of the child at the time and place of the child's birth and must meet all other statutory requirements in order to transmit U.S. citizenship to the child at birth. (*Gestational mother is the woman who carries and gives birth to the child)*

DNA testing is often the best way to establish a genetic or blood relationship after the child is born.

*Even if local law recognizes a surrogacy agreement and finds that U.S. parents are the legal parents of a child conceived and born abroad through ART, **if the child does not have a biological connection to a U.S. citizen parent, the child will not be a U.S. citizen at birth.***

*In addition to establishing a biological relationship to the child, U.S. citizen parents must also establish that other transmission requirements have been met, such as having had certain periods of **physical presence** or a residence in the United States prior to the birth of the child. For more information about specific requirements, visit INA Sections 301 and 309.*

For the full discussion, see U.S. State Department, Assisted Reproductive Technology (ART) and Surrogacy Abroad (https://travel.state.gov/content/travel/en/ legal/travel-legal-considerations/us-citizenship/Assisted-Reproductive-Technology-ART-Surrogacy-Abroad.html) (emphasis in original).

On this basis, the Department declined to acknowledge the citizenship of, and did not issue a passport to, a child born to two U.S. citizen fathers where the child's only genetic link was to the U.S. citizen father who did not satisfy the residency requirement. Sarah Mervosh, Both Parents Are American. The U.S. Says Their Baby Isn't, N.Y. Times, May 21, 2019 (available at https://www.nytimes. com/2019/05/21/us/gay-couple-children-citizenship.html). The Department also declined to issue a passport to one of two twins of a same-sex couple when one twin was conceived using sperm from his non-U.S. citizen father, while the other was conceived using sperm from his U.S. citizen father. That family successfully sued in federal court with a federal district court judge, holding that the law did not require that a child born to married parents prove a biological relationship with both parents. Sarah Mervosh, Twins Were Born to a Gay Couple. Only One Child Was Recognized as a U.S. Citizen, Until Now, N.Y. Times, Feb. 22, 2019 (https://www.nytimes.com/2019/02/22/us/gay-couple-twin-sons-citizenship.html?login=email&auth=login-email). And a lawsuit is underway in federal district court in Washington D.C. challenging the Department's denial of a passport to one of two twin children of a U.S. citizen mother and her Italian wife. The Department granted a passport to the child who was conceived and carried by the U.S. citizen, but not the child conceived and carried by the Italian citizen. The lawsuit contends that both children are U.S. citizens under INA § 301(g), and that the Department is erroneously denying citizenship to one child by treating him as a child born out of wedlock, notwithstanding the legal marriage of his parents. A link to the complaint can be found here: https://www.immigrationequality.org/ wp-content/uploads/2018/01/Blixt-Complaint-Filed.pdf.

Review the INA's definition of "child" to determine the bases for the State Department's policy and the plaintiffs' legal challenges to the policy.

Section III.A.2.c. SIJS

Addendum: *Page 410-411:* The INA defines the age of a child as under 21. In the past, the federal government routinely extend SIJ status to youth in states that had a like definition of a child - defining children to include individuals under the age of 21. In the Spring of 2018, the Trump Administration tried to change that policy, declining to grant SIJS status to young people who had been over the age of 18 but under 21 when they began the application process. This meant that many young people in New York (as well as in other states with similar laws) were denied SIJS notwithstanding the fact that the state defined these individuals as children. See Liz Robbins, *A Rule is Changed for Young Immigrants, and Green Card Hopes Fade*, New York Times, April 18, 2018.

In a March 2019 ruling, Judge John G. Koeltl of the U.S. District Court of the Southern District of New York granted a motion for class certification filed by a group of New York plaintiffs challenging the policy. The judge also granted the plaintiffs' motion for summary judgment, striking down the Trump Administration's policy of denying SIJ status to New York residents between the age of 18 and 21. After finding that the policy was a final agency action reviewable by a federal district court, Judge Koeltl concluded: "Because the agency's policy is contrary to the plain language of the of the SIJ statute, lacks reasoned explanation, is premised on erroneous interpretations of state law, and was not enacted with adequate notice, the policy is arbitrary and capricious, 'in excess of statutory jurisdiction,' and 'without observance of procedure required by law.' See 5 U.S.C. §706(2)(A), (C)-(D). Accordingly the policy must be set aside."

A link to the full decision is here:

https://static1.squarespace.com/static/59578aade110eba6434f4b72/t/5c8c65 894785d34f4980665c/1552704910483/special_immigrant_juvenile_status.pdf

IV. Employment-Based Visas [mislabled as 3 in current print edition]

Addendum: The updated data on employment visas for August 2019 (to replace the information at page 414) is as follows: The wait time for Indian immigrants for a second preference visa is about 10 years and for a third preference visa is about 10 years. (https://travel.state.gov/content/travel/en/legal/visa-law0/visa-bulletin/2019/visa-bulletin-for-august-2019.html)

Errata: The citation at the end of the last full paragraph should read: 20 C.F.R. § 656.1

At page 415, the section titled "First preferences:…" should be labeled "A" not "1". The three subsections that follow at pages 415, 416, and 417 should be numbered 1, 2 and 3, not lettered a, b, and c.

Errata: In Section B on page 418 (mislabeled "b" in the current print edition), subsection 1 describes in greater detail the labor certification process needed to obtain a second preference visa (EB-2). There is a typo in subsection 1 in the second sentence of the second full paragraph on page 419, which should read in full: "The minimum requirements for the offered position may not be unduly restrictive in terms of the years or types of experience required. Employers can determine appropriate qualifications by using O*NET (Occupational Information Network), and online database of occupations."

Section C on page 421 is mislabeled "c" in the current print edition). Section D on page 422 (is mislabeled "d" in the current print edition, and Section E on page 422 is mislabeled "e" in the current print edition.

V.   Diversity Visas [Erratum: mislabled as IV on page 423 of the current print edition]

Errata: In the second full paragraph of this section, the reference to the INA should be to section 203(c) (not (d)) and the code reference should be to section 1153(c) (not 153(d)).

VI.   Adjustment of Status [Erratum: mislabled as V on page 428 of the current print edition]

On page 439, add the following after note 2:

3. Parole in Place

Since President Trump took office, the government has aggressively worked to dismantle many humanitarian and discretionary based programs including DACA and TPS for several countries. And with the way things are headed, there are no signs of abatement. However, there are a few discretionary options that, for the time being, are still intact—one of the most popular but least understood being Military Parole in Place.

Parole in Place is a discretionary decision made by USCIS to allow certain individuals who may have entered the United States without inspection to remain here temporarily. This is accomplished through the government's exercise of section 212(d)(5)(A) of the Immigration and Nationality Act, which authorizes parole on a case-by-case basis for those who have demonstrated urgent humanitarian reasons or a significant public benefit. Military Parole in Place (or PIP) is a formalized protocol for entertaining parole requests for family members of the US Armed Forces and veterans.

In order to be eligible, the individual must be a spouse, widow(er), parent, son or daughter of an active duty member of the US armed forces; an individual in the Selected Reserve of the Ready Reserve; or a former member of the US armed forces (who was not dishonorably discharged). In addition to proof of relationship and proof of the family member's military status, the individual must submit evidence demonstrating that a favorable exercise of discretion is warranted. Furthermore, the applicant must be physically present in the US and generally speaking, not be convicted of a criminal offense or otherwise pose a threat to public safety. Interestingly, if an applicant has entered the US lawfully (i.e., using a visitor's visa) but then overstayed, he/she will not be considered for PIP, since the person has technically already been admitted to the US.

If approved, the individual will be granted temporary authorization to stay in the United States. Parole is granted in increments of one year and insulates the individual from removal/deportation (provided the person follows the law and does not commit conduct that would render him/her deportable). A PIP parolee will also become eligible to apply for work authorization which can lead to an issuance of a social security number and also enable one to apply for a driver license in many states.

Another important aspect of PIP is that the person will be given an I-94 as evidence of their parole status. For individuals who would otherwise not qualify for adjustment of status due to a lack of inspection, PIP may serve as a much-needed mechanism to address the admission eligibility requirement. To illustrate: under section 245(a), only those individuals who have been "inspected, admitted, or paroled" are eligible to seek adjustment of status inside the US. As a result, those who may have evaded inspection when entering the country (colloquially referred to as "ewi's") are not statutorily eligible to apply inside the US. However, if a person is subsequently granted PIP, he or she may then use the I-94 proof of parole to satisfy this prong. Of course, the individual still needs to meet all the other requirements of 245(a) in addition to showing that no grounds of inadmissibility apply. But the point is that military PIP may allow individuals to regularize their immigration status when that would otherwise not be possible under our current immigration system.

Unfortunately, on June 27, 2019, the Trump administration announced that it will scale back protections for undocumented family members of U.S. troops. According to immigration lawyers familiar with the plan, the Parole in Place program—which grants legal residence and benefits to the spouses, children, and parents of active military members—is "being terminated," and lawyers are scrambling to submit applications for eligible clients before it's too late.

The program was designed to ensure that a soldier deployed on active duty would not have to be distracted by concerns about a family member back home in the U.S. being deported. Parole in Place status is often sought by individuals who immigrated to the U.S. long ago, who now have grown children enlisted in the military. It can also be used by the spouses or children of active duty military.

Chapter 7

INADMISSIBILITY

Section II.A.3

Notes and Questions after II.A.3 (p. 446)
Delete note 1. Discussions of the President Trump's entry ban and related issues and litigation are now covered at page 458.

Section II.B

Errata p. 458: The textbook currently states that the Court "declined to apply Mandel," but it would be more accurate to say that Justice Scalia's opinion did not apply Mandel. The concurrence did discuss and apply the test.

Addendum: After note 3 on page 458, add the following:

4. The *Mandel* case played an important role in the *Hawaii v. Trump* litigation and ultimately helped to provide the basis for the majority's decision that the travel ban was a constitutional exercise of presidential power insofar as the ban was premised upon a facially legitimate and bona fide national security justification. Justice Sotomayor's dissent questioned whether the case was even applicable, given that Mandel was subject to an individual waiver denial and the Hawaii case involved a blanket group ban. Please read *Hawaii v. Trump*, which is included in this supplement as **Appendix A,** at this time.

5. Ongoing litigation in the case of *Emani v. Nielson,* currently pending in the Northern District of California, alleges that individuals from banned countries whose individual cases fit the categories purportedly eligible for waiver under Presidential Proclamation 9645 (the final version of President Trump's travel ban) are being illegitimately denied such waivers. The case will help reveal how closely courts are willing to look behind purported "national security" justifications in individual cases under the ban.

On page 458, change note number 4 to 6 (to reflect the inclusion of the notes and case above).

Addendum: In the **Notes and Questions** on page 479, add the following text after Note 2:

In Matter of M-H-Z-, 26 I&N Dec. 757 (BIA 2016), the Board held that the material support bar contains no exception for duress. Of course, the Attorney General still has the authority to issue waivers even if immigration courts find the material support bar applies, but this narrows the path for arguing duress.

In 2018, in Matter of A-C-M, 27 I&N Dec. 303 (BIA 2018), (attached here as **Appendix B**), the Board defined the term "material" in the case of a Salvadoran woman who cooked, cleaned and washed the clothes of guerillas in El Salvador. The Board found that her work was "material" support, writing "we conclude that an alien provides "material support" to a terrorist organization, regardless of whether it was intended to aid the organization, if the act has a logical and reasonably foreseeable tendency to promote, sustain, or maintain the organization, even if only to a de minimis degree."

The Board also found that her work was "forced labor" performed under threat of violence—the essence of duress—but nevertheless applied the bar. At footnotes 5 and 6 of the original opinion (notes 2 and 3 in the except), the Board discusses the fact that the Attorney General can provide a waiver in cases such as these, where the bar applies. Read **Appendix B** now.

Section II.C (p. 480)

Clarification: The last paragraph on page 480 is discussing a single kind of waiver—the waiver available under section 212(h). Some readers have found the use of the plural in this paragraph in reference to 212(h) waivers to be confusing.

Section II.D (p. 482-483)

Addendum: Insert the following text at the end of this Section:

On October 18, 2018, the Trump Administration proposed a rule to replace the regulations that had governed the public charge standard since May 26, 1996. The rule proposed to include in the category anyone who received or was likely to receive "any government assistance in the form of cash, checks or other forms of money transfers, or instruments and non-cash government assistance in the form of aid, services or other relief, that is means-tested or is intended to help the individual meet basic living requirements." After a notice and comment period, during which many organizations submitted critical comments, the Administration announced the final rule on August 14, 2019. A copy can be found at: https://www.federalregister.gov/documents/2019/08/14/2019-17142/inadmissibility-on-public-charge-grounds. Barring court action, the new rule will go into effect and apply to applications filed on or after October 1, 2019.

Under the old rule (which is still the law as this supplement goes to press), immigration officers use their discretion to evaluate a host of factors in determining whether an individual is likely to become a public charge. Included among these is consideration of "affidavits of support," whereby a qualifying resident

7. Inadmissibility

sponsor pledges to financially support the person seeking the visa. Officials also consider the applicants historical reliance on a limited set of federal cash aid such as TANF and SSI or long term institutionalized care. Immigrants who have used these kinds of assistance have been allowed a chance to demonstrate that it is not likely they will need these resources for support in the future. Reliance on publicly-funded health care, nutrition, and housing programs have not been considered as negative factors. The number of public charge exclusions under these regulations has been relatively small.

While the existing rule assesses whether an applicant is likely to become *primarily* dependent on the government for income support, the new rule sweeps much broader, potentially covering many working and self-sufficient people who have had periodic need for government support. Receipt of public benefits for more than an aggregate of 12 months over any 36-month period of time is a heavily weighted factor in favor of a public charge determination. The new rule also calls for immigration officials consider the applicant's reliance not only on TANF and SSI, but also, after the effective date, their reliance on publicly-funded health care, nutrition, and housing programs and some new federal programs, including Medicaid and the Supplemental Nutritional Assistance Program (SNAP). Lack of English language proficiency is also a negative factor under the new public charge rule. And affidavits of support will no longer be weighed as strong evidence against a public charge determination. Should it go into effect, the new rule could substantially increase the number of visa applicants excluded on public charge grounds.

Chapter **8**

GROUNDS FOR DEPORTATION/REMOVAL

III. Criminal Grounds

Section III.A.2

Errata page 540: "*Gonzales*" is spelled incorrectly at page 540. Also, the text 5 lines from the bottom of the page should be amended to read "circuit split by holding that a drug possession offense that is a felony under state law." And the sentence starting 3 lines from the bottom should be amended to read "The federal law classification of the crime as a misdemeanor takes the state drug possession offense outside of the ambit of a…."

Errata page 541: In the excerpted paragraph from *Carachuri-Rosendo* beginning "First, and most fundamentally," delete "(emphasis added)" in the fourth line. Nothing is emphasized.

More on the categorical approach. Students are often confused about the categorical and modified categorical approaches. Katherine Brady of the Immigrant Legal Resource Center has a useful practice advisory here: https://www.ilrc.org/sites/default/files/resources/how_to_use_the_categorical_approach_now_april_2017.pdf.

The practice advisory provides excellent explanations and examples to illustrate how to determine whether the charged offense is a statutory match with the removal ground, whether the criminal statute is divisible, and which records can be relied upon to ascertain the crime of conviction in cases involving divisible statutes.

III.A.3   Crimes of Violence

Addendum: At the bottom of page 557 Add: Please read the Dimaya case, which is attached to the supplement as Appendix C.

* * *

Section III.B.2

Addendum: In the last full paragraph on page 561, delete the text beginning with "Indeed, that decision" and add:

Indeed, that decision was rejected by numerous circuit courts of appeal and ultimately withdrawn by Attorney General Mukasey in 2015. But the question of how to analyze this question continues to come up again and again in litigation. For a recent example of a Ninth Circuit analysis, read Barbosa v. Barr (9th Cir. 2019), which is attached to this supplement as **Appendix G.**

Section III.D.   Firearms Offenses

Addendum: At page 568, at the end of Section C, add the following subsection and text:

D. Firearms offenses

Almost any conviction relating to a firearm will render a noncitizen deportable. Some firearms offenses are also aggravated felonies or crimes involving moral turpitude, in which case, the consequences relating to such offenses also apply. For example, firearms offenses may involve "trafficking in firearms" or qualify as crimes of violence under the aggravated felony provision. See INA § 101(a)(43)(c) (making it an aggravated felony to be convicted of "illicit trafficking in firearms or destructive devices") and INA § 101(a)(43)(f) (defining crimes of violence with a sentence of at least a year as aggravated felonies). As previously noted, offenses involving use or threatened use of force often qualify as crimes involving moral turpitude, and many firearms offenses involve these elements.

But even when crimes do not qualify as aggravated felonies or crimes involving moral turpitude, there may be immigration consequences. INA §237(a)(2)(C) states that any noncitizen "who at any time after admission is convicted under any law of purchasing, selling, offering for sale, exchanging, using, owning, possessing, or carrying, or of attempting or conspiring to purchase, sell, offer for sale, exchange, use, own, possess, or carry, any weapon, part, or accessory which is a firearm or destructive device (as defined in section 921(a) of title 18) in violation of any law is deportable."

As with controlled substances, the consequences are severe and automatic if the firearms offense in question also qualifies as an aggravated felony. If an offense merely qualifies as a firearms offense, and not an aggravated felony or moral turpitude crime, relief might be possible.

For a detailed discussion of the state of immigration law in the 9th Circuit as it pertains to firearms, see Immigrant Legal Resource Center, Firearms Offenses, January 2013 (available at https://www.ilrc.org/sites/default/files/resources/n.12-fireams_0.pdf)

Chapter 9

THE DETENTION NIGHTMARE

II. Constitutional Authority

At page 604, add these to the Notes and Questions after number 7:

8. In *Jennings v. Rodriguez*, 138 S. Ct. 830 (2018), the Supreme Court held that 8 USC §§ 1225(b), 1226(a) and 1226(c) do not give detained aliens the right to periodic bond hearings during the course of their detention pending removal their hearings. *Rodriguez* was a class action suit on behalf of individuals held pursuant to four statutory provisions. The first, 8 U.S.C. § 1225(b), applies to individuals arriving at the border who are seeking admission into the United States. Asylum seekers who establish a credible fear of persecution "shall be detained for further consideration of the application." 8 U.S.C. § 1225(b)(1)(B)(ii) (2012). All others seeking admission who are "not clearly and beyond a doubt entitled to be admitted . . . shall be detained" for removal proceedings. Id. § 1225(b)(2)(A). Under the second provision, 8 U.S.C. § 1226(c), "[t]he Attorney General shall take into custody any [noncitizen]" present in the United States who has been convicted of certain enumerated crimes. Id. §1226(c)(1). These individuals may be released "only if the Attorney General decides" it is necessary for witness-protection purposes. Id. § 1226(c)(2). Any other individual in removal proceedings "may be arrested and detained" under § 1226(a) — the third provision — and, pending removal, the Attorney General "may release the [noncitizen] on bond of at least $1,500." Id. § 1226(a). Those denied bond may remain detained until their proceedings end. Finally, under 8 U.S.C. § 1231(a), individuals who have been ordered removed "shall" be detained for up to ninety days while the government effectuates their removal. Id. § 1231(a)(1)–(2). All of the *Rodriguez* class members, regardless of the statute applicable to their circumstances, were required to wait in detention while they argued their cases to stay.

9. In *Matter of M-S-*, 27 I&N Dec. 509 (A.G. 2019), Attorney General William Barr unilaterally overturned a 2005 decision of the Board of Immigration Appeals (Matter of X-K-, 23 I&N Dec. 731). The Attorney General's outrageous decision strips immigration judges of the authority to grant bond to asylum seekers who entered the United States without being inspected at a port of entry but passed their threshold credible fear asylum screening interviews (CFI). These asylum seekers will now be subject to detention without bond for the duration of their asylum proceedings, separated from their loved ones and community. The decision is currently being challenged in the case *Padilla v. ICE*. *See* https://www.aclu.org/cases/padilla-v-ice

IV.   Detention Since 9/11 and the ICE Age

At page 647, add these to the Notes and Questions after number 3:

4. In the summer of 2018, the nation's attention focused on the separation of migrant children from their parents under a so-called "zero-tolerance" policy implemented by the Trump administration. That strategy is discussed in the teaching supplement for Chapter 10 — see especially *Ms. L v. ICE.*

5. During the summer of 2019, a great deal of national attention was focused on the fact that children who were being separated from non-parental relatives were being held in violation of the terms of the TVPRA for way more than 72 hours in CBP facilities. The conditions were particularly disturbing. Bill Hing's account of what he say at the CBP facility located in Clint, Texas, included the following:

> Several of the younger children I interviewed were unbathed and wore dirty clothes. Some did not have socks. Their hair was dirty. I came to realize that the younger children were dirtier than the older children because the smaller ones were hesitant to bathe by themselves; there was also no one who helped them wash their clothes. With only a couple exceptions, none of the children I interviewed were offered clean clothes. All reported that the belongings they carried to the border were thrown away by CBP officers.
>
> . . .
>
> The children were detained in cramped rooms that slept 20–50 persons, depending on the size of the room. Some had beds, others had mats to sleep on. Still others had no mats to sleep on. The children are confined to their rooms all day long, except when the room is cleaned, when they are out to eat, or when they must go the bathroom. . . . Younger kids reported that they were not able to go outside to play on a daily basis. They reported that they could only go outside every two or three days to play.

Hing also described how CBP separated one two-year-old toddler from her aunt. Incredulously, the little girl was expected to take care of herself. A 16-year-old girl confined in the same room cared for the little one out of the kindness.

Dahlia Lithwick, *"Some Did Not Have Socks. Their Hair Was Dirty."* An *interview with an immigration lawyer who visited the detained children in Clint, Texas,* SLATE, July 1, 2019.

For an interview of Bill Hing on the same topic, visit the website of the New American Story Project: https://newamericanstoryproject.org/context/visiting-a-detention-center-for-child-immigrants

6. In early July 2019, the *Flores* Monitor appointed a physician, Dr. Paul Wise, to conduct evaluations and assess health conditions at facilities for CBP and the ORR, which takes cares of unaccompanied migrant children after they've been processed at the border. The doctor was to draft a report with his findings and recommendations by Aug. 5. Litigating U.S. attorneys would then have a

week to respond with comments or objections to the draft report before the final version is submitted to the monitor by Aug. 29. The sides also agreed to find "any remedial steps necessary to bring the conditions of custody and systems of child health care into compliance with the law and the Flores Settlement Agreement."

VI.   Bond and Other Options

At the top of page 663, before part VII, add the following:

D.   Catch and Release

Although the term has been given a pejorative connotation by President Trump and other anti-immigrant groups, the practice of "catch and release" was quite common prior to 2014. Under the practice, those stopped at the border — especially family units — were processed and allowed to go on their way with a Notice to Appear at the immigration court where they were headed.

Given the surge in Central Americans in the past year, in spite of increased detention, there has also been an increase in catch and release practices under the Trump administration. Overwhelmed by the number of families crossing into the southern border, the Trump administration arrested then released more than 125,000 individuals during the first three months of 2019. This occurred in Texas, Arizona, and California, and often the families are simply dropped off at Greyhound bus stations.

See Cedar Attanasio and Astrid Galvin, *U.S. resorts to expanded "catch and release" as migrants surge at border*, THE ASSOCIATED PRESS, April 2, 2019.

E.   Rate of Absconding

Most asylum seekers actually show up for their immigration court hearings, contrary to assertions by the Trump administration. An analysis by Syracuse University in 2019 reveals that most asylum seekers appear at their asylum hearings. Almost six out of every seven families released from custody show up for their initial court hearings. For those who are represented, more than 99 percent appear at every hearing held. *See Most Released Families Attend Immigration Court Hearings*, June 18, 2019, https://trac.syr.edu/immigration/reports/562/. This data, based on Department of Justice data, contradicts allegations by Trump administration officials that most families do not attend their hearings. Relatedly, a study by the Catholic Legal Immigration Network found that many asylum seekers ordered removed in absentia (not present) had legitimate reasons for not appearing, such as lack of notice, incorrect government information, medical problems, or language barriers.

See Tyche Hendricks, *Report: Vast Majority of Asylum-Seeking Families in S.F. Immigration Court Attend All Hearings,* KQED, June 22, 2019.

VII. Detention of Unaccompanied Minors

At page, 670, add the following at the end of the Notes and Questions:

4. The Trump administration is advocating legislation that would treat all UACs the same way that those from Mexico are treated. They would no longer get ORR treatment. Trump now wants to gut out the protections benefiting UACs from Central America. His proposal would subject all unaccompanied children at the border to rapid removal proceedings that are currently used only for minors from Mexico and Canada. Trump also called for children seeking asylum to make their cases before judges, instead of less-adversarial asylum officers. *See* http://www.motherjones.com/politics/2017/10/trump-wants-to-make-it-easier-to-detain-and-deport-unaccompanied-central-american-children/.

Why do you think Trump is making this proposal?

5. Although ORR facilities may be better than ICE facilities, the ORR facilities also have been criticized. For example, one "temporary influx facility" near Homestead Air Reserve Base in south Florida warehoused about 1,600 children (ages 13 to 17) a day until summer of 2019. Legal observers reported seeing "extremely traumatized children," some who could not stop crying. Each child was kept there for an average of 67 days; and the facility costs about $1.2 million a day to operate by private company Comprehensive Health Services. Another facility in the west Texas desert used tents and was finally shuttered after intense criticism.

See John Burnett, *Inside The Largest And Most Controversial Shelter For Migrant Children In The U.S.,* NPR, Feb. 13, 2019.

Here is video of the Homestead facility: https://www.cbsnews.com/news/homestead-migrant-detention-center-exclusive-look-inside-florida-facility-2019-06-28/.

Another private company that makes millions of dollars in contracts with ORR is Southwest Keys. *See Emily Stewart, The multibillion-dollar business of sheltering migrant children, explained,* Vox, June 25, 2018, at https://www.vox.com/2018/6/23/17493380/family-separation-shelter-money-children-southwest-key.

6. On August 15, 2019, the Ninth Circuit Court of Appeals issued a ruling reviewing a dispute over the terms of the Flores Settlement Agreement (Paragraph 12A) relating to "safe and sanitary" conditions. *Flores v. Barr,* __ F.3d __ (9th Cir. 2019), 2019 WL 3820265. In June 2017, after an evidentiary hearing, the district

court found that the government was violating the Flores Settlement Agreement's express requirements to provide adequate access to appropriate food and water and "adequate temperature controls at a reasonable and comfortable range." The court further found that although the Agreement "makes no mention of the words 'soap,' 'towels,' 'showers,' 'dry clothing,' or 'toothbrushes,' . . . these hygiene products fall within the rubric of the Agreement's language requiring 'safe and sanitary' conditions." The district court also determined that although "the word 'sleep' does not appear in the Agreement, . . . whether the government has set up conditions that allow class members to sleep in the [Border Patrol] facilities is relevant to the issue of whether they have acted in a manner that is consistent with concern for the particular vulnerability of minors as well as the Agreement's 'safe and sanitary' requirement." Citing evidence that many minors in Border Patrol custody are forced to sleep on concrete floors, with no bedding aside from pieces of thin polyester foil, and are subjected to cold temperatures, serious overcrowding, and constant lighting, the district court found that the government was violating the Agreement at certain Border Patrol stations by holding children in facilities that deprived them of adequate sleep.

On appeal, the government contended that, by interpreting parts of the Agreement in the body of its opinion to require that Border Patrol stations provide the most basic human necessities — accommodations that allow for adequate sleep, essential hygiene items, and adequate, clean food and water — the district court modified the Agreement's requirement that minors be held in "safe and sanitary" conditions that comport with the "special concern for the particular vulnerability of minors." Incredulously, the government maintained that as the enumerated conditions said nothing about, for example, allowing the children in government custody to sleep or to wash themselves with soap, reading the "safe and sanitary" requirement to cover those requirements is a modification of the Agreement rather than an interpretation of it. The Ninth Circuit emphatically disagreed with the government:

> The district court's interpretation of the Agreement is consistent with the ordinary meaning of the language of paragraph 12A, which does provide a standard sufficiently clear to be enforced. The court found, among other things, that minors (1) were "not receiving hot, edible, or a sufficient number of meals during a given day," (2) "had no adequate access to clean drinking water," (3) experienced "unsanitary conditions with respect to the holding cells and bathroom facilities," (4) lacked "access to clean bedding, and access to hygiene products (i.e., toothbrushes, soap, towels)," and (5) endured "sleep deprivation" as a result of "cold temperatures, overcrowding, lack of proper bedding (i.e., blankets, mats), [and] constant lighting." After so finding, the district court concluded that these conditions fall short of paragraph 12A's requirement that facilities be "safe and sanitary," especially given "the particular vulnerability of minors." Those determinations reflect a common-sense understanding of what the quoted language requires. Assuring that children eat enough edible food, drink clean water, are housed in hygienic facilities with

sanitary bathrooms, have soap and toothpaste, and are not sleep-deprived are without doubt essential to the children's safety. The district court properly construed the Agreement as requiring such conditions rather than allowing the government to decide whether to provide them.

In other words, the Ninth Circuit disagreed with the government's contention that "safe and sanitary" conditions do not include toothbrushes, soap, towels and ensuring the children are not deprived of sleep. Do you agree?

Chapter 10

ENFORCEMENT

I. Introduction (p. 671)

Addendum: After the introduction on page 671, add the following discussion:

On January 25, 2017, President Trump signed two executive orders relating to immigration enforcement. These are included as **Appendix D**. Please review these two orders now.

As you will see, the first order focuses on the border and, among other things: 1) calls for proposals for a southern border wall; 2) orders the expansion of detention capacity to enable the detention of all incoming unauthorized migrants, and to process their asylum requests while they are detained; 3) expands the border patrol; 4) orders the expansion of 287(g) agreements and other leveraging of state and local agencies as immigration enforcement agents; 5) reorients federal criminal enforcement priorities by requiring the Attorney General to " take all appropriate steps to establish prosecution guidelines and allocate appropriate resources to ensure that Federal prosecutors accord a high priority to prosecutions of offenses having a nexus to the southern border."

This order sowed the seeds for the Administration's family separation policy, whereby families arriving together at the border were separated. Adults were detained, placed in removal proceedings, and sometimes also prosecuted for illegal entry in streamlined procedures (more on this below), while children were placed in detention facilities under the supervision of the office of refugee resettlement (ORR). The practice caused a national outcry and spurred litigation ordering the reunification of separated families. Because the federal government lacks sufficient records for many of these families, and because the government fast-tracked the deportation of many of the parents, at the time this goes to press, hundreds of children still remain separated from their parents. An edited version of Judge Dana Sabraw's order concerning the reunification of families is attached as **Appendix E**.

President Trump's second executive order of January 25, 2017, focuses on interior enforcement. It purports to set priorities for enforcement, but includes categories so broad—including individuals charged with (but not convicted of) crimes and individuals who "[i]n the judgment of an immigration officer, otherwise pose a risk to public safety or national security"—that anyone can be a priority. And indeed, in at least some jurisdictions, ICE agents have been acting under orders to arrest all immigrants that they encounter. In July 2018, Marcelo Rochebrun reported:

The head of the Immigration and Customs Enforcement unit in charge of deportations has directed his officers to take action against all undocumented immigrants they may cross paths with, regardless of criminal histories. The guidance appears to go beyond the Trump administration's publicly stated aims, and some advocates say may explain a marked increase in immigration arrests.

In a February memo, Matthew Albence, a career official who heads the Enforcement and Removal Operations division of ICE, informed his 5,700 deportation officers that, "effective immediately, ERO officers will take enforcement action against all removable aliens encountered in the course of their duties."

Marcelo Rochebrun, ICE Officers Told to Take Action Against All Undocumented Immigrants Encountered While on Duty, July 7, 2017 (available at https://www.propublica.org/article/ice-officers-told-to-take-action-against-all-undocumented-immigrants-encountered-while-on-duty). The article includes a link to the memo.

Among other things, the second order also: 1) calls for the expansion of ICE; 2) reiterates the order to expand the use of 287(g) agreements and other leveraging of state and local law enforcement; 3) calls for an end of Federal aid to "sanctuary cities" (more on this below) and requires compilation and dissemination of crimes committed by unauthorized migrants in "sanctuary cities"; 4) terminates the Obama Administration's Priority Enforcement Program and reinstates "Secure Communities," 5) creates an "Office for Victims of Crimes Committed by Removable Aliens"; and 6) calls for reporting of the immigration status of all inmates in federal, state and local prisons and jails.

Although the term "sanctuary city" is defined in the order as a jurisdiction that violates 8 U.S.C. § 1373, the precatory language of the order (and the President and Attorney General, when speaking about the order), more broadly define "sanctuary city" to include jurisdictions that are not cooperating with all federal requests to assist in immigration enforcement. This has prompted federal district courts to enjoin portions of the order purporting to strip such jurisdictions of resources. An edited version of one such order — from litigation in Northern California – is attached as **Appendix F**, which you will read later in the chapter.

II.   Border Apprehensions (p. 671)

Addendum: At page 677, at the end of Part II, add the following text:

President Trump's presidential campaign relied heavily on rhetoric concerning the building of a wall along the entire U.S.-Mexico border. Indeed, "build the wall" became a staple chant at Trump rallies both before and after the election. There is a virtual consensus among experts that a physical wall along the U.S.-Mexico border would be both extremely expensive and relatively ineffective in preventing unauthorized migration. Yet the theme continues to capture the imagination. Pratheepan Gulasekarem argues that "the wall" serves an expressive function that both legitimates and naturalizes the enforcement of penalties against unauthorized migrants. He writes:

> In addition to normalizing border regulation and sanctifying the background legal framework, the border wall helps intensify perception of the very problem it purports to address. Borrowing again from expressive law theory, Professor Dan Kahan notes that when the government engages in dramatic gestures to make individuals aware of certain penalties, the gestures themselves cause individuals to believe that the phenomenon requiring the penalty is prevalent. In Kahan's example, the raising of tax penalties and the government's gestures to make taxpayers aware of those enhancements create the perception that more taxpayers than before are evading taxes. The same theory is easily applied in the immigration context. Once created, a border wall is visible reassurance that the incidence of unlawful entry, the possibility of a Mexican invasion into the United States, and the likelihood that terrorists are using the southern border, are viable and credible existential threats to the nation.
>
> In this way, the bogeyman of the Mexican migrant or clandestine terrorist—the same one that helped lend public support to authorizing the fence in the first instance—is given a second life by the existence of the wall. In this regard, consider the participation of organized private actors in the project of fence building or fixing. The existence of a partial, government-created fence provides the impetus for private actors, like the Minutemen Civil Defense Corps, to help complete or fix the fence. Private actors engage in fence building despite knowledge that their actions are mostly symbolic because they perceive the threat of undocumented migration as important enough to compel government action. So important, in fact, that perceived government failure or delay in providing a solution cannot be idly tolerated; the concerned citizenry must help defend nationhood and sovereignty on its own.
>
> The attempt to naturalize the border through ancient iconography undermines the fact that borders are constructed and therefore capable of deconstruction. Once the possibility of deconstruction is marginalized, entry without inspection across the southern border resembles *malum in se* rather than *malum prohibitum*; the sovereign may discover and deport those individuals with minimal regard to their claims of belonging. Concurrently, the ability of border fortification to substantiate and elevate public perception of a migration problem solidifies support for the exercise of sovereign power, even to the extent of the public demanding solutions beyond the scope of the individual nation-state sovereign.

Pratheepan Gulasekaram, *Why a Wall*, 2 U.C. IRVINE L. REV. 147, 180-81 (2012) (citations omitted).

Congress's refusal to provide President Trump's requested appropriations for a border wall resulted in a government shut down at the end of 2018 that began in December 2018 and lasted 35 days—the longest government shutdown in history. In the end, Congress did not bend and the government reopened without appropriation of Trump's desired border wall funds. But on February 15, 2019, President Trump did an end-run around Congress by declaring a "national emergency" that required the reallocation of billions of dollars of previously appropriated military construction funds toward the construction of a border wall. Relying on section 8005 of the Department of Defense Appropriations Act of 2019 and related provisions, DoD reprogrammed approximately $2.5 billion from DoD to DHS for the purpose of building border barriers at various points along the Southern border. Section 8005 authorized the Secretary of Defense to transfer funds for military purposes if the Secretary determines that the transfer is "for higher priority items, based on unforeseen military requirements" and "the item for which funds are requested has [not] been denied by the Congress." Pub. L. No. 115-245, § 8005, 132 Stat. 2981, 2999 (2018) (hereinafter "section 8005").

The Sierra Club and the Southern Border Communities Coalition challenged the reprogramming and obtained an injunction in federal district court. The injunction was upheld by the 9th Circuit. Sierrra Club v. Trump (9th Cir. July 3, 2019) (http://cdn.ca9.uscourts.gov/datastore/general/2019/07/03/19-16102-order.pdf). On July 26, 2019, however, the Supreme Court granted the federal government's motion for a stay of the injunction, allowing the border wall process to proceed pending further litigation. Trump v. Sierra Club (2019) (http://cdn.ca9.uscourts.gov/datastore/general/2019/07/03/19-16102-order.pdf).

III.   Border Prosecutions (p. 677)

Addendum: At page 679 before Part IV, add the following text:

Operation Streamline has been revitalized and expanded by the Trump Administration in 2018, consonant with the President's January 25, 2017, executive order. The program has been expanded into California and continues to operate in Texas and Arizona. Defense attorneys in California are now raising questions about whether pleas under streamlined procedures are "voluntary" as required by law. See, e.g., Simon Campbell, Defense attorneys challenge judges over Trump immigration policies, The Guardian, August 20, 2018 (available at https://www.theguardian.com/us-news/2018/aug/20/defense-attorneys-challenge-judges-over-trump-immigration-policies).

The push to prosecute immigration crimes is affecting other enforcement efforts. TRAC, which compiles public immigration statistics, reported in August 2018 that "[i]n March 2018, immigration prosecutions dominated so that in the five federal districts along the southwest border only one in seven prosecutions (14%) were for any non-immigration crimes. But by June 2018, this ratio had shrunk so just one in seventeen prosecutions (6%) were for anything other than immigration offenses." (The full discussion is available at http://trac.syr.edu/immigration/reports/524/).

IV. Border Policing (P. 679)

IV.C. Interior Policing

Note 3 discusses the Obama administration's shift from raids to "silent raids." **Addendum:** At page 721, after note 3, add the following text: The Trump Administration has made a return to higher profile physical raids. See, e.g., Clark Mindock, US immigration agents double number of workplace raids, spreading fear and tearing families apart, The Independent, June 3, 2018 (available at https://www.independent.co.uk/news/world/americas/trump-immigration-ice-us-workplace-raids-irs-mexico-a8379886.html) (noting the Trump administration's announcement of a doubling of raids between October 2017 and March of 2018).

In the middle of page 721, after note 3, add the following:

4. Know Your Rights Presentations. The *Delgado* decisions forms much of the basis for know your rights presentations that are conducted by countless community based organizations and attorneys throughout the country. In *Delgado*, the Court stated that the workers did not need to respond to questions by immigration agents; in fact, the workers could have calmly walked out of the facility because there was not a seizure. Know your rights presentations inform audiences that individuals have the right to remain silent, they have a right to an attorney, that they can resist sorting commands (e.g., "those of you without documents go to this area"), and that they can get up and leave. Only when immigration agents have a warrant signed by a federal judge or magistrate do the individuals have to comply. Various resources for these presentations are readily available online, *see, e.g.,* https://www.aclu.org/know-your-rights/immigrants-rights/

Also, "red cards" in different languages are often distributed to individuals. These red cards can be handed to an immigration officer and contain language such as

> I do not wish to speak with you, answer your questions, or sign or hand you any documents based on my 5th Amendment rights under the United States Constitution. I do not give you permission to enter my home based on my 4th Amendment rights under the United States Constitution unless you have a warrant to enter, signed by a judge or magistrate with my name on it that you slide under the door. I do not give you permission to search any of my belongings based on my 4th Amendment rights. I choose to exercise my constitutional rights.

See https://www.ilrc.org/red-cards

A. *Enlisting State and Local Law Enforcement*

Addendum: At the end of the chapter (p. 726), add the following text:

The Trump Administration early on attempted to secure the enforcement cooperation of state and local law enforcement agents by ordering a reduction of law enforcement funds for "sanctuary cities," as you saw in Section 9 of President Trump's interior January 25, 2017 Executive Order concerning interior enforcement in **Appendix D.** Several localities responded by suing the Trump Administration, arguing (among other things) that the threat to reduce significantly federal law enforcement funding to ensure cooperation constituted unconstitutional coercion of state and local officials in violation of the 10th Amendment of the Constitution and the separation of powers. An excerpt from Federal District Court Judge William H. Orrick permanently enjoining the federal spending is attached as **Appendix F**. Please read that decision, *Santa Clara v. Trump*, now.

On August 1, 2018, the Ninth Circuit Court of Appeals affirmed the injunction on separation of powers grounds (although it reversed the nationwide injunction, upholding the injunction only as applied to the counties party to the lawsuit). San Francisco v. Trump, No. 17-17478 (9th Cir., August 1, 2018) (https://www.sccgov.org/sites/cco/overview/Documents/9th-cir-Opinion.pdf).

Chapter 11

RELIEF FROM REMOVAL

I.   Introduction (p. 727)

Jill E. Family, *The Future Relief of Immigration Law*, 9 DREXEL L. REV. 393 (2017) summarizes the limited forms of relief from removal under the immigration laws.

Generally speaking, the Trump administration has tightened eligibility for relief from removal, such as asylum, for noncitizens. Material in this chapter supplement provides background on Deferred Action for Children Arrivals (DACA) and Temporary Protected Status (TPS), forms of relief that the Trump administration has sought to restrict, and INA § 212(h) relief available to an immigrant with a single marijuana possession (30 grams or less) conviction.

As noted in the introduction, criminal convictions can render noncitizens ineligible for certain forms of relief from removal. In *Marinelarena v. Barr*, 930 F.3d 1039 (9th Cir. 2019), the U.S. Court of Appeals for the Ninth Circuit ruled *en banc* that a criminal conviction with ambiguity in the record about whether a noncitizen should be barred from relief from removal under the immigration statute cannot bar a noncitizen from relief.

II.   Cancellation of Removal (p. 728)

Pereira v. Sessions

138 S. Ct. 2105 (2018)

Justice SOTOMAYOR delivered the opinion of the Court.

Nonpermanent residents, like petitioner here, who are subject to removal proceedings and have accrued 10 years of continuous physical presence in the United States, may be eligible for a form of discretionary relief known as cancellation of removal. 8 U.S.C. §1229b(b)(1). Under the so-called "stop-time rule" set forth in §1229b(d)(1)(A), however, that period of continuous physical presence is "deemed to end . . . when the alien is served a notice to appear under section 1229(a)." Section 1229(a), in turn, provides that the Government shall serve non-citizens in removal proceedings with "written notice (in this section referred to as a 'notice to appear') . . . specifying" several required pieces of information, including "[t]he time and place at which the [removal] proceedings will be held." §1229(a)(1)(G)(i).1

The narrow question in this case lies at the intersection of those statutory provisions. If the Government serves a noncitizen with a document that is labeled "notice to appear," but the document fails to specify either the time or place of the removal proceedings, does it trigger the stop-time rule? The answer is as obvious as it seems: No. A notice that does not inform a noncitizen when and where to appear for removal proceedings is not a "notice to appear under section 1229(a)" and therefore does not trigger the stop-time rule. The plain text, the statutory context, and common sense all lead inescapably and unambiguously to that conclusion.

I

A

Under the Illegal Immigration Reform and Immigrant Responsibility Act of 1996 (IIRIRA), 110 Stat. 3009-546, the Attorney General of the United States has discretion to "cancel removal" and adjust the status of certain nonpermanent residents. §1229b(b). To be eligible for such relief, a nonpermanent resident must meet certain enumerated criteria, the relevant one here being that the noncitizen must have "been physically present in the United States for a continuous period of not less than 10 years immediately preceding the date of [an] application" for cancellation of removal. §1229b(b)(1)(A).

IIRIRA also established the stop-time rule at issue in this case. Under that rule, "any period of . . . continuous physical presence in the United States shall be deemed to end . . . when the alien is served a notice to appear under section 1229(a) of this title." §1229b(d)(1)(A). Section 1229(a), in turn, provides that "written notice (in this section referred to as a 'notice to appear') shall be given . . . to the alien . . . specifying":

"(A) The nature of the proceedings against the alien.

"(B) The legal authority under which the proceedings are conducted.

"(C) The acts or conduct alleged to be in violation of law.

"(D) The charges against the alien and the statutory provisions alleged to have been violated.

"(E) The alien may be represented by counsel and the alien will be provided (i) a period of time to secure counsel under subsection (b)(1) of this section and (ii) a current list of counsel prepared under subsection (b)(2) of this section.

"(F) (i) The requirement that the alien must immediately provide (or have provided) the Attorney General with a written record of an address and telephone number (if any) at which the alien may be contacted respecting proceedings under section 1229a of this title.

---

1. The Court uses the term "noncitizen" throughout this opinion to refer to any person who is not a citizen or national of the United States. *See* 8 U.S.C. §1101(a)(3).

"(ii) The requirement that the alien must provide the Attorney General immediately with a written record of any change of the alien's address or telephone number.

"(iii) The consequences under section 1229a(b)(5) of this title of failure to provide address and telephone information pursuant to this subparagraph.

"(G)(i) The time and place at which the [removal] proceedings will be held.

"(ii) The consequences under section 1229a(b)(5) of this title of the failure, except under exceptional circumstances, to appear at such proceedings." §1229(a)(1) (boldface added).

The statute also enables the Government to "change or postpon[e] . . . the time and place of [the removal] proceedings." §1229(a)(2)(A). To do so, the Government must give the noncitizen "a written notice . . . specifying . . . the new time or place of the proceedings" and "the consequences . . . of failing, except under exceptional circumstances, to attend such proceedings." Ibid. The Government is not required to provide written notice of the change in time or place of the proceedings if the noncitizen is "not in detention" and "has failed to provide [his] address" to the Government. §1229(a)(2)(B).

The consequences of a noncitizen's failure to appear at a removal proceeding can be quite severe. If a noncitizen who has been properly served with the "written notice required under paragraph (1) or (2) of section 1229(a)" fails to appear at a removal proceeding, he "shall be ordered removed in absentia" if the Government "establishes by clear, unequivocal, and convincing evidence that the written notice was so provided and that the alien is removable." §1229a(b)(5)(A). Absent "exceptional circumstances," a noncitizen subject to an in absentia removal order is ineligible for some forms of discretionary relief for 10 years if, "at the time of the notice described in paragraph (1) or (2) of section 1229(a)," he "was provided oral notice . . . of the time and place of the proceedings and of the consequences" of failing to appear. §1229a(b)(7). In certain limited circumstances, however, a removal order entered in absentia may be rescinded—e.g., when the noncitizen "demonstrates that [he] did not receive notice in accordance with paragraph (1) or (2) of section 1229(a)." §1229a(b)(5)(C)(ii).

B

In 1997, shortly after Congress passed IIRIRA, the Attorney General promulgated a regulation stating that a "notice to appear" served on a noncitizen need only provide "the time, place and date of the initial removal hearing, where practicable." 62 Fed. Reg. 10332 (1997). Per that regulation, the Department of Homeland Security (DHS), at least in recent years, almost always serves noncitizens with notices that fail to specify the time, place, or date of initial removal hearings whenever the agency deems it impracticable to include such information. See . . . Tr. of Oral Arg. 52-53 (Government's admission that "almost 100 percent" of "notices to appear omit the time and date of the proceeding over the last three years"). Instead, these notices state that the times, places, or dates of the initial hearings are "to be determined.". . . .

In *Matter of Camarillo*, 25 I. & N. Dec. 644 (2011), the Board of Immigration Appeals (BIA) addressed whether such notices trigger the stop-time rule even if they do not specify the time and date of the removal proceedings. The BIA concluded that they do. Id., at 651. It reasoned that the statutory phrase "notice to appear 'under section [1229](a)'" in the stop-time rule "merely specifies the document the DHS must serve on the alien to trigger the 'stop-time' rule," but otherwise imposes no "substantive requirements" as to what information that document must include to trigger the stop-time rule. Id., at 647.

C

Petitioner Wescley Fonseca Pereira is a native and citizen of Brazil. In 2000, at age 19, he was admitted to the United States as a temporary "non-immigrant visitor." . . . After his visa expired, he remained in the United States. Pereira is married and has two young daughters, both of whom are United States citizens. He works as a handyman and, according to submissions before the Immigration Court, is a well-respected member of his community.

In 2006, Pereira was arrested in Massachusetts for operating a vehicle while under the influence of alcohol. On May 31, 2006, while Pereira was detained, DHS served him (in person) with a document labeled "Notice to Appear." . . . That putative notice charged Pereira as removable for overstaying his visa, informed him that "removal proceedings" were being initiated against him, and provided him with information about the "[c]onduct of the hearing" and the consequences for failing to appear. . . . Critical here, the notice did not specify the date and time of Pereira's removal hearing. Instead, it ordered him to appear before an Immigration Judge in Boston "on a date to be set at a time to be set." . . . (underlining in original).

More than a year later, on August 9, 2007, DHS filed the 2006 notice with the Boston Immigration Court. The Immigration Court thereafter attempted to mail Pereira a more specific notice setting the date and time for his initial removal hearing for October 31, 2007, at 9:30 a.m. But that second notice was sent to Pereira's street address rather than his post office box (which he had provided to DHS), so it was returned as undeliverable. Because Pereira never received notice of the time and date of his removal hearing, he failed to appear, and the Immigration Court ordered him removed in absentia. Unaware of that removal order, Pereira remained in the United States.

In 2013, after Pereira had been in the country for more than 10 years, he was arrested for a minor motor vehicle violation (driving without his headlights on) and was subsequently detained by DHS. The Immigration Court reopened the removal proceedings after Pereira demonstrated that he never received the Immigration Court's 2007 notice setting out the specific date and time of his hearing. Pereira then applied for cancellation of removal, arguing that the stop-time rule was not triggered by DHS' initial 2006 notice because the document lacked information about the time and date of his removal hearing.

11.   Relief from Removal

The Immigration Court disagreed, finding the law "quite settled that DHS need not put a date certain on the Notice to Appear in order to make that document effective.". . . The Immigration Court therefore concluded that Pereira could not meet the 10-year physical presence requirement under §1229b(b), thereby rendering him statutorily ineligible for cancellation of removal, and ordered Pereira removed from the country. The BIA dismissed Pereira's appeal. . . .

The Court of Appeals for the First Circuit denied Pereira's petition for review of the BIA's order. 866 F.3d 1 (2017). Applying the framework set forth in *Chevron U.S.A. Inc. v. Natural Resources Defense Council, Inc.*, 467 U.S. 837 (1984), the Court of Appeals first found that the stop-time rule in §1229b(d)(1) is ambiguous because it "does not explicitly state that the date and time of the hearing must be included in a notice to appear in order to cut off an alien's period of continuous physical presence.". . . Then, after reviewing the statutory text and structure, the administrative context, and pertinent legislative history, the Court of Appeals held that the BIA's interpretation of the stop-time rule was a permissible reading of the statute. . . .

II

A

The Court granted *certiorari* in this case . . . to resolve division among the Courts of Appeals on a simple, but important, question of statutory interpretation: Does service of a document styled as a "notice to appear" that fails to specify "the items listed" in §1229(a)(1) trigger the stop-time rule?[4]. . . .

As a threshold matter, the Court notes that the question presented by Pereira, which focuses on all "items listed" in §1229(a)(1), sweeps more broadly than necessary to resolve the particular case before us. . . . [T]he dispositive question in this case is much narrower, but no less vital: Does a "notice to appear" that does not specify the "time and place at which the proceedings will be held," as required by §1229(a)(1)(G)(i), trigger the stop-time rule?

In addressing that narrower question, the Court need not resort to *Chevron* deference, as some lower courts have done, for Congress has supplied a clear and unambiguous answer to the interpretive question at hand. See 467 U.S., at 842-843 ("If the intent of Congress is clear, that is the end of the matter; for the court,

---

4. Compare Orozco-Velasquez v. Attorney General United States, 817 F.3d 78, 83-84 (CA3 2016) (holding that the stop-time rule unambiguously requires service of a "notice to appear" that meets §1229(a)(1)'s requirements), with Moscoso-Castellanos v. Lynch, 803 F.3d 1079, 1083 (CA9 2015) (finding the statute ambiguous and deferring to the BIA's interpretation); O'Garro v. United States Atty. Gen., 605 Fed. Appx. 951, 953 (CA11 2015) (per curiam) (same); Guaman-Yuqui v. Lynch, 786 F.3d 235, 239-240 (CA2 2015) (per curiam) (same); Gonzalez-Garcia v. Holder, 770 F.3d 431, 434-435 (CA6 2014) (same); Yi Di Wang v. Holder, 759 F.3d 670, 674-675 (CA7 2014) (same); Urbina v. Holder, 745 F.3d 736, 740 (CA4 2014) (same). The Court leaves for another day whether a putative notice to appear that omits any of the other categories of information enumerated in §1229(a)(1) triggers the stop-time rule. . . .

as well as the agency, must give effect to the unambiguously expressed intent of Congress"). A putative notice to appear that fails to designate the specific time or place of the noncitizen's removal proceedings is not a "notice to appear under section 1229(a)," and so does not trigger the stop-time rule.

B

The statutory text alone is enough to resolve this case. Under the stop-time rule, "any period of . . . continuous physical presence" is "deemed to end . . . when the alien is served a notice to appear under section 1229(a)." 8 U.S.C. §1229b(d)(1). By expressly referencing §1229(a), the statute specifies where to look to find out what "notice to appear" means. Section 1229(a), in turn, clarifies that the type of notice "referred to as a 'notice to appear'" throughout the statutory section is a "written notice . . . specifying," as relevant here, "[t]he time and place at which the [removal] proceedings will be held." §1229(a)(1)(G)(i). Thus, based on the plain text of the statute, it is clear that to trigger the stop-time rule, the Government must serve a notice to appear that, at the very least, "specif[ies]" the "time and place" of the removal proceedings.

* * *

[C]ommon sense compels the conclusion that a notice that does not specify when and where to appear for a removal proceeding is not a "notice to appear" that triggers the stop-time rule. If the three words "notice to appear" mean anything in this context, they must mean that, at a minimum, the Government has to provide non-citizens "notice" of the information, i.e., the "time" and "place," that would enable them "to appear" at the removal hearing in the first place. Conveying such time-and-place information to a noncitizen is an essential function of a notice to appear, for without it, the Government cannot reasonably expect the noncitizen to appear for his removal proceedings. To hold otherwise would empower the Government to trigger the stop-time rule merely by sending noncitizens a barebones document labeled "Notice to Appear," with no mention of the time and place of the removal proceedings, even though such documents would do little if anything to facilitate appearance at those proceedings. "'We are not willing to impute to Congress . . . such [a] contradictory and absurd purpose,'" United States v. Bryan, 339 U.S. 323, 342 (1950), particularly where doing so has no basis in the statutory text.

* * *

III

* * *

D

Unable to find sure footing in the statutory text, the Government and the dissent pivot away from the plain language and raise a number of practical concerns.

These practical considerations are meritless and do not justify departing from the statute's clear text. . . .

The Government, for its part, argues that the "administrative realities of removal proceedings" render it difficult to guarantee each noncitizen a specific time, date, and place for his removal proceedings. See Brief for Respondent 48. That contention rests on the misguided premise that the time-and-place information specified in the notice to appear must be etched in stone. That is incorrect. As noted above, §1229(a)(2) expressly vests the Government with power to change the time or place of a noncitizen's removal proceedings so long as it provides "written notice . . . specifying . . . the new time or place of the proceedings" and the consequences of failing to appear. . . . Nothing in our decision today inhibits the Government's ability to exercise that statutory authority after it has served a notice to appear specifying the time and place of the removal proceedings.

The dissent raises a similar practical concern, which is similarly misplaced. The dissent worries that requiring the Government to specify the time and place of removal proceedings, while allowing the Government to change that information, might encourage DHS to provide "arbitrary dates and times that are likely to confuse and confound all who receive them." . . . The dissent's argument wrongly assumes that the Government is utterly incapable of specifying an accurate date and time on a notice to appear and will instead engage in "arbitrary" behavior. . . . The Court does not embrace those unsupported assumptions. As the Government concedes, "a scheduling system previously enabled DHS and the immigration court to coordinate in setting hearing dates in some cases." Brief for Respondent 50, n. 15. . . . Given today's advanced software capabilities, it is hard to imagine why DHS and immigration courts could not again work together to schedule hearings before sending notices to appear.

Finally, the dissent's related contention that including a changeable date would "mislead" and "prejudice" noncitizens is unfounded. . . . As already explained, if the Government changes the date of the removal proceedings, it must provide written notice to the noncitizen, §1229(a)(2). This notice requirement mitigates any potential confusion that may arise from altering the hearing date. In reality, it is the dissent's interpretation of the statute that would "confuse and confound" noncitizens . . . by authorizing the Government to serve notices that lack any information about the time and place of the removal proceedings.

E

In a last ditch effort to salvage its atextual interpretation, the Government invokes the alleged purpose and legislative history of the stop-time rule. . . . Even for those who consider statutory purpose and legislative history, however, neither supports the Government's atextual position that Congress intended the stop-time rule to apply when a noncitizen has been deprived notice of the time and place of his removal proceedings. By the Government's own account, Congress enacted the stop-time rule to prevent noncitizens from exploiting administrative delays to "buy time" during which they accumulate periods of continuous presence. Id., at 37-38 (citing H. R. Rep. No. 104-469, pt. 1, p. 122 (1996)). Requiring the Government to furnish time-and-place information in a notice to appear, however, is entirely consistent with that objective because, once a proper notice to appear is served, the stop-time rule is triggered, and a noncitizen would be unable to manipulate or delay removal proceedings to "buy time." At the end of the day, given the clarity of the plain language, we "apply the statute as it is written." [citation omitted].

IV

For the foregoing reasons, the judgment of the Court of Appeals for the First Circuit is reversed, and the case is remanded for further proceedings consistent with this opinion.

It is so ordered.

Justice KENNEDY, concurring.

I agree with the Court's opinion and join it in full. This separate writing is to note my concern with the way in which the Court's opinion in Chevron U.S.A. Inc. v. Natural Resources Defense Council, Inc., 467 U.S. 837 (1984), has come to be understood and applied. The application of that precedent to the question presented here by various Courts of Appeals illustrates one aspect of the problem. . . .

In according *Chevron* deference to the BIA's interpretation, some Courts of Appeals engaged in cursory analysis of the questions whether, applying the ordinary tools of statutory construction, Congress' intent could be discerned, 467 U.S., at 843, n. 9, and whether the BIA's interpretation was reasonable, id., at 845. In *Urbina v. Holder*, for example, the court stated, without any further elaboration, that "we agree with the BIA that the relevant statutory provision is ambiguous." 745 F.3d, at 740. It then deemed reasonable the BIA's interpretation of the statute, "for the reasons the BIA gave in that case." *Ibid.* This analysis suggests an abdication of the Judiciary's proper role in interpreting federal statutes.

The type of reflexive deference exhibited in some of these cases is troubling. And when deference is applied to other questions of statutory interpretation, such as an agency's interpretation of the statutory provisions that concern the scope of its own authority, it is more troubling still. [citation omitted]. Given the concerns raised by some Members of this Court, . . . it seems necessary and appropriate to reconsider, in an appropriate case, the premises that underlie *Chevron* and how courts have implemented that decision. The proper rules for interpreting statutes and determining agency jurisdiction and substantive agency powers should accord with constitutional separation-of powers principles and the function and province of the Judiciary. . . .

Justice ALITO, dissenting.

Although this case presents a narrow and technical issue of immigration law, the Court's decision implicates the status of an important, frequently invoked, once celebrated, and now increasingly maligned precedent, namely, Chevron U.S.A. Inc. v. Natural Resources Defense Council, Inc., 467 U.S. 837 (1984). Under that decision, if a federal statute is ambiguous and the agency that is authorized to implement it offers a reasonable interpretation, then a court is supposed to accept that interpretation. Here, a straightforward application of *Chevron* requires us to accept the Government's construction of the provision at issue. But the Court rejects the Government's interpretation in favor of one that it regards as the best reading of the statute. I can only conclude that the Court, for whatever reason, is simply ignoring *Chevron*.

* * *

NOTES AND QUESTIONS

1.   Kit Johnson summarizes the holding of Pereira v. Sessions as follows:

> *Pereira* held that when a noncitizen receives a document called a notice to appear [NTA], and where that document does not have a time or place listed for the removal proceedings, then it is not a valid notice to appear, and thus it does not "stop time" for purposes of establishing the noncitizen's continuous physical presence in the United States. That clock-stopping question was crucial in *Pereira*, because the petitioner sought cancellation-of-removal relief, which is available only to noncitizens who can establish continuous physical presence in the United States for ten years [under Immigration & Nationality Act § 240A(b), 8 U.S.C. § 1229b(b)].

> Kit Johnson, Pereira v. Sessions: *A Jurisdictional Surprise for Immigration Courts*, 50 Colum. Hum. Rts. L. Rev. 1, 1-2 (2019) (footnotes omitted).

2.   For application of the Court's holding in *Pereira*, see Lopez v. Barr, 925 F.3d 396 (9th Cir. 2019) (holding that deficient notice to appear did not trigger the "stop time" rule for measuring the length of continuous physical presence in the United States).

A.   *Lawful Permanent Residents* (p. 728)

In Re C-V-T-

22 I. & N. Dec. 7 (BIA 1998) (p. 729)

NOTES AND QUESTIONS (PP. 735-36)

For recent Section 240A(a) cancellation cases, see, for example, Ishac v. Barr, 2019 U.S. App. LEXIS 15300 (6th Cir. May 23, 2019 (unpublished memorandum)); Chen v. Sessions, 864 F.3d 536 (7th Cir. 2017).

B.   *Nonpermanent Residents* (p. 736)

In Re Ariadna Angelica Gonzalez Recinas

23 I. & N. Dec. 467 (BIA 2002) (p. 736)

NOTES AND QUESTIONS (PP. 742-43)

Given the Trump administration's attempted termination of Temporary Protected Status (TPS) for citizens of several countries and the attempted rescission of Deferred Action for Childhood Arrivals (DACA), discussed later in this supplement, cancellation of removal under Immigration & Nationality Act (INA) § 240A(b), 8 U.S.C. § 1229b(b) likely will become a more frequently used form of relief from removal.

Note 3 discusses examples of the hardship on a U.S. citizen child of the removal of a noncitizen parent. Deporting parents with U.S. citizen children is common. *See* Claudia Masferrer, Erin R. Hamilton, & Nicole Denier, *Half a Million Minors Now Live in Mexico*, THE CONVERSATION, June 1, 2019, available at http://theconversation.com/half-a-million-american-minors-now-live-in-mexico-119057. The late Judge Harry Pregerson of the U.S. Court of Appeals for the Ninth Circuit dissented in roughly 60 cases, contending that removal of the parents amounted to *de facto* deportation of U.S. citizen children. *See Judge Pregerson Dissents in 60 Cases: Objects to Effective Deportation of U.S. Citizens,* IMMIGRATION PROF BLOG, OCT. 20, 2007, available at http://lawprofessors.type-pad.com/immigration/2007/10/judge-pregerson.html; Alissa Wickham, *9th Circ. Judge Slams "Cruelty" of US Immigration Law*, LAW 360, May 28, 2015, available at https://www.law360.com/articles/660770/9th-circ-judge-slams-cruelty-of-us-immigration-law; *see also* Kim McLane Wardlaw, *The Latino Immigration Experience*, 31 CHICANO-LATINO L. REV. 13, 39 n.156 (2012) (discussing Judge Pregerson's opinions on the de facto removal of U.S. citizen children). In *Aguallo v. Holder*, 425 Fed. Appx. 625, 627 (9th Cir. 2011) (Pregerson, J., dissenting), he wrote that:

> Aguallo's case is another example of the cruelty and coldness of our immigration laws and the suffering inflicted on innocents. When a parent is denied cancellation of removal, the government effectively banishes his children from the only home they know, depriving our country of their talents and denying them a productive future. This de facto expulsion from the country also forces those children to forego their constitutionally protected right to remain in the country of their birth with their family intact, in violation of due process. I cannot be a party to such a cruel result.

III.   Voluntary Departure (p. 743)

"Voluntary departure" under INA § 240B, 8 U.S.C. § 1229(c), allows a non-citizen to return to his or her native country without the entry of a removal order, thus avoiding a statutory bar of 10 years for legal immigration to the United States for noncitizens who have been ordered removed from the United States. *See* INA § 212(a)(9)(A)(ii), 8 U.S.C. § 1183(a)(9)(A)(ii).

For analysis of voluntary departure eligibility for a noncitizen in a subsequent "illegal re-entry" case under 8 U.S.C. § 1326, see United Stated v. Brown, 354 F. Supp. 3d 362 (S.D.N.Y 2018), *appeal dismissed*, 2019 U.S. App. LEXIS 20642 (2d Cir. Jan. 28, 2019).

In Re Eloy Arguelles-Campos

22 I&N Dec. 811 (BIA 1999) (p. 743)

NOTES AND QUESTIONS (PP. 751-52)

IV.   Victims of Domestic Violence (p. 752)

Hernandez v. Ashcroft

345 F.3d 824 (9th Cir. 2003) (p. 753)

NOTES AND QUESTIONS (P. 767)

As mentioned in note 2, for a period of time, the U.S. government moved toward interpreting the immigration laws with greater sensitivity toward the circumstances of women fleeing domestic violence. For example, gender-based asylum claims, including those founded on domestic violence, became more generously treated by the BIA and courts. However, Attorney Generals Jeff Sessions and William Barr intervened to overrule Board of Immigration Appeals (BIA) precedent and narrow asylum eligibility. *See Matter of L-E-A-*, 27 I. & N. Dec. 581 (AG 2019) (overruling BIA precedent to narrow members of a "particular social group" eligible for asylum); *Matter of A-B-*, 27 I. & N. Dec. 316 (AG 2018) (overruling BIA precedent to narrow eligibility for establishing membership in a particular social group for asylum-seekers who flee domestic or gang violence).

V.   Relief for Trafficking Victims (p. 768)

Jennifer M. Chacón, *Tensions and Trade-Offs: Protecting Trafficking Victims in the Era of Immigration Enforcement*
158 U. PA. L. REV. 1609, 1609-1615 (2010) (p. 768).

NOTES AND QUESTIONS (PP. 770-71)

For criticism of the current relief available to noncitizen survivors of trafficking and crime, see REFUGEES INT'L, REPORT: ABUSED, BLAMED, AND REFUSED: PROTECTION DENIED TO WOMEN AND CHILDREN TRAFFICKED OVER THE U.S. SOUTHERN BORDER (May 21, 2019), available at https://www.refugeesinternational. org/reports/2019/5/21/abused-blamed-and-refused-protection-denied-to-women-and-children-trafficked-over-the-us-southern-border.

United States v. Sabhnami

599 F.3d 215 (2d Cir. 2010) (p. 771)

Muchira v. Al-Rawaf, 850 F.3d 605 (4th Cir.), *cert. denied*, 138 S. Ct. 448 (2017) offers another example of the involuntary servitude of a noncitizen.

VI.   Special Immigrant Juvenile Status (p. 773)

Special Immigrant Juvenile Status (SIJS) status permits undocumented juveniles found by state courts to be abused, abandoned, or neglected to remain lawfully in the United States. *See* Immigration Act of 1990, Pub. L. No. 101-649, § 153, 104 Stat. 4978, 5005-06; Pub. L. No. 105-119, 111 Stat. 2460 (1997). To secure a predicate order necessary for SIJS status, the child's advocate must (1) identify the appropriate state court; (2) initiate an appropriate action under state law; and (3) persuade the court to render judgment that will be sufficient for immigration purposes. *Compare Matter of Marcelina M.-G. v. Israel S.*, 112 A.D.3d 100 (N.Y. App. Div. 2013) (granting predicate order), *with Matter of Hei Ting C.*, 109 A.D.3d 100 (N.Y. App. Div. 2013) (denying predicate order). Court practices related to SIJS vary from state to state and even from county to county within the same state. *See* Immigrant Legal Resource Center, *Frequently Asked Questions in 1-Parent Special Immigrant Juvenile Status Cases in California Family Courts*, Apr. 13, 2016, available at https://www.ilrc.org/sites/default/files/resources/faqs_familyctsijs_final_4.15.16.pdf. Some state courts are hostile to SIJS. For example, courts in Florida routinely deny SIJS applications; according to one practitioner, "if you bring [an SIJS] petition [in Florida], it will be dismissed offhand" in many counties. *See* Ashley Cleek, *Florida Judges Are Turning Their Backs on Abused Young Immigrants*, NATION, Jan. 22, 2018, available at https://www.thenation.com/article/florida-judges-are-turning-their-backs-on-abused-young-immigrants/

With the sporadic increases in the numbers of unaccompanied minors entering the United States without inspection, SIJS relief has grown in importance. *See* Lenni Benson, *Administrative Chaos: Responding to Child Refugees – U.S. Immigration Process in Crisis*, 75 WASH. & LEE L. REV. 1288, 1296-99 (2018); Richard F. Storrow, *Unaccompanied Minors at the U.S.-Mexico Border: The Shifting Sands of Special Immigrant Juvenile Status*, 33 GEO. IMMIGR. L.J. 1 (2018). In 2014, large numbers of unaccompanied minors came to the United States because of widespread violence in Central America and the Obama administration responded with detention of families. *See* Flores v. Lynch, 828 F.3d 898, 901 (9th Cir. 2016). The Trump administration responded to a new wave of Central American asylum seekers with family separation, family detention, and various other enforcement-oriented measures. Public criticism and litigation followed. As with other forms of relief, the Trump administration has tightened scrutiny of SIJS applications. *See* Mica Rosenberg, *New Trump Immigration Efforts to Stop Child Border Crossers*, REUTERS, Nov. 2, 2017, available at https://www.reuters.com/article/us-trump-effect-immigration-children/new-trump-immigration-efforts-aim-to-stop-child-border-crossers-idUSKBN1D309S; *see, e.g.*, Perez v. Cissna, 914 F.3d 846 (4th Cir.) (rejecting SIJS claims), *vacated and rehearing en banc granted*, 2019 U.S. App. LEXIS 14479 (4th Cir. May 15, 2019).

> Consider one SIJS case:
>
> In October 2015, Lucia, 13, was raped and impregnated. When she told her parents, they called her a "cualquiera," or "slut," and tried to send her from their home in Florida back to Guatemala. A case worker had to inform Lucia's parents that they couldn't dispatch their daughter against her wishes to another country. Unable to discard her, Lucia's parents forbade her from reporting her rape to the local police. Instead, they demanded that she extort her rapist. But ICE deported him before he could be blackmailed. Finally, when she was four or five months pregnant, Lucia's parents told her she needed to pay her "debts," so Lucia dropped out of high school and got a job at a plant nursery. At that time, her parents began to charge her $350 a month in rent.
>
> To Lucia's attorney, . . . her story was an obvious example of parental neglect and abuse, and Lucia, an undocumented minor, should therefore be eligible to apply for a green card under a program called Special Immigrant Juvenile Status (SIJS). . . .
>
> Cleek, *supra*.

In In re B.Y.G.M., 176 So.3d 290 (Fla. App. 2015), a 17-year-old Salvadoran claimed that her father abandoned her as an infant and that she had grown up with her grandparents. She was living with her mother in Florida. The federal statute allows for children to apply for SIJS when "reunification with one or both parents is not viable." In denying SIJS relief, the Florida courts found that the child's abandonment was "too remote" and "did not cause B.Y.G.M. any harm." *See also* In the Interest of B.R.C.M. (Fla. App. 2015), available at https://caselaw.findlaw.com/fl-district-court-of-appeal/1722131.html.

Special Immigrant Juveniles are classified under the Immigration and Nationality Act as employment-based immigrants and are limited in number. *See* 8 U.S.C. § 1153(b)(4); Deborah S. Gonzalez, *Sky is the Limit: Protecting Unaccompanied Minors by Not Subjecting Them to Numerical Limitations*, 49 ST. MARY'S L.J. 555 (2018).

VII.   Registry, "Amnesty," Legalization (p. 775)

A.   *Registry* (p. 775)

B.   *"Amnesty?"* (p. 755)

As discussed in the materials in the casebook, there has been debate over the creation of a path to legalization for undocumented immigrants. The excerpt of Hiroshi Motomura, *What is "Comprehensive Immigration Reform"? Taking the Long View*, 63 ARK. L. REV. 225 (2010) discusses various issues surrounding legalization of undocumented immigrants. Muneer I. Ahmad, *Beyond Earned Citizenship*, 52 HARV. C.R.–C.L. L. REV. 257 (2017) and Bill Ong Hing, *The Case for Amnesty*, 3 STAN. J. C.R.–C.L. REV. 233 (2007) support the creation of a path to legal status for undocumented immigrants. President Trump consistently has expressed opposition to any "amnesty" for undocumented immigrants.

C.   Private Bills and Deferred Action (p. 784)

D.   Adjustment of Status (p. 784)

Hernandez v Ashcroft

345 F.3d 824 (9th Cir. 2003) (p. 784).

For recent examples of courts reviewing requests for adjustment of status, compare Ramirez v. Brown, 852 F.3d 954 (9th Cir. 2017) (granting adjustment), *with* Xiao Lu Ma v. Sessions, 907 F.3d 1191 (9th Cir. 2018) (denying adjustment).

11. **Relief from Removal**

NOTES AND QUESTIONS (PP. 791-92)

E.   *Stays of Removal* (**p. 792**)

Leiva-Perez v. Holder
640 F.3d 962 (9th Cir. 2011) (p. 792)

NOTES AND QUESTIONS (P. 800)

For another application of *Nken v. Holder*, 556 U.S. 418 (2009), in granting a stay of removal, see You v. Nelson 321 F. Supp. 3d 451 (S.D.N.Y. 2018).

* * *

National controversy ensued when the Trump administration attempted to restrict two limited forms of relief, known as DACA and TPS. The dismantling, like many of the administration's immigration initiatives, would disparately impact noncitizens of color. *See* Rose Cuison Villazor & Kevin R. Johnson, *The Trump Administration and the War on Immigration Diversity*, 54 WAKE FOREST L. REV. 575, 607-08, 615-16 (2019).

DACA

President Obama's Deferred Action for Childhood Arrivals (DACA) policy provided limited relief to undocumented immigrants brought to the United States as children. *See Consideration of Deferred Action for Childhood Arrivals (DACA)*, U.S. Citizenship & Immigr. Servs., available at http://www.uscis.gov/humanitarian/consideration-deferred-action-childhood-arrivals-daca (last updated Feb. 14, 2018). DACA provided relief to hundreds of thousands of young undocumented immigrants. *See* Jens Manuel Krogstad, *DACA Has Shielded Nearly 790,000 Young Unauthorized Immigrants from Deportation*, PEW RES. CTR. (Sept. 1, 2017), available at http://www.pewresearch.org/fact-tank/2017/09/01/unauthorized-immigrants-covered-by-daca-face-uncertain-future/. Citizens of Mexico, El Salvador, Guatemala, and Honduras constituted nearly 90% of all DACA recipients. *See Top Countries of Origin for DACA Recipients*, PEW RES. CTR. (Sept. 25, 2017), available at http://www.pewresearch.org/fact-tank/2017/09/25/key-facts-about-unauthorized-immigrants-enrolled-in-daca/ft_17-09-25_daca_topcountries/.

Commentators have debated the lawfulness of DACA. *Compare* Patricia L. Bellia, *Faithful Execution and Enforcement Discretion*, 164 U. PA. L. REV. 1753, 1757–58 (2016) (questioning lawfulness of President Obama's deferred action policies), *and* Peter Margulies, *The Boundaries of Executive Discretion: Deferred*

Action, Unlawful Presence, and Immigration Law, 64 Am. U.L. Rev. 1183, 1198–99 (2015) (to the same effect), *with* Michael Kagan, *A Taxonomy of Discretion: Refining the Legality Debate about Obama's Executive Actions on Immigration*, 92 Wash. U.L. Rev. 1083, 1087 (2015) (defending lawfulness of deferred action policies), *and* Anil Kalhan, *Deferred Action, Supervised Enforcement Discretion, and the Rule of Law Basis for Executive Action on Immigration*, 63 UCLA L. Rev. Disc. 58, 58 (2015) (to the same effect).

In 2014, President Obama attempted to extend deferred action relief to undocumented parents of U.S. citizens and lawful immigrants through Deferred Action for Parents of Americans (DAPA). The proposed expansion sparked political debate, along with a legal challenge that permanently derailed the program. *See* United States v. Texas, 136 S. Ct. 2271 (2016) (affirming, by an equally divided Court, injunction barring DAPA's implementation). For analysis of the legal issues presented in *United States v. Texas*, see Josh Blackman, *Gridlock*, 130 Harv. L. Rev. 241, 279-302 (2016).

During the 2016 presidential campaign, Donald Trump promised to dismantle DACA. *See, e.g.*, James Pfiffner & Joshua Lee, *Trump Pledged to Reverse Obama's Executive Orders. Here's How Well Past Presidents Have Fulfilled that Pledge*, Wash. Post (Jan. 23, 2017), available at https://www.washingtonpost.com/news/monkey-cage/wp/2017/01/23/trump-pledged-to-reverse-obamas-executive-orders-heres-how-well-past-presidents-have-fulfilled-that-pledge/?utm_term=.021829d4d67c. In 2017, Attorney General Jeff Sessions announced DACA's rescission. Courts enjoined the rescission. *See* Casa de Md. v. U.S. Dep't of Homeland Sec., 924 F.3d 684 (4th Cir. 2019); Regents of Univ. of Cal. v. Dep't of Homeland Sec., 908 F.3d 476 (9th Cir 2018); NAACP v. Trump, 315 F. Supp. 3d 457 (D.D.C. 2018); Vidal v. Nielsen, 295 F. Supp. 3d 127 (E.D.N.Y. 2018). The Supreme Court granted *certiorari* to review the rescission of DACA. *See* Dep't of Homeland Sec. v. Univ. of Cal., 139 S.Ct. 2779 (2019).

Kevin R. Johnson, *Lessons About the Future of Immigration Law from the Rise and Fall of DACA*, 52 UC Davis L. Rev. 343 (2018) considers the long term impacts of DACA.

TPS

Changing what had been in place throughout the Obama administration, President Trump ended Temporary Protected Status (TPS), a form of relief providing noncitizens fleeing natural disaster or civil strife with temporary safe haven in the United States, for noncitizens of a number of developing nations. *See* INA § 244, 8 U.S.C. § 1254a(a)(1). The Trump administration's announcement of the end of TPS for nationals of El Salvador, for example, threatened to strip relief from nearly two hundred thousand Salvadorans currently living in the United States. *See* Press Release, Dep't of Homeland Sec., Secretary of Homeland Security Kirsten M. Nielsen Announcement on Temporary Protected Status for El Salvador (Jan. 8, 2018), available at https://www.dhs.gov/news/2018/01/08/secretary-homeland-security-kirstjen-m-nielsen-announcement-temporary-protected.

President Trump previously had disparaged Salvadorans. *See* Josh Dawsey, *Trump Derides Protections for Immigrants from "Shithole" Countries*, WASH. POST, Jan. 12, 2018, available at https://www.washingtonpost.com/politics/trump-attacks-protections-for-immigrants-from-shithole-countries-in-oval-office-meeting/2018/01/11/bfc0725c-f711-11e7-91af-31ac729add94_story.html?utm_term=.927f98699037. The Trump administration also ended TPS for Haitians, Hondurans, Nicaraguans, and Sudanese noncitizens. *See* Termination of the Designation of Honduras for Temporary Protected Status, 83 Fed. Reg. 26,074 (June 5, 2018); Termination of the Designation of Haiti for Temporary Protected Status, 83 Fed. Reg. 2648 (Jan. 18, 2018); Termination of the Designation of Nicaragua for Temporary Protected Status, 82 Fed. Reg. 59,636 (Dec. 15, 2017); Termination of the Designation of Sudan for Temporary Protected Status, 82 Fed Reg. 47,228 (Oct. 11, 2017). The Administration extended TPS for noncitizens from South Sudan. *See* Extension of South Sudan for Temporary Protected Status, 82 Fed. Reg. 44,205 (Sept. 21, 2017).

The Trump administration's cancellation of TPS for citizens of a number of nations has encountered criticism and resistance. *See, e.g.*, Susan Ferriss, *Trump's TPS Cancellations Could Lead More than 300,000 to Become Undocumented*, CTR. FOR PUB. INTEGRITY (May 5, 2018), available at https://www.publicintegrity.org/2018/05/04/21736/honduras-temporary-protected-status. Civil right groups sued, claiming that the Administration's termination of TPS for Salvadorans and Haitians, among other things, was racially discriminatory. *See Black and Latino Immigrants File Federal Lawsuit to Block Trump's Termination of TPS*, LAWYERS' COMM. FOR CIV. RTS. & ECON. JUST., available at http://lawyerscom.org/black-and-latino-immigrants-file-federal-lawsuit-to-block-trumps-termination-of-tps. A federal district court enjoined the end of TPS for citizens of El Salvador, Haiti, Nicaragua, and Sudan, finding that the change in policy and possible racial discrimination raised substantial legal questions. *See* Ramos v. Nielsen, 336 F. Supp. 3d 1075, 1097–98 (N.D. Cal. 2018). In so doing, the court recounted various discriminatory statements about immigrants made by President Trump. *See id.* at 1098; *see also* Centro Presente v. U.S. Dep't of Homeland Security, 332 F. Supp. 3d 393, 400–01 (D. Mass. 2018) (reviewing evidence of racial animus motivating the decision to end TPS for nationals of El Salvador, Haiti, and Honduras).

Congress has considered bills that would provide relief to noncitizens stripped of TPS. *See* Rafael Bernal, *Trump Immigration Measures Struggle in the Courts*, THE HILL (Oct. 5, 2018), available at https://thehill.com/latino/410012-trump-immigration-measures-struggle-in-the-courts (referring "to six legislative proposals in the current Congress that would either extend TPS benefits or give current beneficiaries permanent residency"); *see, e.g.*, American Dream and Promise Act, H.R. 6, 116th Cong. (2019).

In a *Matter of D-A-C-*, 27 I. & N. Dec. 575 (BIA 2019), the Board of Immigration Appeals dismissed the appeal of a Salvadoran with a criminal record denied TPS on discretionary grounds.

Cancellation of removal may be available to noncitizens who lose TPS status.

Section 212(h) Relief

INA § 212(h), 8 U.S.C. § 1182(h) allows for waiver from removal for a "single offense of simple possession of 30 grams or less of marijuana." *See* Kate Aschenbrenner Rodriguez, *Irreconcilable Similarities: The Inconsistent Analysis of 212(c) and 212(h) Waivers*, 69 OKLA L. REV. 111 (2017); *see, e.g.*, Sambare v. Attorney General, 925 F.3d 124 (3d Cir. 2019); Poveda v. U.S. Att. Gen., 692 F.3d 1168 (11th Cir. 2012); Matter of J-H-J-, 26 I. & N. Dec. 563 (BIA 2015).

Importantly, a waiver under Section 212(h) of the Immigration and Nationality Act is available under certain circumstances to a lawful permanent resident (LPR) who has been convicted of an aggravated felony. Section 212(h) permits the waiver of certain grounds of inadmissibility to allow a noncitizen to apply or reapply "for a visa, for admission to the United States, or adjustment of status." The language does not bar LPRs who have proceeded abroad from seeking such a relief when returning even if they are not re-applying for adjustment of status in conjunction with the waiver. Thus, in *Matter of Abosi*, 24 I. & N. Dec. 204, 207 (BIA 2007), the Board ruled that an LPR who has departed and is returning is not required to file an application for adjustment of status in conjunction with a waiver request. However, "a § 212(h) waiver for an alien within the United States is available only in connection with an application for adjustment of status. . . ." *Mtoched v. Lynch*, 786 F.3d 1210, 1218 (9th Cir. 2015); *see Garcia-Mendez v. Lynch*, 788 F.3d 1058, 1065 (9th Cir. 2015) (holding "that an applicant for special rule cancellation does not, by virtue of that status, become eligible to seek a section 212(h) waiver"); *see also Poveda v. U.S. Atty. Gen.*, 692 F.3d 1168, 1176 (11th Cir. 2012) (finding that the Board of Immigration Appeals' interpretation of Section 212(h) requiring noncitizens within the United States to apply for an adjustment of his status to receive a hardship waiver, is reasonable). If the LPR is married to a U.S. citizen, for example, the U.S. citizen can petition for the respondent and the respondent can apply for adjustment of status in removal proceedings and obtain a Section 212(h) waiver of the criminal conviction from the immigration judge. However, a waiver is not automatic and the LPR must satisfy the extreme hardship requirement.

The possibility of obtaining a Section 212(h) waiver of an aggravated felony through adjustment of status does not apply to a LPR who initially entered the United States as a LPR. If they enter as a refugee or some other method and subsequently became a permanent resident through adjustment of status and then commits an aggravated felony, a Section 212(h) waiver is possible if the person is once again eligible for adjustment of status. *See Matter of J-H-J-*, 26 I. & N. Dec. 563 (BIA 2015).

Chapter 12

REMOVAL PROCEEDINGS AND IMMIGRATION JUDGES

I.   Removal Hearings and the Right to Counsel

At the top of page 823, add the following at the end of the Notes and Questions:

5. Catholic Legal Immigration Network reports on the nationwide effect of this case:

Appointed Counsel and Bond Hearings for the Mentally Disabled
By Debbie Smith
https://cliniclegal.org/resources/articles-clinic/
appointed-counsel-and-bond-hearings-mentally-disabled

Jose, an unrepresented noncitizen who did not learn to speak until he was six or seven years old, does not know his own birthday or age, has trouble recognizing numbers and counting, and cannot tell time, spent four and a half years in immigration detention after his immigration case was closed. CLINIC has long advocated for the right of immigrants like Jose to appointed counsel, especially in cases involving unaccompanied children, asylum seekers, and other vulnerable populations. On April 22, 2013, the government issued instructions to be implemented nationally to identify detained mentally incompetent noncitizens and appoint counsel for such individuals. The ICE and EOIR memos preceded by one day the April 23, 2013 federal district court order in *Franco-Gonzalez v. Holder*, 10 CV 02211 DMG (C.D. CA August 2, 2010), a permanent injunction that required the government to appoint counsel and provide bond hearings for detained seriously mentally ill noncitizens in Arizona, California and Washington. The new ICE and EOIR policies, while encouraging, are only a first step towards ensuring that at-risk noncitizens receive legal representation in immigration proceedings.

ICE Memo
The April 22, 2013 ICE memo directs the establishment of procedures to ensure that mentally incompetent noncitizens in ICE detention are identified and that information about these individuals is provided to the immigration court. By sharing this information, the immigration judges hearing cases involving seriously mentally ill respondents will be able to rule on their competency and invoke the new EOIR procedures for appointment of counsel. The ICE memo specifies that all immigration detention facilities must have the following procedures in place by December 31, 2013.

Identification and Assessment Procedures: As of April 22, 2013, all immigration detention facilities that are staffed by ICE Health Service Corps are required to develop procedures to screen every immigration detainee when he or she enters the detention center. Detainees also will receive a more thorough medical and mental health assessment within 14 days of entering the detention facility. In the case of private detention centers where ICE holds detainees, DHS staff is required to begin work immediately with the detention facilities' medical staff to develop procedures to identify detainees with serious mental conditions. The required procedures include creating a national telephone hotline for detainees and family members to report and provide information about those detained. Once a detained individual is identified, ICE will request that either a qualified mental health provider complete a mental health review report or the facility provide the detainee's medical records to ICE for review.

Information-Sharing: DHS staff must also immediately develop procedures to transmit all documents related to the mental competency of an unrepresented detained individual to the ICE attorney (Office of Chief Counsel - OCC) in order for OCC to inform the immigration court of the individual's mental incompetency.

EOIR Memo

The EOIR April 22, 2013 memo requires Immigration Judges to implement several procedures to provide the following protections for mentally incompetent individuals.

Competency Hearings: Immigration Judges must conduct competency hearings when medical records or other evidence reflects that the individual appearing in immigration court may have a serious mental disorder or condition causing the individual to be unable to represent himself/herself in removal proceedings.

Mental Competency Examinations: Immigration Judges may order an independent mental competency examination and the production of a psychiatric or psychological report if unable to decide whether an individual is competent to represent himself or herself following a competency hearing. EOIR will be working with DHS to obtain these reports. Although the Immigration Judge will make the ultimate decision regarding competency, the independent evaluation will assist in this determination.

Appointment of Counsel: Immigration Judges may appoint counsel to represent an individual found to be mentally incompetent in removal and/or bond proceedings. EOIR will provide qualified legal counsel in such situations.

Steven Lang, Program Director, Office of Legal Access Programs at EOIR noted at the CLINIC Convening in May, 2013 that EOIR had signed contracts with several immigration legal services providers, including our CLINIC affiliate, Esperanza Immigrant Rights Project in Los Angeles, to provide legal representation to mentally incompetent detainees.

Bond Hearings: Unrepresented mentally incompetent detainees who have been held in detention for six months or longer will be provided a bond hearing.

Franco-Gonzalez Class Action Case

On April 23, 2013, federal district judge Dolly M. Gee granted a permanent injunction in the *Franco-Gonzalez v. Holder* class action lawsuit brought in 2010, a lawsuit that began with Mr. Franco-Gonzalez's petition for writ of habeas corpus. The ruling, covering three states—Arizona, California and Washington—requires immigration courts to provide legal representation for detained immigrants with mental disabilities "in all aspects of their immigration proceedings," and bond hearings for detained immigrants with mental disorders or disabilities who have been detained for more than six months. The government's April 22, 2013 policy expands the *Franco-Gonzalez* order nationwide. For the first time immigrants unable to afford legal representation who are mentally disabled will have an opportunity to present their cases with the assistance of counsel and request release under bond.

6. The Vera Institute of Justice has taken responsibility to work with DOJ on ensuring that *Franco* class members obtain representation. Christi Thompson of The Marshall Project writes:

In contrast to President Trump's crackdown on immigration, one federal protection for immigrants has been quietly expanded in recent months. A growing number of courtrooms are providing free legal representation for detainees who have a serious mental illness or disability. As of March 2017, 21 immigration courts across the country were operating a federal program that provides lawyers to immigrants in deportation proceedings who were incapable of representing themselves, according to a spokesperson for the Executive Office for Immigration Review, the Department of Justice office in charge of immigration courts.

It's an unusual program in a system that generally does not guarantee access to an attorney. Only 14 percent of immigrants in detention have a lawyer, and judges have asserted that even toddlers are capable of appearing in court alone. Research shows that having an attorney has a significant effect on whether someone is deported. So far, over 850 lawyers have been appointed to detainees through the program, according to EOIR.

The program began in 2013 during a federal court case, when a district judge ordered immigration courts in Washington, California and Arizona to provide detainees with representation if they were found to be mentally incompetent. A lead plaintiff in the class-action suit, José Antonio Franco González, could not get counsel to guide him through deportation hearings despite having the cognitive ability of a 2-year-old, according to some measures. His case was in limbo: he could not present his case, but there was no lawyer the court could provide him. He was held in detention for nearly five years while his case went nowhere. The Franco ruling was the first time a court found that a group of immigrants were entitled to lawyers.

The court's order only applied to the three states. But that same week, the Department of Justice announced a policy that was supposed to provide similar services nationwide. For several years, however, the program was only available in a few courtrooms outside the West Coast. That meant that many immigrants were still having to appear in court alone even if they had a serious mental disability, and risked languishing in detention for years as their case stalled.

That finally changed this year, as the program grew to include courtrooms across the country. Several other sites are planned for rollout soon, according to an Executive Office for Immigration Review spokesperson. EOIR could not say what explained the lag. The current program, called the National Qualified Representative Program, is being run by the Vera Institute of Justice through a contract with the Executive Office of Immigration Review. Vera in turn retains attorneys, many of whom work for immigration advocacy groups.

"They're incredibly challenging cases," said Lauren Dasse, executive director of the nonprofit Florence Immigrant and Refugee Rights Project, which represents clients in detention centers in Arizona. "Before Franco, we heard some judges would ask attorneys to take cases, and we would take them on in-house or place them with pro bono attorneys. We can all remember those clients."

Significant gaps in protection remain. The court-appointed monitor's reports produced after the Franco case detail the ways that an immigrant with mental disabilities may still be denied an attorney. It is up to an immigration judge — and not a licensed psychologist — to determine whether someone is competent. A judge can choose to order an evaluation, but many judges rarely do. The monitor also found that the screening forms used in detention centers failed to flag every case. And it sometimes took months to identify a detainee as mentally ill.

"We're concerned people are being missed at the screening stage in detention centers. The forms at the facilities are extremely lacking," said Talia Inlender, a senior staff attorney at pro bono law firm Public Counsel and co-counsel on the Franco case. "And immigration judges who are not psychologists are making competency determinations without a medical expert. In the criminal justice system, that almost never happens."

A federal judge ruled in June to extend the monitoring of compliance with Franco for another year.

In 2015, as part of the Franco settlement, immigration authorities agreed that the protections would be retroactive for certain cases. Those with mental disabilities who had been ordered deported from those three states without counsel within a certain time frame could petition to reopen their case — if they could be found, notified, and walked through the legal process.

Christie Thompson, *One Bit of Good News for Immigrants in Detention — As a federal program grows, more mentally ill immigrants have access to attorneys*, The Marshall Project, July 5, 2017, https://www.themarshallproject.org/2017/07/05/one-bit-of-good-news-for-immigrants-in-detention

7. Mental Competence of Respondent's Not in Detention. *Franco* applies to respondents who are detained. What if a respondent who is not mentally competent is not in detention? Is there a right to government-appointed counsel?

Matter of M-A-M-

25 I&N Dec. 474 (BIA 2011)

In a decision dated June 16, 2010, an Immigration Judge found the respondent removable under sections 237(a)(2)(A)(ii) and (B)(i) of the Immigration and Nationality Act, 8 U.S.C. §§ 1227(a)(2)(A)(ii) and (B)(i) (2006), and concluded that he is ineligible for relief from removal. The respondent has appealed from that decision and has submitted a motion to remand, arguing, in part, that the Immigration Judge did not assess his mental competency. In this decision, we set forth a framework for Immigration Judges to determine whether a respondent is sufficiently competent to proceed and whether the application of safeguards is warranted. The record will be remanded to the Immigration Judge.

I.   FACTUAL AND PROCEDURAL HISTORY

The respondent is a native and citizen of Jamaica who was admitted to the United States as a lawful permanent resident on February 19, 1971, when he was 10 years old. On July 31, 2008, the Department of Homeland Security ("DHS") served the respondent with a Notice to Appear (Form I-862), charging that he is removable under section 237(a)(2)(A)(ii) of the Act on the basis of his conviction for two or more crimes involving moral turpitude. The DHS subsequently amended the allegations and lodged additional charges, charging the respondent with removability under section 237(a)(2)(B)(i) of the Act, as an alien convicted of a controlled substance violation, and under section 237(a)(2)(A)(iii), as an alien convicted of a drug-trafficking aggravated felony pursuant to section 101(a)(43)(B) of the Act, 8 U.S.C. § 1101(a)(43)(B) (2006).

When the respondent first appeared before an Immigration Judge for a master calendar hearing on September 14, 2009, he had difficulty answering basic questions, such as his name and date of birth, and he told the Immigration Judge that he had been diagnosed with schizophrenia. He also indicated that he needed medication. At the second hearing, on October 21, 2009, the respondent indicated that he had a history of mental illness that was not being treated in detention. The respondent requested a change of venue to be closer to his attorney and family, but the request was denied. Additional hearings were held on November 4, 2009, December 7, 2009, January 25, 2010, and April 1, 2010. During those hearings, further reference was made to the respondent's mental illness and he asked to see a psychiatrist.

On June 16, 2010, a different Immigration Judge convened the final merits hearing. At that time, psychiatric evaluations and reports about the respondent from New York State's Office of Mental Health were included in the record. The Immigration Judge asked the respondent about his mental health and treatment. Specifically, the Immigration Judge asked the respondent whether he was able to proceed with the hearing, and the respondent answered that he would do the best he could.

Initially, the respondent indicated that he could not represent himself but, upon further questioning by the Immigration Judge, said he "believed" that he could answer the questions put to him by the Immigration Judge and the DHS attorney. The Immigration Judge proceeded with the merits hearing, asking the respondent questions about his entry into the United States, his criminal convictions, and his fear of returning to Jamaica. Throughout the proceedings, the respondent appeared pro se.

In her decision, the Immigration Judge summarized the respondent's mental health history but did not make an explicit finding regarding his mental competency. The Immigration Judge found the respondent removable on the charges relating to his convictions for crimes involving moral turpitude and controlled substance violations, but not on the aggravated felony charge. The Immigration

Judge denied the respondent's application for cancellation of removal under section 240A(a) of the Act, 8 U.S.C. § 1229b(a) (2006), in the exercise of discretion. She also denied his applications for asylum and withholding of removal because the respondent did not establish a nexus or harm that was sufficiently severe to constitute persecution. The Immigration Judge also found the respondent ineligible for protection under the Convention Against Torture . . .

II.   ISSUES

This case presents three questions related to mental competency determinations: (1) When should Immigration Judges make competency determinations? (2) What factors should Immigration Judges consider and what procedures should they employ to make those determinations? (3) What safeguards should Immigration Judges prescribe to ensure that proceedings are sufficiently fair when competency is not established?

III.   ANALYSIS

. . .[O]ur goal is to ensure that proceedings are as fair as possible in an unavoidably imperfect situation. To that end, this decision will provide a framework for analyzing cases in which issues of mental competency are raised.

A. Presumption of Competency

As a threshold matter, we find that an alien is presumed to be competent to participate in removal proceedings. *See, e.g., Munoz-Monsalve v. Mukasey,* 551 F.3d 1, 6 (1st Cir. 2008) . . .

Absent indicia of mental incompetency, an Immigration Judge is under no obligation to analyze an alien's competency. *Munoz-Monsalve v. Mukasey,* 551 F.3d at 6 . . .

The Act and the regulations contemplate circumstances in which competency concerns trigger the application of appropriate safeguards . . .

B. Legal Authority

1. Statutory and Regulatory Provisions

The Act acknowledges that aliens in proceedings may be mentally incompetent. Specifically, the Act provides as follows:

> If it is impracticable by reason of an alien's mental incompetency for the alien to be present at the proceeding, the Attorney General shall prescribe safeguards to protect the rights and privileges of the alien.

Section 240(b)(3) of the Act, 8 U.S.C. § 1229a(b)(3) (2006). The Act's invocation of safeguards presumes that proceedings can go forward, even where the alien is incompetent, provided the proceeding is conducted fairly.

12. Removal Proceedings and Immigration Judges

The regulations provide guidance regarding the treatment of aliens who lack mental competency. An incompetent alien must be served with the Notice to Appear in person. 8 C.F.R. § 103.5a(c)(2) (2010). If the alien is confined in a penal or mental institution or hospital, service generally must be made on the alien, as well as the person in charge of the institution, although if the alien is incompetent, service can only be made on the person in charge of the institution where the alien is confined. 8 C.F.R. § 103.5a(c)(2)(i). If the alien is not confined, service must be made on the person with whom the alien resides. 8 C.F.R. § 103.5a(c)(2)(ii). Further, "whenever possible, service shall also be made on the near relative, guardian, committee, or friend." *Id.*

Additional requirements are prescribed in the regulations to ensure that an incompetent alien is afforded an adequate opportunity to present his or her case during a hearing. Immigration Judges may not accept an admission of removability from an unrepresented respondent who is incompetent and unaccompanied. 8 C.F.R. § 1240.10(c) (2010). When it is impracticable for the respondent to be present at the hearing because of mental incompetency, the attorney, legal representative or guardian, near relative, or friend who was served with a copy of the Notice to Appear is permitted to appear on behalf of the respondent. 8 C.F.R. §§ 1240.4, 1240.43 (2010). If such a person cannot be found or fails or refuses to appear, the regulations provide that the "custodian of the respondent shall be requested to appear on behalf of the respondent." *Id.*

If an Immigration Judge determines that a respondent lacks sufficient competency to proceed with the hearing, the Immigration Judge will evaluate which available measures would result in a fair hearing. Immigration Judges "shall prescribe safeguards to protect the rights and privileges of the alien." Section 240(b)(3) of the Act; *see also* 8 C.F.R. § 1003.10(b) (2010).

Although the Act and the regulations provide direction for handling cases in which competency is an issue, they do not set forth the process that an Immigration Judge should use to assess the competency of an alien appearing in Immigration Court. This decision sets out a framework for that purpose.

2. Competency for Purposes of Immigration Proceedings

. . .

Unlike in criminal proceedings, a lack of competency in civil immigration proceedings does not mean that the hearing cannot go forward; rather, procedural fairness is required. In immigration proceedings, the Fifth Amendment entitles aliens to due process of law. *Reno v. Flores*, 507 U.S. 292, 306 (1993). Included in the rights that the Due Process Clause requires in removal proceedings is the right to a full and fair hearing. *Matter of M-D-*, 23 I&N Dec. 540, 542 (BIA 2002) (citing *Landon v. Plasencia*, 459 U.S. 21, 32-33 (1982)). "A removal hearing must be conducted in a manner that satisfies principles of fundamental fairness." *Matter of Beckford*, 22 I&N Dec. 1216, 1225 (BIA 2000); *see also Shaughnessey v. United States ex rel. Mezei*, 345 U.S. 206, 212 (1953) (stating that immigration proceedings must conform to traditional standards of fairness encompassed in due process).

To meet traditional standards of fundamental fairness in determining whether an alien is competent to participate in immigration proceedings, Immigration Judges must accord aliens the specific "rights and privileges" prescribed in the Act. Section 240(b)(3) of the Act. For example, aliens "shall have the privilege of being represented" at no expense to the Government. Sections 240(b)(4)(A), 292 of the Act, 8 U.S.C. §§ 1229a(b)(4)(A), 1362 (2006). In addition, the Act requires that an alien have a "reasonable opportunity" to examine and present evidence and to cross-examine witnesses. Section 240(b)(4)(B) of the Act; *see also* 8 C.F.R. § 1240.10(a)(4). Therefore, the test for determining whether an alien is competent to participate in immigration proceedings is whether he or she has a rational and factual understanding of the nature and object of the proceedings, can consult with the attorney or representative if there is one, and has a reasonable opportunity to examine and present evidence and cross-examine witnesses.

C. Framework for Cases Presenting Competency Issues

1. *Indicia of Incompetency*
In cases involving aliens with issues of mental competency, Immigration Judges will need to consider whether there is good cause to believe that the alien lacks sufficient competency to proceed without safeguards. Indicia of incompetency include a wide variety of observations and evidence. For example, the Immigration Judge or the parties may observe certain behaviors by the respondent, such as the inability to understand and respond to questions, the inability to stay on topic, or a high level of distraction. Second, the record may contain evidence of mental illness or incompetency. This could include direct assessments of the respondent's mental health, such as medical reports or assessments from past medical treatment or from criminal proceedings, as well as testimony from medical health professionals. It may also include evidence from other relevant sources, such as school records regarding special education classes or individualized education plans; reports or letters from teachers, counselors, or social workers; evidence of participation in programs for persons with mental illness; evidence of applications for disability benefits; and affidavits or testimony from friends or family members.

. . . The DHS has an obligation to provide the court with relevant materials in its possession that would inform the court about the respondent's mental competency. 8 C.F.R. § 1240.2(a) (2010) ("[DHS] counsel shall present on behalf of the government evidence material to the issues of deportability or inadmissibility and any other issues that may require disposition by the immigration judge."); *see also Matter of S-M-J-*, 21 I&N Dec. 722, 726-27 (BIA 1997) (discussing generally the DHS's role in introducing evidence), *disapproved of on other grounds, Ladha v. INS*, 215 F.3d 889 (9th Cir. 2000).

Mental competency is not a static condition. "It varies in degree. It can vary over time. It interferes with an individual's functioning at different times in different ways." *Indiana v. Edwards*, 554 U.S. 164, 175 (2008). As a result, Immigration

12. Removal Proceedings and Immigration Judges

Judges need to consider indicia of incompetency throughout the course of proceedings to determine whether an alien's condition has deteriorated or, on the other hand, whether competency has been restored.

Even if an alien has been deemed to be medically competent, there may be cases in which an Immigration Judge has good cause for concern about the ability to proceed, such as where the respondent has a long history of mental illness, has an acute illness, or was restored to competency, but there is reason to believe that the condition has changed. In such cases, Immigration Judges should apply appropriate safeguards.

On the other hand, we also recognize that there are many types of mental illness that, even though serious, would not prevent a respondent from meaningfully participating in immigration proceedings. In other words, a diagnosis of mental illness does not automatically equate to a lack of competency.

2. *Measures To Assess Competency*

When there are indicia of incompetency, an Immigration Judge must take measures to determine whether a respondent is competent to participate in proceedings. The approach taken in any particular case will vary based on the circumstances of the case.

For instance, an Immigration Judge may modify the questions posed to the respondent to make them very simple and direct. The inquiries made should include questions about where the hearing is taking place, the nature of the proceedings, and the respondent's state of mind. In addition, an Immigration Judge might ask the respondent whether he or she currently takes or has taken medication to treat a mental illness and what the purpose and effects of that medication are. Proceedings may also be continued to allow the parties to gather and submit evidence relevant to these matters, such as medical treatment reports, documentation from criminal proceedings, or letters and testimony from other third party sources that bear on the respondent's mental health.

Another measure available to Immigration Judges is a mental competency evaluation. *See, e.g., Matter of J-F-F-,* 23 I&N Dec. 912, 915 (A.G. 2006) (noting that at the Immigration Judge's request, the DHS arranged for a psychiatric evaluation of a detained alien, which led the psychiatrist to conclude that the alien understood the proceedings and wanted to proceed with the hearing). Immigration Judges can also permit a family member or close friend to assist the respondent in providing information. In addition, Immigration Judges can docket or manage the case to facilitate the respondent's ability to obtain medical treatment and/or legal representation. For example, a continuance or motion to change venue may be granted to enable a respondent to be closer to family or available treatment programs. Immigration Judges can continue proceedings to allow for further evaluation of competency or an assessment of changes in the respondent's condition.

The Immigration Judge must weigh the results from the measures taken and determine, under the test for competency set out above, whether the respondent is sufficiently competent to proceed with the hearing without safeguards. *Cf. Matter of Sinclitico,* 15 I&N Dec. 320 (BIA 1975) (finding that the respondent was not sufficiently competent to voluntarily relinquish his citizenship where he did not seem to understand the questions asked of him, his answers to questions were not responsive, there was medical evidence of mental illness, and the respondent's brother testified regarding his mental illness). The Immigration Judge must also articulate that determination and his or her reasoning.

3. *Safeguards*

If an Immigration Judge determines that a respondent lacks sufficient competency to proceed with the hearing, the statute provides that the Immigration Judge "shall prescribe safeguards to protect the rights and privileges of the alien." Section 240(b)(3) of the Act. Based on the statutory and regulatory parameters, we conclude that Immigration Judges have discretion to determine which safeguards are appropriate, given the particular circumstances in a case before them.

[T]he regulations provide guidance regarding safeguards to protect aliens who otherwise lack sufficient competency to meaningfully participate in proceedings. For example, the regulations prohibit Immigration Judges from accepting an admission of removability from an unrepresented alien who is incompetent and provide that when an alien is mentally incompetent, the attorney, near relative, or friend who was served with a copy of the Notice to Appear is permitted to appear on the respondent's behalf. 8 C.F.R. §§ 1240.4, 1240.10(c), 1240.43. If such a person cannot be found or fails or refuses to appear, the regulations provide that the respondent's custodian "shall be requested to appear on behalf of the respondent." 8 C.F.R. §§ 1240.4, 1240.43.

Case law also provides guidance to Immigration Judges for determining how they may fairly proceed when an alien lacks competency. We have held that an alien's due process rights were not violated in a deportation hearing where he was represented by an attorney who was able to introduce evidence and cross-examine witnesses, a doctor testified regarding his medical condition, and the respondent appeared to testify intelligently and rationally. *Matter of H-,* 6 I&N Dec. 358 (BIA 1954). In addition, the Attorney General has stated that "[i]t is appropriate for Immigration Judges to aid in the development of the record, and directly question witnesses." *Matter of J-F-F-,* 23 I&N Dec. at 922 . . .

Several Federal circuit courts have also considered the fairness of proceedings involving aliens with indicia of mental incompetency. For example, the United States Court of Appeals for the Ninth Circuit held that the due process rights of an alien with a mental illness were not violated where he was represented by counsel and was accompanied by a State court-appointed conservator who testified fully on his behalf. *Nee Hao Wong v. INS,* 550 F.2d 521, 523 (9th Cir. 1977). Similarly, the Tenth Circuit concluded that procedural safeguards were in place and the alien had an opportunity to be heard at a meaningful time and in a meaningful manner where the alien was represented and was able to answer the questions posed to him and provide his version of the facts. *Brue v. Gonzales,* 464 F.3d 1227, 1232-34 (10th Cir. 2006). The Eighth Circuit also held that an Immigration Judge was not required to determine competency where the respondent answered the charges against him, testified in support of his claim for withholding of removal, arranged for two witnesses to appear on his behalf, was aware of the nature and object of the proceedings, and vigorously resisted removal. *Mohamed v. Gonzales*, 477 F.3d 522, 526-27 (8th Cir. 2007). In addition, the First Circuit concluded that an alien's due process rights were not violated where he was represented, his attorney does not request an evaluation, and the record did not contain evidence of a lack of competency. *Munoz-Monsalve v. Mukasey*, 551 F.3d at 6-8.

Drawing guidance from the regulations and legal precedent, we note that there are a number of safeguards available to Immigration Judges, some of which they may have already taken when initially assessing the respondent's competency. Examples of appropriate safeguards include, but are not limited to, refusal to accept an admission of removability from an unrepresented respondent; identification and appearance of a family member or close friend who can assist the respondent and provide the court with information; docketing or managing the case to facilitate the respondent's ability to obtain legal representation and/or medical treatment in an effort to restore competency; participation of a guardian in the proceedings; continuance of the case for good cause shown; closing the hearing to the public; waiving the respondent's appearance; actively aiding in the development of the record, including the examination and cross-examination of witnesses; and reserving appeal rights for the respondent. The Immigration Judge will consider the facts and circumstances of an alien's case to decide which of these or other relevant safeguards to utilize. The Immigration Judge must articulate his or her reasoning for the decision.

In some cases, even where the court and the parties undertake their best efforts to ensure appropriate safeguards, concerns may remain. In these cases, the Immigration Judge may pursue alternatives with the parties, such as administrative closure, while other options are explored, such as seeking treatment for the respondent.[3]

D. Summary of Legal Framework

To summarize, if there are no indicia of incompetency in an alien's case, no further inquiry regarding competency is required. The test for determining whether an alien is competent to participate in immigration proceedings is whether he or she has a rational and factual understanding of the nature and object of the proceedings, can consult with the attorney or representative if there is one, and has a reasonable opportunity to examine and present evidence and cross-examine witnesses. If there are indicia of incompetency, the Immigration Judge must make further inquiry to determine whether the alien is competent for purposes of immigration proceedings. If the alien lacks sufficient competency to proceed, the Immigration Judge will evaluate and apply appropriate safeguards. The Immigration Judge must articulate the rationale for his or her decision.

IV. CONCLUSION

In this case, there is good cause to believe that the respondent lacked sufficient competency to proceed with the hearing. The record includes several psychiatric reports that diagnose him with mental illness, and during criminal proceedings, the respondent was found to be unfit to proceed with a trial. Additionally, before the Immigration Judge, the respondent had difficulty answering questions, discussed his illness and need for medication, and asked to see a psychiatrist.

Given these circumstances, we will remand the record to the Immigration Judge to apply the framework articulated here. On remand, the Immigration Judge should take steps to assess the respondent's competency, make a finding regarding his competency, apply safeguards as warranted, and articulate her reasoning. The parties will have an opportunity on remand to present evidence relevant to an evaluation of the respondent's competency and any other appropriate issues.

. . .

NOTES AND QUESTIONS

1. Do you agree with the BIA that a person not mentally competent should not be guaranteed counsel at government expense? Why or why not? The BIA does say that the IJ must make sure certain "safeguards" are in place. What are those safeguards?

2. Is the process of determining competence satisfactory? If the respondent is not competence, are the safeguards to assure fairness and due process adequate?

III. Immigration Judges' Powers and Responsibilities

At the top of page 859, add the following at the end of the Notes and Questions:

5. Immigration Judge Performance Quotas. The Trump administration has placed pressure on immigration judges to be more efficient.

From the Catholic Legal Immigration Network (CLINIC): https://cliniclegal.org/resources/doj-requires-immigration-judges-meet-quotas.

Victoria Neilson, *DOJ requires immigration judges to meet quotas*, Oct. 2017:

> Media outlets recently reported new requirements for immigration judges to meet case closing quotas as part of their performance review. When news of the potential quotas was leaked late last year, the National Association of Immigration Judges immediately condemned the idea.

12.   Removal Proceedings and Immigration Judges

"That is a huge, huge, huge encroachment on judicial independence…It's trying to turn immigration judges into assembly-line workers," Dana Leigh Marks, spokeswoman and former president of the association said to the Washington Post. She was also an immigration judge for more than 30 years.

The American Bar Association has decried evaluating individual judges based on case completion numbers, stating that "such quotas have serious implications for decisional independence." Instead the ABA recommends establishing the immigration courts as Article 1 courts, independent of any executive agency and less susceptible to political currents. The New York City Bar Association has likewise proclaimed, "What the attorney general calls 'efficiency' can never be a substitute for fundamental rights."

What do the performance review standards require?

Under the new standards, which are set to go into effect on Oct. 1, 2018, to receive a "satisfactory" review an immigration judge must:
- Complete 700 cases per year, and
- Maintain a remand rate (from the Board of Immigration Appeals and circuit courts) of fewer than 15 percent per year.

Additionally, for a "satisfactory" review an immigration judge must meet at least half of the following benchmarks:

- Issue decisions within three days of completing a merits hearing in 85 percent of non-status detained removal decisions
- Issue decisions within 10 days of completing a merits hearing in 85 percent of non-status non-detained removal decisions (unless completion is prohibited by statute, such as cancellation caps)
- Decide motions within 20 days of receipt in 85 percent of their cases
- Make bond decisions on the day of the hearing in 90 percent of cases
- Complete individual hearings on the initial scheduled hearing date in 95 percent of the cases (unless the Department of Homeland Security does not produce a detained respondent), and
- Issue decisions in 100 percent of cases on the day of the initial hearing in credible fear and reasonable fear reviews (unless DHS does not produce a detained respondent).

The memo includes further metrics, as expected, for judges who "need improvement" and whose work is "unsatisfactory" based on lower numbers and percentages of the above.

Why does the performance evaluation of judges matter to immigrants?

Immigration judges are part of the executive branch of government. Falling within the Department of Justice, all immigration judges ultimately report to Attorney General Jeff Sessions. Immigration is a hot-button political issue, and Sessions frequently gives speeches that are openly contemptuous of protections for asylum seekers and youthful border crossers. In one such speech, he recently referred to complex immigration laws as "loopholes" six times in a four-paragraph speech.

As anyone who has practiced in immigration court knows, each case is different and many cases require complex legal analysis and lengthy testimony. Case completion goals of 700 per year translates into completing—issuing a removal order or granting relief such as asylum, cancellation or adjustment—nearly three cases per day. (700 divided by 48, assuming four weeks' vacation, divided by five = 2.92.); and that number does not account for the hours an immigration judge must spend conducting master calendar hearings, bond hearings, attending trainings and reviewing case files. It is hard to imagine how a judge could ever give fair consideration to three cases per day, while simultaneously preparing for upcoming hearings, writing decisions on complex cases and responding to motions (within newly proscribed time limits.)

It seems clear that the only way to meet these quotas would be to greatly reduce the number of cases that are set for trial, and to increase removal orders. Sessions is currently considering two cases, in which he will issue precedential appellate decisions as to whether judges can control their own dockets through administrative closure of cases and under what circumstances judges can grant continuances for U.S. Citizenship and Immigration Services to adjudicate related applications for relief.

These attacks on the independence of the immigration courts, and the pressure being applied to judges to speed up deportations, make the work of attorneys and accredited representatives more important than ever. Earlier this week, in *Sessions v. Dimaya*, the Supreme Court reiterated "the grave nature of deportation, [which is] — a 'drastic measure,' often amounting to lifelong 'banishment or exile.'" The attorney general should take these words to heart and ensure that whatever decision an immigration judge reaches in a particular case, he or she does so after careful consideration and judicious application of the law to the facts, and not because a timer has gone off in the courtroom.

What is the purpose of these enforcement standards?

6. Removal Proceedings Via Videoconferencing. EOIR has increased the use of videoconferencing to conduct removal hearings, where the respondent remains in a detention center and the immigration judge is in a completely different city. EOIR contends that this procedure is necessary because of serious overcrowding in the immigration courts. The situation creates real problems for respondents who are foreclosed from the opportunity to have personal contact with the immigration judge—contact that could make a big difference in terms of credibility and even empathy. This can create challenges for courtroom interpreters as well. In one case, the interpreter could not understand the respond as he "sobbed" throughout his testimony and his voice was muffled by the sound quality. *See* Christina Goldbaum, *Videoconferencing in Immigration Court: High-Court Solution or Rights Violation?*, NY Times, Feb. 12, 2019.

The use of videoconferencing has exploded at the border. In mid-September, 2019, tent courts were set up in Laredo and Brownsville, Texas, to expedite hearings for more than 40,000 individuals who had been forced to remain in Mexico pending their hearing. The Laredo court was to handle as many as 300 cases a day in four courtrooms. Initial master hearings would be held for 50 individuals at a time in each courtroom with folding tables, set up so the respondents could see the image of the immigration judge located in a different city. *See* Cedar Attanasio, *Tent courts set to open on border for US asylum seekers*, Associated Press, Sept. 10, 2019.

12.   Removal Proceedings and Immigration Judges

A 2015 study by the U.C.L.A. law professor Ingrid Eagly found that deportation proceedings of detained immigrants heard by videoconference were adjudicated more quickly, in fewer days and with fewer trials, than those heard in person. But detained immigrants whose cases were heard through videoconferencing were also more likely to be deported. Professor Eagly article reports the findings of the first empirical study of the use of televideo technology to remotely adjudicate the immigration cases of litigants held in U.S. detention centers. Comparing the outcomes of televideo and in-person cases in federal immigration courts, it reveals an outcome paradox: detained televideo litigants were more likely than detained in-person litigants to be deported, but judges did not deny respondents' claims in televideo cases at higher rates. Instead, these inferior results were associated with the fact that detained litigants assigned to televideo courtrooms exhibited depressed engagement with the adversarial process — they were less likely to retain counsel, to apply to remain lawfully in the United States, or to seek an immigration benefit known as voluntary departure.

Drawing on interviews of stakeholders and court observations from the highest-volume detained immigration courts in the country, Professor Eagly advances several explanations for why televideo litigants might be less likely than other detained litigants to take advantage of procedures that could help them. These reasons include litigants' perception that televideo is unfair and illegitimate, technical challenges in litigating claims over a screen, remote litigants' lower-quality interactions with other courtroom actors, and the exclusion of a public audience from the remote courtroom. This findings begin an important conversation about technology's threat to meaningful litigant participation in the adversarial process. Ingrid Eagly, *Remove Adjudication in Immigration*, 109 Northwestern Univ. L. Rev. 933 (2015).

7. Immigration Judge's Responsibility to Inform Respondent of Apparent Eligibility for Relief. A pertinent part of 8 C.F.R. § 1240.11(a)(2) provides: "The immigration judge shall inform the alien of his or her apparent eligibility to apply for any of the benefits enumerated in this chapter and shall afford the alien an opportunity to make application during the hearing . . ." The Ninth Circuit addressed the "apparent eligibility" language in the regulation in the next case

C.J.L.G. v. Barr

___F.3d___ (9th Cir. May 3, 2019)

Before: Sidney R. Thomas, Chief Judge, and Susan P. Graber, M. Margaret McKeown, William A. Fletcher, Richard A. Paez, Marsha S. Berzon, Johnnie B. Rawlinson, Consuelo M. Callahan, Sandra S. Ikuta, Jacqueline H. Nguyen and Andrew D. Hurwitz, Circuit Judges.
    Concurrence by Judge Paez;
    Concurrence by Judge Berzon;
    Dissent by Judge Callahan

OPINION

HURWITZ, Circuit Judge:

I. Background

A gang held 14-year-old C.J.L.G. ("CJ") at gunpoint in his native Honduras and threatened to kill his family after he rejected recruitment attempts. CJ and his mother Maria then fled their homeland and sought asylum in the United States. Although finding CJ credible, an immigration judge ("IJ") denied his request for asylum and ordered him removed. The Board of Immigration Appeals ("BIA") dismissed CJ's appeal.

CJ petitions for review, arguing, among other things, that the IJ erred by failing to recognize he was an at-risk child potentially eligible for relief as a Special Immigrant Juvenile ("SIJ") and to so advise him. Because we conclude that the IJ erroneously failed to advise CJ about his eligibility for SIJ status, we grant the petition.

At his initial hearing before an IJ in November 2014, CJ appeared with Maria but without counsel. When the IJ informed them that she would "not appoint an attorney for [CJ]" but that they had "the right to find an attorney . . . at [their] own expense," Maria said she did not "have money to pay for an attorney" but requested time to find one. Maria was unable to find counsel despite several continuances, and ultimately agreed to represent CJ herself. When Maria explained that CJ feared returning to Honduras "because of the gangs," the IJ gave her an asylum application and questioned her about her son. In response to one question, Maria stated that CJ's father had left her long ago.

In June 2015, Maria filed the asylum application on CJ's behalf. She also sought withholding of removal and protection under the Convention Against Torture. The IJ accepted the application and set CJ's case for a hearing.

At that hearing, CJ testified that gang members threatened to kill him and other family members on three occasions after he rejected recruitment attempts. On the third occasion, CJ was held at gunpoint and given one day to decide whether to join the gang; he and Maria then fled Honduras. CJ testified that it had been "many years" since he had any contact with his father.

The IJ expressly found CJ credible but denied his applications for relief from removal. On appeal to the BIA, now represented by counsel, CJ contended that the IJ had erred by failing to appoint counsel or advise him about SIJ status. The BIA dismissed the appeal, concluding that, although the IJ must "inform the respondent of any apparent forms of relief from removal," CJ had not established eligibility for SIJ status . . .

A three-judge panel denied CJ's petition for review. . . . A majority of active judges voted to grant CJ's petition for rehearing en banc, and the panel opinion was vacated . . .

II. Discussion

A.

An IJ is required to inform a petitioner subject to removal proceedings of "apparent eligibility to apply for any of the benefits enumerated in this chapter." 8 C.F.R. § 1240.11(a)(2). One of the benefits listed "in this chapter" is SIJ status. *Id.* § 1245.1(a), (e)(2)(vi)(B)(3).

Congress created SIJ status in 1990 to provide a path to lawful permanent residency for certain at-risk children. Immigration Act of 1990, Pub. L. No. 101-649, 104 Stat. 4978, 5005–06; *see Bianka M. v. Superior Court*, 5 Cal.5th 1004, 236 Cal. Rptr.3d 610, 423 P.3d 334, 337–38 (2018). A child seeking SIJ protection must first obtain a state-court order declaring him dependent or placing him under the custody of a court-appointed "individual or entity." 8 U.S.C. § 1101(a)(27)(J)(i). The state court issuing the order must find that (1) "reunification with 1 or both . . . parents is not viable due to abuse, neglect, abandonment, or a similar basis found under State law;" and (2) it would not be in the child's "best interest to be returned to [his] parent's previous country." *Id.* § 1101(a)(27)(J)(i)–(ii).

After obtaining a state court order, the child must obtain the consent of the Secretary of Homeland Security to the granting of SIJ status by filing an I-360 petition with the United States Citizenship and Immigration Services ("USCIS"). *See id.* § 1101(a)(27)(J)(iii); 6 USCIS Policy Manual, pt. J, ch. 2(A), ch. 4(E)(1) (current as of Apr. 19, 2019). In reviewing an I-360 petition, "USCIS relies on the expertise of the juvenile court . . . and does not reweigh the evidence," but may deny relief if it determines that the state court order had no reasonable factual basis or was sought "primarily or solely to obtain an immigration benefit." 6 USCIS Policy Manual, pt. J, ch. 2(D)(5); *see* H.R. Rep. No. 105-405, at 130H.R. Rep. No. 105-405, at 130 (1997) (Conf. Rep.).

If USCIS grants the petition, the child may apply for adjustment of status. 6 USCIS Policy Manual, pt. J, ch. 4(A). A "visa must be immediately available" when he applies. 8 C.F.R. § 1245.2(a)(2)(i)(A); *see* 8 U.S.C. § 1153(b)(4) (establishing quota for SIJ visas). A child who is not in removal proceedings applies to USCIS for adjustment of status, *see* 8 C.F.R. § 245.2(a)(1), but one in removal proceedings must seek it from the IJ, *id.* § 1245.2(a)(1)(i); 6 USCIS Policy Manual, pt. J, ch. 4(A) n.2. If the child was the subject of a removal order before obtaining SIJ status, he cannot adjust status unless the IJ also vacates the removal order. *See* 8 U.S.C. § 1182(a)(9)(A)(ii) (providing that a person under a removal order is inadmissible). The IJ has discretion both in deciding whether to reopen removal proceedings, *see* 8 C.F.R. § 1003.2(a), and in whether to grant a subsequent adjustment application, *see* 8 U.S.C. § 1255(a).

B.

The "apparent eligibility" standard of 8 C.F.R. § 1240.11(a)(2) is triggered whenever the facts before the IJ raise a "reasonable possibility that the petitioner may be eligible for relief." *Moran-Enriquez v. INS*, 884 F.2d 420, 423 (9th Cir. 1989). A failure to advise can be excused only when the petitioner's eligibility for relief is not "plausible." *See United States v. Rojas-Pedroza*, 716 F.3d 1253, 1265–67 (9th Cir. 2013) (finding no prejudice from the IJ's failure to advise about eligibility to apply for voluntary departure because it was not "plausible" IJ would grant it); *United States v. Arrieta*, 224 F.3d 1076, 1082–83 (9th Cir. 2000) (finding prejudice from the IJ's advisement failure because excludability waiver under 8 U.S.C. § 1182(h) was "plausible").

The information presented during CJ's proceedings made it reasonably possible that he could establish eligibility for SIJ status. Maria's comment that CJ's father left her "a long time ago," and CJ's statement that he had no paternal contact for "many years" demonstrated that reunification with one parent might be impossible "due to . . . abandonment." *See* 8 U.S.C. § 1101(a)(27)(J)(i). And CJ's testimony about the death threats he received from the gang showed that returning to Honduras might not be in his "best interest." *See id.* § 1101(a)(27)(J)(ii). Indeed, once he became aware of his potential eligibility for SIJ status, CJ obtained the required state-court order and has now filed an I-360 petition.

The government does not suggest that it was not reasonably possible at the time of CJ's hearing that he could obtain SIJ status or that the IJ was not aware of the facts suggesting CJ's eligibility for relief. Rather, it contends that SIJ status is not a form of relief from removal covered by 8 C.F.R. § 1240.11(a)(2). That argument fails. A successful SIJ application plainly can lead to relief from removal, *see* 6 USCIS Policy Manual, pt. J, ch. 4(A), and SIJ regulations are among those in the referenced subchapter, 8 C.F.R. § 1245.1(a), (e)(2)(vi)(B)(3).

In the alternative, the government argues that the IJ is only required to advise a juvenile of potential eligibility for SIJ relief *after* the child has obtained a state-court order, an approved I-360 petition from USCIS, and an immediately available visa. "We do not read the regulation so grudgingly. [It] obviously is meant to prompt the IJ to help an alien explore legal avenues of relief that might not be apparent to him or his attorney." *Moran-Enriquez*, 884 F.2d at 423. To adopt the government's position here would require a minor to complete all but the final step for SIJ status—seeking adjustment of status from the IJ—before triggering the IJ's duty to advise him of SIJ eligibility. This is a nonsensical approach. It would eviscerate the utility of advice by the IJ and substantially undermine the core purpose of the IJ's duty to advise—to inform a minor of rights and avenues of relief *of which he may not yet be aware.*

To be sure, CJ's eventual ability to obtain SIJ status depended on future decisions by a state court and USCIS. But the regulation speaks of "apparent eligibility," not certain entitlement. 8 C.F.R. § 1240.11(a)(2). We have made plain that "[t]he regulations do not require . . . a reviewing court to conclude that an alien would certainly qualify for relief." *Bui v. INS*, 76 F.3d 268, 271 (9th Cir. 1996). Thus, in *Bui*, we held that an IJ was required to advise Bui about potential eligibility for a waiver of excludability under 8 U.S.C. § 1182(h) even though the record did not show he could satisfy every element necessary to obtain relief. *Id.*

To obtain the waiver, Bui had to show he had a U.S. citizen or permanent resident relative, and that the relative would suffer extreme hardship were Bui deported. *Id.* And, to adjust his status, Bui needed both the waiver and an immediately available visa approved by USCIS. *Id.* at 270–71 (citing 8 U.S.C. §§ 1182(h), 1255(a)). Although the record contained no evidence of hardship and the government argued that no visa would be available, the IJ nonetheless had a duty to advise because the record "raised an inference of the existence of relatives and the possibility of relief." *Id.* at 271. Indeed, we had previously explained that the advisement duty "[b]y definition" involves situations where, as here, the petitioner does not "make a complete showing of eligibility." *Moran-Enriquez*, 884 F.2d at 423; *see also Arrieta*, 224 F.3d at 1082–83 (holding that failure to advise was prejudicial because, "although the evidence produced by Mr. Arrieta does not guarantee that he would have been granted [the] waiver, it provides the 'something more' that makes it plausible that he would have received one").

C.

. . .

[A]lthough the IJ could not have granted CJ relief from removal at the time of the hearing, she could have continued the proceedings to allow him to apply for SIJ status. Indeed, the BIA recently held that an IJ should do so when the child is "actively pursuing" the state-court order.[6] *See In re Zepeda-Padilla*, 2018 WL 1897722, at *1–2 (B.I.A. Feb. 16, 2018) (unpublished). The record makes plain that, once CJ was informed of eligibility for that status, he vigorously—and successfully— pursued the required order. And, had the IJ granted a continuance while CJ navigated the SIJ process, he would not currently be subject to a removal order.

. . . [T]he IJ should exercise that discretion in light of CJ's apparent eligibility for SIJ status, something overlooked at the time of his hearing, and may now also consider how far he has proceeded in the process. We therefore grant the petition for review, vacate the removal order, and remand for a new hearing before the IJ.[7]

PETITION GRANTED.

PAEZ, Circuit Judge, joined by FLETCHER and BERZON, Circuit Judges, concurring:

I concur in the majority's opinion—as far as it goes. I agree that the Immigration Judge ("IJ") had a duty to advise CJ of his apparent eligibility for Special Immigrant Juvenile ("SIJ") relief. I write separately because I disagree with the majority's decision to remain silent on the issue of a child's right to counsel in immigration removal proceedings. As the majority acknowledges, CJ's asylum, withholding of removal, and Convention Against Torture ("CAT") claims may come back to this court. I would reach the fundamental question raised in this proceeding: whether the Fifth Amendment's guaranty of due process entitles children to appointed counsel in immigration proceedings. I would hold that it does, for indigent children under age 18 who are seeking asylum, withholding of removal, CAT, or another form of relief for which they may be eligible, such as SIJ status.[1]

I.

The majority states that because CJ now has counsel, we need not address his argument that appointed counsel is constitutionally required for indigent children in removal proceedings. That was the critical issue raised in the petition for rehearing en banc. In *J.E.F.M. v. Lynch*, we stated that the only proper way for immigrant children to pursue their right to counsel claims was by exhausting the administrative process of their removal orders and then seeking review in federal court. 837 F.3d 1026, 1038 (9th Cir. 2016). "Following discussion at oral argument, to facilitate a test case," the government provided counsel in *J.E.F.M.* with "notice of any minor without counsel that the government is aware of ordered removed by an immigration judge following a merits hearing." *Id.* at 1037 n.10. We described such a case as one where "a right-to-counsel claim [would be] teed up for appellate review." *Id.* at 1038. Now, we have that case, and the majority inexplicably punts the question yet again.

. . .

II.

. . .

"The importance of counsel, particularly in asylum cases where the law is complex and developing, can neither be overemphasized nor ignored." *Reyes-Palacios v. I.N.S.*, 836 F.2d 1154, 1155 (9th Cir. 1988). For immigrant children, that is especially true. In *Jie Lin v. Ashcroft*, we held that a child was denied effective assistance of counsel, in violation of due process, by counsel's inept performance. 377 F.3d 1014, 1034 (9th Cir. 2004). There, the counsel's "lack of preparation prevented her from researching and presenting basic *legal* arguments fundamental to the asylum claim" and "her lack of investigation left her unable to present critical *facts* to support Lin's claim." *Id.* at 1024; *see also id.* at 1024–27. CJ's case poses the question: If an attorney's failure to investigate and research her child client's case can be a Fifth Amendment violation, *id.* at 1024, then how can a child without any counsel have a proceeding that comports with due process?

. . .

I cannot ignore this mockery of judicial and administrative processes. There are thousands of very real children in removal proceedings without counsel. Data from August 2017 shows that four out of every ten children whose cases began in 2016 were unrepresented, where there were over 33,000 new cases—and that number rose to three out of every four children whose cases began in 2017, where there were about 19,000 new cases. Transactional Records Access Clearinghouse,

Children: Amid a Growing Court Backlog Many Still Unrepresented (Sept. 28, 2017), https://trac.syr.edu/immigration/reports/482/. Many of them are fleeing persecution. CJ is fleeing threats from gangs, and his case demonstrates a child's need for counsel in removal proceedings so that the proceedings may be constitutionally "full and fair," especially where the child's proceedings are made even more complex by virtue of the child's potential eligibility for relief through SIJ status or asylum. *Oshodi*, 729 F.3d at 889.

. . .

IV.

Children do not need to be "left to thread their way alone through the labyrinthine maze of immigration laws." *J.E.F.M.*, 837 F.3d at 1040 (McKeown, J., specially concurring). In fact, due process prohibits this reality. I would recognize a due process right to counsel for indigent children in removal proceedings. Based on the record presented, I would limit the class of indigent children under 18 who are required appointed counsel to those who are seeking asylum, withholding of removal, CAT, or another form of relief for which they are apparently eligible, such as SIJ status. As the Supreme Court said when recognizing a right to appointed counsel for children in another context, "[u]nder our Constitution, the condition of being a boy does not justify a kangaroo court." *In re Gault*, 387 U.S. at 28, 87 S.Ct. 1428.

NOTES AND QUESTIONS

1. The Ninth Circuit held that the "apparent eligibility" standard of 8 C.F.R. § 1240.11(a)(2) is triggered whenever the facts before the IJ raise a "reasonable possibility that the petitioner may be eligible for relief." A failure to advise can be excused only when the petitioner's eligibility for relief is not "plausible." Does the approach make sense? Why?

Chapter 13

ASYLUM

III. Well-Founded Fear of Persecution

At the end of page 881, add the following:

So, if the applicant has established past persecution, there is a presumption of a well-founded fear of persecution in the future and the burden shifts to the DHS to prove by a preponderance of the evidence that there are changed country conditions, or that the applicant could avoid future persecution by relocating, and that it would be reasonable to do so under all of the circumstances. *Matter of D-I-M-*, 24 I&N Dec. 448 (BIA 2008).

Credible death threats alone can constitute past persecution. *See, e.g., Tairou v. Whitaker*, 909 F.3d 702 (4th Cir. 2018), *Navas v. INS*, 217 F.3d 646 (9th Cir. 2000). The Ninth Circuit has held that the threats must "so menacing as to cause significant actual suffering or harm, *Lim v. INS*, 224 F.3d 929, 936 (9th Cir. 2000); *see also Duran-Rodriguez v. Barr*, 918 F.3d 1025 (9th Cir. 2019).

Humanitarian asylum. An asylum applicant who has established past persecution but no longer a well-founded fear of persecution may nevertheless warrant a discretionary grant of humanitarian asylum based not only on compelling reasons arising out of the severity of the past persecution, but also on a "reasonable possibility that he or she may suffer other serious harm" upon removal to his or her country under 8 C.F.R. § 1208.13(b)(1)(iii)(B).

Examples:

In *Matter of L-S-*, 25 I&N Dec. 705 (BIA 2012), the respondent is a native and citizen of Albania who has requested asylum, maintaining that he was persecuted over many years in his country on account of his political opinion. In a decision dated September 29, 2004, an Immigration Judge found the respondent removable and denied his applications for relief based on his persecution claim, finding that he failed to establish past persecution and that, in any case, circumstances in Albania had changed so that he no longer had a well-founded fear of persecution. The BIA affirmed, but after review by the Eighth Circuit, the case was remanded to the BIA.

The facts concern the respondent's account of how he and his family were imprisoned by the Communist-era Albanian Government in an internment camp between 1980 and 1981 on account of the respondent's criticism of the communist system then present in his country. The respondent described austere conditions in the camp, which involved spending long hours at hard labor and having to live in a barracks while interned. What drinking water was available was often of poor quality. The respondent asserted that prisoners were constantly supervised and were not permitted to communicate with each other. He described how being labeled a "dissident" caused him difficulty obtaining work after his release, although he did eventually secure a hard-labor job at a stone quarry.

The respondent explained how he joined an Albanian democratic movement in 1990 and became a member of the Democratic Party in Kucova in 1991. Three of his brothers were active in the movement as well. The respondent related that secret police warned him against engaging in democratic political activities and that they threatened him with disappearance. Socialist Party members also threatened him physically. According to the respondent, in May 1997, he was beaten unconscious by unknown individuals on account of his political activity, and in June 1997, he was again beaten by a police officer and a civilian police employee. The respondent endured another similar beating later that month. After the Socialist Party won the election that subsequently ensued, the respondent's employment was terminated.

The respondent also described difficulties that his politically active brothers experienced, including the 1998 bombing of one brother's house and the bombing of his other brother's store later that year. According to the respondent, during the election season of 2000, masked men carrying machine guns shot at his apartment, wounding his son in the leg. Police supposedly told the respondent they would investigate, but no actions were taken. The respondent's three politically active brothers were reportedly granted asylum in the United States.

The respondent indicated that his children remained in hiding in Albania with their grandparents. He acknowledged that Albania held parliamentary elections in 2005 and that members of the Democratic Party, which he had supported, won the prime minister's office and obtained a majority of the seats in the country's single-house parliament. The respondent asserted, however, that there would be no place for him to live in Albania. He believed that his former political opponents were still there and remained armed, and he recalled the mistreatment and death threats he had received from the secret police. The respondent also claimed that he experienced fear, panic attacks, depression, and sleep problems, along with nightmares about his experiences in Albania. He provided evidence that he had been prescribed the psychotropic medications Haldol, benztropine, and temazepam.

In finding that conditions had changed in Albania, the Immigration Judge noted how power in the country had shifted to the respondent's political party. Persuaded by the State Department's recent report on conditions in Albania, the Immigration Judge found that there was no evidence of politically motivated disappearances and no political prisoners, even though there were occasional arbitrary arrests by the police. The Immigration Judge concluded that the State Department's report was more persuasive than some contrary information submitted by the respondent. The BIA previously upheld the Immigration

13. Asylum

Judge's determination regarding changed country conditions—as they relate to the respondent's original basis for asylum—and that issue was no longer before the BIA.

The BIA's decision continued:

A. Humanitarian Asylum

We emphasize that every asylum applicant who arrives at this stage of the analysis has demonstrated past persecution and thus has proven that he or she is a "refugee." Sections 101(a)(42)(A), 208(a)(1) of the Act, 8U.S.C. §§ 1101(a)(42)(A), 1158(a)(1) (2006). However, not all refugees are eligible to receive asylum in the United States. In particular, those for whom the presumption of a well-founded fear has been rebutted and who have not shown any other basis for a well-founded fear of persecution will not qualify for asylum. *See* 8 C.F.R. §§ 1208.13(b)(1)(i)-(ii), (2). Nonetheless, because the regulations provide additional avenues for asylum for an applicant who has suffered past persecution but who no longer has a well-founded fear, adjudicators—when presented with a case in this procedural posture—should consider whether such an applicant is eligible for a humanitarian grant of asylum under the provisions of 8 C.F.R. § 1208.13(b)(1)(iii)(A) or (B).

We note that an asylum applicant, such as the respondent, bears the burden of proof to show that either form of humanitarian asylum is warranted. Specifically, the regulation provides that an applicant who has already shown past persecution may still be granted asylum, even when the presumption of a well-founded fear of future persecution has been rebutted, by establishing either: (1) that he has "compelling reasons," arising out of the severity of the past persecution, for being unable or unwilling to return to his country under § 1208.13(b)(1)(iii)(A); *or* (2) that there is a "reasonable possibility" that he may suffer "other serious harm" upon removal to his country under § 1208.13(b)(1)(iii)(B). *See also Ben Hamida v. Gonzales*, 478 F.3d 734, 740-41 (6th Cir. 2007) (stating that to establish eligibility under either prong, the applicant must first show that he or she suffered persecution on account of a protected ground). A grant of asylum under either approach is considered to be a form of humanitarian asylum, but each is distinct. We will consider each of these forms of asylum in turn.

B. Asylum Based on Severity of Past Persecution

We have previously considered the form of humanitarian asylum currently set forth in 8 C.F.R. § 1208.13(b)(1)(iii)(A), involving "compelling reasons" arising out of the severity of the past persecution, which is the first basis for the Eighth Circuit's remand in this case. For example, in *Matter of Chen*, 20 I&N Dec. at 21, we stated that even though the applicant did not have a well-founded fear of persecution, his genuine subjective fear of returning to his country, his history of mistreatment in the People's Republic of China, and the mistreatment and death of his father there were relevant considerations to his claim. The applicant's suffering began when he was 8 years old and continued until his adulthood. He endured considerable physical, psychological, and social harm, as a result of which he was permanently physically and emotionally scarred. Based on these humanitarian factors, we concluded that asylum should be granted in the exercise of discretion.

Similarly, in *Matter of B-*, 21 I&N Dec. 66, 72 (BIA 1995), we found that humanitarian asylum was appropriate where an applicant had been imprisoned for political reasons for some 13 months under "deplorable" conditions. The applicant faced the routine use of various forms of physical torture and psychological abuse, including beatings and electrical shocks, inadequate diet and medical care, and the integration of political prisoners with criminal and mentally ill prisoners. We recognized that these experiences were likely exacerbated by his separation from his family and the fact that his missing father's fate was unknown.

In *Matter of N-M-A-*, 22 I&N Dec. 312 (BIA 1998), we noted that "asylum is warranted for 'humanitarian reasons' *only* if [the applicant] demonstrates that in the past [he] or his family has suffered under atrocious forms of persecution." *Id.* at 325 (alteration in original) (quoting *Kazlauskas v. INS*, 46 F.3d 902 (9th Cir. 1995)) (internal quotation marks omitted). In that case we declined to extend asylum on a humanitarian basis to an applicant who had experienced a month-long detention and beatings and had the knowledge that his father who had disappeared was likely dead. Instead, we found that the applicant had not demonstrated compelling reasons for being unable or unwilling to return to his country in light of the degree of harm suffered, the length of time over which the harm was inflicted, and the lack of evidence of severe psychological trauma stemming from the harm. *Id.* at 326. This approach, which was the only form of humanitarian asylum available when these cases were decided, is now embodied in 8 C.F.R. § 1208.13(b)(1)(iii)(A).

More recently, in *Matter of S-A-K- & H-A-H-*, 24 I&N Dec. at 46, we found the applicants eligible for humanitarian asylum under this provision because they had suffered "an atrocious form of persecution that results in continuing physical pain and discomfort." The claimants in that case had undergone female genital mutilation in Somalia with aggravating circumstances.

Prior to the regulatory change adding § 1208.13(b)(1)(iii)(B), discussed below, adjudicators would generally end their analysis of humanitarian asylum here, considering whether to exercise discretion to grant relief if the requisite severity of past harm had been shown. However, even after 2001 when the "other serious harm" provision in the regulation went into effect, adjudicators and the parties have not always focused on this second avenue for humanitarian asylum. *See, e.g.*, *Precetaj v. Holder*, 649 F.3d 72, 75 (1st Cir. 2011) (parenthetically noting the "other serious harm" provision as an alternative basis for humanitarian asylum, but citing law that predated it and discussing only relief based on the severity of past persecution); *Mehmeti v. U.S. Att'y Gen.*, 572 F.3d 1196, 1200-01 (11th Cir. 2009) (noting both provisions of the regulation but applying only § 1208.13(b)(1)(iii)(A)); *Ngarurih v. Ashcroft*, 371 F.3d 182, 190 (4th Cir. 2004) (noting both the "compelling reasons" and "other serious harm" avenues for humanitarian asylum, but focusing only on the former).7 While such cases may offer guidance under § 1208.13(b)(1)(iii)(A), they do not address the "other serious harm" aspect of § 1208.13(b)(1)(iii)(B).

C. Asylum Based on a Reasonable Possibility of "Other Serious Harm"

If an Immigration Judge determines that an asylum applicant has not demonstrated "compelling reasons" to grant humanitarian asylum, there remains the additional avenue for relief under 8 C.F.R. § 1208.13(b)(1)(iii)(B) based on a "reasonable possibility" of "other serious harm." As with the "compelling reasons" provision of the regulation, the applicant bears the burden of proof to show why asylum should be granted on this basis in the exercise of discretion.

To date, there has been little legal guidance interpreting the meaning of "other serious harm" under the regulation. Prior to the 2001 change that added this provision, the regulation already permitted asylum grants for "compelling reasons" based on the severity of past persecution, that is, the so-called "*Chen* grants." *See* Asylum Procedures, 65 Fed. Reg. 76,121, 761,33 (final rule Dec. 6, 2000) (effective Jan. 5, 2001); *see also* 8 C.F.R. § 208.13(b)(1)(ii) (1991). Nonetheless, as the Supplementary Information to the proposed regulation change states, the Attorney General found that approach alone to be too limited:

The Department recognizes, however, that the existing regulation may represent an overly restrictive approach to the exercise of discretion in cases involving past persecution, but no well-founded fear of future persecution. The Department believes it is appropriate to *broaden the standards for the exercise of discretion in such cases.*

Executive Office for Immigration Review; New Rules Regarding Procedures for Asylum and Withholding of Removal, 63 Fed. Reg. 31,945, 31,947 (proposed Jun. 11, 1998) (Supplementary Information) (emphasis added). This was the rationale for adding the "other serious harm" language to 8 C.F.R. § 1208.13(b)(1)(iii). The changed regulation not only endorsed the approach to humanitarian asylum that is based on the severity of past harm, but it also made the consideration of a reasonable possibility of other serious harm a specific, additional, and separate avenue for relief. *Id.* (citing the ongoing civil strife in Afghanistan discussed in *Matter of B-*, 21 I&N Dec. 66, as an example of "other serious harm").

According to the Supplementary Information to the regulation, "other serious harm" need not be inflicted on account of race, religion, nationality, membership in a particular social group, or political opinion. 63 Fed. Reg. at 31,947. However, such harm must be so serious that it equals the severity of persecution. Mere economic disadvantage or the inability to practice one's chosen profession would not qualify as "other serious harm." *Id.*

The "other serious harm" provision of the regulation differs in nature from the "compelling reasons" provision. To be eligible for asylum under 8 C.F.R. § 1208.13(b)(1)(iii)(B), an applicant need not show that the harm suffered in the past was atrocious. Instead, the inquiry is forward-looking. When considering the possibility of "other serious harm," the focus should be on current conditions and the potential for new physical or psychological harm that the applicant might suffer.

While "other serious harm" must equal the severity of persecution, it may be wholly unrelated to the past harm. Moreover, pursuant to the regulation, the asylum applicant need only establish a "reasonable possibility" of such "other serious harm"; a showing of "compelling reasons" is not required under this provision. We also emphasize that *no nexus* between the "other serious harm" and an asylum ground protected under the Act need be shown.

Therefore, at this stage of proceedings, adjudicators considering "other serious harm" should be cognizant of conditions in the applicant's country of return and should pay particular attention to major problems that large segments of the population face or conditions that might not significantly harm others but that could severely affect the applicant. Such conditions may include, but are not limited to, those involving civil strife, extreme economic deprivation beyond economic disadvantage, or situations where the claimant could experience severe mental or emotional harm or physical injury.

Some circuit court cases have provided examples of situations that might involve "other serious harm." *See, e.g., Pllumi v. Att'y Gen. of U.S.*, 642 F.3d 155, 162-63 (3d Cir. 2011) (cautioning, where the applicant claimed that medical treatment in Albania was insufficient to treat his severe injuries, that while countries' differing health care standards were not a basis for asylum, "it is conceivable that, in extreme circumstances, harm resulting from the unavailability of necessary medical care could constitute 'other serious harm'"); *Kone v. Holder*, 596 F.3d 141,152-53 (2d Cir. 2010) (stating that the Board may consider on remand "whether the mental anguish of a mother who was herself a victim of genital mutilation who faces the choice of seeing her daughter suffer the same fate, or avoiding that outcome by separation from her child, may qualify as such 'other serious harm'"); *Kholyavskiy v. Mukasey*, 540 F.3d 555, 577 (7th Cir. 2008) (remanding for consideration of "other serious harm" if the applicant's psychiatric medications, which he needed for functioning, might be unavailable in his country); *Mohammed v. Gonzales*, 400 F.3d 785, 801 (9th Cir. 2005) (remanding for consideration of possible "other serious harm" in light of Somalia's poverty; the decimation of the applicant's clan, which left female members like the applicant particularly vulnerable; and serious ongoing human rights abuses, including the killing of many civilian citizens in factional fighting); *Belishta v. Ashcroft*, 378 F.3d 1078 (9th Cir. 2004) (noting the applicant's possible eligibility for relief under § 1208.13(b)(1)(iii)(B) where agents of the former Albanian regime—although motivated solely by money—reportedly tried to take the applicant's house, threatened and harassed both her and her family, shot out her windows, and left a bomb on her doorstep); *cf. Boer-Sedano v. Gonzales*, 418 F.3d 1082, 1090-91 (9th Cir. 2005) (finding that a gay man with Acquired Immune Deficiency Syndrome ("AIDS"), who faced unemployment, a lack of health insurance, and the unavailability of necessary medications in Mexico to treat his disease, showed a likelihood of "other serious harm" to make relocation within his country unreasonable when considered in the context of the "social and cultural constraints" placed upon his particular social group).

In light of these cases and the need to examine "other serious harm" factors under the totality of the circumstances in a given situation, we conclude that such determinations are most appropriately made on a case-by-case basis. We cite the above cases as examples and do not necessarily endorse any particular analysis or outcome.

D.   Respondent's Motion To Remand

We now turn to the case before us to address the respondent's motion to remand the record. He has raised an issue concerning his psychiatric treatment— a question that should be first explored by an Immigration Judge. The Eighth Circuit stated that we should not have ruled on the humanitarian asylum claim without the benefit of a fully developed record relating to that claim. The court further stated that the parties should be allowed to supplement the record on remand. In any case, we note that further fact-finding may generally be required to determine whether an applicant might experience "other serious harm" in his or her country of origin. However, we have limited fact-finding authority in deciding appeals. *See* 8 C.F.R. § 1003.1(d)(3) (2011); *see also Matter of S-H-*, 23 I&N Dec. 462 (BIA 2002). Accordingly, subject to the provisions of the court's order and this decision, the respondent's motion to remand will be granted.

On remand, the Immigration Judge should examine the respondent's request for a discretionary grant of humanitarian asylum in light of the severity of his past persecution to determine whether he has shown "compelling reasons" for being unable or unwilling to return to Albania. In this regard, relevant factors include the actual length of the respondent's internment in the early 1980s, the severity of the conditions there, and the passage of time following his release when he lived in his country without much incident until the late 1990s. Moreover, the nature, severity, and duration of the beatings and all mistreatment that the respondent endured, as well as any aftereffects he may now suffer, should be considered to determine if "compelling reasons" exist for granting asylum, notwithstanding the rebuttal of the presumption of a well-founded fear, as contemplated by 8 C.F.R. § 1208.13(b)(1)(iii)(A). In addition to the respondent's experiences in Albania, those of his politically active brothers may be relevant to the inquiry regarding the severity of the respondent's past mistreatment, especially since they have each reportedly been granted asylum. *See* Office of the United Nations High Commissioner for Refugees, *Handbook on Procedures and Criteria for Determining Refugee Status Under the 1951 Convention and the 1967 Protocol Relating to the Status of Refugees* para. 136, at 31 (Geneva, 1992).

If the Immigration Judge finds that the respondent did not demonstrate "compelling reasons" for granting asylum based on the severity of his past persecution, he should also determine whether the respondent has established a "reasonable possibility" that he will suffer "other serious harm" under 8 C.F.R. § 1208.13(b)(1)(iii) (B) in light of the considerations discussed above. As we previously noted, further fact-finding in this regard may be necessary. Under either of the regulatory provisions, the respondent has the burden of proof to show that a grant of humanitarian asylum is warranted, including whether discretion should be favorably exercised.

ORDER: The respondent's motion to remand is granted.

In *Hanna v. Kessler*, 506 F.3d 933 (9th Cir. 2007), Hanna was a native and citizen of Iraq. He was born in Baghdad and is a Chaldean Catholic. Hanna fled Iraq on September 27, 1997 on account of three incidents described below.

In January 1992, Ba'ath party officials arrested and detained Hanna for over a month. Hanna's captors tortured him while he was jailed. Hanna was accused of being anti-government and of belonging to the Assyrian Democratic Party, in part because he was taking extra math classes from a Christian teacher. Government officials also accused Hanna of making and distributing anti-government fliers with his math teacher.

In March 1994, local police falsely accused Hanna of selling "expired" goods, laundering money, and using counterfeit money. He was jailed for fifteen days. Hanna stated that guards beat him and blindfolded him during his detention.

In 1997, members of the Student Affairs Bureau and Party Organization Committee at Hanna's school tried to force Hanna to join the Fedayeen Saddam, a paramilitary organization loyal to Saddam Hussein. Hanna testified that the group told him if he did not join the Fedayeen Saddam he would be accused of sabotaging the government and he would not be allowed to graduate from university. Hanna told the recruiters that he did not want to join the organization because doing so went against the principles of his Christian faith. Although he tried to refuse to join the group, the members told him that he had two days to change his mind.

Hanna was afraid for his life after his interaction with the recruiters. Hanna told his father about the incident, and his father advised him to flee Baghdad before the recruiters were due to return. That night Hanna took a bus to Batnaya in northern Iraq. While he was in Batnaya, Ba'ath party members forced their way into the family home looking for Hanna. The inquisitors hit Hanna's brother in the eye with a gun. A bullet fired at the floor by the intruders ricocheted and hit Hanna's father in the leg, breaking a bone and putting him in the hospital for a month. One of the officers spat in the face of Hanna's mother. The Ba'ath party officials ransacked the house looking for Hanna and left after threatening the family members that harsher consequences would follow if they did not produce Hanna.

Hanna's father wrote Hanna a letter telling him of the incident at the house. The letter advised Hanna that he would likely face execution if he did not flee the country. Hanna then fled Iraq, traveling through Turkey, Greece, Belgium, France, and Mexico before eventually reaching the United States.

The BIA refused to grant relief, however, the Ninth Circuit remanded, advising the BIA to reconsider the asylum denial. Furthermore, the Ninth Circuit considered humanitarian asylum:

> The BIA may grant humanitarian asylum to a victim of past persecution, even where the government has rebutted the applicant's fear of future persecution, if the applicant establishes one of two things. First, the asylum seeker can show

"compelling reasons for being unwilling or unable to return to the country [that he fled] arising out of the severity of the past persecution." 8 C.F.R. § 1208.13(b) (1)(iii)(A). Or, under the second prong of the humanitarian asylum analysis, the asylum seeker can show "a reasonable possibility that he or she may suffer other serious harm upon removal to that country." 8 C.F.R. § 1208.13(b)(1)(iii)(B); see also Belishta v. Ashcroft, 378 F.3d 1078, 1081 (9th Cir.2004).

The BIA held that Hanna "failed to establish that any persecution he may have suffered compels a grant of asylum as a matter of humanitarian concerns." Though we agree that the severity of Hanna's past persecution is not sufficient to qualify for humanitarian asylum under the first prong, the BIA seems to have ignored the second prong of the humanitarian asylum analysis. This prong, as described above, requires only a reasonable possibility that Hanna may suffer serious harm upon removal. Because it appears that Hanna could have qualified for humanitarian asylum based on the likely future harm he would suffer as a Christian upon his return to Iraq and because the BIA does not seem to have considered this prong, we remand to the BIA to consider whether there exists a "reasonable possibility" that Hanna "may suffer other serious harm upon removal" to Iraq.

At the top of page 884, before part IV, add the following:

Asylum can be granted if the persecution emanates from an entity or group that authorities tolerate or cannot effectively control. *See, e.g., Matter of Villalta*, 20 I. & N. Dec. 142 (BIA 1990)(death squads); *Arteaga v. INS*, 836 F.2d 1227, 1232 (9th Cir. 1985)(guerillas); *Singh v. INS*, 94 F.3d 1353, 1359 (9th Cir. 1996) (gangs). *In Re Kasinga*, 21 I. & N. 357 (BIA 1996), involves female genital mutilation and appears later in the chapter. Some governments are unable or unwilling to control gang or even domestic violence against many asylum applicants. That situation was challenged however in *Matter of A-B-*, which is discussed in these notes following the *Kasinga* discussion below.

IV. Statutory Requirements for Asylum

At the top of page 887, add the following prior to the Notes and Questions:

Withholding of Removal. The Supreme Court in *Cardoza-Fonseca* emphasized the distinction between asylum and withholding. The burden of proof for withholding is a higher (is persecution "more likely than not") preponderance standard established in *Stevic*. In fact, most asylum applicants facing removal, apply for withholding of removal as well. There is a one-year time deadline to apply for asylum, while there is no such time deadline for withholding. If the requirements for withholding are met, it *must* be granted. Asylum, on the other hand, is discretionary. Also, a person who has been deported, but who flees back to the United States out of fear, will be ineligible to apply for asylum, but can apply for withholding.

The statutory requirements for withholding are found in 8 U.S.C. § 1231(b)(3):

(3) Restriction on removal to a country where alien's life or freedom would be threatened
(A) In general
Notwithstanding paragraphs (1) and (2), the Attorney General may not remove an alien to a country if the Attorney General decides that the alien's life or freedom would be threatened in that country because of the alien's race, religion, nationality, membership in a particular social group, or political opinion.

(B) Exception: Subparagraph (A) does not apply to an alien deportable under section 1227(a)(4)(D) of this title or if the Attorney General decides that—
(i) the alien ordered, incited, assisted, or otherwise participated in the persecution of an individual because of the individual's race, religion, nationality, membership in a particular social group, or political opinion;
(ii) the alien, having been convicted by a final judgment of a particularly serious crime is a danger to the community of the United States;
(iii) there are serious reasons to believe that the alien committed a serious nonpolitical crime outside the United States before the alien arrived in the United States; or
(iv) there are reasonable grounds to believe that the alien is a danger to the security of the United States.

For purposes of clause (ii), an alien who has been convicted of an aggravated felony (or felonies) for which the alien has been sentenced to an aggregate term of imprisonment of at least 5 years shall be considered to have committed a particularly serious crime. The previous sentence shall not preclude the Attorney General from determining that, notwithstanding the length of sentence imposed, an alien has been convicted of a particularly serious crime. For purposes of clause (iv), an alien who is described in section 1227(a)(4)(B) of this title shall be considered to be an alien with respect to whom there are reasonable grounds for regarding as a danger to the security of the United States.

In addition to establishing a statutory asylum process, the 1980 Refugee Act amended the withholding of deportation provision. See Stevic, 467 U.S., at 421, n. 15. Prior to 1968, the Attorney General had discretion whether to grant withholding of deportation to aliens. In 1968, however, the United States agreed to comply with the substantive provisions of Articles 2 through 34 of the 1951 United Nations Convention Relating to the Status of Refugees. See 19 U.S.T. 6223, 6259–6276, T.I.A.S. No. 6577 (1968); see generally Stevic, at 416–417.

Article 33.1 of the Convention, 189 U.N.T.S. 150, 176 (1954), reprinted in 19 U.S.T. 6259, 6276, which is the counterpart of INA § 241, imposed a mandatory duty on contracting States not to return an alien to a country where his "life or freedom would be threatened" on account of one of the enumerated reasons. This is often referred to as *non-refoulement*. Thus, although the withholding provision did not itself originally constrain the Attorney General's discretion, after 1968, presumably, the dictates of the United Nations Convention were honored. In any event, the 1980 Act removed the Attorney General's discretion in withholding proceedings. INS v. Cardoza-Fonseca, 480 U.S. 421, 429 (1987).

Congress enacted the withholding statute to codify the United States' *non-refoulement* obligations. *See INS v. Stevic*, 467 U.S. 407, 421, 426 n.20 (1984). The *non-refoulement* obligation is not limited to protecting people from final orders of removal to places where their life would be threatened on account of a protected ground, but rather considers any "return" to such territory.

The United States is a party to the 1967 Protocol Relating to the Status of Refugees, which incorporates Articles 2 to 34 of the 1951 Convention Relating to the Status of Refugees. Article 33 of the 1951 Convention provides that: "[n]o Contracting State shall expel or return (*'refouler'*) a refugee in any manner whatsoever to the frontiers of territories where his or freedom would be threatened on account of his race, religion, nationality, membership of a particular social group or political opinion." (emphasis added).

Similarly, Article 3 of the Convention Against Torture states, "No State Party shall expel, return (*'refouler'*) or extradite a person to another State where there are substantial grounds for believing that he would be in danger of being subjected to torture." *See also* Foreign Affairs Reform and Restructuring Act of 1998 (FARRA), Pub. L. No. 105-277, Div. G, Title XXII, § 2242(a) (8 U.S.C. § 1231 note) ("It shall be the policy of the United States not to expel, extradite, or otherwise effect the involuntary return of any person to a country in which there are substantial grounds for believing the person would be in danger of being subjected to torture, regardless of whether the person is physically present in the United States.").

V. Membership in a Particular Social Group

At the top of page 896, add the following to note 8:

In *Matter of L-E-A-*, the Board easily recognized that the respondent's relationship with his father established membership in a PSG, namely "his father's immediate family." *Matter of L-E-A-*, 27 I&N Dec. 40, 43 (BIA 2017). Is this consistent with what comes to mind when you think of a social group. The Ninth Circuit has said that "the family . . . [is] the quintessential particular social group." *Flores-Rios v. Lynch*, 807 F.3d 1123, 1128 (9th Cir. 2015). In reaching its conclusion in *L-E-A-*, the Board relied upon DHS's concession "that the imme-diate family unit of the respondent's father qualifies as a cognizable social group." However, on July 29, 2019, Attorney General William Barr overturned the BIA in *Matter of L-E-A-*, 27 I&N Dec. 581 (A.G. 2019):

> Thus, by the terms of the statutory definition of "refugee," as well as according to long-standing principles set forth in BIA precedent, to qualify as a "particular social group," an applicant must demonstrate that his family group meets each of the immutability, particularity, and social distinction requirements. While many family relationships will be immutable, some family-based group definitions may be too vague or amorphous to meet the particularity requirement—i.e., where an applicant cannot show discernible boundaries to the group. See, e.g., S-E-G-, 24 I&N Dec. at 585 (noting that the "proposed group of 'family members,' which could include fathers, mothers, siblings, uncles, aunts, nieces, nephews, grandparents, cousins, and others, is . . . too amorphous a category" to satisfy the particularity requirement). Further, many family-based social groups will have trouble qualifying as "socially distinct," a requirement that contemplates that the applicant's proposed group be "set apart, or distinct, from other persons within the society in some significant way." M-E-V-G-, 26 I&N Dec. at 238 ("In other words, if the common immutable char-acteristic were known, those with the characteristic in the society in question would be meaningfully distinguished from those who do not have it."). "To have the 'social distinction' necessary to establish a particular social group, there must be evidence showing that society in general perceives, considers, or recognizes persons sharing the particular characteristic to be a group." W-G-R-, 26 I&N Dec. at 217.
>
> . . .
>
> This opinion does not bar all family-based social groups from qualifying for asy-lum. To the contrary, in some societies, an applicant may present specific kinship groups or clans that, based on the evidence in the applicant's case, are particular and socially distinct. See, e.g., Ali v. Ashcroft, 394 F.3d 780, 785 (9th Cir. 2005) (holding that the "persecution Ali suffered was clearly on account of . . . her mem-bership in a particular social group, her clan"); H-, 21 I&N Dec. at 343 (recogniz-ing a Somali subclan as a "particular social group"). But unless an immediate fam-ily carries greater societal import, it is unlikely that a proposed family-based group will be "distinct" in the way required by the INA for purposes of asylum. Moreover, adjudicators should be skeptical of social groups that appear to be "defined prin-cipally, if not exclusively, for the purposes of [litigation] . . . without regard to the question of whether anyone in [a given country] perceives [those] group[s] to exist in any form whatsoever." In re R-A-, 22 I&N Dec. 906, 918 (BIA 1999; A.G. 2001), *remanded for recons. in* Matter of R-A-, 24 I&N Dec. 629 (A.G. 2008).

Where does this decision leave asylum applicants who want to argue family as a social group? Is evidence necessary in each case establishing that the family is socially distinct in the community? How does an applicant do that?

One advocate has offered these questions of asylum applicants who base their PSG on family. The questions relate particularly to the social distinction issue of L-E-A-:

What community within city did you live?
With whom did you live there?
How long had you/abuser live there?
How long had your parents/abusers parents lived there?
Who lived with you and abuser?
What size community was it?
Did people in community know abuser?
Did they know abuser's parents?
When you moved in abuser's house, did community members know you?
Did they ever learn who you were?
How did they learn who you were?
Did you and abuser go outside of the house together?
Did people from the community see you outside together?
Did you and abuser go to church together?
Where was the church?
Did anyone else from family/household go to that church with you?
Did you all walk to church together?
Did other people in the community go to that church?
Did members of the community see you in church with abuser?
Did you participate in other public events with abuser? or his family?
When there were birthdays/baptisms, etc did you and abuser go?
How would abuser introduce you to his friends and family?
In your country, what does being someone's "woman" mean?
Is it common that people live together instead of getting married?

VI.   Women and Gender Claims

On page 918, at the following to note 7:
Unfortunately, *Matter of A-R-C-G-* was overruled by Attorney General Jeff Sessions in *Matter of A-B-*, which is found below.
On page 918, prior to part VII, add the following:

MATTER OF A-B-

27 I. & N. Dec. 316 (A.G. 2018)

. . .

BEFORE THE ATTORNEY GENERAL

On March 7, 2018, I directed the Board of Immigration Appeals ("Board") to refer for my review its decision in this matter, see 8 C.F.R. § 1003.1(h)(1)(i), and I invited the parties and any interested amici to submit briefs addressing questions relevant to that certification. *Matter of A-B-*, 27 I&N Dec. 227 (A.G. 2018). Specifically, I sought briefing on whether, and under what circumstances, being a victim of private criminal activity constitutes a cognizable "particular social group" for purposes of an application for asylum or withholding of removal.

For the reasons set forth in the accompanying opinion, I vacate the Board's December 6, 2016 decision and remand this case to the immigration judge for further proceedings. Consistent with the test developed by the Board over the past several decades, an applicant seeking to establish persecution on account of membership in a "particular social group" must satisfy two requirements. First, the applicant must demonstrate membership in a group, which is composed of members who share a common immutable characteristic, is defined with particularity, and is socially distinct within the society in question. And second, the applicant's membership in that group must be a central reason for her persecution. When, as here, the alleged persecutor is someone unaffiliated with the government, the applicant must show that flight from her country is necessary because her home government is unwilling or unable to protect her.

Although there may be exceptional circumstances when victims of private criminal activity could meet these requirements, they must satisfy established standards when seeking asylum. Such applicants must establish membership in a particular and socially distinct group that exists independently of the alleged underlying harm, demonstrate that their persecutors harmed them on account of their membership in that group rather than for personal reasons, and establish that the government protection from such harm in their home country is so lacking that their persecutors' actions can be attributed to the government. Because *Matter of A-R-C-G-*, 26 I&N Dec. 388 (BIA 2014), recognized a new particular social group without correctly applying these standards, I overrule that case and any other Board precedent to the extent those other decisions are inconsistent with the legal conclusions set forth in this opinion.

OPINION

. . . A recurring question in asylum law is determining whether alleged persecution was based on their membership in a "particular social group." Over the past thirty years, this question has recurred frequently before the Board and the courts of appeals, and the standard has evolved over time.

. . . The prototypical refugee flees her home country because the government has persecuted her — either directly through its own actions or indirectly by being unwilling or unable to prevent the misconduct of non-government actors — based upon a statutorily protected ground. Where the persecutor is not part of the government, the immigration judge must consider both the reason for the harm inflicted on the asylum applicant and the government's role in sponsoring or enabling such actions. An alien may suffer threats and violence in a foreign country for any number of reasons relating to her social, economic, family, or other personal circumstances. Yet the asylum statute does not provide redress for all misfortune. It applies when persecution arises on account of membership in a protected group and the victim may not find protection except by taking refuge in another country.

. . .

. . .[T]he Board decided A-R-C-G-, which recognized "married women in Guatemala who are unable to leave their relationship" as a particular social group — without performing the rigorous analysis required by the Board's precedents. 26 I&N Dec. at 389; *see id.* at 390-95. Instead, the Board accepted the concessions by the Department of Homeland Security ("DHS") that the respondent suffered harm rising to the level of past persecution, that she was a member of a qualifying particular social group, and that her membership in that group was a central reason for her persecution. *Id.* at 395.

I do not believe A-R-C-G- correctly applied the Board's precedents, and I now overrule it. The opinion has caused confusion because it recognized an expansive new category of particular social groups based on private violence. Since that decision, the Board, immigration judges, and asylum officers have relied upon it as an affirmative statement of law, even though the decision assumed its conclusion and did not perform the necessary legal and factual analysis. When confronted with asylum cases based on purported membership in a particular social group, the Board, immigration judges, and asylum officers must analyze the requirements as set forth in this opinion, which restates and where appropriate, elaborates upon, the requirements set forth in *M-E-V-G* and *W-G-R-*.

In this matter, the immigration judge initially denied the respondent's asylum claim, which arises out of allegations of domestic abuse suffered in El Salvador. In reversing the immigration judge's decision, the Board did little more than cite A-R-C-G- in finding that she met her burden of establishing that she was a member of a particular social group. In addition to failing meaningfully to consider that question or whether the respondent's persecution was on account of her membership in that group, the Board gave insufficient deference to the factual findings of the immigration judge.

For these and other reasons, I vacate the Board's decision and remand for further proceedings before the immigration judge consistent with this opinion. In so doing, I reiterate that an applicant for asylum on account of her membership in a purported particular social group must demonstrate: (1) membership in a particular group, which is composed of members who share a common immutable characteristic, is defined with particularity, and is socially distinct within the society in question; (2) that her membership in that group is a central reason for her persecution; and (3) that the alleged harm is inflicted by the government of her home country or by persons that the government is unwilling or unable to control. *See M-E-V-G-*, 26 I&N Dec. at 234-44; *W-G-R-*, 26 I&N Dec. at 209-18, 223-24 & n.8. Furthermore, when the applicant is the victim of private criminal activity, the analysis must also "consider whether government protection is available, internal relocation is possible, and persecution exists countrywide." *M-E-V-G-*, 26 I&N Dec. at 243.

Generally, claims by aliens pertaining to domestic violence or gang violence perpetrated by non-governmental actors will not qualify for asylum.[1] While I do not decide that violence inflicted by non-governmental actors may never serve as the basis for an asylum or withholding application based on membership in a particular social group, in practice such claims are unlikely to satisfy the statutory grounds for proving group persecution that the government is unable or unwilling to address. The mere fact that a country may have problems effectively policing certain crimes–such as domestic violence or gang violence–or that certain populations are more likely to be victims of crime, cannot itself establish an asylum claim.

I.

. . .

The respondent claimed that she was eligible for asylum because she was persecuted on account of her membership in the purported particular social group of "El Salvadoran women who are unable to leave their domestic relationships where they have children in common" with their partners. *Matter of A-B-*, Decision Denying Asylum Application at *8, (Immig. Ct. Dec. 1, 2015). The respondent asserted that her ex-husband, with whom she shares three children, repeatedly abused her physically, emotionally, and sexually during and after their marriage. *Id.* at *2-3).

In December 2015, the immigration judge denied all relief and ordered the respondent removed to El Salvador. The immigration judge denied the respondent's asylum claim for four independent reasons: (1) the respondent was not credible; (2) the group in which she claimed membership did not qualify as a "particular social group" within the meaning of 8 U.S.C. § 1101(a)(42)(A); (3) even if it did, the respondent failed to establish that her membership in a social group was a central reason for her persecution; and (4) she failed to show that the El Salvadoran government was unable or unwilling to help her. *Id.* at *4-15. The respondent appealed the immigration judge's decision to the Board.

In December 2016, the Board reversed and remanded with an order to grant the respondent asylum after the completion of background checks. *Matter of A-B-*,

---

1. Accordingly, few such claims would satisfy the legal standard to determine whether an alien has a credible fear of persecution. *See* 8 U.S.C. § 1225(b)(1)(B)(v) (requiring a "significant possibility, taking into account the credibility of the statements made by the alien in support of the alien's claim and such other facts as are known to the officer, that the alien could establish eligibility for asylum under section 1158 of this title [8 U.S.C. § 1158]").

(BIA Dec. 8, 2016). The Board found the immigration judge's adverse credibility determinations clearly erroneous. *Id.* at *1-2. The Board further concluded that the respondent's particular social group was substantially similar to "married women in Guatemala who are unable to leave their relationship," which the Board had recognized in *Matter of A-R-C-G-*, 26 I&N Dec. at 390. *A-B-* at *2. Moreover, the Board held that the immigration judge clearly erred in finding that the respondent could leave her ex-husband, and that the respondent established that her ex-husband persecuted her because of her status as a Salvadoran woman unable to leave her domestic relationship. *Id.* at *2-3. Finally, the Board determined that the El Salvadoran government was unwilling or unable to protect the respondent. *Id.* at *3-4.

In August 2017, the immigration judge issued an order purporting to certify and administratively return the matter to the Board in light of intervening developments in the law. . .

In particular, the immigration judge cited the Fourth Circuit's opinion in *Velasquez v. Sessions*, 866 F.3d 188 (4th Cir. 2017), which denied the petition for review on the ground that the alien had not established that her alleged persecution was on account of her membership in a particular social group. *A-B-* at *3-4 (Immig. Ct. Aug. 18, 2017) (citing *Velasquez*, 866 F.3d at 197). Distinguishing *A-R-C-G-* because of DHS's concessions there, 866 F.3d at 195 n.5, the court in *Velasquez* reiterated that "'[e]vidence consistent with acts of private violence or that merely shows that an individual has been the victim of criminal activity does not constitute evidence of persecution on a statutorily protected ground." *Id.* at 194 (quoting *Sanchez v. U.S. Att'y Gen.*, 392 F.3d 434, 438 (11th Cir. 2004)). The court further noted, "'the asylum statute was not intended as a panacea for the numerous personal altercations that invariably characterize economic and social relationships." *Id.* at 195 (quoting *Saldarriaga v. Gonzales*, 402 F.3d 461, 467 (4th Cir. 2005)).

In a concurrence, Judge Wilkinson reiterated that the particular social groups protected from persecution under the asylum statute must be understood in the context of the other grounds for protection, which concern specific segments of the population who are marginalized or subjected to social stigma and prejudice. *Id.* at 198 (Wilkinson, J., concurring). Noting that victims of private violence were "seizing upon the 'particular social group' criterion in asylum applications," Judge Wilkinson considered the example of applicants who claim to be the victims of gang violence. Aliens seeking asylum on that basis "are often not 'exposed to more violence or human rights violations than other segments of society,' and 'not in a substantially different situation from anyone who has crossed the gang, or who is perceived to be a threat to the gang's interests." *Id.* at 199 (quoting *Matter of S-E-G-*, 24 I&N Dec. 579, 587 (BIA 2008)). He recognized that the Board "has previously explained that 'victims of gang violence come from all segments of society, and it is difficult to conclude that any "group," as actually perceived by the criminal gangs, is much narrower than the general population." *Id.* (quoting

M-E-V-G-, 26 I&N Dec. at 250). The pervasive nature of this violent criminality, in Judge Wilkinson's view, suggested that membership in a purported particular social group "is often not a central reason for the threats received, but rather is secondary to a grander pattern of criminal extortion that pervades petitioners' societies."

. . .

III.

I turn now to the question of whether, and under what circumstances, being a victim of private criminal activity constitutes persecution on account of membership in a particular social group.[4]

A.

. . .

As the Board and the federal courts have repeatedly recognized, the phrase "membership in a particular social group" is ambiguous. . . .

. . .

C.

. . .

Subsequent Board decisions, including the decision certified here, have read *A-R-C-G-* as categorically extending the definition of a "particular social group" to encompass most Central American domestic violence victims. Like *A-R-C-G-*, these ensuing decisions have not performed the detailed analysis required. For instance, the Board's decision in this case offered only the conclusory statement that the respondent's proposed group was "substantially similar to that which we addressed in *Matter of A-R-C-G-*," and that the "totality of the evidence, including the 2014 El Salvador Human Rights Report, establishes that the group is sufficiently particular and socially distinct in El Salvadoran Society." *A-B-* at *2. The Board's entire analysis of the respondent's proposed particular social group consisted of only two sentences. *Id.* Other Board opinions have similarly treated *A-R-C-G-* as establishing a broad new category of cognizable particular social groups. *See, e.g., Matter of D-M-R-* (BIA June 9, 2015); *Matter of E-M-* (BIA Feb. 18, 2015).

By contrast, several courts of appeals have expressed skepticism about *A-R-C-G-*. In *Velasquez v. Sessions*, the Fourth Circuit concluded that the petitioner's asylum claim concerned personal, private conflict rather than persecution on a protected ground. 866 F.3d at 197. The court distinguished *A-R-C-G-* "because, there, the Government conceded that the mistreatment suffered by the alien was, at least for one central reason, on account of her membership in a cognizable particular social group." 866 F.3d at 195 n.5 (quotation marks and alterations omitted). In *Fuentes-Erazo*, the Eighth Circuit declined to approve a particular social group of "Honduran women in domestic relationships who are unable to leave their relationships" after distinguishing *A-R-C-G-* because there "the petitioner's actual membership in the proposed particular social group was undisputed." 848 F.3d at 853. And in *Jeronimo v. U.S. Attorney General*, 678 F. App'x 796 (11th Cir. 2017), the Eleventh Circuit denied the asylum application of a woman who claimed membership in a group of "indigenous women who live with a domestic partner and who suffer abuse and cannot leave safely from that domestic partner relationship." *Id.* at 802-03. The court recognized that in *A-R-C-G-*, "DHS had conceded the petitioner had suffered past persecution and the persecution was because of membership in a particular social group." *Id.* at 802.

IV.

. . .

B.

. . .

1.

. . .

Social groups defined by their vulnerability to private criminal activity likely lack the particularity required under *M-E-V-G-*, given that broad swaths of society may be susceptible to victimization. For example, groups comprising persons who are "resistant to gang violence" and susceptible to violence from gang members on that basis "are too diffuse to be recognized as a particular social group." *Constanza v. Holder*, 647 F.3d 749, 754 (8th Cir. 2011); *see also, e.g., S-E-G-*, 24 I&N Dec. at 588; *Lizama v. Holder*, 629 F.3d 440, 447 (4th Cir. 2011); *Larios v. Holder*, 608 F.3d 105, 109 (1st Cir. 2010); *Lushaj v. Holder*, 380 F. App'x 41, 43 (2d Cir. 2010); *Barrios v. Holder*, 581 F.3d 849, 855 (9th Cir. 2009). Victims of gang violence often come from all segments of society, and they possess no distinguishing characteristic or concrete trait that would readily identify them as members of such a group.

Particular social group definitions that seek to avoid particularity issues by defining a narrow class--such as "Guatemalan women who are unable to leave their domestic relationships where they have children in common"--will often lack sufficient social distinction to be cognizable as a distinct social group, rather than a description of individuals sharing certain traits or experiences. *See R-A-*, 22 I&N Dec. at 918 (holding that R-A-failed to show that her claimed social group "is a group that is recognized and understood to be a societal faction, or is otherwise a recognized segment of the population, within Guatemala"). A particular social group must avoid, consistent with the evidence, being too broad to have definable boundaries and too narrow to have larger significance in society.

. . .

3.

Finally, DHS conceded the nexus requirement by agreeing that persecution suffered by A-R-C-G- "was, for at least one central reason, on account of her membership in a cognizable particular social group." A-R-C-G-, 26 I&N Dec. at 392, 395. This conclusion simply does not follow from the facts of that case or similar cases. Establishing the required nexus between past persecution and membership in a particular social group is a critical step for victims of private crime who seek asylum. *See* R-A-, 22 I&N Dec. at 920-23. Yet the Board did not evaluate the conclusion that A-R-C-G- was persecuted "on account of" her status as a married woman in Guatemala who was unable to leave her relationship.

. . .

V.

. . .

An asylum applicant has the burden of showing her eligibility for asylum, 8 C.F.R. § 208.13(a), which includes identifying a cognizable social group and establishing group membership, persecution based on that membership, and that the government was unwilling or unable to protect the respondent. The respondent must present facts that undergird *each* of these elements, and the asylum officer, immigration judge, or the Board has the duty to determine whether those facts satisfy all of the legal requirements for asylum.

Of course, if an alien's asylum application is fatally flawed in one respect–for example, for failure to show membership in a proposed social group, *see Guzman-Alvarez v. Sessions*, 701 F. App'x 54, 56-57 (2d Cir. 2017)–an immigration judge or the Board need not examine the remaining elements of the asylum claim. *See, e.g., Perez-Rabanales*, 881 F.3d at 67 ("That ends this aspect of the matter. The petitioner's failure to satisfy both the particularity and the social distinctiveness requirements defeats her attempt to qualify as a refugee through membership in a particular social group.").

Having subjected the Board's decision to plenary review, I also address several additional errors and outline other general requirements relevant to all asylum applications to provide guidance to the Board and immigration judge on remand.

A.

. . .

1.

Here, the Board admitted that the immigration judge identified discrepancies and omissions in the respondent's testimony, but discounted the adverse credibility determination on various grounds including that the supportive affidavits were due greater weight, that the respondent sufficiently explained some discrepancies, and that the discrepancies did not ultimately undermine the respondent's account. In so doing, the Board failed to give adequate deference to the credibility determinations and improperly substituted its own assessment of the evidence.

When an asylum applicant makes inconsistent statements, the immigration judge is uniquely advantaged to determine the applicant's credibility, and the Board may not substitute its own view of the evidence on appeal. *See Xiao Ji Chen v. U.S. Dep't of Justice*, 471 F.3d 315, 334 (2d Cir. 2006) ("[W]here the [immigration judge]'s adverse credibility finding is based on specific examples in the record of inconsistent statements by the asylum applicant about matters material to his claim of persecution, or on contradictory or inherently improbable testimony regarding such matters, a reviewing court will generally not be able to conclude that a reasonable adjudicator was compelled to find otherwise." (quotation omitted)). Under the REAL ID Act, "[t]here is no presumption of credibility" in favor of an asylum applicant. Pub. L. No. 109-13, div. B, §§ 101(a)(3), 119 Stat. 231, 303 (2005) (codified at 8 U.S.C. § 1158(b)(1)(B)(iii)). Furthermore, the identified inconsistencies do not have to be related to an applicant's core asylum claim to support an adverse credibility determination . . .

2.

The Board further erred in concluding that the immigration judge's factual findings concerning the respondent's ability to leave her relationship and El Salvador's ability to protect her were clearly erroneous. *A-B-* at *3. In support of his findings, the immigration judge cited evidence that the respondent was able to divorce and move away from her ex-husband, and that she was able to obtain from the El Salvadoran government multiple protective orders against him.[11] Although the Board questioned the significance of these facts in light of other evidence, it did not establish that the immigration judge's conclusions were "illogical or implausible," or without support from the record. *See Rodriguez*, 683 F.3d at 1170.

Instead, the Board substituted its view of the evidence for that of the immigration judge, again violating the standard of review applicable to the factual determinations of immigration judges.

B.

The Board also erred when it found that the respondent established the required nexus between the harm she suffered and her group membership. . .

The Board stated that "the record indicates that the ex-husband abused [the respondent] from his position of perceived authority, as her ex-husband and the father of her children." *A-B-* at *3. From this, the Board held, in a conclusory fashion, that the "record as a whole supports a finding that the respondent's membership in the particular social group of 'El Salvadoran women who are unable to leave their domestic relationship where they have children in common' is at least one central reason that he ex-husband abused her." *Id.* While citing the standard of review, the Board did not apply it in summarily dismissing the immigration judge's findings. Moreover, the Board's legal analysis was deficient. The Board, required to find "clear error" of a factual finding, pointed to no record evidence that respondent's husband mistreated her in any part "on account of" her membership in the particular social group of "El Salvadoran women who are unable to leave their domestic relationship where they have children in common." The Board cited no evidence that her husband knew any such social group existed, or that he persecuted wife for reasons unrelated to their relationship. There was simply no basis in the Board's summary reasoning for overturning the immigration judge's factual findings, much less finding them clearly erroneous.

C.

The Board also erred when it overruled the immigration judge's finding that the respondent failed to demonstrate that the government of El Salvador was unable or unwilling to protect her from her ex-husband. This inquiry too involved factual findings to which the Board did not give proper deference. No country provides its citizens with complete security from private criminal activity, and perfect protection is not required. In this case, the respondent not only reached out to police, but received various restraining orders and had him arrested on at least one occasion. *See A-B-* at *14-15 (Immig. Ct. Dec. 1, 2015).

For many reasons, domestic violence is a particularly difficult crime to prevent and prosecute, even in the United States, which dedicates significant resources to combating domestic violence. *See, e.g.,* Office of Justice Programs, U.S. Dep't of Justice, Extent, Nature, and Consequences of Intimate Partner Violence (2000). The persistence of domestic violence in El Salvador, however, does not establish that El Salvador was unable or unwilling to protect A-B- from her husband, any more than the persistence of domestic violence in the United States means that our government is unwilling or unable to protect victims of domestic violence. . .

D.

. . .

Furthermore, the Board, immigration judges, and all asylum officers must consider, consistent with the regulations, whether internal relocation in the alien's home country presents a reasonable alternative before granting asylum. Asylum applicants who have "not established past persecution . . . bear the burden of establishing that it would not be reasonable for him or her to relocate, unless the persecution is by a government or government-sponsored." 8 C.F.R. § 1208.13(b)(3)(i). . .

13. Asylum

Finally, there are alternative proper and legal channels for seeking admission to the United States other than entering the country illegally and applying for asylum in a removal proceeding. The asylum statute "is but one provision in a larger web of immigration laws designed to address individuals in many different circumstances," and "[t]o expand that statute beyond its obviously intended focus is to distort the entire immigration framework." *Velasquez*, 866 F.3d at 199 (Wilkinson, J., concurring). Aliens seeking a better life in America are welcome to take advantage of existing channels to obtain legal status before entering the country. In this case, A-B- entered the country illegally, and when initially apprehended by Border Patrol agents, she stated that her reason for entering the country was "to find work and reside" in the United States. Aliens seeking an improved quality of life should seek legal work authorization and residency status, instead of illegally entering the United States and claiming asylum.

VI.

In reaching these conclusions, I do not minimize the vile abuse that the respondent reported she suffered at the hands of her ex-husband or the harrowing experiences of many other victims of domestic violence around the world. I understand that many victims of domestic violence may seek to flee from their home countries to extricate themselves from a dire situation or to give themselves the opportunity for a better life. But the "asylum statute is not a general hardship statute." *Velasquez*, 866 F.3d at 199 (Wilkinson, J., concurring). As Judge Wilkinson correctly recognized, the Board's recent treatment of the term "particular social group" is "at risk of lacking rigor." *Id.* at 198. Nothing in the text of the INA supports the suggestion that Congress intended "membership in a particular social group" to be "some omnibus catch-all" for solving every "heart-rending situation." *Id.*

I therefore overrule *Matter of A-R-C-G-*, 26 I&N Dec. 388 (BIA 2014) and all other opinions inconsistent with the analysis in this opinion, vacate the Board's decision, and remand to the immigration judge for further proceedings consistent with this opinion.

NOTES AND QUESTIONS

1. How does this decision alter how advocates should approach presenting asylum claims based on persecution by non-state actors?

2. Did the decision put forth a blanket rule that the specific group in A-RC-G-, or similar groups, could never be accepted?

3. The decision opines that both domestic violence and gang violence are merely examples of "private violence" against groups that "are often not exposed to more violence or human rights violations than other segments of society." Does this decision jeopardize claims based on gang violence as well?

4. *Grace v. Whitaker.* In response to *Matter of A-B-*, the American Civil Liberties Union, Center for Gender & Refugee Studies, the ACLU of Texas, and the ACLU of D.C. filed a federal lawsuit in August 2018 challenging the USCIS policy memo that attempts to implement *Matter of A-B-*. In December 2018, the federal district court in D.C. issued a decision and injunction permanently blocking the government's general rule against credible fear claims relating to domestic violence or gang violence, as well as multiple other challenged policies. The court found key aspects of Sessions' decision and related policy guidance with respect to expedited removal proceedings, unlawful. For example, the court invalidated Session's requirement that people fleeing persecution by nongovernmental actors need to show that their home country government either "condoned" the persecution or is "completely helpless" to prevent it. The court also struck down the government's new rule that asylum officers can just ignore court of appeals precedents that are inconsistent with *Matter of A-B-*. As a result, the administration is now permanently blocked from applying these unlawful policies to credible fear proceedings going forward. In the court's words: "[B]ecause it is the will of Congress — not the whims of the Executive — that determines the standard for expedited removal, the Court finds that those policies are unlawful."

VII.   Convention Against Torture (CAT) Claims

On page 919, before the Avendano-Hernandez v. Lynch case, add the following:

Relief under CAT: Withholding or Deferral of Removal

The immigration regulations establish two different forms of relief under CAT:

First, a noncitizen who does not come within the bars to withholding such as conviction of a particularly serious crime, commission of serious non-political offense, etc., may seek withholding of removal by establishing that it is more likely than not that he or she would be tortured if removed to the country in question. 8 C.F.R. §208.16(b)(2).

A noncitizen who comes within one of the bars to withholding may only apply for deferral of removal. 8 C.F.R. §208.17(a). In deferral of removal the INS may still order the noncitizen removed to a third country. 8 C.F.R. §208.17(b)(2). Deferral of removal does not require that the noncitizen be released from INS custody or detention. 8 C.F.R. §208.17(b)(1)(ii), (c). In order to be eligible for DCAT, an applicant must show "he is more likely than not to suffer intentionally-inflicted cruel and inhuman treatment that either (1) is not lawfully sanctioned by that country or (2) is lawfully sanctioned by that country, *but* defeats the object and purpose of CAT." *Nuru v. Gonzales*, 404 F.3d 1207, 1221 (9th Cir. 2005).

    If the requirements for CAT are met, protection must be granted.

Chapter 14

JUDICIAL REVIEW

I. Introduction (p. 965)

This section discusses judicial review of immigration decisions and explains the history of judicial deference to the immigration judgments of Congress and the Executive Branch. It further outlines the trend in the modern cases toward ordinary judicial review of immigration decisions. *See* Kevin R. Johnson, *Immigration in the Supreme Court, 2009-13: A New Era of Immigration Law Unexceptionalism*, 68 OKLA. L. REV. 57 (2015); Kate Aschenbrenner Rodriguez, *Eroding Immigration Exceptionalism: Administrative Law in the Supreme Court's Immigration Jurisprudence*, 86 U. CIN. L. REV. 215 (2018); *see also* Jason A. Cade, *Judging Immigration Equity: Deportation and Proportionality in the Supreme Court*, 50 UC DAVIS L. REV. 1029 (2017) (contending that recent Supreme Court immigration decisions suggest the need to review the proportionality of removal based on the misconduct of the noncitizen).

As the Supreme Court first announced in the nineteenth century, Congress has "plenary power" over the immigration laws and courts should not interfere with congressional immigration judgments. The "plenary power" doctrine exemplifies what is referred to as "immigration exceptionalism." *See* Hiroshi Motomura, *Federalism, International Human Rights, and Immigration Exceptionalism*, 70 U. COLO. L. REV. 1361, 1392-94 (1999); Rachel E. Rosenbloom, *The Citizenship Line: Rethinking Immigration Exceptionalism*, 54 B.C. L. REV. 1965, 1981-89 (2013). Although starkly incongruent with modern constitutional law, *see* T. ALEXANDER ALEINIKOFF, SEMBLANCES OF SOVEREIGNTY (2002); GERALD L. NEUMAN, STRANGERS TO THE CONSTITUTION (1996), the plenary power doctrine has never been squarely overruled. *See* Gabriel J. Chin, *Segregation's Last Stronghold: Race Discrimination and the Constitutional Law of Immigration*, 46 UCLA L. REV. 1 (1998) (analyzing the continued vitality of the plenary power doctrine).

In a pair of classic articles, Hiroshi Motomura analyzes techniques frequently employed by the courts to evade the plenary power doctrine and its harsh results. *See* Hiroshi Motomura, *The Curious Evolution of Immigration Law: Procedural Surrogates for Substantive Constitutional Rights*, 92 COLUM. L. REV. 1625 (1992); Hiroshi Motomura, *Immigration Law After a Century of Plenary Power: Phantom Constitutional Norms and Statutory Interpretation*, 100 YALE L.J. 545, 578–580 (1990). Jack Chin later declared the demise of the doctrine. *See* Gabriel J. Chin, *Is There a Plenary Power Doctrine? A Tentative Apology and Prediction for Our Strange but Unexceptional Constitutional Immigration Law*, 14 GEO. IMMIGR. L.J. 257

(2000). The prediction was not immediately accurate. Shortly after publication of Chin's article, the tragic events of September 11 saw the courts pull back from review of the executive's immigration policies pursued in the name of national security.

As it has evolved, the law today generally ensures compliance with due process in the treatment of noncitizens physically present in the United States. *See* Joseph Landau, *Due Process and the Non-Citizen: A Revolution Reconsidered*, 47 Conn. L. Rev. 879, 884-911 (2015); Peter H. Schuck, *The Transformation of Immigration Law*, 84 Colum. L. Rev. 1, 4-5 (1984); *see also* Alina Das, *Administrative Constitutionalism in Immigration Law*, 98 B.U. L. Rev. 485 (2018) (calling on executive branch to enforce constitutional norms in immigration laws); Catherine Y. Kim, *Plenary Power in the Modern Administrative State*, 96 N.C. L. Rev. 77, 79 (2017) (noting that courts "have largely . . . declin[ed] to exempt immigration law from generally applicable standards of judicial review"). *But see* David A. Martin, *Why Immigration's Plenary Power Doctrine Endures*, 68 Okla. L. Rev. 29, 29 (2015) (questioning the alleged normalization of immigration law); David S. Rubenstein & Pratheepan Gulasekaram, *Immigration Exceptionalism*, 111 Nw. U.L. Rev. 583, 584-92 (2017) (to the same effect).

From the ordinary review of removal decisions of the Board of Immigration Appeals to the review of President Trump's "travel ban" by the Supreme Court, *see Trump v. Hawaii*, 138 S. Ct. 2392 (2018), the courts have played an increasingly important role in immigration law similar to the role that they play in other areas of law.

Recent Developments in Judicial Review

Three recent cases exemplify the increasingly important role that courts play in reviewing the immigration laws and Executive Branch immigration policies.

Trump v. Hawaii

(See Appendix A for a more complete version)

In *Trump v. Hawaii*, 138 S. Ct. 2392 (2018), the Court by a 5-4 majority engaged in rationality review and upheld the travel ban barring the admission of noncitizens from several nations populated predominantly by Muslims. The Trump administration defended the measure on national security grounds, which historically have been given great deference by the courts. Four Justices dissented, believing that anti-Muslim animus, not security concerns, motivated the ban. *See Trump v. Hawaii*, 138 S. Ct. at 2429 (Breyer, J., dissenting) (joined by Justice Kagan); *Trump v. Hawaii*, 138 S. Ct. at 2333 (Sotomayor, J., dissenting) (joined by Justice Ginsburg).

The court in *Trump v. Hawaii* engaged in judicial review of the travel ban, even though it was deferential rationality review. Was the review meaningful? For criticism of *Trump v. Hawaii*, see Shoba Sivaprasad Wadhia, *National Security, Immigration and the Muslim Bans*, 75 WASH. & LEE L. REV. 1475 (2018); Jill E. Family, *The Executive Power of Political Emergency: The Travel Ban*, 87 UMKC L. REV. 611 (2019).

Sessions v. Morales-Santana

In *Sessions v. Morales-Santana*, 137 S. Ct. 1678 (2017), the Supreme Court invalidated a gender distinction favoring women over men in the derivative citizenship provisions of the immigration laws. Justice Ginsburg wrote for the Court that the distinction "cannot withstand inspection under a Constitution that requires the Government to respect the equal dignity and status of its male and female citizens." *Id.* at 1698; *see* Kristin A. Collins, *Equality, Sovereignty, and the Family in* Morales-Santana, 131 HARV. L. REV. 170 (2017). This unequivocal holding followed several relatively recent decisions in which the Court struggled with reaching a majority in cases raising similar questions. *See* Nguyen v. INS, 533 U.S. 53 (2001); Miller v. Albright, 523 U.S. 420 (1998); *see also* Flores-Villar v. United States, 564 U.S. 210 (2011) (affirming by an equally divided 4-4 Court a court of appeals' ruling rejecting a constitutional challenge to an immigration provision establishing different standards for children born outside of marriage and outside of the United States to obtain U.S. citizenship, depending on whether the child's mother or father was a U.S. citizen).

Sessions v. Dimaya

138 S. Ct. 1204 (2018)
(See Appendix C for a more complete version)

Justice KAGAN announced the judgment of the Court and delivered the opinion of the Court with respect to Parts I, III, IV-B, and V, and an opinion with respect to Parts II and IVA, in which Justice GINSBURG, Justice BREYER, and Justice SOTOMAYOR join.

Three Terms ago, in *Johnson v. United States*, this Court held that part of a federal law's definition of "violent felony" was impermissibly vague. See 135 S. Ct. 2551 (2015). The question in this case is whether a similarly worded clause in a statute's definition of "crime of violence" suffers from the same constitutional defect. Adhering to our analysis in *Johnson*, we hold that it does.

I

The Immigration and Nationality Act (INA) renders deportable any alien convicted of an "aggravated felony" after entering the United States. 8 U.S.C.

§1227(a)(2)(A)(iii). Such an alien is also ineligible for cancellation of removal, a form of discretionary relief allowing some deportable aliens to remain in the country. See §§1229b(a)(3), (b)(1)(C). Accordingly, removal is a virtual certainty for an alien found to have an aggravated felony conviction, no matter how long he has previously resided here.

The INA defines "aggravated felony" by listing numerous offenses and types of offenses, often with cross-references to federal criminal statutes. §1101(a)(43). . . . According to one item on that long list, an aggravated felony includes "a crime of violence (as defined in section 16 of title 18 . . .) for which the term of imprisonment [is] at least one year." §1101(a)(43)(F). The specified statute, 18 U.S.C. §16, provides the federal criminal code's definition of "crime of violence." Its two parts, often known as the elements clause and the residual clause, cover:

> "(a) an offense that has as an element the use, attempted use, or threatened use of physical force against the person or property of another, or
> "(b) any other offense that is a felony and that, by its nature, involves a substantial risk that physical force against the person or property of another may be used in the course of committing the offense."

Section 16(b), the residual clause, is the part of the statute at issue in this case.

* * *

. . . A native of the Philippines, [James] Dimaya has resided lawfully in the United States since 1992. But he has not always acted lawfully during that time. . . . Following his second [criminal] offense, the Government initiated a removal proceeding against him. Both an Immigration Judge and the Board of Immigration Appeals held that California first-degree burglary is a "crime of violence" under §16(b). "[B]y its nature," the Board reasoned, the offense "carries a substantial risk of the use of force." . . . Dimaya sought review in the Court of Appeals for the Ninth Circuit.

While his appeal was pending, this Court held unconstitutional part of the definition of "violent felony" in the Armed Career Criminal Act (ACCA), 18 U. S. C. §924(e). ACCA prescribes a 15-year mandatory minimum sentence if a person convicted of being a felon in possession of a firearm has three prior convictions for a "violent felony." §924(e)(1). The definition of that statutory term goes as follows:

> "any crime punishable by imprisonment for a term exceeding one year . . . that—
> "(i) has as an element the use, attempted use, or threatened use of physical force against the person of another; or
> "(ii) is burglary, arson, or extortion, involves use of explosives, *or otherwise involves conduct that presents a serious potential risk of physical injury to another.*" §924(e)(2)(B) (emphasis added).

The italicized portion of that definition (like the similar language of §16(b)) came to be known as the statute's residual clause. In *Johnson v. United States*, the Court declared that clause "void for vagueness" under the Fifth Amendment's Due Process Clause. 135 S. Ct. at 2561-2563.

Relying on *Johnson*, the Ninth Circuit held that §16(b), as incorporated into the INA, was also unconstitutionally vague, and accordingly ruled in Dimaya's favor. *See* Dimaya v. Lynch, 803 F.3d 1110, 1120 (2015). Two other Circuits reached the same conclusion, but a third distinguished ACCA's residual clause from §16's.[1] We granted *certiorari* to resolve the conflict. . . .

II

"The prohibition of vagueness in criminal statutes," our decision in *Johnson* explained, is an "essential" of due process, required by both "ordinary notions of fair play and the settled rules of law." . . . The void-for-vagueness doctrine, as we have called it, guarantees that ordinary people have "fair notice" of the conduct a statute proscribes. Papachristou v. Jacksonville, 405 U.S. 156, 162 (1972). And the doctrine guards against arbitrary or discriminatory law enforcement by insisting that a statute provide standards to govern the actions of police officers, prosecutors, juries, and judges. *See* Kolender v. Lawson, 461 U.S. 352, 357-358 (1983). . . .

The Government argues that a less searching form of the void-for-vagueness doctrine applies here than in *Johnson* because this is not a criminal case. . . . As the Government notes, this Court has stated that "[t]he degree of vagueness that the Constitution [allows] depends in part on the nature of the enactment": In particular, the Court has "expressed greater tolerance of enactments with civil rather than criminal penalties because the consequences of imprecision are qualitatively less severe." Hoffman Estates v. Flipside, Hoffman Estates, Inc., 455 U.S. 489, 498-499 (1982). The removal of an alien is a civil matter. *See* Arizona v. United States, 567 U.S. 387, 396 (2012). Hence, the Government claims, the need for clarity is not so strong; even a law too vague to support a conviction or sentence may be good enough to sustain a deportation order. . . .

But this Court's precedent forecloses that argument, because we long ago held that the most exacting vagueness standard should apply in removal cases. In *Jordan v. De George*, we considered whether a provision of immigration law making an alien deportable if convicted of a "crime involving moral turpitude" was "sufficiently definite." 341 U.S. 223, 229 (1951). . . . "[W]e chose to test (and ultimately uphold) it "under the established criteria of the 'void for vagueness' doctrine" applicable to criminal laws. . . . That approach was demanded, we explained, "in view of the grave nature of deportation," *ibid*—a "drastic measure," often amounting to lifelong "banishment or exile,". . . .

---

1. Compare Shuti v. Lynch, 828 F.3d 440 (CA6 2016) (finding §16(b) unconstitutionally vague); United States v. Vivas-Ceja, 808 F.3d 719 (CA7 2015) (same), with United States v. Gonzalez-Longoria, 831 F.3d 670 (CA5 2016) (en banc) (upholding §16(b)).

Nothing in the ensuing years calls that reasoning into question. To the contrary, this Court has reiterated that deportation is "a particularly severe penalty," which may be of greater concern to a convicted alien than "any potential jail sentence." Jae Lee v. United States, 137 S. Ct. 1958, 1968 (2017) (quoting Padilla v. Kentucky, 559 U.S. 356, 365, 368 (2010)). And we have observed that as federal immigration law increasingly hinged deportation orders on prior convictions, removal proceedings became ever more "intimately related to the criminal process." Chaidez v. United States, 568 U.S. 342, 352 (2013) [citation omitted]. What follows, as *Jordan* recognized, is the use of the same standard in the two settings.

For that reason, the Government cannot take refuge in a more permissive form of the void-for-vagueness doctrine than the one *Johnson* employed. To salvage §16's residual clause, even for use in immigration hearings, the Government must instead persuade us that it is materially clearer than its now invalidated ACCA counterpart. That is the issue we next address, as guided by *Johnson's* analysis.

III

[The Court reviews the statutory provision at issue in *Johnson* and the Court's analysis of the constitutional information — Eds.]

* * *

. . . §16(b) has the same "[t]wo features" that "conspire[d] to make [ACCA's residual clause] unconstitutionally vague." . . . It too "requires a court to picture the kind of conduct that the crime involves in 'the ordinary case,' and to judge whether that abstraction presents" some not well-specified-yet-sufficiently-large degree of risk. . . . The result is that §16(b) produces, just as ACCA's residual clause did, "more unpredictability and arbitrariness than the Due Process Clause tolerates." . . .

* * *

V

Johnson tells us how to resolve this case. . . . [N]one of the minor linguistic disparities in the statutes makes any real difference. [J]ust like ACCA's residual clause, §16(b) "produces more unpredictability and arbitrariness than the Due Process Clause tolerates." 135 S. Ct. 2551, 2558. We accordingly affirm the judgment of the Court of Appeals.

It is so ordered.

Justice GORSUCH, concurring in part and concurring in the judgment.

Vague laws invite arbitrary power. Before the Revolution, the crime of treason in English law was so capaciously construed that the mere expression of disfavored opinions could invite transportation or death. The founders cited the crown's abuse of "pretended" crimes like this as one of their reasons for revolution. See Declaration of Independence ¶21. Today's vague laws may not be as invidious, but they can invite the exercise of arbitrary power all the same— by leaving the people in the dark about what the law demands and allowing prosecutors and courts to make it up.

* * *

. . . .Writing for the Court in *Johnson v. United States*, 135 S. Ct. 2551 (2015), Justice Scalia held the residual clause of the Armed Career Criminal Act void for vagueness because it invited "more unpredictability and arbitrariness" than the Constitution allows. . . . Because the residual clause in the statute now before us uses almost exactly the same language as the residual clause in *Johnson*, respect for precedent alone would seem to suggest that both clauses should suffer the same judgment.

But first in *Johnson* and now again today Justice Thomas has questioned whether our vagueness doctrine can fairly claim roots in the Constitution as originally understood. . . . Respectfully, I am persuaded instead that void for vagueness doctrine, at least properly conceived, serves as a faithful expression of ancient due process and separation of powers principles the framers recognized as vital to ordered liberty under our Constitution.

* * *

Perhaps the most basic of due process's customary protections is the demand of fair notice. *See* Connally v. General Constr. Co., 269 U. S. 385, 391 (1926). . . . Criminal indictments at common law had to provide "precise and sufficient certainty" about the charges involved. 4 W. Blackstone, Commentaries on the Laws of England 301 (1769) (Blackstone). Unless an "offence [was] set forth with clearness and certainty," the indictment risked being held void in court. *Id.*, at 302 (emphasis deleted). . . .

The same held true in civil cases affecting a person's life, liberty, or property. . . . A suit began by obtaining a writ—a detailed and specific form of action asking for particular relief.

* * *

Although today's vagueness doctrine owes much to the guarantee of fair notice embodied in the Due Process Clause, it would be a mistake to overlook the doctrine's equal debt to the separation of powers. Art. I, §1. . . . [L]egislators may not "abdicate their responsibilities for setting the standards of the criminal law," Smith v. Goguen, 415 U.S. 566, 575 (1974), by leaving to judges the power to decide "the various crimes includable in [a] vague phrase," Jordan v. De George, 341 U.S. 223, 242 (Jackson, J., dissenting). . . . Nor is the worry only that vague laws risk allowing judges to assume legislative power. Vague laws also threaten to transfer legislative power to police and prosecutors, leaving to them the job of shaping a vague statute's contours through their enforcement decisions. *See* Grayned v. City of Rockford, 408 U.S. 104, 108-109 (1972) ("A vague law impermissibly delegates basic policy matters to policemen, judges, and juries for resolution on an ad hoc and subjective basis").

* * *

Chief Justice ROBERTS, with whom Justice KENNEDY, Justice THOMAS, and Justice ALITO join, dissenting.

In *Johnson v. United States*, we concluded that the residual clause of the Armed Career Criminal Act was unconstitutionally vague, given the "indeterminacy of the wide-ranging inquiry" it required. 135 S. Ct. 2551, 2557 (2015). Today, the Court relies wholly on *Johnson*—but only some of *Johnson* — to strike down another provision, 18 U.S.C. §16(b). Because §16(b) does not give rise to the concerns that drove the Court's decision in *Johnson*, I respectfully dissent.

* * *

Justice THOMAS, with whom Justice KENNEDY and Justice ALITO join as to Parts I-C-2, II-A-1, and II-B, dissenting.

I agree with THE CHIEF JUSTICE that 18 U.S.C. §16(b), as incorporated by the Immigration and Nationality Act (INA), is not unconstitutionally vague. Section 16(b) lacks many of the features that caused this Court to invalidate the residual clause of the Armed Career Criminal Act (ACCA) in *Johnson v. United States*. . . .

While The Chief Justice persuasively explains why respondent cannot prevail under our precedents, I write separately to make two additional points. First, I continue to doubt that our practice of striking down statutes as unconstitutionally vague is consistent with the original meaning of the Due Process Clause. . . . Second, if the Court thinks that §16(b) is unconstitutionally vague because of the "categorical approach," . . . then the Court should abandon that approach—not insist on reading it into statutes and then strike them down. Accordingly, I respectfully dissent.

* * *

NOTES AND QUESTIONS

1. Notably, the Court in *Sessions v. Dimaya* applies standard vagueness doctrine to strike down a removal ground. No Justice sought to invoke the plenary power doctrine to avoid judicial review.

2. Jennifer Lee Koh, *Crimmigration and the Void for Vagueness Doctrine*, 2016 Wis. L. Rev. 1127, analyzes the application of the void for vagueness doctrine to the immigration laws before *Dimaya*.

II. Immigration Regulation and Adjudication (p. 966)

From its first days, the Trump administration has implemented aggressive immigration enforcement policies. *See, e.g.,* Jennifer M. Chacón, *Immigration and the Bully Pulpit*, 130 HARV. L. REV. FORUM 243 (2017), available at https:// harvardlawreview.org//wp-content/uploads/2017/vol120_Chacon.pdf; Bill Ong Hing, *Entering the Trump ICE Age: Contextualizing the New Immigration Enforcement Regime*, 5 TEXAS A&M L. REV. 253 (2018); Kevin R. Johnson, *Immigration and Civil Rights in the Trump Administration: Law and Policy Making by Executive Order*, 57 SANTA CLARA L. REV. 611 (2017). "The Trump administration's sweeping high profile immigration enforcement initiatives – along with its inflammatory anti-immigrant rhetoric – mark the ascendance of immigration restrictionism to the highest levels of the executive branch to an extent that is entirely without modern precedent." Anil Kalhan, *Revisiting the 1996 Experiment in Comprehensive Immigration Severity in the Age of Trump*, 9 DREXEL L. REV. 262, 262 (2017).

In response to the Trump administration's aggressive immigration enforcement efforts, an energized movement for the protection of immigrant rights has emerged. Indeed, a movement grew to "Abolish ICE," Immigration and Customs Enforcement. *See* Matt Ford, *OK, Abolish ICE. What Then?*, NEW REP., July 18, 2018, available at https://newrepublic.com/article/149945/ok-abolish-ice-then.

Recent years have seen a growing backlog of cases in the immigration courts. *See* U.S. Government Accountability Office, *Immigration Courts: Actions Needed to Reduce Case Backlog and Address Long-Standing Management and Operational Challenges* (GAO-17-438) June 17, 2017, available at https://www. gao.gov/products/GAO-17-438. The Trump administration has sought to reduce the backlog. *See* Maria Sacchetti, *DOJ Details Plan to Slash Immigration Court Backlog*, WASH. POST, Nov. 3, 2017, available at https://www.washington-post.com/local/immigration/doj-details-plan-to-slash-immigration-court-back-log/2017/11/03/03fcef34-c0a0-11e7-959c-fe2b598d8c00_story.html?utm_term=. d62d961a027d. The Justice Department imposed a controversial quota system tied to annual performance reviews to help create incentives for immigration judges to decide cases. *See* Nick Miroff, *Trump Administration, Seeking to Speed Deportations, to Impose Quotas on Immigration Judges*, WASH. POST, Apr. 2, 2018, available at https://www.washingtonpost.com/world/national-security/ trump-administration-seeking-to-speed-deportations-to-impose-quotas-on-immi-gration-judges/2018/04/02/a282d650-36bb-11e8-b57c-9445cc4dfa5e_story.htm-l?utm_term=.04d25bae5279. In addition, Attorney General Jeff Sessions and later William Barr issued rulings restricting relief for asylum and pushing immigration courts to close open removal cases. *See, e.g.,* Matter of L-E-A-, 27 I. & N. Dec. 581 (AG 2019) (overruling BIA precedent to restrict particular social group eligible for asylum); *Matter of A-B-*, 27 I. & N. Dec. 316 (AG 2018) (to the same effect); *Matter of Castro-Tum*, 27 I. & N. Dec. 271 (AG 2018) (rejecting administrative closure of removal proceedings and instructing immigration courts to expeditiously decide cases). The administration also proposed expansion of expedited removal, limitations on asylum eligibility for noncitizens who traveled through other nations but failed to apply for asylum, and the "remain in Mexico policy" requiring asylum seekers to remain in Mexico while their claim was being decided.

The fairness and impartiality of the immigration courts continue to be questioned. *See* Amit Jain, *Bureaucrats in Robes: Immigration "Judges" and the Trappings of "Courts"*, 33 GEO. IMMIGR. L.J. 261 (2019); Catherine Y. Kim, *The President's Immigration Courts*, 68 EMORY L.J. 3 (2018); Fatma E. Marouf, *Executive Overreaching in Immigration Adjudication*, 93 TUL. L. REV. 707 (2019). Recent calls have been made for immigration courts to be made independent of the Department of Justice. *See ABA, AILA, FBA, and Immigration Judge Association Call for Independent Immigration Courts*, Immigration Prof blog, July 12, 2019, available at https://lawprofessors.typepad.com/immigration/2019/07/aba-aila-fba-and-immigration-judge-association-call-for-independent-immigration-courts.html.

III.   Constitutional Scope and Limits on Judicial Review of Immigration Decisions (p. 968)

A.   Review of the Right to Enter: The Doctrine of Consular Absolutism (p. 968)

An important exception to the doctrine of consular nonreviewability is laid out by the Supreme Court in *Kleindienst v. Mandel*, 408 U.S. 753 (1972). In that case, which the Ninth Circuit relied on in *Bustamante v. Mukasey*, a U.S. citizen claimed that his First Amendment rights were violated by the denial of a nonimmigrant visa to an academic who advocated communism. The Supreme Court reviewed the visa denial under a narrow standard of review:

> When the Executive exercises this power negatively *on the basis of a facially legitimate and bona fide reason*, the courts will neither look behind the exercise of that discretion, nor test by balancing the justification against the First Amendment interests of those who seek personal communication with the applicant.

Id. at 770 (emphasis added).

In *Trump v. Hawaii*, 138 S. Ct. 2392, 2407 (2018), the Supreme Court assumed, without deciding, that the doctrine of consular nonreviewability did not bar review of the President's "travel ban" on the admission of noncitizens from several predominantly Muslim nations. A majority held that the national security concerns for the ban constituted a "facially legitimate and bona fide reason" under *Kleindienst v. Mandel. See id.* at 2418-20.

Bustamante v. Mukasey

531 F.3d 1059 (9th Cir. 2008) (p. 968)

NOTES AND QUESTIONS (PP. 972-74)

Note 3 discusses *Kerry v. Din*, 135 S. Ct. 2128 (2015), in which the Supreme Court addressed a case in which the consular officer merely cited the "terrorist activity" definition in the immigration statute and denied a visa to a citizen of Afghanistan, who was the husband of a U.S. citizen. A plurality of the Court concluded that the U.S. citizen had no protected liberty interest at stake in having her husband immigrate to the United States and could not challenge the visa denial. Justice Kennedy, joined by Justice Alito, concurred in the judgment; assuming that there in fact was a liberty interest at stake; Justice Kennedy would have found that the reason offered by the consular officer for the visa denial satisfied Due Process. Four Justices dissented, and would have found (1) an interest at stake justifying review; and (2) that the citation to a statutory section was not sufficient explanation of the denial of the visa.

In total, six justices in *Kerry v. Din* would have reviewed the visa denial. Two courts of appeals have held that Justice Kennedy's concurrence in *Kerry v. Din*, which engages in rationality review of visa decisions, controls the judicial review of visa denials. *See* Allen v. Milas, 89 F.3d 1094, 1106 (9th Cir. 2018); Morfin v. Tillerson, 851 F.3d 710, 713 (7th Cir.), *cert. denied*, 138 S. Ct. 380 (2017); Cardenas v. United States, 826 F.3d 1164, 1171-72 (9th Cir. 2016). For a debate over the application of the doctrine of consular nonreviewability after *Kerry v. Din*, see the opinions in the denial of the petition for rehearing en banc in Yafai v. Pompeo, 924 F.3d 969 (7th Cir. 2019).

For analysis of *Kerry v. Din* in addition to the article cited in note 3 on p. 973, see Kerry Abrams, *The Rights of Marriage*: Obergfell, Din *and the Future of Constitutional Law*, 103 CORNELL L. REV. 501 (2018); Peter Margulies, *Bans, Borders, and Sovereignty: Judicial Review of Immigration Law in the Trump Administration*, 2018 MICH. ST. L. REV. 1, 42-43.

B.   Due Process Rights (p. 974)

Landon v. Plasencia

459 U.S. 21 (1982) (p. 974)

NOTES AND QUESTIONS (PP. 981-82)

As discussed previously, in *Trump v. Hawaii*, 138 S. Ct. 2392 (2018), the Supreme Court engaged in rationality review in upholding the "travel ban."

For analysis of due process challenges to expedited removal orders, see Osorio Martinez v. Attorney General, 893 F.3d 153 (3d Cir. 2018).

Two 2018 Supreme Court decisions addressed the substantive due process rights of noncitizens in the United States. In *Sessions v. Dimaya*, 138 S. Ct. 1204 (2018), a 5-4 Court struck down as unconstitutionally vague a criminal removal prevision of the immigration laws. In *Jennings v. Rodriguez*, 138 S. Ct. 830 (2018), the Court found that the immigration statute permitted detention of immigrants pending removal without bond and remanded the case to the lower court to decide the constitutionality of such detention. *See also* Nielsen v. Preap, 139 S. Ct. 954 (2019) (finding that the immigration detention in question was authorized by the immigration statute).

C.   Removal (p. 983)

D.   Limits on Judicial Review (p. 983)

NOTES AND QUESTIONS (PP. 983-84)

Demore v. Kim

538 U.S. 510 (2003) (p. 984)

NOTES AND QUESTIONS (PP. 991-92)

1.   The Modern Use of the Plenary Power Doctrine (p. 992)

The introduction to the supplement reviews recent developments in judicial review and the plenary power doctrine.

E.   Deference to Administrative Agencies (p. 993)

In *Pereira v. Sessions*, 138 S. Ct. 2105 (2018), the Supreme Court in a cancellation of removal found the statutory text clear and refused to apply *Chevron* deference to the BIA's interpretation of the statute case. In a concurring opinion, Justice Kennedy suggested that the time was ripe to revisit the Supreme Court's decision in *Chevron U.S.A., Inc. v. Natural Resources Defense Council, Inc.*, 467 U.S. 837 (1984), which requires deference to agency interpretations of ambiguous provisions of the INA. *See Pereira v. Sessions*, 138 S. Ct. at 2120, 2121 (Kennedy, J., concurring).

For the argument that *Chevron* deference should not apply to the review of crime-based removals, see Rebecca Sharpless, *Zone of Nondefiance*: Chevron *and Deportation for a Crime*, 9 Drexel L. Rev. 323 (2017).

IV. The Modern Immigration and Nationality Act Provisions on Judicial Review (p. 995)

A. Standards of Review (p. 997)

B. Commencing Proceedings or Stays of Removal (p. 997)

C. Class Actions (p. 997)

Orantes-Hernandez v. Thornburgh is an example of a class action used to seek institutional reform of immigration practices. The U.S. government again employed mass detention of women and children in 2014 and 2018/19 to deter immigration from Central America. The Trump administration has aggressively employed detention as a tool of immigration enforcement.

Orantes-Hernandez v. Thornburgh
919 F.2d 549 (9th Cir. 1990) (p. 998)

The settlement in the *Flores* litigation in the 1990s (pp. 1019-20, note 10) later thwarted to President Trump's efforts to detain migrant children pending removal hearings, which was the policy that emerged after the administration generated a firestorm of controversy by separating migrant children from parents at the U.S./ Mexico border. *See* NPR, *The History of the Flores Settlement and Its Effects on Immigration*, June 22, 2018, available at https://www.npr.org/2018/06/22/622678753/the-history-of-the-flores-settlement-and-its-effects-on-immigration. The *Flores* settlement has been invoked to protect child migrants from Central America. *See* Megan Flynn, *Federal Judge Denies Trump Administration's Request to Indefinitely Detain Families*, WASH. POST, July 10, 2018, available at (https://www.washingtonpost.com/news/morning-mix/wp/2018/07/10/federal-judge-denies-trump-administrations-request-to-indefinitely-detain-families/?noredirect=on) (reporting on the district court's refusal to amend the *Flores* settlement to allow the Trump administration to indefinitely detain families, including children).

Class actions regularly have been brought challenging various Trump administration immigration enforcement policies. Courts have enjoined a number of the policies on a nationwide basis, resulting in criticism by officials in the Trump administration. *See, e.g., Attorney General William P. Barr Delivers Remarks to the American Law Institute on Nationwide Injunctions*, U.S. DEP'T OF JUSTICE, May 21, 2019, available at https://www.justice.gov/opa/speech/attorney-general-al-william-p-barr-delivers-remarks-american-law-institute-nationwide. For evaluation of the lawfulness of nationwide injunctions, see Zayn Siddique, *Nationwide Injunctions*, 117 COLUM. L. REV. 2095 (2017).

D. The Nuts and Bolts of Judicial Review (p. 1020)

E. Criminal Grounds (p. 1020)

F. Discretionary Relief (p. 1021)

G. Expedited Removal (p. 1021)

For examination of expedited removal and other removal orders lacking judicial review, see Jennifer Lee Koh, *When Shadow Removals Collide: Searching for Solutions to the Legal Black Holes Created by Expedited Removal and Reinstatement*, 96 WASH U.L. REV. 338 (2018).

In January 2017, President Trump in an executive order stating the intent to expand expedited removal. *See* Executive Order: Border Security and Immigration Improvements §§ 11 (b), (c) (Jan. 25, 2017), available at https://www.whitehouse.gov/presidential-actions/executive-order-border-security-immigration-enforcement-improvements/. In July 2019, the Trump administration released regulations expanding expedited removal to the limits allowed by Congress. *See* 84 Fed. Reg. 35, 409 (July 24, 2019). For analysis of the due process problems posed by expanded expedited removal, see Daniel Kanstroom, *Expedited Removal and Due Process: "A Testing Crucible of Basic Principle" in the Time of Trump*, 75 WASH. & LEE L. REV. 1323 (2018); Vanessa M. Garza, Comment, *Unheard and Deported: The Unconstitutional Denial of Habeas Corpus in Expedited Removal*, 56 HOUS. L. REV. 883 (2019) (reviewing history of expedited removal in light of its possible expansion by the Trump administration).

H. Detention (p. 1022)

Detention is discussed in the section on class actions in connection with *Orantes-Hernandez v. Thornburgh* and the notes that follow.

As part of a "zero tolerance" policy of immigration enforcement, President Trump has moved toward eliminating the possibility that apprehended undocumented migrants might post bond and be released from detention. *See* Executive Order, *supra*, § 5; Kevin R. Johnson, *Immigration and Civil Rights in the Trump*.

Administration: Law and Policy Making by Executive Order, 57 Santa Clara L. Rev. 611, 649-51 (2017). Conditions of detention, as well as allegations of abuse and deaths, and the use of private companies for immigrant detention have provoked criticism. The use of detention has been central to President Trump's immigration enforcement measures and has been subject to many successful legal challenges. The use and conditions of detention continue to be deeply controversial and contested.

Chapter 15

THE RIGHTS OF NONCITIZENS

I. Introduction (p. 1023)

The rights extended to noncitizens have changed over time. For example, some jurisdictions have expanded the right to vote to immigrants, even though it generally has been limited in modern times to U.S. citizens:

> Presently, there are local jurisdictions where noncitizens can vote, albeit not in federal elections. For example, in Maryland, ten jurisdictions as of 2018 have adopted measures providing for noncitizen voting. Cities such as Chicago and San Francisco allow noncitizens to vote in school-board elections. And four cities in Massachusetts have granted legal permanent residents the right to vote in local elections, although state legislation is still needed to effectuate the change. In such instances, the extension of voting rights to noncitizens resulted from organized campaigns that raised fundamental arguments about the nature of democracy and the social contract.

Cheryl J. Harris, *Back to the Future: Recentering the Political Outsider: Response to Professor Bertrall Ross*, 118 Colum. L. Rev. Online 153, 176 (2018) (footnotes omitted). For contemporary analysis of extension of the right to vote to lawful permanent residents in local elections, see Joshua A. Douglas, *The Right to Vote Under Local Law*, 85 Geo. Wash. L. Rev. 1039, 1062-66 (2017); Tara Kini, Comment, *Sharing the Vote: Noncitizen Voting Rights in Local School Board Elections*, 93 Cal. L. Rev. 271 (2005).

At various times, President Trump claimed that undocumented immigrant voted in large numbers. The claim could not be substantiated. *See* Jessica Huseman, *How the Case for Voter Fraud was Tested—and Utterly Failed*, ProPublica, June 19, 2018, available at https://www.propublica.org/article/kris-kobach-voter-fraud-kansas-trial.

In the summer of 2019, President Trump on two occasions threatened to conduct mass immigration raids in major cities across the country. One unintended impact of the threats is that many immigrants were informed of their rights if approached by Immigration and Customs Enforcement officers. *See* Vera Bergengruen, *An Unintended Consequence of Trump's Repeated Threats of Raids: More Immigrants Know Their Rights*, Time, July 18, 2019, available at https://time.com/5629589/immigration-rights-trump-ice-raids/. Mass raids never materialized.

Arrests by Immigration and Customs Enforcement officers of noncitizens at state courthouses have generated considerable controversy. *See, e.g.*, Bing Le,

Constitutional Challenges to Courthouse Civil Arrests of Noncitizens, 43 N.Y.U. L. REV. 295 (2019).

II.   First Amendment Rights (p. 1023)

The free speech rights of immigrants living in the United States under the First Amendment of the U.S. Constitution continue to be contested. *See* Rene Galindo, *The Functions of Dreamer Civil Disobedience*, 24 TEX. HISP. J.L. & POL'Y 41 (2017); Vanessa Canuto, Note, *Immigrants are "People" Too: Constitutionalizing Free Speech Protections for Undocumented Immigrants*, 17 FIRST AMEND. L. REV. 403 (2019); *see also* Jason A. Cade, *Judicial Review of Disproportionate (or Retaliatory) Deportation*, 75 WASH. & LEE L. REV. 1428, 1459-68 (2018) (reviewing possible legal challenges to the U.S. government's removal efforts based on criticism of Trump administration immigration policies).

III.   Public Benefits (p. 1025)

The Affordable Care Act excludes undocumented immigrants from health care coverage. *See* Nat'l Immigration Law Center, Immigrants and the Affordable Care Act (ACA) (last revised Jan. 2014), available at https://www.nilc.org/issues/health-care/immigrantshcr/; Madha D. Makhlouf, *Health Justice for Immigrants*, 4 U. PA. J.L. & PUB. AFF. 235 (2019) (reviewing immigrant access to healthcare). California decided to provide health care to undocumented immigrants. *See* Bobby Allyn, *California is 1st State to Offer Health Benefits to Adult Undocumented Immigrants*, NPR, July 10, 2019, available at https://www.npr.org/2019/07/10/740147546/california-first-state-to-offer-health-benefits-to-adult-undocumented-immigrants.

The Trump administration proposed a regulation that threatens to deny naturalization to immigrants who lawfully receive public benefits. *See* 83 Fed. Reg. 51114 (Oct. 10, 2018). The proposal appears to have inhibited immigrants from lawfully accessing benefit programs out of fear of coming to the attention of U.S. immigration authorities and facing possible removal. *See* Hamutal Bernstein et al., *One in Seven Adults in Immigrant Families Reported Avoiding Public Benefit Programs in 2018* (Urban Inst., 2019), available at https://www.urban.org/research/publication/one-seven-adults-immigrant-families-reported-avoiding-public-benefit-programs-2018.

IV.   Protections for Undocumented Workers (p. 1026)

Hoffman Plastic Compounds, Inc. v. National Labor Relations Board
535 U.S. 137 (2002) (p. 1027)

NOTES AND QUESTIONS (PP. 1033-34)

President Trump and officials in his administration, including former Attorney General Jeff Sessions, have claimed that immigrant workers have driven down the wages of, and taken jobs from, U.S. citizen workers. *See, e.g.*, Josh Boak, *AP Fact Check: Trump Plays on Immigration Myths*, PBS News Hour, Feb. 8, 2019, available at https://www.pbs.org/newshour/politics/ap-fact-check-trump-plays-on-immigration-myths. Might such views lead the Trump administration to not aggresively protect the rights of immigrant workers?

Leticia M. Saucedo, *Employment Authorization, Alienage Discrimination and Executive Authority*, 38 Berkeley J. Emp. & Lab. L. 183 (2017), contends that labor rights should be separate from immigration status and advocates for labor protections for workers who are DACA recipients.

V.   State Employment and Licenses (p. 1034) and (Notes and Comments p. 1035-36)

NOTES AND QUESTIONS (PP. 1035-36)

In re Sergio C. Garcia
315 P.3d 117 (Cal. 2014) (p. 1036)

NOTES AND QUESTIONS (P. 1048)

Since being licensed as an attorney, Sergio Garcia has practiced law in the rural community in California where he has lived most of his life. In 2015, decades after submitting a visa application, Garcia was issued a visa. *See California Attorney Who Fought to Practice Law Finally Gets Green Card*, Guardian, June 4, 2015, available at https://www.theguardian.com/

us-news/2015/jun/04/california-attorney-green-card.   He   later   naturalized
and became a U.S. citizen. *See More Than 25 Years After Coming to
California, Chico Lawyer Earns U.S. Citizenship*, Chico Enterprise
Record, June 21, 2019, available at https://www.chicoer.com/2019/06/21/
more-than-25-years-after-coming-to-california-chico-lawyer-earns-u-s-citizenship/.

For recent developments in the professional licensing of undocumented
immigrants, see Janet M. Calvo, *Professional Licensing and Teacher Certification
for Non-Citizens: Federalism, Equal Protection and a State's Socio-Economic
Interests*, 8 Colum. J. Race & L. 33 (2017); Christopher Connell, Note,
Undocumented Attorneys and the State of the Bar, 26 S. Cal. Interdis. L.J. 569
(2017)).

VI.   Sanctions for the Employment of Undocumented Immigrants and the Anti-Discrimination Provisions of the Immigration Reform and Control Act (p. 1049)

In *United States v. California*, 921 F.3d 865, 879-84 (9th Cir. 2019), the
Ninth Circuit held that the Immigration Reform and Control Act did not preempt a California law requiring an employer to provide notice to employees of an
employment records inspection by U.S. immigration authorities.

VII.   Employment Discrimination (p. 1049)

Espinoza v. Farah Manufacturing Co.
414 U.S. 86 (1973) (p. 1050)

For the argument that the Supreme Court's decision in *Espinoza v. Farah
Manufacturing Co.* should be overruled, see Maria L. Ontiveros, *Immigrant
Workers and Workplace Discrimination: Overturning the Missed Opportunity of
Title VII Under* Espinoza v. Farah, 39 Berkeley J. Emp. & Lab. L. 118 (2018).

NOTES AND QUESTIONS (P. 1054)

VIII.   Elementary and Secondary Education (p. 1055)

Plyler v. Doe
457 U.S. 202 (1982) (p. 1055)

A NOTE ON PLYLER V. DOE (PP. 1065-67)

IX.   Higher Education (p. 1067)

Toll v. Moreno

458 U.S. 1 (1982) (p. 1067)

NOTES AND QUESTIONS (PP. 1072-73)

In *Estrada v. Becker*, 917 F.3d 1298 (11th Cir. 2019), the Eleventh Circuit held that federal immigration law did not preempt a Georgia policy denying Deferred Action for Childhood Arrivals (DACA) recipients admission to the state's most selective colleges.

A.   The DREAM Act (pp. 1074-75)

In 2019, another version of the DREAM Act was introduced in Congress. *See* Christian Penichet-Paul, *Dream Act of 2019: Bill Summary*, NAT'L IMMIGRATION Forum, Mar. 28, 2019, available at https://immigrationforum.org/article/dream-act-of-2019-bill-summary/.

X.   The Civil Rights Implications of State and Local Governments' Involvement in Immigration and Immigrant Enforcement (p. 1075)

A contemporary debate centers on the lawfulness of "sanctuary cities," which the Trump administration has targeted. Forms of cooperation in immigration enforcement between the state, local, and federal governments include, among other initiatives, Section 287(g) agreements and Secure Communities, an enforcement program that the Obama administration discontinued but the Trump administration revived. Federal courts have enjoined efforts by the Trump administration to withhold federal funding from "sanctuary cities." *See* City & Cty of San Francisco v. Trump, 897 F.3d 1225 (9th Cir. 2018); City of Chicago v. Sessions, 888 F.3d 272 (7th Cir. 2018); City of Philadelphia v. Sessions, 280 F. Supp. 3d 579 (E.D. Pa. 2017).

NOTES AND QUESTIONS (P. 1077-80)

XI.   State Regulation of Day Laborers (p. 1080)

For another successful First Amendment challenge to a day laborer regulation ordinance, see Centro de la Comunidad Hispana de Locust Valley v. Town of Oyster Bay, 868 F.3rd 104 (2d Cir. 2017).

XII.   State-Issue Driver's Licenses (p. 1081)

In light of the Trump administration's aggressive immigration enforcement measures, concerns have grown in immigrant communities about the possibility that U.S. immigration enforcement officers might access state driver's license databases to remove undocumented immigrants from the United States. *See* John Dillion, *For Undocumented Immigrants, Getting a Driver's License Could Spell Trouble with ICE*, NPR, Jan. 1, 2019, available at https://www.npr.org/2019/01/01/681241982/for-undocumented-immigrants-getting-a-drivers-license-could-spell-trouble-with-i.

In *Arizona Dream Act Coalition v. Brewer*, 855 F.3d 957 (9th Cir. 2017), *cert. denied*, 138 S. Ct. 1279 (2018), the Ninth Circuit held that Arizona's denial of driver's licenses to DACA recipients was preempted by federal immigration law.

For analysis of driver's license eligibility as a type of "sanctuary," see Jason A. Cade, *Sanctuaries as Equitable Delegation in an Era of Mass Immigration Enforcement*, 113 Nw. U.L. Rev. 433, 483-94 (2018); Hiroshi Motomura, *Arguing About Sanctuary*, 52 U.C. Davis L. Rev. 437, 441-42 (2018).

XIII.   Official English/English-Only Laws (p. 1081)

For recent examination of English only laws, see Andrew Tae-Hyun Kim, *Immigrant Passing*, 105 Ky. L.J. 95, 112-20 (2016/17).

Should the immigration laws give preference to English language proficiency? Why or why not? Both the RAISE Act, S. 354, 115th Cong. § 5 (2017), and President Trump's immigration reform proposal, White House Blog, *President Trump's Bold Immigration Plan for the 21st Century* (May 21, 2019), available at https://www.whitehouse.gov/articles/president-trumps-bold-immigration-plan-21st-century/, would prefer noncitizens with English language ability in the issuance of visas.

TRUMP v. HAWAII

Decided June 26, 2018

ROBERTS, C. J., delivered the opinion of the Court, in which KENNEDY, THOMAS, ALITO, and GORSUCH, JJ., joined. KENNEDY, J., and THOMAS, J., filed concurring opinions. BREYER, J., filed a dissenting opinion, in which KAGAN, J., joined. SOTOMAYOR, J., filed a dissenting opinion, in which GINSBURG, J., joined.

585 U. S. ____ (2018)

Chief Justice ROBERTS delivered the opinion of the Court.

Under the Immigration and Nationality Act, foreign nationals seeking entry into the United States undergo a vetting process to ensure that they satisfy the numerous requirements for admission. The Act also vests the President with authority to restrict the entry of aliens whenever he finds that their entry "would be detrimental to the interests of the United States." 8 U. S. C. §1182(f). Relying on that delegation, the President concluded that it was necessary to impose entry restrictions on nationals of countries that do not share adequate information for an informed entry determination, or that otherwise present national security risks. Presidential Proclamation No. 9645, 82 Fed. Reg. 45161 (2017) (Proclamation). The plaintiffs in this litigation, respondents here, challenged the application of those entry restrictions to certain aliens abroad. We now decide whether the President had authority under the Act to issue the Proclamation, and whether the entry policy violates the Establishment Clause of the First Amendment.

I

A

Shortly after taking office, President Trump signed Executive Order No. 13769, Protecting the Nation From Foreign Terrorist Entry Into the United States. 82 Fed. Reg. 8977 (2017) (EO–1). EO–1 directed the Secretary of Homeland Security to conduct a review to examine the adequacy of information provided by foreign governments about their nationals seeking to enter the United States. §3(a). Pending that review, the order suspended for 90 days the entry of foreign nationals from seven countries—Iran, Iraq, Libya, Somalia, Sudan, Syria, and Yemen— that had been previously identified by Congress or prior administrations as posing heightened terrorism risks. §3(c). The District Court for the Western District of Washington entered a temporary restraining order blocking the entry restrictions, and the Court of Appeals for the Ninth Circuit denied the Government's request to stay that order. Washington v. Trump, 847 F. 3d 1151 (2017) (per curiam).

In response, the President revoked EO–1, replacing it with Executive Order No. 13780, which again directed a worldwide review. 82 Fed. Reg. 13209 (2017) (EO–2). Citing investigative burdens on agencies and the need to diminish the risk that dangerous individuals would enter without adequate vetting, EO–2 also temporarily restricted the entry (with case-by-case waivers) of foreign nationals from six of the countries covered by EO–1: Iran, Libya, Somalia, Sudan, Syria, and Yemen. §§2(c), 3(a). The order explained that those countries had been selected because each "is a state sponsor of terrorism, has been significantly compromised by terrorist organizations, or contains active conflict zones." §1(d). The entry restriction was to stay in effect for 90 days, pending completion of the worldwide review.

These interim measures were immediately challenged in court. The District Courts for the Districts of Maryland and Hawaii entered nationwide preliminary injunctions barring enforcement of the entry suspension, and the respective Courts of Appeals upheld those injunctions, albeit on different grounds. International Refugee Assistance Project (IRAP) v. Trump, 857 F. 3d 554 (CA4 2017); Hawaii v. Trump, 859 F. 3d 741 (CA9 2017) (per curiam). This Court granted certiorari and stayed the injunctions—allowing the entry suspension to go into effect—with respect to foreign nationals who lacked a "credible claim of a bona fide relationship" with a person or entity in the United States. Trump v. IRAP, 582 U. S. ___, ___ (2017) (per curiam) (slip op., at 12). The temporary restrictions in EO–2 expired before this Court took any action, and we vacated the lower court decisions as moot. Trump v. IRAP, 583 U. S. ___ (2017); Trump v. Hawaii, 583 U. S. ___ (2017).

On September 24, 2017, after completion of the worldwide review, the President issued the Proclamation before us—Proclamation No. 9645, Enhancing Vetting Capabilities and Processes for Detecting Attempted Entry Into the United States by Terrorists or Other Public-Safety Threats. 82 Fed. Reg. 45161. The Proclamation (as its title indicates) sought to improve vetting procedures by identifying ongoing deficiencies in the information needed to assess whether nationals of particular countries present "public safety threats." §1(a). To further that purpose, the Proclamation placed entry restrictions on the nationals of eight foreign states whose systems for managing and sharing information about their nationals the President deemed inadequate.

The Proclamation described how foreign states were selected for inclusion based on the review undertaken pursuant to EO–2. As part of that review, the Department of Homeland Security (DHS), in consultation with the State Department and several intelligence agencies, developed a "baseline" for the information required from foreign governments to confirm the identity of individuals seeking entry into the United States, and to determine whether those individuals pose a security threat. §1(c). The baseline included three components. The first, "identity-management information," focused on whether a foreign government ensures the integrity of travel documents by issuing electronic passports, reporting lost or stolen passports, and making available additional identity-related information. Second, the agencies considered the extent to which the country discloses information on criminal history and suspected terrorist links, provides travel document exemplars, and facilitates the U. S. Government's receipt of information about airline passengers and crews traveling to the United States. Finally, the agencies weighed various indicators of national security risk, including whether the foreign state is a known or potential terrorist safe haven and whether it regularly declines to receive returning nationals following final orders of removal from the United States. Ibid.

DHS collected and evaluated data regarding all foreign governments. §1(d). It identified 16 countries as having deficient information-sharing practices and presenting national security concerns, and another 31 countries as "at risk" of similarly failing to meet the baseline. §1(e). The State Department then undertook diplomatic efforts over a 50-day period to encourage all foreign governments to improve their practices. §1(f). As a result of that effort, numerous countries provided DHS with travel document exemplars and agreed to share information on known or suspected terrorists. Ibid.

Following the 50-day period, the Acting Secretary of Homeland Security concluded that eight countries—Chad, Iran, Iraq, Libya, North Korea, Syria, Venezuela, and Yemen—remained deficient in terms of their risk profile and willingness to provide requested information. The Acting Secretary recommended that the President impose entry restrictions on certain nationals from all of those countries except Iraq. §§1(g), (h). She also concluded that although Somalia generally satisfied the information-sharing component of the baseline standards, its "identity management deficiencies" and "significant terrorist presence" presented special circumstances justifying additional limitations. She therefore recommended entry limitations for certain nationals of that country. §1(i). As for Iraq, the Acting Secretary found that entry limitations on its nationals were not warranted given the close cooperative relationship between the U. S. and Iraqi Governments and Iraq's commitment to combating ISIS. §1(g).

After consulting with multiple Cabinet members and other officials, the President adopted the Acting Secretary's recommendations and issued the Proclamation. Invoking his authority under 8 U. S. C. §§1182(f) and 1185(a), the President determined that certain entry restrictions were necessary to "prevent the entry of those foreign nationals about whom the United States Government lacks sufficient information"; "elicit improved identity-management and information-sharing protocols and practices from foreign governments"; and otherwise "advance [the] foreign policy, national security, and counter-terrorism objectives" of the United States. Proclamation §1(h). The President explained that these restrictions would be the "most likely to encourage cooperation" while "protect[ing] the United States until such time as improvements occur." Ibid.

The Proclamation imposed a range of restrictions that vary based on the "distinct circumstances" in each of the eight countries. Ibid. For countries that do not cooperate with the United States in identifying security risks (Iran, North Korea, and Syria), the Proclamation suspends entry of all nationals, except for Iranians seeking nonimmigrant student and exchange-visitor visas. §§2(b)(ii), (d)(ii), (e)(ii). For countries that have information-sharing deficiencies but are nonetheless "valuable counterterrorism partner[s]" (Chad, Libya, and Yemen), it restricts entry of nationals seeking immigrant visas and nonimmigrant business or tourist visas. §§2(a)(i), (c)(i), (g)(i). Because Somalia generally satisfies the baseline standards but was found to present special risk factors, the Proclamation suspends entry of nationals seeking immigrant visas and requires additional scrutiny of nationals seeking nonimmigrant visas. §2(h)(ii). And for Venezuela, which refuses to cooperate in information sharing but for which alternative means are available to identify its nationals, the Proclamation limits entry only of certain government officials and their family members on nonimmigrant business or tourist visas. §2(f)(ii).

The Proclamation exempts lawful permanent residents and foreign nationals who have been granted asylum. §3(b). It also provides for case-by-case waivers when a foreign national demonstrates undue hardship, and that his entry is in the national interest and would not pose a threat to public safety. §3(c)(i); see also §3(c)(iv) (listing examples of when a waiver might be appropriate, such as if the foreign national seeks to reside with a close family member, obtain urgent medical care, or pursue significant business obligations). The Proclamation further directs DHS to assess on a continuing basis whether entry restrictions should be modified or continued, and to report to the President every 180 days. §4. Upon completion of the first such review period, the President, on the recommendation of the Secretary of Homeland Security, determined that Chad had sufficiently improved its practices, and he accordingly lifted restrictions on its nationals. Presidential Proclamation No. 9723, 83 Fed. Reg. 15937 (2018).

B

Plaintiffs in this case are the State of Hawaii, three individuals (Dr. Ismail Elshikh, John Doe #1, and John Doe #2), and the Muslim Association of Hawaii. The State operates the University of Hawaii system, which recruits students and faculty from the designated countries. The three individual plaintiffs are U. S. citizens or lawful permanent residents who have relatives from Iran, Syria, and Yemen applying for immigrant or nonimmigrant visas. The Association is a nonprofit organization that operates a mosque in Hawaii.

Plaintiffs challenged the Proclamation—except as applied to North Korea and Venezuela—on several grounds. As relevant here, they argued that the Proclamation contravenes provisions in the Immigration and Nationality Act (INA), 66 Stat. 187, as amended. Plaintiffs further claimed that the Proclamation violates the Establishment Clause of the First Amendment, because it was motivated not by concerns pertaining to national security but by animus toward Islam.

The District Court granted a nationwide preliminary injunction barring enforcement of the entry restrictions. The court concluded that the Proclamation violated two provisions of the INA: §1182(f), because the President did not make sufficient findings that the entry of the covered foreign nationals would be detrimental to the national interest, and §1152(a)(1)(A), because the policy discriminates against immigrant visa applicants on the basis of nationality. 265 F. Supp. 3d 1140, 1155–1159 (Haw. 2017). The Government requested expedited briefing and sought a stay pending appeal. The Court of Appeals for the Ninth Circuit granted a partial stay, permitting enforcement of the Proclamation with respect to foreign nationals who lack a bona fide relationship with the United States. This Court then stayed the injunction in full pending disposition of the Government's appeal. 583 U. S. ___ (2017).

The Court of Appeals affirmed. The court first held that the Proclamation exceeds the President's authority under §1182(f). In its view, that provision authorizes only a "temporary" suspension of entry in response to "exigencies" that "Congress would be ill-equipped to address." 878 F. 3d 662, 684, 688 (2017). The court further reasoned that the Proclamation "conflicts with the INA's finely reticulated regulatory scheme" by addressing "matters of immigration already passed upon by Congress." Id., at 685, 690. The Ninth Circuit then turned to §1152(a)(1)(A) and determined that the entry restrictions also contravene the prohibition on nationality-based discrimination in the issuance of immigrant visas. The court did not reach plaintiffs' Establishment Clause claim.

We granted certiorari. 583 U. S. ___ (2018).

II

Before addressing the merits of plaintiffs' statutory claims, we consider whether we have authority to do so. The Government argues that plaintiffs' challenge to the Proclamation under the INA is not justiciable. Relying on the doctrine of consular nonreviewability, the Government contends that because aliens have no "claim of right" to enter the United States, and because exclusion of aliens is "a fundamental act of sovereignty" by the political branches, review of an exclusion decision "is not within the province of any court, unless expressly authorized by law." The Government does not argue that the doctrine of consular nonreviewability goes to the Court's jurisdiction, see Tr. of Oral Arg. 13, nor does it point to any provision of the INA that expressly strips the Court of jurisdiction over plaintiffs' claims, see Sebelius v. Auburn Regional Medical Center, 568 U. S. 145, 153 (2013) (requiring Congress to "clearly state[]" that a statutory provision is jurisdictional). As a result, we may assume without deciding that plaintiffs' statutory claims are reviewable, notwithstanding consular nonreviewability or any other statutory nonreviewability issue, and we proceed on that basis.

III

The INA establishes numerous grounds on which an alien abroad may be inadmissible to the United States and ineligible for a visa. See, e.g., 8 U. S. C. §§1182(a)(1) (health-related grounds), (a)(2) (criminal history), (a)(3)(B)(terrorist activities), (a)(3)(C) (foreign policy grounds). Congress has also delegated to the President authority to suspend or restrict the entry of aliens in certain circumstances. The principal source of that authority, §1182(f), enables the President to "suspend the entry of all aliens or any class of aliens" whenever he "finds" that their entry "would be detrimental to the interests of the United States."

The President also invoked his power under 8 U. S. C. §1185(a)(1),which grants the President authority to adopt "reasonable rules, regulations, and orders" governing entry or removal of aliens, "subject to such limitations and exceptions as [he] may prescribe." Because this provision "substantially overlap[s]" with §1182(f), we agree with the Government that we "need not resolve . . . the precise relationship between the two statutes" in evaluating the validity of the Proclamation.

Plaintiffs argue that the Proclamation is not a valid exercise of the President's authority under the INA. In their view, §1182(f) confers only a residual power to temporarily halt the entry of a discrete group of aliens engaged in harmful conduct. They also assert that the Proclamation violates another provision of the INA—8 U. S. C. §1152(a)(1)(A)—because it discriminates on the basis of nationality in the issuance of immigrant visas.

By its plain language, §1182(f) grants the President broad discretion to suspend the entry of aliens into the United States. The President lawfully exercised that discretion based on his findings—following a worldwide, multi-agency review—that entry of the covered aliens would be detrimental to the national interest. And plaintiffs' attempts to identify a conflict with other provisions in the INA, and their appeal to the statute's purposes and legislative history, fail to overcome the clear statutory language.

A

The text of §1182(f) states: "Whenever the President finds that the entry of any aliens or of any class of aliens into the United States would be detrimental to the interests of the United States, he may by proclamation, and for such period as he shall deem necessary, suspend the entry of all aliens or any class of aliens as immigrants or nonimmigrants, or impose on the entry of aliens any restrictions he may deem to be appropriate."

By its terms, §1182(f) exudes deference to the President in every clause. It entrusts to the President the decisions whether and when to suspend entry ("[w]henever [he] finds that the entry" of aliens "would be detrimental" to the national interest); whose entry to suspend ("all aliens or any class of aliens"); for how long ("for such period as he shall deem necessary"); and on what conditions ("any restrictions he may deem to be appropriate"). It is therefore unsurprising that we have previously observed that §1182(f) vests the President with "ample power" to impose entry restrictions in addition to those elsewhere enumerated in the INA.

The Proclamation falls well within this comprehensive delegation. The sole prerequisite set forth in §1182(f) is that the President "find[]" that the entry of the covered aliens "would be detrimental to the interests of the United States." The President has undoubtedly fulfilled that requirement here. He first ordered DHS and other agencies to conduct a comprehensive evaluation of every single country's compliance with the information and risk assessment baseline. The President then issued a Proclamation setting forth extensive findings describing how deficiencies in the practices of select foreign governments—several of which are state sponsors of terrorism—deprive the Government of "sufficient information to assess the risks [those countries' nationals] pose to the United States." Proclamation §1(h)(i). Based on that review, the President found that it was in the national interest to restrict entry of aliens who could not be vetted with adequate information—both to protect national security and public safety, and to induce improvement by their home countries. The Proclamation therefore "craft[ed] . . . country-specific restrictions that would be most likely to encourage cooperation given each country's distinct circumstances," while securing the Nation "until such time as improvements occur."

Plaintiffs believe that these findings are insufficient. They argue, as an initial matter, that the Proclamation fails to provide a persuasive rationale for why nationality alone renders the covered foreign nationals a security risk. And they further discount the President's stated concern about deficient vetting because the Proclamation allows many aliens from the designated countries to enter on nonimmigrant visas.

Such arguments are grounded on the premise that §1182(f) not only requires the President to make a finding that entry "would be detrimental to the interests of the United States," but also to explain that finding with sufficient detail to enable judicial review. That premise is questionable. See Webster v. Doe, 486 U. S. 592, 600 (1988) (concluding that a statute authorizing the CIA Director to terminate an employee when the Director "shall deem such termination necessary or advisable in the interests of the United States" forecloses "any meaningful judicial standard of review"). But even assuming that some form of review is appropriate, plaintiffs' attacks on the sufficiency of the President's findings cannot be sustained. The 12-page Proclamation—which thoroughly describes the process, agency evaluations, and recommendations underlying the President's chosen restrictions—is more detailed than any prior order a President has issued under §1182(f). Contrast Presidential Proclamation No. 6958, 3 CFR 133 (1996) (President Clinton) (explaining in one sentence why suspending entry of members of the Sudanese government and armed forces "is in the foreign policy interests of the United States"); Presidential Proclamation No. 4865, 3 CFR 50–51 (1981) (President Reagan) (explaining in five sentences why measures to curtail "the continuing illegal migration by sea of large numbers of undocumented aliens into the southeastern United States" are "necessary").

Moreover, plaintiffs' request for a searching inquiry into the persuasiveness of the President's justifications is inconsistent with the broad statutory text and the deference traditionally accorded the President in this sphere. "Whether the President's chosen method" of addressing perceived risks is justified from a policy perspective is "irrelevant to the scope of his [§1182(f)] authority." Sale, 509 U. S., at 187–188. And when the President adopts "a preventive measure . . . in the context of international affairs and national security," he is "not required to conclusively link all of the pieces in the puzzle before [courts] grant weight to [his] empirical conclusions." Holder v. Humanitarian Law Project, 561 U. S. 1, 35 (2010).

The Proclamation also comports with the remaining textual limits in §1182(f). We agree with plaintiffs that the word "suspend" often connotes a "defer[ral] till later," Webster's Third New International Dictionary 2303 (1966). But that does not mean that the President is required to prescribe in advance a fixed end date for the entry restrictions. Section 1182(f) authorizes the President to suspend entry "for such period as he shall deem necessary." It follows that when a President suspends entry in response to a diplomatic dispute or policy concern, he may link the duration of those restrictions, implicitly or explicitly, to the resolution of the triggering condition. See, e.g., Presidential Proclamation No. 5829, 3 CFR 88 (1988) (President Reagan) (suspending the entry of certain Panamanian nationals "until such time as . . . democracyhas been restored in Panama"); Presidential Proclamation No. 8693, 3 CFR 86–87 (2011) (President Obama) (suspending the entry of individuals subject to a travel restriction under United Nations Security Council resolutions "until such time as the Secretary of State determines that [the suspension] is no longer necessary"). In fact, not one of the 43 suspension orders issued prior to this litigation has specified a precise end date.

Like its predecessors, the Proclamation makes clear that its "conditional restrictions" will remain in force only so long as necessary to "address" the identified "inadequacies and risks" within the covered nations. Proclamation Preamble, and §1(h); see ibid. (explaining that the aim is to "relax[] or remove[]" the entry restrictions "as soon as possible"). To that end, the Proclamation establishes an ongoing process to engage covered nations and assess every 180 days whether the entry restrictions should be modified or terminated. §§4(a), (b). Indeed, after the initial review period, the President determined that Chad had made sufficient improvements to its identity-management protocols, and he accordingly lifted the entry suspension on its nationals. See Proclamation No. 9723, 83 Fed. Reg. 15937.

Finally, the Proclamation properly identifies a "class of aliens"—nationals of select countries—whose entry is suspended. Plaintiffs argue that "class" must refer to a well-defined group of individuals who share a common "characteristic" apart from nationality. Brief for Respondents 42. But the text of §1182(f), of course, does not say that, and the word "class" comfortably encompasses a group of people linked by nationality. Plaintiffs also contend that the class cannot be "overbroad." Brief for Respondents 42. But that simply amounts to an unspoken tailoring requirement found nowhere in Congress's grant of authority to suspend entry of not only "any class of aliens" but "all aliens."

In short, the language of §1182(f) is clear, and the Proclamation does not exceed any textual limit on the President's authority.

B

Confronted with this "facially broad grant of power," 878 F. 3d, at 688, plaintiffs focus their attention on statutory structure and legislative purpose. They seek support in, first, the immigration scheme reflected in the INA as a whole, and, second, the legislative history of §1182(f) and historical practice. Neither argument justifies departing from the clear text of the statute.

1

Plaintiffs' structural argument starts with the premise that §1182(f) does not give the President authority to countermand Congress's considered policy judgments. The President, they say, may supplement the INA, but he cannot supplant it. And in their view, the Proclamation falls in the latter category because Congress has already specified a two-part solution to the problem of aliens seeking entry from countries that do not share sufficient information with the United States. First, Congress designed an individualized vetting system that places the burden on the alien to prove his admissibility. See §1361. Second, instead of banning the entry of nationals from particular countries, Congress sought to encourage information sharing through a Visa Waiver Program offering fast-track admission for countries that cooperate with the United States. See §1187. We may assume that §1182(f) does not allow the President to expressly override particular provisions of the INA. But plaintiffs have not identified any conflict between the statute and the Proclamation that would implicitly bar the President from addressing deficiencies in the Nation's vetting system. To the contrary, the Proclamation supports Congress's individualized approach for determining admissibility. The INA sets forth various inadmissibility grounds based on connections to terrorism and criminal history, but those provisions can only work when the consular officer has sufficient (and sufficiently reliable) information to make that determination. The Proclamation promotes the effectiveness of the vetting process by helping to ensure the availability of such information.

Plaintiffs suggest that the entry restrictions are unnecessary because consular officers can simply deny visas in individual cases when an alien fails to carry his burden of proving admissibility—for example, by failing to produce certified records regarding his criminal history. Brief for Respondents 48. But that misses the point: A critical finding of the Proclamation is that the failure of certain countries to provide reliable information prevents the Government from accurately determining whether an alien is inadmissible or poses a threat. Proclamation §1(h). Unless consular officers are expected to apply categorical rules and deny entry from those countries across the board, fraudulent or unreliable documentation may thwart their review in individual cases. And at any rate, the INA certainly does not require that systemic problems such as the lack of reliable information be addressed only in a progression of case-by-case admissibility determinations. One of the key objectives of the Proclamation is to encourage foreign governments to improve their practices, thus facilitating the Government's vetting process overall. Ibid.

Nor is there a conflict between the Proclamation and the Visa Waiver Program. The Program allows travel without a visa for short-term visitors from 38 countries that have entered into a "rigorous security partnership" with the United States.

DHS, U. S. Visa Waiver Program (Apr. 6,2016), http://www.dhs.gov/visa-waiver-program (as last visited June 25, 2018). Eligibility for that partnership involves "broad and consequential assessments of [the country's] foreign security standards and operations." Ibid. A foreign government must (among other things) undergo a comprehensive evaluation of its "counterterrorism, law enforcement, immigration enforcement, passport security, and border management capabilities," often including "operational site inspections of airports, seaports, land borders, and passport production and issuance facilities." Ibid.

Congress's decision to authorize a benefit for "many of America's closest allies," ibid., did not implicitly foreclose the Executive from imposing tighter restrictions on nationals of certain high-risk countries. The Visa Waiver Program creates a special exemption for citizens of countries that maintain exemplary security standards and offer "reciprocal [travel] privileges" to United States citizens. 8 U. S. C. §1187(a)(2)(A). But in establishing a select partnership covering less than 20% of the countries in the world, Congress did not address what requirements should govern the entry of nationals from the vast majority of countries that fall short of that gold standard—particularly those nations presenting heightened terrorism concerns. Nor did Congress attempt to determine—as the multi-agency review process did—whether those high-risk countries provide a minimum baseline of information to adequately vet their nationals. Once again, this is not a situation where "Congress has stepped into the space and solved the exact problem." Tr. of Oral Arg. 53.

Although plaintiffs claim that their reading preserves for the President a flexible power to "supplement" the INA, their understanding of the President's authority is remarkably cramped: He may suspend entry by classes of aliens "similar in nature" to the existing categories of inadmissibility—but not too similar—or only in response to "some exigent circumstance" that Congress did not already touch on in the INA.

In any event, no Congress that wanted to confer on the President only a residual authority to address emergency situations would ever use language of the sort in §1182(f). Fairly read, the provision vests authority in the President to impose additional limitations on entry beyond the grounds for exclusion set forth in the INA—including in response to circumstances that might affect the vetting system or other "interests of the United States."

Because plaintiffs do not point to any contradiction with another provision of the INA, the President has not exceeded his authority under §1182(f).

2

Plaintiffs seek to locate additional limitations on the scope of §1182(f) in the statutory background and legislative history. Given the clarity of the text, we need not consider such extra-textual evidence. See State Farm Fire & Casualty Co. v. United States ex rel. Rigsby, 580 U. S. ___, ___ (2016) (slip op., at 9). At any rate, plaintiffs' evidence supports the plain meaning of the provision. Drawing on legislative debates over §1182(f), plaintiff ssuggest that the President's suspension power should be limited to exigencies where it would be difficult for Congress to react promptly. Precursor provisions enacted during the First and Second World Wars confined the President's exclusion authority to times of "war" and "national emergency." See Act of May 22, 1918, §1(a), 40Stat. 559; Act of June 21, 1941, ch. 210, §1, 55 Stat. 252.When Congress enacted §1182(f) in 1952, plaintiffs note, it borrowed "nearly verbatim" from those predecessor statutes, and one of the bill's sponsors affirmed that the provision would apply only during a time of crisis. According to plaintiffs, it therefore follows that Congress sought to delegate only a similarly tailored suspension power in §1182(f).

If anything, the drafting history suggests the opposite. In borrowing "nearly verbatim" from the pre-existing statute, Congress made one critical alteration—it removed the national emergency standard that plaintiffs now seek to reintroduce in another form. Weighing Congress's conscious departure from its wartime statutes against an isolated floor statement, the departure is far more probative. See NLRB v. SW General, Inc., 580 U. S. ___, ___ (2017) (slip op., at 16) ("[F]loor statements by individual legislators rank among the least illuminating forms of legislative history."). When Congress wishes to condition an exercise of executive authority on the President's finding of an exigency or crisis, it knows how to say just that. See, e.g., 16 U. S. C. §824o–1(b); 42 U. S. C. §5192; 50 U. S. C. §§1701, 1702. Here, Congress instead chose to condition the President's exercise of the suspension authority on a different finding: that the entry of an alien or class of aliens would be "detrimental to the interests of the United States."

Plaintiffs also strive to infer limitations from executive practice. By their count, every previous suspension order under §1182(f) can be slotted into one of two categories. The vast majority targeted discrete groups of foreign nationals engaging in conduct "deemed harmful by the immigration laws." And the remaining entry restrictions that focused on entire nationalities—namely, President Carter's response to the Iran hostage crisis and President Reagan's suspension of immigration from Cuba—were, in their view, designed as a response to diplomatic emergencies "that the immigration laws do not address."

Even if we were willing to confine expansive language in light of its past applications, the historical evidence is more equivocal than plaintiffs acknowledge. Presidents have repeatedly suspended entry not because the covered nationals themselves engaged in harmful acts but instead to retaliate for conduct by their governments that conflicted with U. S. foreign policy interests. See, e.g., Exec. Order No. 13662, 3 CFR 233 (2014) (President Obama) (suspending entry of Russian nationals working in the financial services, energy, mining, engineering, or defense sectors, in light of the Russian Federation's "annexation of Crimea and its use of force in Ukraine"); Presidential Proclamation No. 6958, 3 CFR 133 (1997) (President Clinton) (suspending entry of Sudanese governmental and military personnel, citing "foreign policy interests of the United States" based on Sudan's refusal to comply with United Nations resolution). And while some of these reprisals were directed at subsets of aliens from the countries at issue, others broadly suspended entry on the basis of nationality due to ongoing diplomatic disputes. For example, President Reagan invoked §1182(f) to suspend entry "as immigrants" by almost all Cuban nationals, to apply pressure on the Cuban Government. Presidential Proclamation No. 5517, 3 CFR 102 (1986). Plaintiffs try to fit this latter order within their carve-out for emergency action, but the proclamation was based in part on Cuba's decision to breach an immigration agreement some 15 months earlier.

More significantly, plaintiffs' argument about historical practice is a double-edged sword. The more ad hoc their account of executive action—to fit the history into their theory—the harder it becomes to see such a refined delegation in a statute that grants the President sweeping authority to decide whether to suspend entry, whose entry to suspend, and for how long.

C

Plaintiffs' final statutory argument is that the President's entry suspension violates §1152(a)(1)(A), which provides that "no person shall . . . be discriminated against in the issuance of an immigrant visa because of the person's race, sex, nationality, place of birth, or place of residence." They contend that we should interpret the provision as prohibiting nationality-based discrimination throughout the entire immigration process, despite the reference in §1152(a)(1)(A) to the act of visa issuance alone. Specifically, plaintiffs argue that §1152(a)(1)(A) applies to the predicate question of a visa applicant's eligibility for admission and the subsequent question whether the holder of a visa may in fact enter the country. Any other conclusion, they say, would allow the President to circumvent the protections against discrimination enshrined in §1152(a)(1)(A).

As an initial matter, this argument challenges only the validity of the entry restrictions on immigrant travel. Section 1152(a)(1)(A) is expressly limited to the issuance of "immigrant visa[s]" while §1182(f) allows the President to suspend entry of "immigrants or nonimmigrants." At a minimum, then, plaintiffs' reading would not affect any of the limitations on nonimmigrant travel in the Proclamation.

In any event, we reject plaintiffs' interpretation because it ignores the basic distinction between admissibility determinations and visa issuance that runs throughout the INA. Section 1182 defines the pool of individuals who are admissible to the United States. Its restrictions come into play at two points in the process of gaining entry (or admission) into the United States. First, any alien who is inadmissible under §1182 (based on, for example, health risks, criminal history, or foreign policy consequences) is screened out as "ineligible to receive a visa." 8 U.S.C. §1201(g). Second, even if a consular officer issues a visa, entry into the United States is not guaranteed. As every visa application explains, a visa does not entitle an alien to enter the United States "if, upon arrival," an immigration officer determines that the applicant is "inadmissible under this chapter, or any other provision of law"—including §1182(f). §1201(h).

Sections 1182(f) and 1152(a)(1)(A) thus operate in different spheres: Section 1182 defines the universe of aliens who are admissible into the United States (and therefore eligible to receive a visa). Once §1182 sets the boundaries of admissibility into the United States, §1152(a)(1)(A) prohibits discrimination in the allocation of immigrant visas based on nationality and other traits. The distinction between admissibility—to which §1152(a)(1)(A) does not apply—and visa issuance—to which it does—is apparent from the text of the provision, which specifies only that its protections apply to the "issuance" of "immigrant visa[s]," without mentioning admissibility or entry. Had Congress instead intended in §1152(a)(1)(A) to constrain the President's power to determine who may enter the country, it could easily have chosen language directed to that end. See, e.g., §§1182(a)(3)(C)(ii), (iii) (providing that certain aliens "shall not be excludable or subject to restrictions or conditions on entry . . . because of the alien's past, current, or expected beliefs, statements, or associations" (emphasis added)). "The fact that [Congress] did not adopt [a] readily available and apparent alternative strongly supports" the conclusion that §1152(a)(1)(A) does not limit the President's delegated authority under §1182(f). Knight v. Commissioner, 552 U. S. 181, 188 (2008).

Common sense and historical practice confirm as much. Section 1152(a)(1)(A) has never been treated as a constraint on the criteria for admissibility in §1182. Presidents have repeatedly exercised their authority to suspend entry on the basis of nationality. As noted, President Reagan relied on §1182(f) to suspend entry "as immigrants by all Cuban nationals," subject to exceptions. Proclamation No. 5517, 51 Fed. Reg. 30470 (1986). Likewise, President Carter invoked §1185(a)(1) to deny and revoke visas to all Iranian nationals. See Exec. Order No. 12172, 3 CFR 461 (1979), as amended by Exec. Order No.12206, 3 CFR 249 (1980); Public Papers of the Presidents, Jimmy Carter, Sanctions Against Iran, Vol. 1, Apr. 7,1980, pp. 611–612 (1980); see also n. 1, supra.

On plaintiffs' reading, those orders were beyond the President's authority. The entry restrictions in the Proclamation on North Korea (which plaintiffs do not challenge in this litigation) would also be unlawful. Nor would the President be permitted to suspend entry from particular foreign states in response to an epidemic confined to a single region, or a verified terrorist threat involving nationals of a specific foreign nation, or even if the United States were on the brink of war.

In a reprise of their §1182(f) argument, plaintiffs attempt to soften their position by falling back on an implicit exception for Presidential actions that are "closely drawn" to address "specific fast-breaking exigencies." Brief for Respondents 60–61. Yet the absence of any textual basis for such an exception more likely indicates that Congress did not intend for §1152(a)(1)(A) to limit the President's flexible authority to suspend entry based on foreign policy interests. In addition, plaintiffs' proposed exigency test would require courts, rather than the President, to determine whether a foreign government's conduct rises to the level that would trigger a supposed implicit exception to a federal statute. The text of §1152(a)(1)(A) offers no standards that would enable courts to assess, for example, whether the situation in North Korea justifies entry restrictions while the terrorist threat in Yemen does not.

* * * The Proclamation is squarely within the scope of Presidential authority under the INA. Indeed, neither dissent even attempts any serious argument to the contrary, despite the fact that plaintiffs' primary contention below and in their briefing before this Court was that the Proclamation violated the statute.

IV

A

We now turn to plaintiffs' claim that the Proclamation was issued for the unconstitutional purpose of excluding Muslims. Because we have an obligation to assure ourselves of jurisdiction under Article III, we begin by addressing the question whether plaintiffs have standing to bring their constitutional challenge.

In a case arising from an alleged violation of the Establishment Clause, a plaintiff must show, as in other cases, that he is "directly affected by the laws and practices against which[his] complaints are directed." School Dist. of Abington Township v. Schempp, 374 U. S. 203, 224, n. 9 (1963). That is an issue here because the entry restrictions apply not to plaintiffs themselves but to others seeking to enter the United States.

Plaintiffs first argue that they have standing on the ground that the Proclamation "establishes a disfavored faith" and violates "their own right to be free from federal [religious] establishments." Brief for Respondents 27–28 (emphasis deleted). They describe such injury as "spiritual and dignitary." Id., at 29.

We need not decide whether the claimed dignitary interest establishes an adequate ground for standing. The three individual plaintiffs assert another, more concrete injury: the alleged real-world effect that the Proclamation has had in keeping them separated from certain relatives who seek to enter the country. We agree that a person's interest in being united with his relatives is sufficiently concrete and particularized to form the basis of an Article III injury in fact. This Court has previously considered the merits of claims asserted by United States citizens regarding violations of their personal rights allegedly caused by the Government's exclusion of particular foreign nationals. See Kerry v. Din, 576 U. S. ___, ___ (2015) (plurality opinion) (slip op., at 15); id., at ___ (KENNEDY, J., concurring in judgment) (slip op., at 1); Kleindienst v. Mandel, 408 U. S. 753, 762 (1972). Likewise, one of our prior stay orders in this litigation recognized that an American individual who has "a *bona fide* relationship with a particular person seeking to enter the country . . . can legitimately claim concrete hardship if that person is excluded." Trump v. IRAP, 582 U. S., at ___ (slip op., at 13).

The Government responds that plaintiffs' Establishment Clause claims are not justiciable because the Clause does not give them a legally protected interest in the admission of particular foreign nationals. But that argument—which depends upon the scope of plaintiffs' Establishment Clause rights—concerns the merits rather than the justiciability of plaintiffs' claims. We therefore conclude that the individual plaintiffs have Article III standing to challenge the exclusion of their relatives under the Establishment Clause.

Appendix A. Trump v. Hawaii

B

The First Amendment provides, in part, that "Congress shall make no law respecting an establishment of religion, or prohibiting the free exercise thereof." Our cases recognize that "[t]he clearest command of the Establishment Clause is that one religious denomination cannot be officially preferred over another." Larson v. Valente, 456 U. S. 228, 244 (1982). Plaintiffs believe that the Proclamation violates this prohibition by singling out Muslims for disfavored treatment. The entry suspension, they contend, operates as a "religious gerrymander," in part because most of the countries covered by the Proclamation have Muslim-majority populations. And in their view, deviations from the information-sharing baseline criteria suggest that the results of the multi-agency review were "foreordained." Relying on Establishment Clause precedents concerning laws and policies applied domestically, plaintiffs allege that the primary purpose of the Proclamation was religious animus and that the President's stated concerns about vetting protocols and national security were but pretexts for discriminating against Muslims.

At the heart of plaintiffs' case is a series of statements by the President and his advisers casting doubt on the official objective of the Proclamation. For example, while a candidate on the campaign trail, the President published a "Statement on Preventing Muslim Immigration" that called for a "total and complete shutdown of Muslims entering the United States until our country's representatives can figure out what is going on." App. 158. That statement remained on his campaign website until May 2017. Id., at 130–131. Then-candidate Trump also stated that "Islam hates us" and asserted that the United States was "having problems with Muslims coming into the country." Id., at 120–121, 159. Shortly after being elected, when asked whether violence in Europe had affected his plans to "ban Muslim immigration," the President replied, "You know my plans. All along, I've been proven to be right." Id., at 123.

One week after his inauguration, the President issued EO–1. In a television interview, one of the President's campaign advisers explained that when the President "first announced it, he said, 'Muslim ban.' He called me up. He said, 'Put a commission together. Show me the right way to do it legally.'" Id., at 125. The adviser said he assembled a group of Members of Congress and lawyers that "focused on, instead of religion, danger. . . . [The order] is based on places where there [is] substantial evidence that people are sending terrorists into our country." Id., at 229.

Plaintiffs also note that after issuing EO–2 to replace EO–1, the President expressed regret that his prior order had been "watered down" and called for a "much tougher version" of his "Travel Ban." Shortly before the release of the Proclamation, he stated that the "travel ban . . . should be far larger, tougher, and more specific," but "stupidly that would not be politically correct." Id., at 132–133. More recently, on November 29, 2017, the President re-tweeted links to three anti-Muslim propaganda videos. In response to questions about those videos, the President's deputy press secretary denied that the President thinks

Muslims are a threat to the United States, explaining that "the President has been talking about these security issues for years now, from the campaign trail to the White House" and "has addressed these issues with the travel order that he issued earlier this year and the companion proclamation." IRAP v. Trump, 883 F. 3d 233, 267 (CA4 2018).

The President of the United States possesses an extraordinary power to speak to his fellow citizens and on their behalf. Our Presidents have frequently used that power to espouse the principles of religious freedom and tolerance on which this Nation was founded. In 1790 George Washington reassured the Hebrew Congregation of Newport, Rhode Island that "happily the Government of the United States . . . gives to bigotry no sanction, to persecution no assistance [and] requires only that they who live under its protection should demean themselves as good citizens." 6 Papers of George Washington 285 (D. Twohig ed. 1996). President Eisenhower, at the opening of the Islamic Center of Washington, similarly pledged to a Muslim audience that "America would fight with her whole strength for your right to have here your own church," declaring that "[t]his concept is indeed a part of America." Public Papers of the Presidents, Dwight D. Eisenhower, June 28, 1957, p. 509 (1957). And just days after the attacks of September 11, 2001, President George W. Bush returned to the same Islamic Center to implore his fellow Americans—Muslims and non-Muslims alike— to remember during their time of grief that "[t]he face of terror is not the true faith of Islam," and that America is "a great country because we share the same values of respect and dignity and human worth." Public Papers of the Presidents, George W. Bush, Vol. 2, Sept. 17, 2001, p. 1121 (2001). Yet it cannot be denied that the Federal Government and the Presidents who have carried its laws into effect have—from the Nation's earliest days—performed unevenly in living up to those inspiring words.

Plaintiffs argue that this President's words strike at fundamental standards of respect and tolerance, in violation of our constitutional tradition. But the issue before us is not whether to denounce the statements. It is instead the significance of those statements in reviewing a Presidential directive, neutral on its face, addressing a matter within the core of executive responsibility. In doing so, we must consider not only the statements of a particular President, but also the authority of the Presidency itself.

The case before us differs in numerous respects from the conventional Establishment Clause claim. Unlike the typical suit involving religious displays or school prayer, plaintiffs seek to invalidate a national security directive regulating the entry of aliens abroad. Their claim accordingly raises a number of delicate issues regarding the scope of the constitutional right and the manner of proof. The Proclamation, moreover, is facially neutral toward religion. Plaintiffs therefore ask the Court to probe the sincerity of the stated justifications for the policy by reference to extrinsic statements—many of which were made before the President took the oath of office. These various aspects of plaintiffs' challenge inform our standard of review.

Appendix A.   Trump v. Hawaii

C

For more than a century, this Court has recognized that the admission and exclusion of foreign nationals is a "fundamental sovereign attribute exercised by the Government's political departments largely immune from judicial control." Fiallo v. Bell, 430 U. S. 787, 792 (1977); see Harisiades v. Shaughnessy, 342 U. S. 580, 588–589 (1952) ("[A]ny policy toward aliens is vitally and intricately interwoven with contemporaneous policies in regard to the conduct of foreign relations [and] the war power."). Because decisions in these matters may implicate "relations with foreign powers," or involve "classifications defined in the light of changing political and economic circumstances," such judgments "are frequently of a character more appropriate to either the Legislature or the Executive." Mathews v. Diaz, 426 U. S. 67, 81 (1976). Nonetheless, although foreign nationals seeking admission have no constitutional right to entry, this Court has engaged in a circumscribed judicial inquiry when the denial of a visa allegedly burdens the constitutional rights of a U. S. citizen. In Kleindienst v. Mandel, the Attorney General denied admission to a Belgian journalist and self-described "revolutionary Marxist," Ernest Mandel, who had been invited to speak at a conference at Stanford University. 408 U. S., at 756–757. The professors who wished to hear Mandel speak challenged that decision under the First Amendment, and we acknowledged that their constitutional "right to receive information" was implicated. Id., at 764–765. But we limited our review to whether the Executive gave a "facially legitimate and bona fide" reason for its action. Id., at 769. Given the authority of the political branches over admission, we held that "when the Executive exercises this [delegated] power negatively on the basis of a facially legitimate and bona fide reason, the courts will neither look behind the exercise of that discretion, nor test it by balancing its justification" against the asserted constitutional interests of U. S.citizens. Id., at 770.

Mandel's narrow standard of review "has particular force" in admission and immigration cases that overlap with "the area of national security." Din, 576 U. S., at ___ (KENNEDY, J., concurring in judgment) (slip op., at 3). For one, "[j]udicial inquiry into the national-security realm raises concerns for the separation of powers" by intruding on the President's constitutional responsibilities in the area of foreign affairs. Ziglar v. Abbasi, 582 U. S. ___, ___ (2017) (slip op., at 19) (internal quotation marks omitted).For another, "when it comes to collecting evidence and drawing inferences" on questions of national security, "the lack of competence on the part of the courts is marked." Humanitarian Law Project, 561 U. S., at 34.

The upshot of our cases in this context is clear: "Any rule of constitutional law that would inhibit the flexibility" of the President "to respond to changing world conditions should be adopted only with the greatest caution," and our inquiry into matters of entry and national security is highly constrained. Mathews, 426 U. S., at 81–82. We need not define the precise contours of that inquiry in this case. A conventional application of Mandel, asking only whether the policy is facially legitimate and bona fide, would put an end to our review. But the Government has suggested that it may be appropriate here for the inquiry to extend beyond the facial neutrality of the order. See Tr. of Oral Arg. 16–17, 25–27 (describing Mandel as "the starting point" of the analysis). For our purposes today, we assume that we may look behind the face of the Proclamation to the extent of applying rational basis review. That standard of review considers whether the entry policy is plausibly related to the Government's stated objective to protect the country and improve vetting processes. See Railroad Retirement Bd. v. Fritz, 449 U. S. 166, 179 (1980). As a result, we may consider plaintiffs' extrinsic evidence, but will uphold the policy so long as it can reasonably be understood to result from a justification independent of unconstitutional grounds.

D

Given the standard of review, it should come as no surprise that the Court hardly ever strikes down a policy as illegitimate under rational basis scrutiny. On the few occasions where we have done so, a common thread has been that the laws at issue lack any purpose other than a "bare . . . desire to harm a politically unpopular group." Department of Agriculture v. Moreno, 413 U. S. 528, 534 (1973). In one case, we invalidated a local zoning ordinance that required a special permit for group homes for the intellectually disabled, but not for other facilities such as fraternity houses or hospitals. We did so on the ground that the city's stated concerns about (among other things) "legal responsibility" and "crowded conditions" rested on "an irrational prejudice" against the intellectually disabled. Cleburne v. Cleburne Living Center, Inc., 473 U. S. 432, 448–450 (1985) (internal quotation marks omitted). And in another case, this Court overturned a state constitutional amendment that denied gays and lesbians access to the protection of antidiscrimination laws. The amendment, we held, was "divorced from any factual context from which we could discern a relationship to legitimate state interests," and "its sheer breadth [was] so discontinuous with the reasons offered for it" that the initiative seemed "inexplicable by anything but animus." Romer v. Evans, 517 U. S. 620, 632, 635 (1996). The Proclamation does not fit this pattern. It cannot be said that it is impossible to "discern a relationship to legitimate state interests" or that the policy is "inexplicable by anything but animus." Indeed, the dissent can only attempt to argue otherwise by refusing to apply anything resembling rational basis review. But because there is persuasive evidence that the entry suspension has a legitimate grounding in national security concerns, quite apart from any religious hostility, we must accept that independent justification.

The Proclamation is expressly premised on legitimate purposes: preventing entry of nationals who cannot be adequately vetted and inducing other nations to improve their practices. The text says nothing about religion. Plaintiffs and the dissent nonetheless emphasize that five of the seven nations currently included in the Proclamation have Muslim-majority populations. Yet that fact alone does not support an inference of religious hostility, given that the policy covers just 8% of the world's Muslim population and is limited to countries that were previously designated by Congress or prior administrations as posing national security risks.

Appendix A.   Trump v. Hawaii

The Proclamation, moreover, reflects the results of a worldwide review process undertaken by multiple Cabinet officials and their agencies. Plaintiffs seek to discredit the findings of the review, pointing to deviations from the review's baseline criteria resulting in the inclusion of Somalia and omission of Iraq. But as the Proclamation explains, in each case the determinations were justified by the distinct conditions in each country. It is, in any event, difficult to see how exempting one of the largest predominantly Muslim countries in the region from coverage under the Proclamation can be cited as evidence of animus toward Muslims.

The dissent likewise doubts the thoroughness of the multi-agency review because a recent Freedom of Information Act request shows that the final DHS report "was a mere 17 pages." Post, at 19. Yet a simple page count offers little insight into the actual substance of the final report, much less predecisional materials underlying it. See 5 U. S. C. §552(b)(5) (exempting deliberative materials from FOIA disclosure).

More fundamentally, plaintiffs and the dissent challenge the entry suspension based on their perception of its effectiveness and wisdom. They suggest that the policy is overbroad and does little to serve national security interests. But we cannot substitute our own assessment for the Executive's predictive judgments on such matters, all of which "are delicate, complex, and involve large elements of prophecy." Chicago & Southern Air Lines, Inc. v. Waterman S. S. Corp., 333 U. S. 103, 111 (1948). While we of course "do not defer to the Government's reading of the First Amendment," the Executive's evaluation of the underlying facts is entitled to appropriate weight, particularly in the context of litigation involving "sensitive and weighty interests of national security and foreign affairs." Humanitarian Law Project, 561 U. S., at 33–34.

Three additional features of the entry policy support the Government's claim of a legitimate national security interest. First, since the President introduced entry restrictions in January 2017, three Muslim-majority countries—Iraq, Sudan, and Chad—have been removed from the list of covered countries. The Proclamation emphasizes that its "conditional restrictions" will remain in force only so long as necessary to "address" the identified "inadequacies and risks," Proclamation Preamble, and §1(h), and establishes an ongoing process to engage covered nations and assess every 180 days whether the entry restrictions should be terminated, §§4(a), (b). In fact, in announcing the termination of restrictions on nationals of Chad, the President also described Libya's ongoing engagement with the State Department and the steps Libya is taking "to improve its practices." Proclamation No. 9723, 83 Fed. Reg. 15939.

Second, for those countries that remain subject to entry restrictions, the Proclamation includes significant exceptions for various categories of foreign nationals. The policy permits nationals from nearly every covered country to travel to the United States on a variety of nonimmigrant visas. See, e.g., §§2(b)–(c), (g), (h) (permitting student and exchange visitors from Iran, while restricting only business and tourist nonimmigrant entry for nationals of Libya and Yemen, and imposing no restrictions on nonimmigrant entry for Somali nationals). These carve-outs for nonimmigrant visas are substantial: Over the last three fiscal years—before the Proclamation was in effect—the majority of visas issued to nationals from the covered countries were nonimmigrant visas. The Proclamation also exempts permanent residents and individuals who have been granted asylum. §§3(b)(i), (vi).

Third, the Proclamation creates a waiver program open to all covered foreign nationals seeking entry as immigrants or nonimmigrants. According to the Proclamation, consular officers are to consider in each admissibility determination whether the alien demonstrates that (1) denying entry would cause undue hardship; (2) entry would not pose a threat to public safety; and (3) entry would be in the interest of the United States. §3(c)(i); see also §3(c)(iv) (listing examples of when a waiver might be appropriate, such as if the foreign national seeks to reside with a close family member, obtain urgent medical care, or pursue significant business obligations). On its face, this program is similar to the humanitarian exceptions set forth in President Carter's order during the Iran hostage crisis. See Exec. Order No. 12206, 3 CFR 249; Public Papers of the Presidents, Jimmy Carter, Sanctions Against Iran, at 611–612 (1980) (outlining exceptions). The Proclamation also directs DHS and the State Department to issue guidance elaborating upon the circumstances that would justify a waiver.

Finally, the dissent invokes Korematsu v. United States, 323 U. S. 214 (1944). Whatever rhetorical advantage the dissent may see in doing so, Korematsu has nothing to do with this case. The forcible relocation of U. S. citizens to concentration camps, solely and explicitly on the basis of race, is objectively unlawful and outside the scope of Presidential authority. But it is wholly inapt to liken that morally repugnant order to a facially neutral policy denying certain foreign nationals the privilege of admission. The entry suspension is an act that is well within executive authority and could have been taken by any other President—the only question is evaluating the actions of this particular President in promulgating an otherwise valid Proclamation.

The dissent's reference to Korematsu, however, affords this Court the opportunity to make express what is already obvious: Korematsu was gravely wrong the day it was decided, has been overruled in the court of history, and—to be clear—"has no place in law under the Constitution." 323 U. S., at 248 (Jackson, J., dissenting).

* * *

Under these circumstances, the Government has set forth a sufficient national security justification to survive rational basis review. We express no view on the soundness of the policy. We simply hold today that plaintiffs have not demonstrated a likelihood of success on the merits of their constitutional claim.

V

Because plaintiffs have not shown that they are likely to succeed on the merits of their claims, we reverse the grant of the preliminary injunction as an abuse of discretion. The case now returns to the lower courts for such further proceedings as may be appropriate.

Our disposition of the case makes it unnecessary to consider the propriety of the nationwide scope of the injunction issued by the District Court.

The judgment of the Court of Appeals is reversed, and the case is remanded for further proceedings consistent with this opinion.

It is so ordered.

JUSTICE KENNEDY, concurring.

I join the Court's opinion in full.

There may be some common ground between the opinions in this case, in that the Court does acknowledge that in some instances, governmental action may be subject to judicial review to determine whether or not it is "inexplicable by anything but animus," Romer v. Evans, 517 U. S. 620, 632 (1996), which in this case would be animosity to a religion. Whether judicial proceedings may properly continue in this case, in light of the substantial deference that is and must be accorded to the Executive in the conduct of foreign affairs, and in light of today's decision, is a matter to be addressed in the first instance on remand. And even if further proceedings are permitted, it would be necessary to determine that any discovery and other preliminary matters would not themselves intrude on the foreign affairs power of the Executive.

In all events, it is appropriate to make this further observation. There are numerous instances in which the statements and actions of Government officials are not subject to judicial scrutiny or intervention. That does not mean those officials are free to disregard the Constitution and the rights it proclaims and protects. The oath that all officials take to adhere to the Constitution is not confined to those spheres in which the Judiciary can correct or even comment upon what those officials say or do. Indeed, the very fact that an official may have broad discretion, discretion free from judicial scrutiny, makes it all the more imperative for him or her to adhere to the Constitution and to its meaning and its promise.

The First Amendment prohibits the establishment of religion and promises the free exercise of religion. From these safeguards, and from the guarantee of freedom of speech, it follows there is freedom of belief and expression. It is an urgent necessity that officials adhere to these constitutional guarantees and mandates in all their actions, even in the sphere of foreign affairs. An anxious world must know that our Government remains committed always to the liberties the Constitution seeks to preserve and protect, so that freedom extends outward, and lasts.

THOMAS, J., concurring.

I join the Court's opinion, which highlights just a few of the many problems with the plaintiffs' claims. There are several more. Section 1182(f) does not set forth any judicially enforceable limits that constrain the President. Nor could it, since the President has inherent authority to exclude aliens from the country. Further, the Establishment Clause does not create an individual right to be free from all laws that a "reasonable observer" views as religious or antireligious. The plaintiffs cannot raise any other First Amendment claim, since the

179

alleged religious discrimination in this case was directed at aliens abroad. See United States v. Verdugo-Urquidez, 494 U. S. 259, 265 (1990). And, even on its own terms, the plaintiffs' proffered evidence of anti-Muslim discrimination is unpersuasive.

Merits aside, I write separately to address the remedy that the plaintiffs sought and obtained in this case. The District Court imposed an injunction that barred the Government from enforcing the President's Proclamation against anyone, not just the plaintiffs. Injunctions that prohibit the Executive Branch from applying a law or policy against anyone—often called "universal" or "nationwide" injunctions—have become increasingly common. District courts, including the one here, have begun imposing universal injunctions without considering their authority to grant such sweeping relief. These injunctions are beginning to take a toll on the federal court system—preventing legal questions from percolating through the federal courts, encouraging forum shopping, and making every case a national emergency for the courts and for the Executive Branch.

I am skeptical that district courts have the authority to enter universal injunctions. These injunctions did not emerge until a century and a half after the founding. And they appear to be inconsistent with longstanding limits one quitable relief and the power of Article III courts. If their popularity continues, this Court must address their legality.

[Thomas undertakes a detailed historical analysis of the nationwide or universal injunction and concludes:]

In sum, universal injunctions are legally and historically dubious. If federal courts continue to issue them, this Court is dutybound to adjudicate their authority to do so.

JUSTICE BREYER, with whom JUSTICE KAGAN joins, dissenting.

The question before us is whether Proclamation No.9645 is lawful. If its promulgation or content was significantly affected by religious animus against Muslims, it would violate the relevant statute or the First Amendment itself. If, however, its sole ratio decidendi was one of national security, then it would be unlikely to violate either the statute or the Constitution. Which is it? Members of the Court principally disagree about the answer to this question, i.e., about whether or the extent to which religious animus played a significant role in the Proclamation's promulgation or content.

In my view, the Proclamation's elaborate system of exemptions and waivers can and should help us answer this question. That system provides for case-by-case consideration of persons who may qualify for visas despite the Proclamation's general ban. Those persons include lawful permanent residents, asylum seekers, refugees, students, children, and numerous others. There are likely many such persons, perhaps in the thousands. And I believe it appropriate to take account of their Proclamation-granted status when considering the Proclamation's lawfulness. The Solicitor General asked us to consider the Proclamation "as" it is "written" and "as" it is "applied," waivers and exemptions included.

Appendix A. Trump v. Hawaii

On the one hand, if the Government is applying the exemption and waiver provisions as written, then its argument for the Proclamation's lawfulness is strengthened. For one thing, the Proclamation then resembles more closely the two important Presidential precedents on point, President Carter's Iran order and President Reagan's Cuba proclamation, both of which contained similar categories of persons authorized to obtain case-by-case exemptions. For another thing, the Proclamation then follows more closely the basic statutory scheme, which provides for strict case-by-case scrutiny of applications. It would deviate from that system, not across the board, but where circumstances may require that deviation.

Further, since the case-by-case exemptions and waivers apply without regard to the individual's religion, application of that system would help make clear that the Proclamation does not deny visas to numerous Muslim individuals (from those countries) who do not pose a security threat. And that fact would help to rebut the First Amendment claim that the Proclamation rests upon anti-Muslim bias rather than security need. Finally, of course, the very fact that Muslims from those countries would enter the United States (under Proclamation-provided exemptions and waivers) would help to show the same thing.

On the other hand, if the Government is not applying the system of exemptions and waivers that the Proclamation contains, then its argument for the Proclamation's lawfulness becomes significantly weaker. For one thing, the relevant precedents—those of Presidents Carter and Reagan—would bear far less resemblance to the present Proclamation. Indeed, one might ask, if those two Presidents thought a case-by-case exemption system appropriate, what is different about present circumstances that would justify that system's absence?

For another thing, the relevant statute requires that there be "find[ings]" that the grant of visas to excluded persons would be "detrimental to the interests of theUnited States." §1182(f). Yet there would be no such findings in respect to those for whom the Proclamation itself provides case-by-case examination (followed by the grant of a visa in appropriate cases).

And, perhaps most importantly, if the Government is not applying the Proclamation's exemption and waiver system, the claim that the Proclamation is a "Muslim ban," rather than a "security-based" ban, becomes much stronger. How could the Government successfully claim that the Proclamation rests on security needs if it is excluding Muslims who satisfy the Proclamation's own terms? At the same time, denying visas to Muslims who meet the Proclamation's own security terms would support the view that the Government excludes them for reasons based upon their religion.

Unfortunately there is evidence that supports the second possibility, i.e., that the Government is not applying the Proclamation as written. The Proclamation provides that the Secretary of State and the Secretary of Homeland Security "shall coordinate to adopt guidance" for consular officers to follow when deciding whether to grant a waiver. §3(c)(ii). Yet, to my knowledge, no guidance has issued.

An examination of publicly available statistics also provides cause for concern. The State Department reported that during the Proclamation's first month, two waivers were approved out of 6,555 eligible applicants. Letter from M. Waters, Assistant Secretary Legislative Affairs, to Sen. Van Hollen (Feb. 22, 2018). In its reply brief, the Government claims that number increased from 2 to 430 during the first four months of implementation. Reply Brief 17. That number, 430, however, when compared with the number of pre-Proclamation visitors, accounts for a miniscule percentage of those likely eligible for visas, in such categories as persons requiring medical treatment, academic visitors, students, family members, and others belonging to groups that, when considered as a group(rather than case by case), would not seem to pose security threats.

Amici have suggested that there are numerous applicants who could meet the waiver criteria.

Other data suggest the same. The Proclamation does not apply to asylum seekers or refugees. §§3(b)(vi), 6(e). Yet few refugees have been admitted since the Proclamation took effect. While more than 15,000 Syrian refugees arrived in the United States in 2016, only 13 have arrived since January 2018. Dept. of State, Bureau of Population,Refugees, and Migration, Interactive Reporting, Refugee Processing Center, http://ireports.wrapsnet.org. Similarly few refugees have been admitted since January from Iran (3), Libya (1), Yemen (0), and Somalia (122). Ibid.

The Proclamation also exempts individuals applying for several types of nonimmigrant visas: lawful permanent residents, parolees, those with certain travel documents, dual nationals of noncovered countries, and representatives of governments or international organizations. If nonimmigrant visa applications under the Proclamation resemble those in 2016, 16 percent of visa applicants would be eligible for exemptions. In practice, however, only 258 student visas were issued to applicants from Iran (189), Libya (29), Yemen (40), and Somalia (0) in the first three months of 2018. See Dept. of State, Nonimmigrant Visa Issuances by Nationality, Jan., Feb., and Mar. 2018. This is less than a quarter of the volume needed to be on track for 2016 student visa levels.

Anecdotal evidence further heightens these concerns. For example, one amicus identified a child with cerebral palsy in Yemen. The war had prevented her from receiving her medication, she could no longer move or speak, and her doctors said she would not survive in Yemen. Her visa application was denied. Her family received a form with a check mark in the box unambiguously confirming that "'a waiver will not be granted in your case.'" Letter from L. Blatt to S. Harris, Clerk of Court (May 1, 2018).But after the child's case was highlighted in an amicus brief before this Court, the family received an update from the consular officer who had initially denied the waiver. It turns out, according to the officer, that she had all along determined that the waiver criteria were met. But, the officer explained, she could not relay that information at the time because the waiver required review from a supervisor, who had since approved it. The officer said that the family's case was now in administrative processing and that she was attaching a "'revised refusal letter indicating the approval of the waiver.'" Ibid. The new form did not actually approve the waiver (in fact, the form contains no box saying "granted"). But a different box was now checked, reading: "'The consular officer is reviewing your eligibility for a waiver under the Proclamation. . . . This can be a lengthy process, and until the consular officer canmake an individualized determination of [the relevant] factors, your visa application will remain refused under Section 212(f) [of the Proclamation].'" Ibid. One is left to wonder why this second box, indicating continuing review, had not been checked at the outset if in fact the child's case had remained under consideration all along. Though this is but one incident and the child was admitted after considerable international attention in this case, it provides yet more reason to believe that waivers are not being processed in an ordinary way.

Finally, in a pending case in the Eastern District of New York, a consular official has filed a sworn affidavit asserting that he and other officials do not, in fact, have discretion to grant waivers.

Declarations, anecdotal evidence, facts, and numbers taken from amicus briefs are not judicial factfindings. The Government has not had an opportunity to respond, and a court has not had an opportunity to decide. But, given the importance of the decision in this case, the need for assurance that the Proclamation does not rest upon a "Muslim ban," and the assistance in deciding the issue that answers to the "exemption and waiver" questions may provide, I would send this case back to the District Court for further proceedings. And, I would leave the injunction in effect while the matter is litigated. Regardless, the Court's decision today leaves the District Court free to explore these issues on remand.

If this Court must decide the question without this further litigation, I would, on balance, find the evidence of antireligious bias, including statements on a website taken down only after the President issued the two executive orders preceding the Proclamation, along with the other statements also set forth in JUSTICE SOTOMAYOR's opinion, a sufficient basis to set the Proclamation aside. And for these reasons, I respectfully dissent.

JUSTICE SOTOMAYOR, with whom JUSTICE GINSBURG joins, dissenting.

The United States of America is a Nation built upon the promise of religious liberty. Our Founders honored that core promise by embedding the principle of religious neutrality in the First Amendment. The Court's decision today fails to safeguard that fundamental principle. It leaves undisturbed a policy first advertised openly and unequivocally as a "total and complete shutdown of Muslims entering the United States" because the policy now masquerades behind a façade of national-security concerns. But this repackaging does little to cleanse Presidential Proclamation No. 9645 of the appearance of discrimination that the President's words have created. Based on the evidence in the record, a reasonable observer would conclude that the Proclamation was motivated by anti-Muslim animus. That alone suffices to show that plaintiffs are likely to succeed on the merits of their Establishment Clause claim. The majority holds otherwise by ignoring the facts, misconstruing our legal precedent, and turning a blind eye to the pain and suffering the Proclamation inflicts upon countless families and individuals, many of whom are United States citizens. Because that troubling result runs contrary to the Constitution and our precedent, I dissent.

I

Plaintiffs challenge the Proclamation on various grounds, both statutory and constitutional. Ordinarily, when a case can be decided on purely statutory grounds, we strive to follow a "prudential rule of avoiding constitutional questions." Zobrest v. Catalina Foothills School Dist., 509 U. S. 1, 8 (1993). But that rule of thumb is far from categorical, and it has limited application where, as here, the constitutional question proves far simpler than the statutory one. Whatever the merits of plaintiffs' complex statutory claims, the Proclamation must be enjoined for a more fundamental reason: It runs afoul of the Establishment Clause's guarantee of religious neutrality.

A

The Establishment Clause forbids government policies "respecting an establishment of religion." U. S. Const., Amdt. 1. The "clearest command" of the Establishment Clause is that the Government cannot favor or disfavor one religion over another. Larson v. Valente, 456 U. S. 228, 244 (1982); Church of Lukumi Babalu Aye, Inc. v. Hialeah, 508 U. S. 520, 532 (1993) ("[T]he First Amendment forbids an official purpose to disapprove of a particular religion"). Consistent with that clear command, this Court has long acknowledged that governmental actions that favor one religion "inevitabl[y]" foster "the hatred, disrespect and even contempt of those who [hold] contrary beliefs." Engel v. Vitale, 370 U. S. 421, 431 (1962). That is so, this Court has held, because such acts send messages to members of minority faiths "'that they are outsiders, not full members of the political community.'" Santa Fe Independent School Dist. v. Doe, 530 U. S. 290, 309 (2000). To guard against this serious harm, the Framers mandated a strict "principle of denominational neutrality." Larson, 456 U. S., at 246; Board of Ed. of Kiryas Joel Village School Dist. v. Grumet, 512 U. S. 687, 703 (1994) (recognizing the role of courts in "safeguarding a principle at the heart of the Establishment Clause, that government should not prefer one religion to another, or religion to irreligion").

"When the government acts with the ostensible and predominant purpose" of disfavoring a particular religion, "it violates that central Establishment Clause value of official religious neutrality, there being no neutrality when the government's ostensible object is to take sides." McCreary County v. American Civil Liberties Union of Ky., 545 U. S. 844, 860 (2005). To determine whether plaintiffs have proved an Establishment Clause violation, the Court asks whether a reasonable observer would view the government action as enacted for the purpose of disfavoring a religion.

In answering that question, this Court has generally considered the text of the government policy, its operation, and any available evidence regarding "the historical background of the decision under challenge, the specific series of events leading to the enactment or official policy in question, and the legislative or administrative history, including contemporaneous statements made by" the decisionmaker. At the same time, however, courts must take care not to engage in "any judicial psychoanalysis of a drafter's heart of hearts." Id., at 862.

B

1

Although the majority briefly recounts a few of the statements and background events that form the basis of plaintiffs' constitutional challenge, ante, at 27–28, that highly abridged account does not tell even half of the story. The full record paints a far more harrowing picture, from which a reasonable observer would readily conclude that the Proclamation was motivated by hostility and animus toward the Muslim faith.

During his Presidential campaign, then-candidate Donald Trump pledged that, if elected, he would ban Muslims from entering the United States. Specifically, on December 7, 2015, he issued a formal statement "calling for a total and complete shutdown of Muslims entering the United States." App. 119. That statement, which remained on his campaign website until May 2017 (several months into his Presidency), read in full:

> "Donald J. Trump is calling for a total and complete shutdown of Muslims entering the United States until our country's representatives can figure out what is going on. According to Pew Research, among others, there is great hatred towards Americans by large segments of the Muslim population. Most recently, a poll from the Center for Security Policy released data showing '25% of those polled agreed that violence against Americans here in the United States is justified as a part of the global jihad' and 51% of those polled 'agreed that Muslims in America should have the choice of being governed according to Shariah.' Shariah authorizes such atrocities as murder against nonbelievers who won't convert, beheadings and more unthinkable acts that pose great harm to Americans, especially women."
>
> "Mr. Trum[p] stated, 'Without looking at the various polling data, it is obvious to anybody the hatred is beyond comprehension. Where this hatred comes from and why we will have to determine. Until we are able to determine and understand this problem and the dangerous threat it poses, our country cannot be the victims of the horrendous attacks by people that believe only in Jihad, and have no sense of reason or respect of human life. If I win the election for President, we are going to Make America Great Again.' —
>
> Donald J. Trump."

On December 8, 2015, Trump justified his proposal during a television interview by noting that President Franklin D. Roosevelt "did the same thing" with respect to the internment of Japanese Americans during World War II. In January 2016, during a Republican primary debate, Trump was asked whether he wanted to "rethink [his] position" on "banning Muslims from entering the country."

He answered, "No." A month later, at a rally in South Carolina, Trump told an apocryphal story about United States General John J. Pershing killing a large group of Muslim insurgents in the Philippines with bullets dipped in pigs' blood in the early 1900's. In March 2016, he expressed his belief that "Islam hates us. . . . [W]e can't allow people coming into this country who have this hatred of the United States . . . [a]nd of people that are not Muslim." That same month, Trump asserted that "[w]e're having problems with the Muslims, and we're having problems with Muslims coming into the country." He therefore called for surveillance of mosques in the United States, blaming terrorist attacks on Muslims' lack of "assimilation" and their commitment to "sharia law." A day later, he opined that Muslims "do not respect us at all" and "don't respect a lot of the things that are happening throughout not only our country, but they don't respect other things." *Ibid.*

As Trump's presidential campaign progressed, he began to describe his policy proposal in slightly different terms. In June 2016, for instance, he characterized the policy proposal as a suspension of immigration from countries "where there's a proven history of terrorism." He also described the proposal as rooted in the need to stop "importing radical Islamic terrorism to the West through a failed immigration system." Asked in July 2016 whether he was "pull[ing] back from" his pledged Muslim ban, Trump responded, "I actually don't think it's a rollback. In fact, you could say it's an expansion." He then explained that he used different terminology because "[p]eople were so upset when [he] used the word Muslim."

A month before the 2016 election, Trump reiterated that his proposed "Muslim ban" had "morphed into a[n] extreme vetting from certain areas of the world." Then, on December 21, 2016, President-elect Trump was asked whether he would "rethink" his previous "plans to create a Muslim registry or ban Muslim immigration." He replied: "You know my plans. All along, I've proven to be right."

On January 27, 2017, one week after taking office, President Trump signed Executive Order No. 13769. As he signed it, President Trump read the title, looked up, and said "We all know what that means." That same day, President Trump explained to the media that, under EO–1, Christians would be given priority for entry as refugees into the United States. In particular, he bemoaned the fact that in the past, "[i]f you were a Muslim [refugee from Syria] you could come in, but if you were a Christian, it was almost impossible." Considering that past policy "very unfair," President Trump explained that EO–1 was designed "to help" the Christians in Syria. The following day, one of President Trump's key advisers candidly drew the connection between EO–1 and the "Muslim ban" that the President had pledged to implement if elected. According to that adviser, "[W]hen [Donald Trump] first announced it, he said, 'Muslim ban.' He called me up. He said, 'Put a commission together. Show me the right way to do it legally.'"

On February 3, 2017, the United States District Court for the Western District of Washington enjoined the enforcement of EO–1. The Ninth Circuit denied the Government's request to stay that injunction. Rather than appeal, the Government declined to continue defending EO–1 in court and instead announced that the President intended to issue a new executive order to replace EO–1.

On March 6, 2017, President Trump issued that new executive order, which, like its predecessor, imposed temporary entry and refugee bans. See Exec. Order No. 13,780, 82 Fed. Reg. 13209 (EO–2). One of the President's senior advisers publicly explained that EO–2 would "have the same basic policy outcome" as EO–1, and that any changes would address "very technical issues that were brought up by the court." App. 127. After EO–2 was issued, the White House Press Secretary told reporters that, by issuing EO–2, President Trump "continue[d] to deliver on . . . his most significant campaign promises." Id., at 130. That statement was consistent with President Trump's own declaration that "I keep my campaign promises, and our citizens will be very happy when they see the result." Id., at 127–128.

Before EO–2 took effect, federal District Courts in Hawaii and Maryland enjoined the order's travel and refugee bans.

While litigation over EO–2 was ongoing, President Trump repeatedly made statements alluding to a desire to keep Muslims out of the country. For instance, he said at a rally of his supporters that EO–2 was just a "watered down version of the first one" and had been "tailor[ed]" at the behest of "the lawyers." App. 131. He further added that he would prefer "to go back to the first [executive order] and go all the way" and reiterated his belief that it was "very hard" for Muslims to assimilate into Western culture. During a rally in April 2017, President Trump recited the lyrics to a song called "The Snake," a song about a woman who nurses a sick snake back to health but then is attacked by the snake, as a warning about Syrian refugees entering the country. And in June 2017, the President stated on Twitter that the Justice Department had submitted a "watered down, politically correct version" of the "original Travel Ban" "to S[upreme] C[ourt]." The President went on to tweet: "People, the lawyers and the courts can call it whatever they want, but I am calling it what we need and what it is, a TRAVEL BAN!" He added: "That's right, we need a TRAVEL BAN for certain DANGEROUS countries, not some politically correct term that won't help us protect our people!" Then, on August 17, 2017, President Trump issued yet another tweet about Islam, once more referencing the story about General Pershing's massacre of Muslims in the Philippines: "Study what General Pershing . . .did to terrorists when caught. There was no more Radical Islamic Terror for 35 years!"

In September 2017, President Trump tweeted that "[t]he travel ban into the United States should be far larger, tougher and more specific—but stupidly, that would not be politically correct!" Later that month, on September 24, 2017, President Trump issued Presidential Proclamation No. 9645, 82 Fed. Reg. 45161 (2017) (Proclamation), which restricts entry of certain nationals from six Muslim-majority countries. On November 29, 2017, President Trump "retweeted" three anti-Muslim videos, entitled "Muslim Destroys a Statue of Virgin Mary!", "Islamist mob pushes teenage boy off roof and beats him to death!", and "Muslim migrant beats up Dutch boy on crutches!" Those videos were initially tweeted by a British political party whose mission is to oppose "all alien and destructive politic[al] or religious doctrines, including . . . Islam." When asked about these videos, the White House Deputy Press Secretary connected them to the Proclamation, responding that the "President has been talking about these security issues for years now, from the campaign trail to the White House" and "has addressed these issues with the travel order that he issued earlier this year and the companion proclamation."

2

As the majority correctly notes, "the issue before us is not whether to denounce" these offensive statements. Rather, the dispositive and narrow question here is whether a reasonable observer, presented with all "openly available data," the text and "historical context" of the Proclamation, and the "specific sequence of events" leading to it, would conclude that the primary purpose of the Proclamation is to disfavor Islam and its adherents by excluding them from the country. The answer is unquestionably yes.

Taking all the relevant evidence together, a reasonable observer would conclude that the Proclamation was driven primarily by anti-Muslim animus, rather than by the Government's asserted national-security justifications.

Notably, the Court recently found less pervasive official expressions of hostility and the failure to disavow them to be constitutionally significant. Cf. Masterpiece Cakeshop, Ltd. v. Colorado Civil Rights Comm'n, 584 U. S. ___, ___ (2018) (slip op., at 18) ("The official expressions of hostility to religion in some of the commissioners' comments—comments that were not disavowed at the Commission or by the State at any point in the proceedings that led to the affirmance of the order—were inconsistent with what the Free Exercise Clause requires"). It should find the same here.

Ultimately, what began as a policy explicitly "calling for a total and complete shutdown of Muslims entering the United States" has since morphed into a "Proclamation" putatively based on national-security concerns. But this new window dressing cannot conceal an unassailable fact: the words of the President and his advisers create the strong perception that the Proclamation is contaminated by impermissible discriminatory animus against Islamand its followers.

II

Rather than defend the President's problematic statements, the Government urges this Court to set them aside and defer to the President on issues related to immigration and national security. The majority accepts that invitation and incorrectly applies a watered-down legal standard in an effort to short circuit plaintiffs' Establishment Clause claim.

The extent to which Mandel and Din apply at all to this case is unsettled, and there is good reason to think they do not. Indeed, even the Government agreed at oral argument that where the Court confronts a situation involving "all

Appendix A. Trump v. Hawaii

kinds of denigrating comments about" a particular religion and a subsequent policy that is designed with the purpose of disfavoring that religion but that "dot[s] all the i's and . . . cross[es] all the t's," Mandel would not "pu[t] an end to judicial review of that set of facts."

In light of the Government's suggestion "that it may be appropriate here for the inquiry to extend beyond the facial neutrality of the order," the majority rightly declines to apply Mandel's "narrow standard of review" and "assume[s] that we may look behind the face of the Proclamation." In doing so, however, the Court, without explanation or precedential support, limits its review of the Proclamation to rational-basis scrutiny. That approach is perplexing, given that in other Establishment Clause cases, including those involving claims of religious animus or discrimination, this Court has applied a more stringent standard of review. The Proclamation is plainly unconstitutional under that heightened standard.

But even under rational-basis review, the Proclamation must fall. That is so because the Proclamation is "'divorced from any factual context from which we could discern a relationship to legitimate state interests,' and 'its sheer breadth [is] so discontinuous with the reasons offered for it'" that the policy is "'inexplicable by anything but animus.'" The President's statements, which the majority utterly fails to address in its legal analysis, strongly support the conclusion that the Proclamation was issued to express hostility toward Muslims and exclude them from the country. Given the overwhelming record evidence of anti-Muslim animus, it simply cannot be said that the Proclamation has a legitimate basis.

This Court's Establishment Clause precedents require that, if a reasonable observer would understand an executive action to be driven by discriminatory animus, the action be invalidated. That reasonable-observer inquiry includes consideration of the Government's asserted justifications for its actions. The Government's invocation of a national-security justification, however, does not mean that the Court should close its eyes to other relevant information. Deference is different from unquestioning acceptance. Thus, what is "far more problematic" in this case is the majority's apparent willingness to throw the Establishment Clause out the window and forgo any meaningful constitutional review at the mere mention of a national-security concern.

The majority insists that the Proclamation furthers two interrelated national-security interests: "preventing entry of nationals who cannot be adequately vetted and inducing other nations to improve their practices." But the Court offers insufficient support for its view "that the entry suspension has a legitimate grounding in [those] national security concerns, quite apart from any religious hostility." Indeed, even a cursory review of the Government's asserted national-security rationale reveals that the Proclamation is nothing more than a "'religious gerrymander.'" Lukumi, 508 U. S., at 535.

The majority first emphasizes that the Proclamation "says nothing about religion." Ante, at 34. Even so, the Proclamation, just like its predecessors, overwhelmingly targets Muslim-majority nations. Given the record here, including all the President's statements linking the Proclamation to his apparent hostility toward Muslims, it is of no moment that the Proclamation also includes minor restrictions on two non-Muslim majority countries, North Korea and Venezuela, or that the Government has removed a few Muslim-majority countries from the list of covered countries since EO–1 was issued. Consideration of the entire record supports the conclusion that the inclusion of North Korea and Venezuela, and the removal of other countries, simply reflect subtle efforts to start "talking territory instead of Muslim," precisely so the Executive Branch could evade criticism or legal consequences for the Proclamation's otherwise clear targeting of Muslims. The Proclamation's effect on North Korea and Venezuela, for example, is insubstantial, if not entirely symbolic.

The majority next contends that the Proclamation "reflects the results of a worldwide review process undertaken by multiple Cabinet officials." Ante, at 34. At the outset, there is some evidence that at least one of the individuals involved in that process may have exhibited bias against Muslims.

But, even setting aside those comments, the worldwide review does little to break the clear connection between the Proclamation and the President's anti-Muslim statements.

Ignoring all this, the majority empowers the President to hide behind an administrative review process that the Government refuses to disclose to the public. Furthermore, evidence of which we can take judicial notice indicates that the multiagency review process could not have been very thorough. Ongoing litigation under the Freedom of Information Act shows that the September 2017 report the Government produced after its review process was a mere 17 pages. See Brennan Center for Justice v. United States Dept. of State, No. 17–cv–7520 (SDNY), Doc. No. 31–1, pp. 2–3. That the Government's analysis of the vetting practices of hundreds of countries boiled down to such a short document raises serious questions about the legitimacy of the President's proclaimed national-security rationale.

Beyond that, Congress has already addressed the national-security concerns supposedly undergirding the Proclamation through an "extensive and complex" framework governing "immigration and alien status." Arizona v. United States, 567 U. S. 387, 395 (2012).

In addition to vetting rigorously any individuals seeking admission to the United States, the Government also rigorously vets the information-sharing and identity-management systems of other countries, as evidenced by the Visa Waiver Program, which permits certain nationals from a select group of countries to skip the ordinary visa-application process.

Put simply, Congress has already erected a statutory scheme that fulfills the putative national-security interests the Government now puts forth to justify the Proclamation. Tellingly, the Government remains wholly unable to articulate any credible national-security interest that would go unaddressed by the current statutory scheme absent the Proclamation. The Government also offers no evidence that this current vetting scheme, which involves a highly searching consideration of individuals required to obtain visas for entry into the United States and a highly searching consideration of which countries are eligible for inclusion in the Visa Waiver Program, is inadequate to achieve the Proclamation's proclaimed objectives of "preventing entry of nationals who cannot be adequately vetted and inducing other nations to improve their [vetting and information-sharing] practices."

For many of these reasons, several former national-security officials from both political parties—including former Secretary of State Madeleine Albright, former State Department Legal Adviser John Bellinger III, former Central Intelligence Agency Director John Brennan,and former Director of National Intelligence James Clapper—have advised that the Proclamation and its predecessor orders "do not advance the national-security or foreign policy interests of the United States, and in fact do serious harm to those interests."

Moreover, the Proclamation purports to mitigate national-security risks by excluding nationals of countries that provide insufficient information to vet their nationals. 82 Fed. Reg. 45164. Yet, as plaintiffs explain, the Proclamation broadly denies immigrant visas to all nationals of those countries, including those whose admission would likely not implicate these information deficiencies. In addition, the Proclamation permits certain nationals from the countries named in the Proclamation to obtain nonimmigrant visas, which undermines the Government's assertion that it does not already have the capacity and sufficient information to vet these individuals adequately.

Equally unavailing is the majority's reliance on the Proclamation's waiver program. Ante, at 37, and n. 7. As several amici thoroughly explain, there is reason to suspect that the Proclamation's waiver program is nothingmore than a sham.

In sum, none of the features of the Proclamation highlighted by the majority supports the Government's claim that the Proclamation is genuinely and primarily rooted in a legitimate national-security interest. What the unrebutted evidence actually shows is that a reasonable observer would conclude, quite easily, that the primary purpose and function of the Proclamation is to disfavor Islam by banning Muslims from entering our country.

III

As the foregoing analysis makes clear, plaintiffs are likely to succeed on the merits of their Establishment Clause claim. To obtain a preliminary injunction, however, plaintiffs must also show that they are "likely to suffer irreparable harm in the absence of preliminary relief," that "the balance of equities tips in [their] favor," and that "an injunction is in the public interest." Winter v. Natural Resources Defense Council, Inc., 555 U. S. 7, 20 (2008). Plaintiffs readily clear those remaining hurdles.

IV

The First Amendment stands as a bulwark against official religious prejudice and embodies our Nation's deep commitment to religious plurality and tolerance.

That constitutional promise is why, "[f]or centuries now, people have come to this country from every corner of the world to share in the blessing of religious freedom." Town of Greece v. Galloway, 572 U. S., at ___ (KAGAN, J., dissenting) (slip op., at 1). Instead of vindicating those principles, today's decision tosses them aside. In holding that the First Amendment gives way to an executive policy that a reasonable observer would view as motivated by animus against Muslims, the majority opinion upends this Court's precedent, repeats tragic mistakes of the past, and denies countless individuals the fundamental right of religious liberty. Just weeks ago, the Court rendered its decision in Masterpiece Cakeshop, 584 U. S. ___, which applied the bedrock principles of religious neutrality and tolerance in considering a First Amendment challenge to government action. See id., at ___ (slip op., at 17) ("The Constitution 'commits government itself to religious tolerance, and upon even slight suspicion that proposals for state intervention stem from animosity to religion or distrust of its practices, all officials must pause to remember their own high duty to the Constitution and to the rights it secures'" (quoting Lukumi, 508 U. S., at 547)); Masterpiece, 584 U. S., at ___ (KAGAN, J., concurring) (slip op., at 1)("[S]tate actors cannot show hostility to religious views; rather, they must give those views 'neutral and respectful consideration'"). Those principles should apply equally here. In both instances, the question is whether a government actor exhibited tolerance and neutrality in reaching a decision that affects individuals' fundamental religious freedom. But unlike in Masterpiece, where a state civil rights commission was found to have acted without "the neutrality that the Free Exercise Clause requires," id., at ___ (slip op., at 17), the government actors in this case will not be held accountable for breaching the First Amendment's guarantee of religious neutrality and tolerance. Unlike in Masterpiece, where the majority considered the state commissioners' statements about religion to be persuasive evidence of unconstitutional government action, id., at ___–___ (slip op., at 12–14), the majority here completely sets aside the President's charged statements about Muslims as irrelevant. That holding erodes the foundational principles of religious tolerance that the Court elsewhere has so emphatically protected, and it tells members of minority religions in our country "'that they are outsiders, not full members of the political community.'" Santa Fe, 530 U. S., at 309.

Today's holding is all the more troubling given the stark parallels between the reasoning of this case and that of Korematsu v. United States, 323 U. S. 214 (1944). In Korematsu, the Court gave "a pass [to] an odious, gravely injurious racial classification" authorized by an executive order. Adarand Constructors, Inc. v. Peña, 515 U. S. 200, 275 (1995) (GINSBURG, J., dissenting). As here, the Government invoked an ill-defined national-security threat to justify an exclusionary policy of sweeping proportion. As here, the exclusion order was rooted in dangerous stereotypes about, inter alia, a particular group's supposed inability to assimilate and desire to harm the United States. As here, the Government was unwilling to reveal its own intelligence agencies' views of the alleged security concerns to the very citizens it purported to protect. And as here, there was strong evidence that impermissible hostility and animus motivated the Government's policy.

Although a majority of the Court in Korematsu was willing to uphold the Government's actions based on a barren invocation of national security, dissenting Justices warned of that decision's harm to our constitutional fabric. Justice Murphy recognized that there is a need for great deference to the Executive Branch in the context of national security, but cautioned that "it is essential that there be definite limits to [the government's] discretion," as "[i]ndividuals must not be left impoverished of their constitutional rights on a plea of military necessity that has neither substance nor support." 323 U. S., at 234 (Murphy, J., dissenting). Justice Jackson lamented that the Court's decision upholding the Government's policy would prove to be "a far more subtle blow to liberty than the promulgation of the order itself," for although the executive order was not likely to be long lasting, the Court's willingness to tolerate it would endure.

In the intervening years since Korematsu, our Nation has done much to leave its sordid legacy behind. Today, the Court takes the important step of finally overruling Korematsu, denouncing it as "gravely wrong the day it was decided." This formal repudiation of a shameful precedent is laudable and long overdue. But it does not make the majority's decision here acceptable or right. By blindly accepting the Government's misguided invitation to sanction a discriminatory policy motivated by animosity toward a disfavored group, all in the name of a superficial claim of national security, the Court redeploys the same dangerous logic underlying Korematsu and merely replaces one "gravely wrong" decision with another.

Our Constitution demands, and our country deserves, a Judiciary willing to hold the coordinate branches to account when they defy our most sacred legal commitments. Because the Court's decision today has failed in that respect, with profound regret, I dissent.

MATTER OF A-C-M

27 I&N Dec. 303 (BIA 2018)

June 6, 2018

BEFORE: Board Panel: PAULEY and COLE, Board Members. Concurring and Dissenting Opinion: WENDTLAND, Board Member

PAULEY, Board Member:

In a decision dated August 8, 2016, an Immigration Judge granted the respondent's request for deferral of removal under the Convention Against Torture and Other Cruel, Inhuman or Degrading Treatment or Punishment, adopted and opened for signature Dec. 10, 1984, G.A. Res. 39/46, 39 U.N. GAOR Supp. No. 51, at 197, U.N. Doc. A/RES/39/708 (1984) (entered into force June 26, 1987; for the United States Apr. 18, 1988) ("Convention Against Torture"). The Department of Homeland Security ("DHS") has appealed from that decision. The respondent filed a cross-appeal challenging the Immigration Judge's denial of her applications for Temporary Protected Status, cancellation of removal under section 240A(b) of the Immigration and Nationality Act, 8 U.S.C. § 1229b(b) (2012), asylum, withholding of removal, and protection under the Convention Against Torture. The respondent's cross-appeal will be dismissed and the record will be remanded to the Immigration Judge.

I.   FACTUAL AND PROCEDURAL HISTORY

The respondent is a native and citizen of El Salvador who claims that she entered the United States without inspection in 1991. She was subsequently granted Temporary Protected Status, departed the country on advance parole, and returned on March 7, 2004, seeking admission. The DHS initiated removal proceedings against her, charging that she is removable as an alien without a valid entry document under section 212(a)(7)(A)(i)(I) of the Act, 8 U.S.C. § 1182(a)(7)(A)(i)(I) (2006).

In proceedings before the Immigration Judge, the respondent applied for cancellation of removal. The DHS argued that she was ineligible for that relief under section 240A(c)(4) of the Act based on her undisputed testimony that she was kidnapped by guerillas in El Salvador in 1990 and was coerced into undergoing weapons training and performing forced labor in the form of cooking, cleaning, and washing their clothes.

In a decision dated December 15, 2011, the Immigration Judge found the respondent removable but granted her application for cancellation of removal. The

DHS appealed. In a decision dated January 14, 2014, we concluded that the respondent is ineligible for cancellation, finding that she is inadmissible under section 212(a)(3)(B)(i)(VIII) of the Act because she received military-type weapons training from the guerrillas, who we determined were a terrorist organization in 1990. Further, we found no basis for the Immigration Judge's assertion that there is a self-defense or duress exception in section 212(a)(3)(B) of the Act. We therefore sustained the DHS's appeal and remanded the record for the Immigration Judge to consider whether the respondent is eligible for any other relief or protection from removal.

On remand, the respondent applied for asylum, withholding of removal, and protection under the Convention Against Torture. The DHS conceded that although the respondent is barred from establishing eligibility for cancellation of removal based on her military/weapons training, section 208(b)(2)(A)(v) of the Act, 8 U.S.C. § 1158(b)(2)(A)(v) (2012), does not bar her from seeking asylum.

The Immigration Judge incorporated by reference the respondent's credible testimony and all the documents submitted at her cancellation of removal hearing. In her August 8, 2016, decision, the Immigration Judge found that the respondent is ineligible for asylum and withholding of removal based on the material support bar in section 212(a)(3)(B)(iv)(VI) of the Act. The Immigration Judge stated that, but for the material support bar, she would have granted the respondent's asylum application on humanitarian grounds pursuant to Matter of Chen, 20 I&N Dec. 16 (BIA 1989), noting the horrific harm she experienced from the guerrillas in El Salvador because, in addition to being kidnapped and required to perform cooking and cleaning for the guerrillas under threat of death, the respondent was forced to witness her husband, a sergeant in the Salvadoran Army, dig his own grave before being killed. However, the Immigration Judge granted the respondent's request for deferral of removal pursuant to the Convention Against Torture.

II.   ISSUE

The principal issue on appeal is whether the respondent is subject to the "material support" bar in section 212(a)(3)(B)(iv)(VI) of the Act. Specifically, we must decide if the statutory definition of "material support" has any limitation based on the extent and type of support rendered.

III.   ANALYSIS

A.   Statutory Provisions

Section 208(b)(2)(A)(v) of the Act bars the Attorney General from granting asylum to an alien who is inadmissible under sections 212(a)(3)(B)(i)(I), (II),

(III), (IV) or (VI), or is removable under section 237(a)(4)(B) of the Act, 8 U.S.C. § 1227(a)(4)(B) (2012). The Attorney General is also barred from granting withholding of removal to an alien when "there are reasonable grounds to believe that the alien is a danger to the security of the United States." Section 241(b)(3)(B)(iv) of the Act, 8 U.S.C. § 1231(b)(3)(B)(iv) (2012). For purposes of that provision, an alien who is described in section 237(a)(4)(B) of the Act—that is, inter alia, any alien who has engaged, is engaged, or at any time after admission engages in any terrorist activity, as that term is defined in section 212(a)(3)(B)(iv)—"shall be considered to be an alien with respect to whom there are reasonable grounds for regarding as a danger to the security of the United States." Section 241(b)(3)(B) of the Act.

As relevant to the respondent, section 212(a)(3)(B)(iv)(VI) of the Act provides that a person engages in terrorist activity when she "commit[s] an act that [she] knows, or reasonably should know, affords material support" to a terrorist organization, as that term is defined in section 212(a)(3)(B)(vi). Section 212(a)(3)(B)(iv)(VI)(dd) of the Act requires "only that the [alien] afford material support to a terrorist organization, with the sole exception being a showing by clear and convincing evidence that the actor did not know, and should not reasonably have known, that the organization was of that character." Matter of S-K-, 23 I&N Dec. 936, 943–44 (BIA 2006), remanded, 24 I&N Dec. 289 (A.G. 2007), clarified, 24 I&N Dec. 475 (BIA 2008). If the evidence indicates that the terrorism bar applies to an alien, he or she has the burden of proving by a preponderance of the evidence that the bar is not applicable. See 8 C.F.R. § 1240.8(d) (2018); see also Matter of M-B-C-, 27 I&N Dec. 31, 36–37 (BIA 2017); Matter of S-K-, 23 I&N Dec. at 939.

B.   Material Support Bar

The respondent argues on appeal that the Immigration Judge erred by finding that she is subject to the material support bar, claiming that any assistance she provided to the guerrillas in El Salvador was de minimis and therefore not "material." She further asserts that even if the material support bar is applicable to her, she is entitled to a duress exception. However, in Matter of M-H-Z-, 26 I&N Dec. 757 (BIA 2016), we ruled that the "material support bar" in section 212(a)(3)(B)(iv)(VI) of the Act does not include an implied exception for an alien whose material support to a terrorist organization was provided under duress. The United States Court of Appeals for the Second Circuit, in whose jurisdiction this case arises, has deferred to our interpretation. See Hernandez v. Sessions, 884 F.3d 107, 109 (2d Cir. 2018). Consequently, we will not address that issue further.

We must therefore decide whether the phrase "material support" contains a quantitative requirement. The respondent and the dissent contend that an insignificant degree of support provided by an alien to a terrorist organization does not constitute "material" support. We hold that no such quantitative limitation exists in the bar.

We first observe that, while not dispositive, the fact that the Board and the Federal courts have uniformly rejected a duress exception to the material support bar counsels against adopting the interpretation that the respondent and the dissent support. The essence of a duress defense is that it negates culpability for one's actions, even if those actions are otherwise criminal. See Dixon v. United States, 548 U.S. 1, 6–7 (2006); United States v. Bailey, 444 U.S. 394, 409–10 (1980). A person who voluntarily renders assistance has acted culpably and would seem to present a greater threat than one whose aid was only involuntarily given. It therefore appears unlikely that Congress intended to impose the bar on an alien who was coerced into giving material support to a terrorist organization but to exempt one who willingly provided such assistance, even if it was small in degree.

In Matter of S-K-, 23 I&N Dec. at 943, we stated that we were "unaware of any legislative history which indicates a limitation on the definition of the term 'material support.'" We also agreed with the DHS that it is plausible that the list in section 212(a)(3)(B) of the Act was intended to "cover virtually all forms of assistance, even small monetary contributions." Id. at 945. However, we ultimately found it unnecessary to address the alien's argument that the term "material" should be given "independent content," because the amount of money she provided was sufficiently substantial to have an effect on the terrorist organization's ability to accomplish its goals. Id.

We agree with the Third Circuit that the word "material" in the phrase "material support" must be "ascribed some meaning." Sesay v. Att'y Gen. of U.S., 787 F.3d 215, 222 (3d Cir. 2015). However, we conclude that the meaning does not relate to a quantitative requirement. We reiterate that there is no legislative history to support taking a quantitative approach and separating out what amount of support is necessary to make it "material." If an alien affords material support to a terrorist organization, he or she is subject to the bar, regardless of how limited that support is in amount.

This interpretation does not render the word "material" superfluous. Without that qualification, the bar could have been construed to apply to a person who merely expressed general "support" for a terrorist organization, which would have raised substantial freedom of expression concerns. Cf. Holder v. Humanitarian Law Project, 561 U.S. 1, 38–39 (2010) (upholding a conviction under the criminal analogue to the material support bar in the face of a First Amendment challenge).

In sum, "material support" is a term of art that "relates to the type of aid provided," that is, aid of a material and normally tangible nature,[1] and it is not quantitative. Boim v. Quranic Literacy Inst. and Holy Land Found. for Relief and Dev., 291 F.3d 1000, 1015 (7th Cir. 2002); see also Singh-Kaur v. Ashcroft, 385 F.3d 293, 298–99 (3d Cir. 2004) (noting that "material support" is a broad concept that is not limited to the enumerated examples and deferring to our determination that

---

1. [Footnote 3 in original] The Court in Humanitarian Law Project, 561 U.S. at 36–40, considered that speech in the form of "training" could be prohibited.

the "provision of food and setting up tents" was within the definition of "material support"); Matter of S-K-, 23 I&N Dec. at 945 (observing that "Congress has not expressly indicated its intent to provide an exception for contributions which are de minimis").

The Third Circuit has defined "material support" as anything that has a "logical connection" to the aims of the terrorist organization, but the act need not be done for the specific purpose of aiding in a terrorist act. Singh-Kaur, 385 F.3d at 298–301; see also Black's Law Dictionary 1066 (9th ed. 2009) (defining "material" as "[h]aving some logical connection with the consequential facts"). We agree that Congress intended to use the adjective "material" in a relational sense — that is, to denote a necessary logical relationship between an act and a forbidden consequence. Thus, we conclude that an alien provides "material support" to a terrorist organization, regardless of whether it was intended to aid the organization, if the act has a logical and reasonably foreseeable tendency to promote, sustain, or maintain the organization, even if only to a de minimis degree.

Our view that the phrase "material support" has no quantitative component is also borne out by the fact that Congress, through section 212(d)(3)(B)(i) of the Act, has conferred upon the Secretary of Homeland Security the authority to grant a waiver regarding the application of the material support bar in order to address excusable violations including, among other things, support provided under duress or to only a de minimis degree. See, e.g., Annachamy v. Holder, 733 F.3d 254, 261–64 (9th Cir. 2013), overruled on other grounds by Abdisalan v. Holder, 774 F.3d 517, 526 (9th Cir. 2014) (as amended Jan. 6, 2015); Barahona v. Holder, 691 F.3d 349, 354–55 (4th Cir. 2012). As relevant here, the DHS has construed the waiver to apply specifically in situations where an alien has afforded only "insignificant material support" to an undesignated terrorist organization, a member of such an organization, or an individual the applicant knew, or reasonably should have known, had committed or planned to commit a terrorist activity. Exercise of Authority Under Section 212(d)(3)(B)(i) of the Immigration and Nationality Act, 79 Fed. Reg. 6913, 6913 (Feb. 5, 2014).[2]

In Matter of S-K-, 23 I&N Dec. at 941, we noted that the inclusion of the waiver was a means of balancing the "harsh provisions" of the material support bar. By creating the waiver, Congress effectively addressed the over-inclusive nature of the bar by allowing the Secretary to consider each situation in a more

---

2. [Footnote 5 in original] The DHS has also determined that the waiver applies to "an alien who provided limited material support . . . that involves (1) certain routine commercial transactions or certain routine social transactions . . ., (2) certain humanitarian assistance, or (3) substantial pressure that does not rise to the level of duress." Exercise of Authority Under Section 212(d)(3)(B)(i) of the Immigration and Nationality Act, 79 Fed. Reg. 6914, 6914 (Feb. 5, 2014). Thus, the waiver is available to cover the kinds of activities that the dissent argues should not be considered to be "material support," such as providing water or medical care.

holistic manner. See Sesay, 787 F.3d at 223 n.8 (noting that in recent years, the Secretaries of State and Homeland Security have continued to expand the categories of activities eligible for waiver).[3]

Obviously, if providing merely an "insignificant" amount of support did not constitute "material support," the DHS would not have found a need for a waiver addressing this type of circumstance. The fact that the waiver covers such situations is clear evidence that the DHS regards the bar as extending to the provision of even "insignificant" support, contrary to the contention of the respondent and the dissent. While the DHS's position is not binding on either the Board or the Federal courts, it is nevertheless entitled to some weight. See Davis v. United States, 495 U.S. 472, 484 (1990); Udall v. Tallman, 380 U.S. 1, 16 (1965). Thus, regardless of how sympathetic the circumstances of an alien's case may be, we find no support for concluding that Congress intended to provide a quantitative exclusion from the term "material support." See generally Matter of C-T-L-, 25 I&N Dec. 341, 345 (BIA 2010) (stating that we do not generally view statutory language in isolation, but must read the words "in their context and with a view to their place in the overall statutory scheme" (citations omitted)).

We therefore conclude that, on the facts before us, the respondent afforded material support when she aided guerillas in continuing their mission of armed and violent opposition to the Salvadoran Government in 1990. See Humanitarian Law Project, 561 U.S. at 28–29 (citing Congress' finding that any "contribution" to a terrorist organization facilitates terrorist activity and holding that such a "contribution" is not limited to monetary aid); Humanitarian Law Project v. Reno, 205 F.3d 1130, 1136 (9th Cir. 2000) (stating that "giving support intended to aid an

---

3. [Footnote 6 in original] Implementation of the section 212(d)(3)(B)(i) material support exemption has been delegated from the Secretaries to the U.S. Citizenship and Immigration Services ("USCIS") in consultation with the U.S. Immigration and Customs Enforcement ("ICE"). See Exercise of Authority Under Sec. 212(d)(3)(B)(i) of the Immigration and Nationality Act, 72 Fed. Reg. 9955, 9955 (Mar. 6, 2007). The DHS announced that USCIS, in consultation with ICE, will consider a case for an exemption only after an order of removal is administratively final. See Fact Sheet: Department of Homeland Security Implements Exemption Authority for Certain Terrorist-Related Inadmissibility Grounds for Cases with Administratively Final Orders of Removal, USCIS (Oct. 23, 2008), https://www.uscis.gov/sites/default/files/USCIS/Laws/TRIG/USCIS_Process_Fact_Sheet_-_Cases_in_Removal_Proceedings.pdf. After an administratively final order is issued, ICE will forward to USCIS those cases where relief or protection was denied solely on the basis of one of the terrorist-related inadmissibility grounds for which exemption authority has been exercised by the Secretary. Id. Pursuant to the Secretaries' exercise of authority under section 212(d)(3)(B)(i) of the Act, "USCIS will consider whether certain aliens are eligible for and warrant a discretionary exemption for the provision of the following types of certain limited material support: certain routine commercial transactions; certain routine social transactions; certain humanitarian assistance; or material support provided under sub-duress pressure." USCIS Policy Memorandum, PM-602-0112, 2015 WL 2439341 (May 8, 2015) (regarding "Implementation of the Discretionary Exemption Authority under Section 212(d)(3)(B)(i) of the Immigration and Nationality Act for the Provision of Certain Limited Material Support"). We emphasize that the DHS adjudicates section 212(d)(3)(B)(i) waivers only as a last resort, when it is clear that the terrorism bar is the sole ground for an alien's removability or ineligibility for relief.

organization's peaceful activities frees up resources that can be used for terrorist acts"); Matter of S-K-, 24 I&N Dec. at 477–78 (reaffirming Matter of S-K-, 23 I&N Dec. at 944–46). While the respondent's assistance may have been relatively minimal, if she had not provided the cooking and cleaning services she was forced to perform, another person would have needed to do so.

The dissent, in addition to arguing that the amount of support afforded by an alien to a terrorist organization must reach a certain level to be considered "material," asserts that the support provided must be of a certain type in order to be covered by the material support bar. We find this issue, which was not raised by the respondent, to be relatively straightforward.

In several nonprecedential decisions, some of which have been reviewed by the Federal courts of appeals, we have found that "material support" includes activities, both voluntary and involuntary, such as fundraising, making payments of money, providing food and shelter, and performing physical labor. See, e.g., Tahir v. Lynch, 654 F. App'x 512, 515 (2d Cir. 2016) (designing and printing communications materials, such as brochures, posters, and banners); Annachamy, 733 F.3d at 257 (making a monetary contribution and performing physical labor); Barahona, 691 F.3d at 351 (allowing the use of a home for shelter and meal preparation); Haile v. Holder, 658 F.3d 1122, 1124 (9th Cir. 2011) (fundraising and supplying provisions and secret documents); Singh-Kaur, 385 F.3d at 294 (providing food and shelter). The term is broadly defined and is not limited to the enumerated examples in the statute under section 212(a)(3)(B)(iv)(VI) of the Act. See, e.g., Alturo v. U.S. Att'y Gen., 716 F.3d 1310, 1314 (11th Cir. 2013) (per curiam) (citing Singh-Kaur, 385 F.3d at 298–99).

The dissent nevertheless asserts that, although not an exclusive list, the acts enumerated in section 212(a)(3)(B)(iv)(VI) of the Act imply that only certain kinds of support qualify as "material."[4] This argument is refuted by the above-cited examples. Moreover, as we have noted, the examples of types of material support listed in the statute are not exhaustive but are "intended to illustrate a broad concept rather than narrowly circumscribe a term with exclusive categories." Matter of S-K-, 23 I&N Dec. at 944 (quoting Singh-Kaur, 385 F.3d at 298). We have further observed that the court in Singh-Kaur "rejected the alien's arguments that because a similar statute criminalizing such support to terrorists included a longer list of examples, including lodging, congressional intent was to limit the types of support that would qualify to those listed." Id.

In fact, no court has held that the kind of support an alien provides, if related to promoting the goals of a terrorist organization, is exempt from the material support bar, and we discern no basis to import such a limitation. Indeed, the

---

4. [Footnote 7 in original] Section 212(a)(3)(B)(iv)(VI) identifies acts that afford material support as "including" the following: "a safe house, transportation, communications, funds, transfer of funds or other material financial benefit, false documentation or identification, weapons (including chemical, biological, or radiological weapons), explosives, or training."

Supreme Court has stated that even "[m]aterial support meant to 'promot[e] peaceable, lawful conduct' can further terrorism by foreign groups in multiple ways." Humanitarian Law Project, 561 U.S. at 30 (alteration in original) (citation omitted).

The dissent invokes the canon of ejusdem generis, which provides that when "general words in a statute follow the enumeration of particular classes of persons or things, the general words will be construed as applicable only to persons or things of the same general nature or class as those enumerated." Matter of L-, 9 I&N Dec. 14, 21 (BIA 1960). But canons of statutory construction are merely general guides and should not be applied where the context dictates otherwise. See, e.g., Envt'l. Def. v. Duke Energy Corp., 549 U.S. 561, 574 (2007); Atl. Cleaners & Dyers v. United States, 286 U.S. 427, 433 (1932). Here, Congress has considered that combatting terrorism is a high priority and that any contributions to terrorist organizations further their terrorism. See Humanitarian Law Project, 561 U.S. at 28–32. The context therefore plainly counsels against a limitation being placed on the type of support rendered by an alien.

Because the material support bar applies, we will dismiss the respondent's cross-appeal. As noted, the Immigration Judge determined that, but for the "material support" bar, the respondent would have been eligible for asylum on humanitarian grounds under Matter of Chen, 20 I&N Dec. 16. The DHS does not dispute this finding. For the reasons enumerated by the Immigration Judge, we agree.

C.   Convention Against Torture

The DHS argues that the Immigration Judge erred by granting the respondent's application for deferral of removal under the Convention Against Torture because the respondent did not demonstrate that it is more likely than not that she will be tortured if removed to El Salvador. Our review of the Immigration Judge's decision reflects that she has not provided sufficient fact-finding and analysis regarding the respondent's request for protection under the Convention Against Torture. We cannot meaningfully address the DHS's arguments absent sufficient legal analysis by the Immigration Judge or adequate factual findings, which we are without authority to make in the first instance. See Matter of S-H-, 23 I&N Dec. 462, 463 (BIA 2002) (remanding to the Immigration Judge because of insufficient factual findings and legal analysis); Matter of A-P-, 22 I&N Dec. 468, 477 (BIA 1999) (stating that the Immigration Judge is "responsible for the substantive completeness of the decision").

It is also unclear whether the Immigration Judge applied the correct legal standard in assessing the merits of the respondent's claim for protection under the Convention Against Torture. Such relief is available only if it is more likely than not that an individual will suffer from torture "inflicted by or at the instigation of or with the consent or acquiescence of a public official or other person acting in an official capacity." 8 C.F.R. § 1208.18(a)(1) (2018); see also Khouzam v.

Ashcroft, 361 F.3d 161, 170–71 (2d Cir. 2004) (noting that an applicant for protection under the Convention Against Torture must show that torture will be perpetrated with a government official's consent, acquiescence, or willful blindness).

The Immigration Judge's analysis was conclusory, stating only that the respondent met her burden to show that she was subject to torture and that deferral of removal was warranted. Under these circumstances, we conclude that a remand is necessary for the Immigration Judge to provide factual and legal analyses for her decision. Upon remand, the Immigration Judge may conduct further proceedings, as appropriate, and give the parties an opportunity to supplement the record with additional relevant evidence and argument. She should issue a new decision taking into consideration the totality of all the evidence presented in this matter. In remanding, we offer no opinion as to the ultimate outcome in this case.

ORDER: The respondent's cross-appeal is dismissed.

FURTHER ORDER: The record is remanded to the Immigration Judge for further proceedings consistent with the foregoing opinion and for the entry of a new decision.

CONCURRING AND DISSENTING OPINION: Linda S. Wendtland, Board Member

I concur with the majority to the extent that it holds that the record should be remanded for further proceedings and the entry of a new decision with regard to the respondent's eligibility for protection under the Convention Against Torture.

However, I respectfully dissent from the majority's conclusion that the respondent is subject to the bar to asylum and withholding of removal for applicants who have provided "material support" to a terrorist organization, and I would sustain the respondent's cross-appeal in that regard. See sections 208(b)(2)(A)(v), 212(a)(3)(B)(i)(I), (iv)(VI), 237(a)(4)(B), 241(b)(3)(B)(iv) of the Immigration and Nationality Act, 8 U.S.C. §§ 1158(b)(2)(A)(v), 1182(a)(3)(B)(i)(I), (iv)(VI), 1227(a)(4)(B), 1231(b)(3)(B)(iv) (2012).

The primary question presented by this case is whether the respondent's activities are of the kind and magnitude that would meet the threshold requirement of "material." I would conclude that they are not.

To prevent Congress' use of the word "material" from being superfluous, that word must have an independent meaning. Had Congress intended the word "material" to add little or nothing to the threshold requirements, it presumably would have simply prohibited "support." Far from having done so, Congress went into detail about the kinds of activities that the general term "material support" entails. Specifically, section 212(a)(3)(B)(iv)(VI) of the Act states that "material support" includes "a safe house, transportation, communications, funds, transfer of funds or other material financial benefit, false documentation or identification, weapons (including chemical, biological, or radiological weapons), explosives, or training."

Admittedly, this is not an exclusive list. Nevertheless, the listed specific examples imply that certain kinds and levels of support are required in order to constitute "material" support. See Matter of S-K-, 23 I&N Dec. 936, 945 (BIA

2006) (acknowledging that the respondent's "argument that 'material' should be given independent content is by no means frivolous," but finding it unnecessary to resolve the issue), remanded, 24 I&N Dec. 289 (A.G. 2007), clarified, 24 I&N Dec. 475 (BIA 2008). It is a well-settled canon of statutory construction that general statutory terms like "material support" "should be understood to refer to items belonging to the same class that is defined by the more specific terms in the list." Holder v. Hall, 512 U.S. 874, 917 (1994) (emphasis added); see also Federal Land Bank of St. Paul v. Bismarck Lumber Co., 314 U.S. 95, 100 (1941) (concluding that the use of the word "including" in a statutory definition conveys that other kindred items may be included within that definition, even if the items are not explicitly listed).

I cannot conclude that the menial and incidental tasks that the respondent performed—as a slave—for Salvadoran guerrillas, including cooking, cleaning, and washing clothes, are of "the same class" as the enumerated forms of assistance set forth in the statute. The enumerated examples all involve items that either can directly be used to plan or carry out terrorist activities or, in the case of funds, have the liquidity and fungibility to readily be diverted to such use. Cooking and cleaning services for individuals who happen to belong to a terrorist organization cannot validly be placed in the same category as items that can be used to plan and carry out the organization's goals. If Congress had intended to include such incidental services in the definition of "material support," there would have been no need—and, indeed, it would have been counterproductive—to list multiple specific examples that relate directly to terrorist activity.

Similarly, I cannot conclude that the incidental assistance the respondent afforded to the guerillas provides "material" support in the logical sense of having at least some importance to promoting, sustaining, or maintaining the organization's goals. See Haile v. Holder, 658 F.3d 1122, 1129 (9th Cir. 2011) (concluding that the definition of "material support" was broad enough to include collecting funds, supplying provisions, and passing along secret documents (citing Matter of S-K-, 23 I&N Dec. at 943)). "A word in a statute may or may not extend to the outer limits of its definitional possibilities. Interpretation of a word or phrase depends upon reading the whole statutory text, considering the purpose and context of the statute, and consulting any precedents or authorities that inform the analysis." Dolan v. U.S. Postal Serv., 546 U.S. 481, 486 (2006). I do not believe, as the majority apparently does, that Congress intended that any support—no matter how small, dissimilar to the statutorily enumerated examples, or indeed immaterial—would bar an asylum applicant from relief. The majority's apparent interpretation of "material," as referencing anything and everything that "another person would have needed to do" if the respondent had not done it, is without effective limits and would lead to absurd results. Matter of A-C-M-, 27 I&N Dec. 302, 310 (BIA 2018).

For example, under the majority's strained interpretation, providing a glass of water to a thirsty individual who happened to belong to a terrorist organization would constitute material support of that organization, because the individual otherwise would have needed to obtain water from another source. Providing medical care to a flu-stricken member of a terrorist organization would also qualify as material support, since the individual otherwise would have needed to seek help from another doctor. Myriad other everyday activities that involve the crossing of paths with individuals who happen to be members of terrorist organizations would also be covered, such as selling such a member groceries on the same terms as are applied to the public generally, or cooking breakfast or doing laundry for one's spouse who is a member. All of these examples, like the majority's application of the bar to the minimal and menial activities in which the respondent has engaged, essentially read the word "material" out of the statute and render it superfluous, an outcome with which I cannot agree. See, e.g., Dole Food Co. v. Patrickson, 538 U.S. 468, 476–77 (2003) (declining to construe a "statute in a manner that is strained and, at the same time, would render a statutory term superfluous"); Singh-Kaur v. Ashcroft, 385 F.3d 293, 298 (3d Cir. 2004).

In view of our relatively recent holding in Matter of M-H-Z-, 26 I&N Dec. 757 (BIA 2016), that the material support bar contains no exception for duress, "it is especially important to give meaning to the statutory limit of 'material.' That term calls for [I]mmigration [J]udges, the Board, and the courts to strike a balance written into the Act." Jabateh v. Lynch, 845 F.3d 332, 348 (7th Cir. 2017) (Hamilton, J., concurring in part and concurring in the judgment). Individuals arriving in this country from "some of the most dangerous and chaotic places on earth . . . may not have been able to avoid all contact with terrorist groups and their members, but we should not interpret the statute to exclude on this basis those who did not provide 'material' support to them," since "[m]any deserving asylum-seekers could be barred otherwise." Id. Unlike the majority, which apparently would apply the bar without any meaningful limit, I would not decline to carry out our responsibility to strike the foregoing critical balance.

Nor do I believe that Congress intended to relegate the respondent, who did not afford support that qualifies as "material," to the statutory waiver process under section 212(d)(3)(B)(i) of the Act, which is intended only for those individuals whose support did meet the threshold materiality requirement. And given my view that the respondent's conduct does not come within the "material support" bar in the first place, I need not reach the question whether the respondent reasonably should have known that the guerrillas in 1990 in El Salvador were a terrorist organization.

SESSIONS v. DIMAYA

594 U. S. ___ (2018)

JUSTICE KAGAN announced the judgment of the Court and delivered the opinion of the Court with respect to Parts I, III, IV–B, and V, and an opinion with respect to Parts II and IV–A, in which JUSTICE GINSBURG, JUSTICE BREYER, and JUSTICE SOTOMAYOR join.

Three Terms ago, in Johnson v. United States, this Court held that part of a federal law's definition of "violent felony" was impermissibly vague. See 576 U. S. ___ (2015). The question in this case is whether a similarly worded clause in a statute's definition of "crime of violence" suffers from the same constitutional defect. Adhering to our analysis in Johnson, we hold that it does.

I

The Immigration and Nationality Act (INA) renders deportable any alien convicted of an "aggravated felony" after entering the United States. 8 U. S. C. §1227(a)(2)(A)(iii). Such an alien is also ineligible for cancellation of removal, a form of discretionary relief allowing some deportable aliens to remain in the country. See §§1229b(a)(3), (b)(1)(C). Accordingly, removal is a virtual certainty for an alien found to have an aggravated felony conviction, no matter how long he has previously resided here.

The INA defines "aggravated felony" by listing numerous offenses and types of offenses, often with cross-references to federal criminal statutes. §1101(a)(43). According to one item on that long list, an aggravated felony includes "a crime of violence (as defined in section16 of title 18 . . .) for which the term of imprisonment [is]at least one year." §1101(a)(43)(F). The specified statute,18 U. S. C. §16, provides the federal criminal code's definition of "crime of violence." Its two parts, often known as the elements clause and the residual clause, cover:

"(a) an offense that has as an element the use, attempted use, or threatened use of physical force against the person or property of another, or

"(b) any other offense that is a felony and that, by its nature, involves a substantial risk that physical force against the person or property of another may be used in the course of committing the offense."

Section 16(b), the residual clause, is the part of the statute at issue in this case.

To decide whether a person's conviction "falls within the ambit" of that clause, courts use a distinctive form of what we have called the categorical approach. Leocal v. Ashcroft, 543 U. S. 1, 7 (2004). The question, we have explained, is not whether "the particular facts" underlying a conviction posed the substantial risk that §16(b) demands. Ibid. Neither is the question whether the statutory elements of a crime require (or entail) the creation of such a risk in each case that the crime covers.[1] The §16(b) inquiry instead turns on the "nature of the offense" generally speaking. Ibid. (referring to §16(b)'s "by its nature" language). More precisely, §16(b) requires a court to ask whether "the ordinary case" of an offense poses the requisite risk. James v. United States, 550 U. S. 192, 208 (2007); see infra, at 7.

In the case before us, Immigration Judges employed that analysis to conclude that respondent James Dimaya is deportable as an aggravated felon. A native of the Philippines, Dimaya has resided lawfully in the United States since 1992. But he has not always acted lawfully during that time. Twice, Dimaya was convicted of first-degree burglary under California law. See Cal. Penal Code Ann. §§459, 460(a). Following his second offense, the Government initiated a removal proceeding against him. Both an Immigration Judge and the Board of Immigration Appeals held that California first-degree burglary is a "crime of violence" under §16(b). "[B]y its nature," the Board reasoned, the offense "carries a substantial risk of the use of force." Dimaya sought review in the Court of Appeals for the Ninth Circuit.

While his appeal was pending, this Court held unconstitutional part of the definition of "violent felony" in the Armed Career Criminal Act (ACCA), 18 U. S. C. §924(e). ACCA prescribes a 15-year mandatory minimum sentence if a person convicted of being a felon in possession of a firearm has three prior convictions for a "violent felony." §924(e)(1). The definition of that statutory term goes as follows:

"any crime punishable by imprisonment for a term exceeding one year . . . that—

"(i) has as an element the use, attempted use, or threatened use of physical force against the person of another; or

"(ii) is burglary, arson, or extortion, involves use of explosives, or otherwise involves conduct that presents a serious potential risk of physical injury to another."

§924(e)(2)(B) (emphasis added).

The italicized portion of that definition (like the similar language of §16(b)) came to be known as the statute's residual clause. In Johnson v. United States, the Court declared that clause "void for vagueness" under the Fifth Amendment's Due Process Clause. 576 U. S., at ___–___ (slip op., at 13–14).

---

1. The analysis thus differs from the form of categorical approach used to determine whether a prior conviction is for a particular listed offense (say, murder or arson). In that context, courts ask what the elements of a given crime always require—in effect, what is legally necessary for a conviction. See, e.g., Descamps v. United States, 570 U. S. 254, 260–261 (2013); Moncrieffe v. Holder, 569 U. S. 184, 190–191 (2013).

Appendix C.   Sessions v. Dimaya

Relying on Johnson, the Ninth Circuit held that §16(b),as incorporated into the INA, was also unconstitutionally vague, and accordingly ruled in Dimaya's favor. See Dimaya v. Lynch, 803 F. 3d 1110, 1120 (2015). Two other Circuits reached the same conclusion, but a third distinguished ACCA's residual clause from §16's. We granted certiorari to resolve the conflict. Lynch v. Dimaya, 579 U. S. ___ (2016).

II

"The prohibition of vagueness in criminal statutes," our decision in Johnson explained, is an "essential" of due process, required by both "ordinary notions of fair play and the settled rules of law." 576 U. S., at ___ (slip op., at 4). The void-for-vagueness doctrine, as we have called it, guarantees that ordinary people have "fair notice" of the conduct a statute proscribes. Papachristou v. Jacksonville, 405 U. S. 156, 162 (1972). And the doctrine guards against arbitrary or discriminatory law enforcement by insisting that a statute provide standards to govern the actions of police officers, prosecutors, juries, and judges. See Kolender v. Lawson, 461 U. S. 352, 357– 358 (1983). In that sense, the doctrine is a corollary of the separation of powers—requiring that Congress, rather than the executive or judicial branch, define what conduct is sanctionable and what is not.

The Government argues that a less searching form of the void-for-vagueness doctrine applies here than in Johnson because this is not a criminal case. As the Government notes, this Court has stated that "[t]he degree of vagueness that the Constitution [allows] depends in part on the nature of the enactment": In particular, the Court has "expressed greater tolerance of enactments with civil rather than criminal penalties because the consequences of imprecision are qualitatively less severe." Hoffman Estates v. Flipside, Hoffman Estates, Inc., 455 U. S. 489, 498–499 (1982). The removal of an alien is a civil matter. See Arizona v. United States, 567 U. S. 387, 396 (2012). Hence, the Government claims, the need for clarity is not so strong; even a law too vague to support a conviction or sentence may be good enough to sustain a deportation order.

But this Court's precedent forecloses that argument, because we long ago held that the most exacting vagueness standard should apply in removal cases. In Jordan v. De George, we considered whether a provision of immigration law making an alien deportable if convicted of a "crime involving moral turpitude" was "sufficiently definite." 341 U. S. 223, 229 (1951). That provision, we noted, "is not a criminal statute" (as §16(b) actually is). Id., at 231; supra, at 1–2. Still, we chose to test (and ultimately uphold) it "under the established criteria of the 'void for vagueness' doctrine" applicable to criminal laws. 341 U. S., at 231. That approach was demanded, we explained, "in view of the grave nature of deportation," ibid.—a "drastic measure," often amounting to lifelong "banishment or exile," ibid. (quoting Fong Haw Tan v. Phelan, 333 U. S. 6, 10 (1948)).

Nothing in the ensuing years calls that reasoning into question. To the contrary, this Court has reiterated that deportation is "a particularly severe penalty," which may be of greater concern to a convicted alien than "any potential jail sentence." Jae Lee v. United States, 582 U. S. ___, ___ (2017) (slip op., at 11) (quoting Padilla v. Kentucky, 559 U. S. 356, 365, 368 (2010)). And we have observed that as federal immigration law increasingly hinged deportation orders on prior convictions, removal proceedings became ever more "intimately related to the criminal process." Chaidez v. United States, 568 U. S. 342, 352 (2013) (quoting Padilla, 559 U. S., at 365). What follows, as Jordan recognized, is the use of the same standard in the two settings.

For that reason, the Government cannot take refuge in a more permissive form of the void-for-vagueness doctrine than the one *Johnson* employed. To salvage §16's residual clause, even for use in immigration hearings, the Government must instead persuade us that it is materially clearer than its now-invalidated ACCA counterpart. That is the issue we next address, as guided by Johnson's analysis.

III

Johnson is a straightforward decision, with equally straightforward application here. Its principal section begins as follows: "Two features of [ACCA's] residual clause conspire to make it unconstitutionally vague." The opinion then identifies each of those features and explains how their joinder produced "hopeless indeterminacy," inconsistent with due process. And with that reasoning, Johnson effectively resolved the case now before us. For §16's residual clause has the same two features as ACCA's, combined in the same constitutionally problematic way.

Consider those two, just as Johnson described them:

"In the first place," Johnson explained, ACCA's residual clause created "grave uncertainty about how to estimate the risk posed by a crime" because it "tie[d] the judicial assessment of risk" to a hypothesis about the crime's "ordinary case." Under the clause, a court focused on neither the "real-world facts" nor the bare "statutory elements" of an offense. Instead, a court was supposed to "imagine" an "idealized ordinary case of the crime"—or otherwise put, the court had to identify the "kind of conduct the 'ordinary case' of a crime involves." But how, Johnson asked, should a court figure that out? By using a "statistical analysis of the state reporter? A survey? Expert evidence? Google? Gut instinct?" ACCA provided no guidance, rendering judicial accounts of the "ordinary case" wholly "speculative." Johnson gave as its prime example the crime of attempted bur-glary. One judge, contemplating the "ordinary case," would imagine the "violent encounter" apt to ensue when a "would-be burglar [was] spotted by a police officer [or]private security guard." Another judge would conclude that "any confrontation" was more "likely to consist of [an observer's] yelling 'Who's there?' . . . and the burglar's running away." But how could either judge really know?

Appendix C.   Sessions v. Dimaya

"The residual clause," Johnson summarized, "offer[ed] no reliable way" to discern what the ordinary version of any offense looked like. And without that, no one could tell how much risk the offense generally posed.

Compounding that first uncertainty, Johnson continued, was a second: ACCA's residual clause left unclear what threshold level of risk made any given crime a "violent felony." The Court emphasized that this feature alone would not have violated the void-for-vagueness doctrine: Many perfectly constitutional statutes use imprecise terms like "serious potential risk" (as in ACCA's residual clause) or "substantial risk" (as in §16's). The problem came from layering such a standard on top of the requisite "ordinary case" inquiry. As the Court explained:

"[W]e do not doubt the constitutionality of laws that call for the application of a qualitative standard such as 'substantial risk' to real-world conduct; the law is full of instances where a man's fate depends on his estimating rightly . . . some matter of degree[.] The residual clause, however, requires application of the 'serious potential risk' standard to an idealized ordinary case of the crime. Because the elements necessary to determine the imaginary ideal are uncertain[,] this abstract inquiry offers significantly less predictability than one that deals with the actual . . . facts."

So much less predictability, in fact, that ACCA's residual clause could not pass constitutional muster. As the Court again put the point, in the punch line of its decision: "By combining indeterminacy about how to measure the risk posed by a crime with indeterminacy about how much risk it takes for the crime to qualify as a violent felony, the residual clause" violates the guarantee of due process.

Section 16's residual clause violates that promise in just the same way. To begin where Johnson did, §16(b) also calls for a court to identify a crime's "ordinary case" in order to measure the crime's risk. The Government explicitly acknowledges that point here. And indeed, the Government's briefing in *Johnson* warned us about that likeness, observing that §16(b) would be "equally susceptible to [an] objection" that focused on the problems of positing a crime's ordinary case. . . .

And §16(b) also possesses the second fatal feature of ACCA's residual clause: uncertainty about the level of risk that makes a crime "violent." In ACCA, that threshold was "serious potential risk"; in §16(b), it is "substantial risk." But the Government does not argue that the latter formulation is any more determinate than the former, and for good reason. As THE CHIEF JUSTICE's valiant attempt to do so shows, that would be slicing the baloney mighty thin. And indeed, Johnson as much as equated the two phrases: Return to the block quote above, and note how Johnson—as though anticipating this case—refers to them interchangeably, as alike examples of imprecise "qualitative standard[s]." Once again, the point is not that such a non-numeric standard is alone problematic: In Johnson's words, "we do not doubt" the constitutionality of applying §16(b)'s "substantial risk [standard] to real-world conduct." The difficulty comes, in §16's residual clause just as in ACCA's, from applying such a standard to "a judge-imagined abstraction"—i.e., "an idealized ordinary case of the crime." It is then that the standard ceases to work in a way consistent with due process.

In sum, §16(b) has the same "[t]wo features" that "conspire[d] to make [ACCA's residual clause] unconstitutionally vague." It too "requires a court to picture the kind of conduct that the crime involves in 'the ordinary case,' and to judge whether that abstraction presents" some not-well-specified-yet-sufficiently large degree of risk. The result is that §16(b) produces, just as ACCA's residual clause did, "more unpredictability and arbitrariness than the Due Process Clause tolerates."

IV

The Government and dissents offer two fundamentally different accounts of how §16(b) can escape unscathed from our decision in Johnson. JUSTICE THOMAS accepts that the ordinary-case inquiry makes §16(b) "impossible to apply." Post, at 27. His solution is to overthrow our historic understanding of the statute: We should now read §16(b), he says, to ask about the risk posed by a particular defendant's particular conduct. In contrast, the Government, joined by THE CHIEF JUSTICE, accepts that §16(b), as long interpreted, demands a categorical approach, rather than a case-specific one. They argue only that "distinctive textual features" of §16's residual clause make applying it "more predictable" than its ACCA counter- part. We disagree with both arguments.

A

The essentials of Justice Thomas's position go as follows. Section 16(b)... cannot demand an inquiry merely into the elements of a crime, because that is the province of §16(a). But that still leaves a pair of options: the categorical, ordinary-case approach and the "underlying-conduct approach," which asks about the specific way in which a defendant committed a crime. According to Justice Thomas, each option is textually viable (although he gives a slight nod to the latter based on §16(b)'s use of the word "involves"). What tips the scales is that only one—the conduct approach—is at all "workable." The difficulties of the ordinary-case inquiry, JUSTICE THOMAS rightly observes, underlie this Court's view that §16(b) is too vague. So abandon that inquiry, JUSTICE THOMAS urges. After all, he reasons, it is the Court's "plain duty," under the constitutional avoidance canon, to adopt any reasonable construction of a statute that escapes constitutional problems. For anyone who has read Johnson, that argument will ring a bell. The dissent there issued the same invitation, based on much the same reasoning, to jettison the categorical approach in residual-clause cases. 576 U. S., at ___–___ (slip op., at 9–13) (opinion of ALITO, J.). The Court declined to do so. It first noted that the Government had not asked us to switch to a fact-based inquiry. It then observed that the Court "had good reasons" for originally adopting the categorical approach, based partly on ACCA's text (which, by the way, uses the word "involves" identically) and partly on the "utter impracticability" of the alternative. Id., at ___ (slip op., at 13) (majority opinion).

The same is true here—except more so.

[S]uch an approach would generate its own constitutional questions. As Justice Thomas relates, post, at 22, 28, this Court adopted the categorical approach in part to "avoid[] the Sixth Amendment concerns that would arise from sentencing courts' making findings of fact that properly belong to juries." Justice Thomas thinks that issue need not detain us here because "the right of trial by jury ha[s] no application in a removal proceeding." But although this particular case involves removal, §16(b) is a criminal statute, with criminal sentencing consequences. And this Court has held (it could hardly have done otherwise) that "we must interpret the statute consistently, whether we encounter its application in a criminal or noncriminal context." And that means the avoidance canon cannot serve, as he would like, as the interpretive tie breaker.

In any event, §16(b)'s text creates no draw: Best read, it demands a categorical approach. Our decisions have consistently understood language in the residual clauses of both ACCA and §16 to refer to "the statute of conviction, not to the facts of each defendant's conduct." Taylor v. United States, 495 U. S. 575, 601 (1990); see Leocal, 543 U. S., at 7 (Section 16 "directs our focus to the 'offense' of conviction . . . rather than to the particular facts"). Simple references to a "conviction," "felony," or "offense," we have stated, are "read naturally" to denote the "crime as generally committed." Nijhawan v. Holder, 557 U. S. 29, 34 (2009). And the words "by its nature" in §16(b) make that meaning all the clearer. The statute, recall, directs courts to consider whether an offense, by its nature, poses the requisite risk of force. An offense's "nature" means its "normal and characteristic quality." Webster's Third New International Dictionary 1507 (2002). So §16(b) tells courts to figure out what an offense normally—or, as we have repeatedly said, "ordinarily"—entails, not what happened to occur on one occasion. And the same conclusion follows if we pay attention to language that is missing from §16(b). As we have observed in the ACCA context, the absence of terms alluding to a crime's circumstances, or its commission, makes a fact-based interpretation an uncomfortable fit. Congress had wanted judges to look into a felon's actual conduct, "it presumably would have said so; other statutes, in other contexts, speak in just that way."

And finally, the "utter impracticability"—and associated inequities—of such an interpretation is as great in the one statute as in the other. This Court has often described the daunting difficulties of accurately "reconstruct[ing]," often many years later, "the conduct underlying [a] conviction." Ibid.; Descamps, 570 U. S., at 270; Taylor, 495 U. S., at 601–602. According to Justice Thomas, we need not worry here because immigration judges have some special factfinding talent, or at least experience, that would mitigate the risk of error attaching to that endeavor in federal courts. But we cannot see putting so much weight on the superior fact-finding prowess of (notoriously overburdened) immigration judges.

B

Agreeing that is so, the Government (joined by the Chief Justice) takes a narrower path to the same desired result. It points to three textual discrepancies between ACCA's residual clause and §16(b), and argues that they make §16(b) significantly easier to apply. But each turns out to be the proverbial distinction without a difference.

1

The Government first—and foremost—relies on §16(b)'s express requirement (absent from ACCA) that the risk arise from acts taken "in the course of committing the offense." Because of that "temporal restriction," a court applying §16(b) may not "consider risks arising after" the offense's commission is over . . . thereby demand[ing] a "significantly more focused inquiry" than did ACCA's residual clause. Id., at 32. To assess that claim, start with the meaning of §16(b)'s "in the course of" language. That phrase, understood in the normal way, includes the conduct occurring throughout a crime's commission—not just the conduct sufficient to satisfy the offense's formal elements.... [A] court applying §16(b) gets to consider everything that is likely to take place for as long as a crime is being committed.

[W]ith or without §16(b)'s explicit temporal language, a court applying the section would do the same thing—ask what usually happens when a crime goes down.

And that is just what courts did when applying ACCA's residual clause—and for the same reason. True, that clause lacked an express temporal limit. But not a single one of this Court's ACCA decisions turned on conduct that might occur after a crime's commission. Thus, the analyses under ACCA's residual clause and §16(b) coincide.

The upshot is that the phrase "in the course of " makes no difference as to either outcome or clarity. The phrase, then, cannot cure the statutory indeterminacy Johnson described.

Second, the Government (and again, the Chief Justice's dissent) observes that §16(b) focuses on the risk of "physical force" whereas ACCA's residual clause asked about the risk of "physical injury." The §16(b) inquiry, the Government says, "trains solely" on the conduct typically involved in a crime. By contrast, the Government continues, ACCA's residual clause required a second inquiry: After describing the ordinary criminal's conduct, a court had to "speculate about a chain of causation that could possibly result in a victim's injury."

But once more, we struggle to see how that statutory distinction would matter. To begin with, the first of the Government's two steps—defining the conduct in the ordinary case—is almost always the difficult part. Once that is accomplished, the assessment of consequences tends to follow as a matter of course. So, for example, if a crime is likely enough to lead to a shooting, it will also belikely enough to lead to an injury. And still more important, §16(b) involves two steps as well—and essentially the same ones. In interpreting statutes like §16(b), this Court has made clear that "physical force" means "force capable of causing physical pain or injury." Johnson v. United States, 559 U. S. 133, 140 (2010) (defining the term for purposes of deciding what counts as a "violent" crime). So under §16(b) too, a court must not only identify the conduct typically involved in a crime, but also gauge its potential consequences. Or said a bit differently, evaluating the risk of "physical force" itself entails considering the risk of "physical injury." For those reasons, the force/injury distinction is unlikely to affect a court's analysis of whether a crime qualifies as violent. All the same crimes might—or, then again, might not—satisfy both requirements. Accordingly, this variance in wording cannot make ACCA's residual clause vague and §16(b) not.

Third, the Government briefly notes that §16(b), unlike ACCA's residual clause, is not preceded by a "confusing list of exemplar crimes." (The Chief Justice's dissent reiterates this argument, with some additional references to our caselaw.) Here, the Government is referring to the offenses ACCA designated as violent felonies independently of the residual clause (i.e., burglary, arson, extortion, and use of explosives). According to the Government, those crimes provided "contradictory and opaque indications" of what non-specified offenses should also count as violent. §16(b)lacks any such enumerated crimes, the Government concludes, it avoids the vagueness of ACCA's residual clause.

We readily accept a part of that argument. This Court for several years looked to ACCA's listed crimes for help in giving the residual clause meaning. But to no avail. As the Government relates (and Johnson explained), the enumerated crimes were themselves too varied to provide such assistance.

But the Government's conclusion does not follow. To say that ACCA's listed crimes failed to resolve the residual clause's vagueness is hardly to say they caused the problem. Had they done so, Johnson would not have needed to strike down the clause. It could simply have instructed courts to give up on trying to interpret the clause by reference to the enumerated offenses. That Johnson went so much further—invalidating a statutory provision rather than construing it independently of an-other—demonstrates that the list of crimes was not the culprit. And indeed, Johnson explicitly said as much.

***

V

Johnson tells us how to resolve this case. That decision held that "[t]wo features of [ACCA's] residual clause con-spire[d] to make it unconstitutionally vague." Because the clause had both an ordinary-case requirement and an ill-defined risk threshold, it necessarily "devolv[ed] into guesswork and intuition," invited arbitrary enforcement, and failed to provide fair notice. Section 16(b) possesses the exact same two features. And none of the minor linguistic disparities in the statutes makes any real difference. So just like ACCA's residual clause, §16(b) "produces more unpredictability and arbitrariness than the Due Process Clause tolerates." We accordingly affirm the judgment of the Court of Appeals.

It is so ordered.

JUSTICE GORSUCH, concurring in part and concurring in the judgment.

Vague laws invite arbitrary power. Before the Revolution, the crime of treason in English law was so capaciously construed that the mere expression of disfavored opinions could invite transportation or death. The founders cited the crown's abuse of "pretended" crimes like this as one of their reasons for revolution. See Declaration of Independence ¶21. Today's vague laws may not be as invidious, but they can invite the exercise of arbitrary power all the same—by leaving the people in the dark about what the law demands and allowing prosecutors and courts to make it up.

The law before us today is such a law. Before holding a lawful permanent resident alien like James Dimaya subject to removal for having committed a crime, the Immigration and Nationality Act requires a judge to determine that the ordinary case of the alien's crime of conviction involves a substantial risk that physical force may be used. But what does that mean? Just take the crime at issue in this case, California burglary, which applies to everyone from armed home intruders to door-to-door salesmen peddling shady products. How, on that vast spectrum, is anyone supposed to locate the ordinary case and say whether it includes a substantial risk of physical force? The truth is, no one knows. The law's silence leaves judges to their intuitions and the people to their fate. In my judgment, the Constitution demands more.

I begin with a foundational question. Writing for the Court in Johnson v. United States, 576 U. S. ___ (2015), Justice Scalia held the residual clause of the Armed Career Criminal Act void for vagueness because it invited "more unpredictability and arbitrariness" than the Constitution allows. Because the residual clause in the statute now before us uses almost exactly the same language as the residual clause in Johnson, respect for precedent alone would seem to suggest that both clauses should suffer the same judgment. But first in Johnson and now again today Justice Thomas has questioned whether our vagueness doctrine can fairly claim roots in the Constitution as originally understood. For its part, the Court has yet to offer a reply. I believe our colleague's challenge is a serious and thoughtful one that merits careful attention. At day's end, though, it is a challenge to which I find myself unable to subscribe. Respectfully, I am persuaded instead that void for vagueness doctrine, at least properly conceived, serves as a faithful expression of ancient due process and separation of powers principles the framers recognized as vital to ordered liberty under our Constitution. Consider first the doctrine's due process underpinnings. The Fifth and Fourteenth Amendments guarantee that "life, liberty, or property" may not be taken "without due process of law." That means the government generally may not deprive a person of those rights without affording him the benefit of (at least) those "customary procedures to which freemen were entitled by the old law of England."

Admittedly, some have suggested that the Due Process Clause does less work than this, allowing the government to deprive people of their liberty through whatever procedures (or lack of them) the government's current laws may tolerate. But in my view the weight of the historical evidence shows that the clause sought to ensure that the people's rights are never any less secure against governmental invasion than they were at common law. Lord Coke took this view of the English due process guarantee. 1 E. Coke, The Second Part of the Institutes of the Laws of England 50 (1797). John Rutledge, our second Chief Justice, explained that Coke's teachings were carefully studied and widely adopted by the framers, becoming "'almost the foundations of our law.'" Klopfer v. North Carolina, 386 U. S. 213, 225 (1967). And many more students of the Constitution besides—from Justice Story to Justice Scalia—have agreed that this view best represents the original understanding of our own Due Process Clause. See, e.g., Murray's Lessee v. Hoboken Land & Improvement Co., 18 How. 272, 277 (1856); 3 J. Story, Commentaries on the Constitution of the United States §1783, p. 661 (1833); Pacific Mut., supra, at 28–29 (opinion of Scalia, J.); Eberle, Procedural Due Process: The Original Understanding, 4 Const. Comment. 339, 341 (1987).

Perhaps the most basic of due process's customary protections is the demand of fair notice. See Connally v. General Constr. Co., 269 U. S. 385, 391 (1926); see also Note, Textualism as Fair Notice, 123 Harv. L. Rev. 542, 543 (2009) ("From the inception of Western culture, fair notice has been recognized as an essential element of therule of law"). Criminal indictments at common law had to provide "precise and sufficient certainty" about the charges involved. 4 W. Blackstone, Commentaries on the Laws of England 301 (1769) (Blackstone). Unless an "offence [was] set forth with clearness and certainty," the indictment risked being held void in court. Id., at 302 (emphasis deleted); 2 W. Hawkins, Pleas of the Crown, ch. 25, §§99, 100, pp. 244–245 (2d ed. 1726) ("[I]t seems to have been anciently the common practice, where an indictment appeared to be [in]sufficient, either for its uncertainty orthe want of proper legal words, not to put the defendant to answer it").

The same held true in civil cases affecting a person's life, liberty, or property. A civil suit began by obtaining a writ—a detailed and specific form of action asking for particular relief. Bellia, Article III and the Cause of Action, 89 Iowa L. Rev. 777, 784–786 (2004); Subrin, How Equity Conquered Common Law: The Federal Rules of Civil Procedure in Historical Perspective, 135 U. Pa. L. Rev. 909, 914–915 (1987). Because the various civil writs were clearly defined, English subjects served with one would know with particularity what legal requirement they were alleged to have violated and, accordingly, what would be at issue in court. Id., at 917; Moffitt, Pleadings in the Age of Settlement, 80 Ind. L. J. 727, 731 (2005). And a writ risked being held defective if it didn't provide fair notice. Goldington v. Bassingburn, Y. B. Trin. 3 Edw. II, f. 27b (1310) (explaining that it was "the law of the land" that "no one [could] be taken by surprise" by having to "answer in court for what [one] has not been warned to answer").

The requirement of fair notice applied to statutes too. Blackstone illustrated the point with a case involving a statute that made "stealing sheep, or other cattle" a felony. 1 Blackstone 88 (emphasis deleted). Because the term "cattle" embraced a good deal more then than it does now (including wild animals, no less), the court held the statute failed to provide adequate notice about what it did and did not cover—and so the court treated the term "cattle" as a nullity. Ibid. All of which, Blackstone added, had the salutary effect of inducing the legislature to reenter the field and make itself clear by passing a new law extending the statute to "bulls, cows, oxen," and more "by name."

This tradition of courts refusing to apply vague statutes finds parallels in early American practice as well. In The Enterprise, 8 F. Cas. 732 (No. 4,499) (CC NY 1810), for example, Justice Livingston found that a statute setting the circumstances in which a ship may enter a port during an embargo was too vague to be applied, concluding that "the court had better pass" the statutory terms by "as unintelligible and useless" rather than "put on them, at great uncertainty, a very harsh signification, and one which the legislature may never have designed." Id., at 735. In United States v. Sharp, 27 F. Cas. 1041 (No.16,264) (CC Pa. 1815), Justice Washington confronted a statute which prohibited seamen from making a "revolt." Id., at 1043. But he was unable to determine the meaning of this provision "by any authority . . . either in the common, admiralty, or civil law." Ibid. As a result, he declined to "recommend to the jury, to find the prisoners guilty of making, or endeavouring to make a revolt, however strong the evidence may be."

Nor was the concern with vague laws confined to the most serious offenses like capital crimes. Courts refused to apply vague laws in criminal cases involving relatively modest penalties. See, e.g., McJunkins v. State, 10 Ind. 140, 145 (1858). They applied the doctrine in civil cases too. See, e.g., Drake v. Drake, 15 N. C. 110, 115 (1833); Commonwealth v. Bank of Pennsylvania, 3 Watts & Serg.173, 177 (Pa. 1842). As one court put it, "all laws" "ought to be expressed in such a manner as that its meaning may be unambiguous, and in such language as may be readily understood by those upon whom it is to operate." McConvill v. Mayor and Aldermen of Jersey City, 39 N. J. L. 38, 42 (1876).

These early cases, admittedly, often spoke in terms of construing vague laws strictly rather than declaring them void. But in substance void the law is often exactly what these courts did: rather than try to construe or interpret the statute before them, judges frequently held the law simply too vague to apply. Blackstone, for example, did not suggest the court in his illustration should have given a narrowing construction to the term "cattle," but argued against giving it any effect at all. 1 Blackstone 88.

What history suggests, the structure of the Constitution confirms. Many of the Constitution's other provisions presuppose and depend on the existence of reasonably clear laws. Take the Fourth Amendment's requirement that arrest warrants must be supported by probable cause, and consider what would be left of that requirement if the alleged crime had no meaningful boundaries. Or take the Sixth Amendment's mandate that a defendant must be informed of the accusations against him and allowed to bring witnesses in his defense, and consider what use those rights would be if the charged crime was so vague the defendant couldn't tell what he's alleged to have done and what sort of witnesses he might need to rebut that charge. Without an assurance that the laws supply fair notice, so much else of the Constitution risks becoming only a "parchment barrie[r]" against arbitrary power. The Federalist No. 48, p. 308 (C. Rossiter ed. 1961) (J. Madison).

Although today's vagueness doctrine owes much to the guarantee of fair notice embodied in the Due Process Clause, it would be a mistake to overlook the doctrine's equal debt to the separation of powers. The Constitution assigns "[a]ll legislative Powers" in our federal government to Congress. Art. I, §1. It is for the people, through their elected representatives, to choose the rules that will govern their future conduct. See The Federalist No. 78, at 465 (A. Hamilton) ("The legislature . . . prescribes the rules by which the duties and rights of every citizen are to be regulated"). Meanwhile, the Constitution assigns to judges the "judicial Power" to decide "Cases" and "Controversies." Art. III, §2. That power does not license judges to craft new laws to govern future conduct, but only to "discer[n] the course prescribed by law" as it currently exists and to "follow it" in resolving disputes between the people over past events. Osborn v. Bank of United States, 9 Wheat. 738, 866 (1824).

From this division of duties, it comes clear that legislators may not "abdicate their responsibilities for setting the standards of the criminal law," Smith v. Goguen, 415 U. S. 566, 575 (1974), by leaving to judges the power to decide "the various crimes includable in [a] vague phrase," Jordan v. De George, 341 U. S. 223, 242 (1951) (Jackson, J., dissenting). For "if the legislature could set a net large enough to catch all possible offenders, and leave it to the courts to step inside and say who could be rightfully detained, and who should be set at large[,] [t]his would, to some extent, substitute the judicial for the legislative department of government." Kolender v. Lawson, 461 U. S. 352, 358, n. 7 (1983) (internal quotation marks omitted). Nor is the worry only that vague laws risk allowing judges to assume legislative power. Vague laws also threaten to transfer legislative power to police and prosecutors, leaving to them the job of shaping a vague statute's contours through their enforcement decisions. See Grayned v. City of Rockford, 408 U. S. 104, 108–109 (1972).

These structural worries are more than just formal ones. Under the Constitution, the adoption of new laws restricting liberty is supposed to be a hard business, the product of an open and public debate among a large and diverse number of elected representatives. Allowing the legislature to hand off the job of lawmaking risks substituting this design for one where legislation is made easy, with a mere handful of unelected judges and prosecutors free to "condem[n] all that [they] personally disapprove and for no better reason than [they] disapprove it." Jordan, supra, at 242 (Jackson, J., dissenting). Nor do judges and prosecutors act in the open and accountable forum of a legislature, but in the comparatively obscure confines of cases and controversies. See, e.g., A. Bickel, The Least Dangerous Branch: The Supreme Court at the Bar of Politics 151 (1962) ("A vague statute delegates to administrators, prosecutors, juries, and judges the authority of ad hoc decision, which is in its nature difficult if not impossible to hold to account, because of its narrow impact"). For just these reasons, Hamilton warned, while "liberty can have nothing to fear from the judiciary alone," it has "every thing to fear from" the union of the judicial and legislative powers. The Federalist No. 78, at 466. No doubt, too, for reasons like these this Court has held "that the more important aspect of vagueness doctrine 'is not actual notice, but . . . the requirement that a legislature establish minimal guidelines to govern law enforcement'" and keep the separate branches within their proper spheres. Kolender, supra, at 358 (quoting Goguen, supra, at 575 (emphasis added)).

Persuaded that vagueness doctrine enjoys a secure footing in the original understanding of the Constitution, the next question I confront concerns the standard of review. What degree of imprecision should this Court tolerate in a statute before declaring it unconstitutionally vague? For its part, the government argues that where(as here) a person faces only civil, not criminal, consequences from a statute's operation, we should declare the law unconstitutional only if it is "unintelligible." But in the criminal context this Court has generally insisted that the law must afford "ordinary people . . . fair notice of the conduct it punishes." Johnson, 576 U. S., at ___ (slip op., at 3). And I cannot see how the Due Process Clause might often require any less than that in the civil context either. Fair notice of the law's demands, as we've seen, is "the first essential of due process." Connally, 269 U. S., at 391. And as we've seen, too, the Constitution sought to preserve a common law tradition that usually aimed to ensure fair notice before any deprivation of life, liberty, or property could take place, whether under the banner of the criminal or the civil law. See supra, at 2–7.

First principles aside, the government suggests that at least this Court's precedents support adopting a less-than-fair-notice standard for civil cases. But even that much I do not see. [T]the happenstance that a law is found in the civil or criminal part of the statute books cannot be dispositive. To be sure, this Court has also said that what qualifies as fair notice depends "in part on the nature of the enactment." Hoffman Estates, 455 U. S., at 498. And the Court has sometimes "expressed greater tolerance of enactments with civil rather than criminal penalties because the consequences of imprecision are qualitatively less severe." Id., at 498–499. But to acknowledge these truisms does nothing to prove that civil laws must always be subject to the government's emaciated form of review.

In fact, if the severity of the consequences counts when deciding the standard of review, shouldn't we also take account of the fact that today's civil laws regularly impose penalties far more severe than those found in many criminal statutes? Ours is a world filled with more and more civil laws bearing more and more extravagant punishments. Today's "civil" penalties include confiscatory rather than compensatory fines, forfeiture provisions that allow homes to be taken, remedies that strip persons of their professional licenses and livelihoods, and the power to commit persons against their will indefinitely. Some of these penalties are routinely imposed and are routinely graver than those associated with misdemeanor crimes—and often harsher than the punishment for felonies. And not only are "punitive civil sanctions . . . rapidly expanding," they are "sometimes more severely punitive than the parallel criminal sanctions for the same conduct." Mann, Punitive Civil Sanctions: The Middleground BetweenCriminal and Civil Law, 101 Yale L. J. 1795, 1798 (1992) (emphasis added). Given all this, any suggestion that criminal cases warrant a heightened standard of review does more to persuade me that the criminal standard should be set above our precedent's current threshold than to suggest the civil standard should be buried below it.

Retreating to a more modest line of argument, the government emphasizes that this case arises in the immigration context and so implicates matters of foreign relations where the Executive enjoys considerable constitutional authority. But to acknowledge that the President has broad authority to act in this general area supplies no justification for allowing judges to give content to an impermissibly vague law.

Alternatively still, Justice Thomas suggests that, at least at the time of the founding, aliens present in this country may not have been understood as possessing any rights under the Due Process Clause. For support, he points to the Alien Friends Act of 1798. An Act Concerning Aliens §1, 1 Stat. 571; post, at 6–12 (opinion of THOMAS, J.). But the Alien Friends Act—better known as the "Alien" part of the Alien and Sedition Acts—is one of the most notorious laws in our country's history. It was understood as a temporary war measure, not one that the legislature would endorse in a time of tranquility. See, e.g., Fehlings, Storm on the Constitution: The First Deportation Law, 10 Tulsa J. Comp. & Int'l L. 63, 70–71 (2002). Yet even then it was widely condemned as unconstitutional by Madison and many others. It also went unenforced, may have cost the Federalist Party its existence, and lapsed a mere two years after its enactment. With this fuller view, it seems doubtful the Act tells us a great deal about aliens' due process rights at the founding.

Besides, none of this much matters. Whether Madison or his adversaries had the better of the debate over the constitutionality of the Alien Friends Act, Congress is surely free to extend existing forms of liberty to new classes of persons—liberty that the government may then take only after affording due process. And, of course, that's exactly what Congress eventually chose to do here. Decades ago, it enacted a law affording Mr. Dimaya lawful permanent residency in this country, extending to him a statutory liberty interest others traditionally have enjoyed to remain in and move about the country free from physical imprisonment and restraint. See Dimaya v. Lynch, 803 F. 3d 1110, 1111 (CA9 2015); 8 U. S. C. §§1101(20), 1255. No one suggests Congress had to enact statutes of this sort. And exactly what processes must attend the deprivation of a statutorily afforded liberty interest like this may pose serious and debatable questions. Cf. Murray's Lessee, 18 How., at 277 (approving summary procedures in another context). But however summary those procedures might be, it's hard to fathom why fair notice of the law—the most venerable of due process's requirements—would not be among them.

This Court already and long ago held that due process requires affording aliens the "opportunity, at some time, to be heard" before some lawful authority in advance of removal—and it's unclear how that opportunity might be meaningful without fair notice of the law's demands. The Japanese Immigrant Case, 189 U. S. 86, 101 (1903). Nor do the cases Justice Thomas cites hold that a statutory right to lawful permanent residency in this country can be withdrawn without due process. Rather, each merely holds that the particular statutory removal procedures under attack comported with due process.

Today, a plurality of the Court agrees that we should reject the government's plea for a feeble standard of review, but for a different reason. My colleagues suggest the law before us should be assessed under the fair notice standard because of the special gravity of its civil deportation penalty. But, grave as that penalty may be, I cannot see why we would single it out for special treatment when (again) so many civil laws today impose so many similarly severe sanctions. Why, for example, would due process require Congress to speak more clearly when it seeks to deport a lawfully resident alien than when it wishes to subject a citizen to indefinite civil commitment, strip him of a business license essential to his family's living, or confiscate his home? I can think of no good answer.

***

With the fair notice standard now in hand, all that remains is to ask how it applies to the case before us. And here at least the answer comes readily for me: to the extent it requires an "ordinary case" analysis, the portion of the Immigration and Nationality Act before us fails the fair notice test for the reasons Justice Scalia identified in Johnson and the Court recounts today….Johnson held that a law that asks so much of courts while offering them so little by way of guidance is unconstitutionally vague. And I do not see how we might reach a different judgment here.

***

Having said this much, it is important to acknowledge some limits on today's holding too. I have proceeded on the premise that the Immigration and Nationality Act, as it incorporates §16(b) of the criminal code, commands courts to determine the risk of violence attending the ordinary case of conviction for a particular crime. I have done so because no party before us has argued for a different way to read these statutes in combination; because our precedent seemingly requires this approach; and because the government itself has conceded (repeatedly) that the law compels it. Johnson, supra, at ___ (slip op., at

13); Taylor v. United States, 495 U. S. 575, 600 (1990); Brief for Petitioner 11, 30, 32, 36, 40, 47 (conceding that an ordinary case analysis is required). But any more than that I would not venture. In response to the problems engendered by the ordinary case analysis, Justice Thomas suggests that we should overlook the government's concession about the propriety of that approach; reconsider our precedents endorsing it; and read the statute as requiring us to focus on the facts of the alien's crime as committed rather than as the facts appear in the ordinary case of conviction. But normally courts do not rescue parties from their concessions, maybe least of all concessions from a party as able to protect its interests as the federal government. And normally, too, the crucible of adversarial testing is crucial to sound judicial decision making. We rely on it to "yield insights (or reveal pitfalls) we cannot muster guided only by our own lights." Maslenjak v. United States, 582 U. S. ___, ___ (2017) (GORSUCH, J., concurring in part and concurring in judgment) (slip op., at 2).

While sometimes we may or even must forgo the adversarial process, I do not see the case for doing so today. While I remain open to different arguments about our precedent and the proper reading of language like this, I would address them in another case, whether involving the INA or a different statute, where the parties have a chance to be heard and we might benefit from their learning.

It's important to note the narrowness of our decision today in another respect too. Vagueness doctrine represents a procedural, not a substantive, demand. It does not forbid the legislature from acting toward any end it wishes, but only requires it to act with enough clarity that reasonable people can know what is required of them and judges can apply the law consistent with their limited office. Our history surely bears examples of the judicial misuse of the so-called "substantive component" of due process to dictate policy on matters that belonged to the people to decide. But concerns with substantive due process should not lead us to react by withdrawing an ancient procedural protection compelled by the original meaning of the Constitution.

Today's decision sweeps narrowly in yet one more way. By any fair estimate, Congress has largely satisfied the procedural demand of fair notice even in the INA provision before us. The statute lists a number of specific crimes that can lead to a lawful resident's removal—for example, murder, rape, and sexual abuse of a minor. 8 U. S. C. §1101(a)(43)(A). Our ruling today does not touch this list. We address only the statute's "residual clause" where Congress ended its own list and asked us to begin writing our own. Just as Blackstone's legislature passed a revised statute clarifying that "cattle" covers bulls and oxen, Congress remains free at any time to add more crimes to its list. It remains free, as well, to write a new residual clause that affords the fair notice lacking here. Congress might, for example, say that a conviction for any felony carrying a prison sentence of a specified length opens an alien to removal. Congress has done almost exactly this in other laws. See, e.g., 18 U. S. C. §922(g). What was done there could be done here.

But those laws are not this law. And while the statute before us doesn't rise to the level of threatening death for "pretended offences" of treason, no one should be surprised that the Constitution looks unkindly on any law so vague that reasonable people cannot understand its terms and judges do not know where to begin in applying it. A government of laws and not of men can never tolerate that arbitrary power. And, in my judgment, that foundational principle dictates today's result. Because I understand them to be consistent with what I have said here, I join Parts I, III, IV–B, and V of the Court's opinion and concur in the judgment.

CHIEF JUSTICE ROBERTS, with whom JUSTICE KENNEDY, JUSTICE THOMAS, and JUSTICE ALITO join, dissenting.

In Johnson v. United States, we concluded that the residual clause of the Armed Career Criminal Act was unconstitutionally vague, given the "indeterminacy of the wide-ranging inquiry" it required. Today, the Court relies wholly on Johnson—but only some of Johnson—to strike down another provision, 18 U. S. C. §16(b). Because §16(b) does not give rise to the concerns that drove the Court's decision in Johnson, I respectfully dissent.

I

The parties begin by disputing whether a criminal or more relaxed civil vagueness standard should apply in resolving Dimaya's challenge….I see no need to resolve which standard applies, because I would hold that §16(b) is not unconstitutionally vague even under the standard applicable to criminal laws.

II

This is not our first encounter with §16(b). In Leocal v. Ashcroft, 543 U. S. 1 (2004), we were asked to decide whether either subsection of §16 covers a particular category of state crimes, specifically DUI offenses involving no more than negligent conduct. 543 U. S., at 6. Far from finding §16(b) "hopeless[ly] indetermina[te]," we considered the provision clear and unremarkable: "while §16(b) is broader than §16(a) in the sense that physical force need not actually be applied," the provision "simply covers offenses that naturally involve a person acting in disregard of the risk that physical force might be used against another in committing an offense," Leocal, 543 U. S., at 10–11. Applying that standard to the state offense at issue, we concluded— unanimously—that §16(b) "cannot be read to include [a]conviction for DUI causing serious bodily injury under Florida law." Id., at 11.

Leocal thus provides a model for how courts should assess whether a particular crime "by its nature" involves a risk of the use of physical force. At the outset, our opinion set forth the elements of the Florida DUI statute, which made it a felony "for a person to operate a vehicle while under the influence and, 'by reason of such operation, caus[e] . . . [s]erious bodily injury to another.'"

Our §16(b) analysis, in turn, focused on those specific elements in concluding that a Florida offender's acts would not naturally give rise to the requisite risk of force "in the course of committing the offense."

Appendix C.   Sessions v. Dimaya

The Court holds that the same provision we had no trouble applying in Leocal is in fact incapable of reasoned application. The sole justification for this turnabout is the resemblance between the language of §16(b) and the language of the residual clause of the Armed Career Criminal Act (ACCA) that was at issue in Johnson.

Section 16(b) does not present the same ambiguities. The two provisions do correspond to some extent....But the Court too readily dismisses the significant textual distinctions between §16(b) and the ACCA residual clause.

To begin, §16(b) yields far less uncertainty "about how to estimate the risk posed by a crime." Johnson, 576 U. S., at ___ (slip op., at 5). There are three material differences between §16(b) and the ACCA residual clause in this respect. First, the ACCA clause directed the reader to consider whether the offender's conduct presented a "potential risk" of injury....Section 16(b), on the other hand, asks about "risk" alone, a familiar concept of everyday life. It therefore calls for a commonsense inquiry that does not compel a court to venture beyond the offense elements to consider contingent and remote possibilities.

Second, §16(b) focuses exclusively on the risk that the offender will "use[]" "physical force" "against" another person or another person's property. Thus, unlike the ACCA residual clause, "§16(b) plainly does not encompass all offenses which create a 'substantial risk' that injury will result from a person's conduct

Third, §16(b) has a temporal limit that the ACCA residual clause lacked: The "substantial risk" of force must arise "in the course of committing the offense."

Those three distinctions—the unadorned reference to "risk," the focus on the offender's own active employment of force, and the "in the course of committing" limitation—also mean that many hard cases under ACCA are easier under §16(b). Take the firearm possession crime from Johnson itself, which had as its constituent elements (1) unlawfully (2) possessing (3) a short-barreled shotgun. None of those elements, "by its nature," carries "a substantial risk" that the possessor will use force against another "in the course of committing the offense." Nothing inherent in the act of firearm possession, even when it is unlawful, gives rise to a substantial risk that the owner will then shoot someone. See United States v. Serafin, 562 F. 3d 1105, 1113 (CA10 2009) (recognizing that "Leocal instructs [a court] to focus not on whether possession willlikely result in violence, but instead whether one possessing an unregistered weapon necessarily risks the needto employ force to commit possession"). Yet short-barreled shotgun possession presented a closer question under the ACCA residual clause, because the "serious potential risk" language seemingly directed us to consider "the circumstances and conduct that ordinarily attend theoffense," in addition to the offense itself. Johnson, 576

U. S., at ___ (ALITO, J., dissenting) (slip op., at 17); see id., at ___–___ (slip op., at 19–20) (reasoning that the crimemust qualify because "a person who chooses to break the law and risk the heavy criminal penalty incurred by possessing a notoriously dangerous weapon is [likely] to use that weapon in violent ways").

The enumerated offenses, and our Court's failed attempts to make sense of them, were essential to Johnson's conclusion that the residual clause "leaves uncertainty about how much risk it takes for a crime to qualify as a violent felony." As Johnson explained, the issue was not that the statute employed a fuzzy standard. That kind of thing appears in the statute books all the time. In the majority's retelling today, the difficulty inhered solely in the fact that the statute paired such a standard withthe ordinary case inquiry. But that account sidesteps much of Johnson's reasoning. Our opinion emphasized that the word "otherwise" "force[d]" courts to interpret the amorphous standard "in light of" the four enumerated crimes, which are "not much more similar to one another in kind than in degree of risk posed."

III

The more constrained inquiry required under §16(b)—which asks only whether the offense elements naturally carry with them a risk that the offender will use force in committing the offense—does not itself engender "grave uncertainty about how to estimate the risk posed by a crime." And the provision's use of a commonplace substantial risk standard—one not tied to a list of crimes that lack a unifying feature—does not give rise to intolerable "uncertainty about how much risk it takes for a crime to qualify." That should be enough to reject Dimaya's facial vagueness challenge. I would adhere to that careful holding and not reflexively extend the decision to a different statute whose reach is, on the whole, far more clear.

The Court does the opposite, and the ramifications of that decision are significant. First, of course, today's holding invalidates a provision of the Immigration and Nationality Act—part of the definition of "aggravated felony"—on which the Government relies to "ensure that dangerous criminal aliens are removed from the United States." Brief for United States 54. Contrary to the Court's back-of-the-envelope assessment, the Government explains that the definition is "critical" for "numerous" immigration provisions. Brief for United States 12.

In addition, §16 serves as the universal definition of "crime of violence" for all of Title 18 of the United States Code. Its language is incorporated into many procedural and substantive provisions of criminal law, including provisions concerning racketeering, money laundering, domestic violence, using a child to commit a violent crime, and distributing information about the making or use of explosives. See 18 U. S. C. §§25(a)(1), 842(p)(2), 1952(a),1956(c)(7)(B)(ii), 1959(a)(4), 2261(a), 3561(b). Of special concern, §16 is replicated in the definition of "crime of violence" applicable to §924(c), which prohibits using or carrying a firearm "during and in relation to any crime of violence," or possessing a firearm "in furtherance of any such crime." §§924(c)(1)(A), (c)(3). Though I express no view on whether §924(c) can be distinguished from the provision we consider here, the Court's holding calls into question convictions under what the Government warns us is an "oft-prosecuted offense." Brief for United States 12.

Because Johnson does not compel today's result, I respectfully dissent.

JUSTICE THOMAS, with whom JUSTICE KENNEDY and JUSTICE ALITO join as to Parts I–C–2, II–A–1, and II–B, dissenting.

I agree with THE CHIEF JUSTICE that 18 U. S. C. §16(b), as incorporated by the Immigration and Nationality Act(INA), is not unconstitutionally vague. Section 16(b) lacks many of the features that caused this Court to invalidate the residual clause of the Armed Career Criminal Act (ACCA) in Johnson v. United States, 576 U. S. ___ (2015). ACCA's residual clause—a provision that this Court had applied four times before Johnson—was not unconstitutionally vague either. But if the Court insists on adhering to Johnson, it should at least take Johnson at its word that the residual clause was vague due to the "'sum'" of its specific features. By ignoring this limitation, the Court jettisons Johnson's assurance that its holding would not jeopardize "dozens of federal and state criminal laws."

While THE CHIEF JUSTICE persuasively explains why respondent cannot prevail under our precedents, I write separately to make two additional points. First, I continue to doubt that our practice of striking down statutes as unconstitutionally vague is consistent with the original meaning of the Due Process Clause. Second, if the Court thinks that §16(b) is unconstitutionally vague because of the "categorical approach," then the Court should abandon that approach—not insist on reading it into statutes and then strike them down. Accordingly, I respectfully dissent.

I

I continue to harbor doubts about whether the vagueness doctrine can be squared with the original meaning of the Due Process Clause—and those doubts are only amplified in the removal context. I am also skeptical that the vagueness doctrine can be justified as a way to prevent delegations of core legislative power in this context. But I need not resolve these questions because, if the vagueness doctrine has any basis in the Due Process Clause, it must be limited to cases in which the statute is unconstitutionally vague as applied to the person challenging it. That is not the case for respondent, whose prior convictions for first-degree residential burglary in California fall comfortably within the scope of §16(b).

A

The Fifth Amendment's Due Process Clause provides that no person shall be "deprived of life, liberty, or property, without due process of law." Section 16(b), as incorporated by the INA, cannot violate this Clause unless the following propositions are true: The Due Process Clause requires federal statutes to provide certain minimal procedures, the vagueness doctrine is one of those procedures, and the vagueness doctrine applies to statutes governing the removal of aliens. Although I need not resolve any of these propositions today, each one is questionable. I will address them in turn.

1

First, the vagueness doctrine is not legitimate unless the "law of the land" view of due process is incorrect. Under that view, due process "require[s] only that our Government . . . proceed . . . according to written constitutional and statutory provision[s] before depriving someone of life, liberty, or property." Nelson v. Colorado, 581 U. S. ___, ___, n. 1 (2017) (Thomas, J. dissenting) (slip op., at 2, n. 1) (internal quotation marks omitted). More than a half century after the founding, the Court rejected this view of due process in Murray's Lessee v. Hoboken Land & Improvement Co., 18 How. 272 (1856). But the textual and historical support for the law-of-the-land view is not insubstantial.

2

Even under Murray's Lessee, the vagueness doctrine is legitimate only if it is a "settled usag[e] and mod[e] of proceeding existing in the common and statute law of England, before the emigration of our ancestors." Id., at 277. That proposition is dubious. Until the end of the 19th century, "there is little indication that anyone . . . believed that courts had the power under the Due Process Claus[e] to nullify statutes on [vagueness] ground[s]." Johnson, supra, at ___ (opinion of Thomas, J.) (slip op., at 11). That is not because Americans were unfamiliar with vague laws. Rather, early American courts, like their English predecessors, addressed vague laws through statutory construction instead of constitutional law. They invoked the rule of lenity and declined to apply vague penal statutes on a case-by-case basis. The modern vagueness doctrine, which claims the judicial authority to "strike down" vague legislation on its face, did not emerge until the turn of the 20th century.

The difference between the traditional rule of lenity and the modern vagueness doctrine is not merely semantic. Most obviously, lenity is a tool of statutory construction, which means States can abrogate it—and many have.

Tellingly, the modern vagueness doctrine emerged at a time when this Court was actively interpreting the Due Process Clause to strike down democratically enacted laws—first in the name of the "liberty of contract," then in the name of the "right to privacy." That the vagueness doctrine "develop[ed] on the federal level concurrently with the growth of the tool of substantive due process" does not seem like a coincidence.

This Court also has a bad habit of invoking the Due Process Clause to constitutionalize rules that were traditionally left to the democratic process. If vagueness is another example of this practice, then that is all the more reason to doubt its legitimacy.

3

Even assuming the Due Process Clause prohibits vague laws, this prohibition might not apply to laws governing the removal of aliens. The Founders were familiar with English law, where "'the only question that ha[d] ever been made in regard to the power to expel aliens [was] whether it could be exercised by the King without the consent of Parliament.'" Demore v. Kim, 538 U. S. 510, 538 (2003) (O'Connor, J., concurring in part and concurring in judgment) (quoting Fong Yue Ting v. United States, 149 U. S. 698, 709 (1893)). And, in this country, the notion that the Due Process Clause governed the removal of aliens was not announced until the 20th century.

Less than a decade after the ratification of the Bill of Rights, the founding generation had an extensive debate about the relationship between the Constitution and federal removal statutes. In 1798, the Fifth Congress enacted the Alien Acts. One of those Acts, the Alien Friends Act, gave the President unfettered discretion to expel any aliens "he shall judge dangerous to the peace and safety of the United States, or shall have reasonable grounds to suspect are concerned in any treasonable or secret machinations against the government thereof."

The Jeffersonian Democratic-Republicans, who viewed the Alien Friends Act as a threat to their party and the institution of slavery, raised a number of constitutional objections. Some of the Jeffersonians argued that the Alien Friends Act violated the Fifth Amendment's Due Process Clause.

The Federalists gave two primary responses to this due process argument. First, the Federalists argued that the rights of aliens were governed by the law of nations, not the Constitution. The law of nations imposed no enforceable limits on a nation's power to remove aliens.

Second, the Federalists responded that the expulsion of aliens "did not touch life, liberty, or property." The founding generation understood the phrase "life, liberty, or property" to refer to a relatively narrow set of core private rights that did not depend on the will of the government. Quasi-private rights—"privileges" or "franchises" bestowed by the government on individuals—did not qualify and could be taken away without judicial process. Removing a resident alien from the country did not affect "life, liberty, or property," the Federalists argued, until the alien became a naturalized citizen.

After the Alien Friends Act lapsed in 1800, Congress did not enact another removal statute for nearly a century. The States enacted their own removal statutes during this period, see G. Neuman, Strangers to the Constitution 19–43 (1996), and I am aware of no decision questioning the legality of these statutes under State due-process or law of-the-land provisions. Beginning in the late 19th century, the Federal Government reinserted itself into the regulation of immigration. When this Court was presented with constitutional challenges to Congress' removal laws, it initially rejected them for many of the same reasons that Marshall and the Federalists had cited in defense of the Alien Friends Act. Although the Court rejected the Federalists' argument that resident aliens do not enjoy constitutional rights, see Wong Wing v. United States, 163 U. S. 228, 238 (1896), it agreed that civil deportation statutes do not implicate "life, liberty, or property," see, e.g., Harisiades v. Shaughnessy, 342 U. S. 580, 584–585 (1952) ("[T]hat admission for permanent residence confers a 'vested right' on the alien [is] not founded in precedents of this Court"); United States ex rel. Turner v. Williams, 194 U. S. 279,

290 (1904) ("[T]he deportation of an alien who is found to be here in violation of law is not a deprivation of liberty without due process of law"); Fong Yue Ting, 149 U. S., at 730 ("[Deportation] is but a method of enforcing the return to his own country of an alien who has not complied with[statutory] conditions . . . . He has not, therefore, been deprived of life, liberty, or property without due process of law"); id., at 713–715 (similar). Consistent with this understanding, "federal immigration laws from 1891 until 1952 made no express provision for judicial review." Demore, 538 U. S., at 538 (opinion of O'Connor, J.).

It was not until the 20th century that this Court held that nonpenal removal statutes could violate the Due Process Clause. See Wong Yang Sung v. McGrath, 339 U. S. 33, 49 (1950). That ruling opened the door for the Court to apply the then-nascent vagueness doctrine to immigration statutes. But the Court upheld vague standards in immigration laws that it likely would not have tolerated in criminal statutes. See, e.g., Boutilier v. INS, 387 U. S. 118, 122 (1967) ("'psychopathic personality'"); Jordan v. De George, 341 U. S. 223, 232 (1951) ("'crime involving moral turpitude'"); cf. Mahler, supra, at 40 ("'undesirable residents'"). Until today, this Court has never held that an immigration statute is unconstitutionally vague.

I agree that the Constitution prohibits Congress from delegating core legislative power to another branch. But I locate that principle in the Vesting Clauses of Articles I, II, and III—not in the Due Process Clause. In my view, impermissible delegations of legislative power violate this principle, not just delegations that deprive individuals of "life, liberty, or property," Amdt. 5.

Respondent does not argue that §16(b), as incorporated by the INA, is an impermissible delegation of power. See Brief for Respondent 50 (stating that "there is no delegation question" in this case). I would not reach that question here, because this case can be resolved on narrower grounds. See Part I–C, infra. But at first blush, it is not at all obvious that the nondelegation doctrine would justify wholesale invalidation of §16(b).

If §16(b) delegates power in this context, it delegates power primarily to the Executive Branch entities that administer the INA—namely, the Attorney General, immigration judges, and the Board of Immigration Appeals (BIA). But Congress does not "delegate" when it merely authorizes the Executive Branch to exercise a power that it already has. And there is some founding-era evidence that "the executive Power," Art. II, §1, includes the power to deport aliens.

Blackstone—one of the political philosophers whose writings on executive power were "most familiar to the Framers," Prakash & Ramsey, The Executive Power OverForeign Affairs, 111 Yale L. J. 231, 253 (2001)—described the power to deport aliens as executive and located it with the King. Alien friends, Blackstone explained, are "liable to be sent home whenever the king sees occasion." Commentaries on the Laws of England 252 (1765). When our Constitution was ratified, moreover, "[e]minent English judges, sitting in the Judicial Committee of the Privy Council, ha[d] gone very far in supporting the . . . expulsion, by the executive authority of a colony, of aliens." Demore, 538 U. S., at 538 (opinion of O'Connor, J.) (quoting Fong Yue Ting, 149 U. S., at 709). Some of the Federalists defending the Alien Friends Act similarly argued that the President had the power to remove aliens. More recently, this Court recognized that "[r]emoval decisions" implicate "our customary policy of deference to the President in matters of foreign affairs" because they touch on "our relations with foreign powers and require consideration of changing political and economic circumstances." Jama v. Immigration and Customs Enforcement, 543 U. S. 335, 348 (2005) (internal quotation marks omitted). Taken together, this evidence makes it difficult to confidently conclude that the INA, through §16(b), delegates core legislative power to the Executive.

Instead of the Executive, perhaps §16(b) impermissibly delegates power to the Judiciary, since the Courts of Appeals often review the BIA's application of §16(b). I assume that, at some point, a statute could be so devoid of content that a court tasked with interpreting it "would simply be making up a law—that is, exercising legislative power." Lawson, Delegation and Original Meaning, 88 Va. L. Rev. 327, 339 (2002); see id., at 339–340 (providing examples such as a gibberish-filled statute or a statute that requires "'goodness and niceness'"). But I am not confident that our modern vagueness doctrine—which focuses on whether regulations of individual conduct provide "fair warning," are "clearly defined," and do not encourage "arbitrary and discriminatory enforcement," Grayned, 408 U. S., at 108; Kolender, 461 U. S., at 357— accurately demarcates the line between legislative and judicial power. The Founders understood that the interpretation of legal texts, even vague ones, remained an exercise of core judicial power.

C

1

I need not resolve these historical questions today, as this case can be decided on narrower grounds. If the vagueness doctrine has any basis in the original meaning of the Due Process Clause, it must be limited to case-by case challenges to particular applications of a statute. That is what early American courts did when they applied the rule of lenity. See id., at ___ (slip op., at 10). And that is how early American courts addressed constitutional challenges to statutes more generally.

In my view, §16(b) is not vague as applied to respondent. When respondent committed his burglaries in 2007and 2009, he was "sufficiently forewarned . . . that the statutory consequence . . . is deportation." De George, 341 U. S., at 232. At the time, courts had "unanimous[ly]" concluded that residential burglary is a crime of violence, and not "a single opinion . . . ha[d] held that [it] is not." United States v. M. C. E., 232 F. 3d 1252, 1255–1256 (CA9 2000)....In Leocal v. Ashcroft, 543 U. S. 1 (2004), this Court unanimously agreed that burglary is the "classic example" of a crime of violence under §16(b), because it "involves a substantial risk that the burglar will use force against a victim in completing the crime." That same risk is present with respect to respondent's statute of conviction—first-degree residential burglary, Cal. Penal Code Ann. §§459, 460(a) (West 1999).

Drawing on Johnson and the decision below, the Court suggests that residential burglary might not be a crime of violence because "'only about seven percent of burglaries actually involve violence.'" But this statistic—which measures actual violence against a member of the household, see id., at 1, 12—is woefully under-inclusive. It excludes other potential victims besides household members—for example, "a police officer, or a bystande[r] who comes to investigate," James, supra, at 203. And §16(b) requires only a risk of physical force, no tactual physical force, and that risk would seem to be present whenever someone is home during the burglary. Further, Johnson is not conclusive because, unlike ACCA's residual clause, §16(b) covers offenses that involve a substantial risk of physical force "against the person or property of another." (Emphasis added.) Surely the ordinary case of residential burglary involves at least one of these risks. According to the statistics referenced by the Court, most burglaries involve either a forcible entry (e.g., breaking a window or slashing a door screen), an attempted forcible entry, or an unlawful entry when someone is home. See Bureau of Justice Statistics, supra, at 2 (Table 1). Thus, under any metric, respondent's convictions for first-degree residential burglary are crimes of violence under §16(b).

3

Finally, if facial vagueness challenges are ever appropriate, I adhere to my view that a law is not facially vague "'[i]f any fool would know that a particular category of conduct would be within the reach of the statute, if there is an unmistakable core that a reasonable person would know is forbidden by the law.'" Morales, 527 U. S., at 112 (THOMAS, J., dissenting) (quoting Kolender, 461 U. S., at 370–371 (White, J., dissenting)). The residual clause of ACCA had such a core. And §16(b) has an even wider core, as the Chief Justice explains. Thus, the Court should not have invalidated §16(b), either on its face or as applied to respondent.

II

Even taking the vagueness doctrine and Johnson at face value, I disagree with the Court's decision to invalidate §16(b). The sole reason that the Court deems §16(b) unconstitutionally vague is because it reads the statute as incorporating the categorical approach—specifically, the "ordinary case" approach from ACCA's residual clause. Although the Court mentions "[t]wo features" of §16(b) that make it vague—the ordinary-case approach and an imprecise risk standard—the Court admits that the second feature is problematic only in combination with the first. Ante, at 8. Without the ordinary-case approach, the Court "do[es] not doubt" the constitutionality of §16(b). Ante, at 10. But if the categorical approach renders §16(b) unconstitutionally vague, then constitutional avoidance requires us to make a reasonable effort to avoid that interpretation. And a reasonable alternative interpretation is available: Instead of asking whether the ordinary case of an alien's offense presents a substantial risk of physical force, courts should ask whether the alien's actual underlying conduct presents a substantial risk of physical force. I will briefly discuss the origins of the categorical approach and then explain why the Court should abandon it for §16(b).

A
1

The categorical approach originated with Justice Blackmun's opinion for the Court in Taylor v. United States, 495 U. S. 575 (1990). Taylor gave a few reasons why the categorical approach was the correct reading of ACCA, but the "heart of the decision" was the Court's concern with limiting the amount of evidence that the parties could introduce at sentencing. Shepard v. United States, 544 U. S. 13, 23 (2005). Specifically, the Court was worried about potential violations of the Sixth Amendment. If the parties could introduce evidence about the defendant's underlying conduct, then sentencing proceedings might devolve into a full-blown minitrial, with factfinding by the judge instead of the jury.

2

I disagreed with the Court's decision to extend the categorical approach to ACCA's residual clause. See James, 550 U. S., at 231–232 (dissenting opinion). The categorical approach was an "'unnecessary exercise,'" I explained, because it created the same Sixth Amendment problem that it tried to avoid. Id., at 231. Absent waiver, a defendant has the right to have a jury find "every fact that is by law a basis for imposing or increasing punishment," including the fact of a prior conviction. In my view, if the Government wants to enhance a defendant's sentence based on his prior convictions, it must put those convictions in the indictment and prove them to a jury beyond a reasonable doubt.

B

My objection aside, the ordinary-case approach soon created problems of its own. The Court's attempt to avoid the Scylla of the Sixth Amendment steered it straight into the Charybdis of the Fifth. The ordinary-case approach that was created to honor the individual right to a jury is now, according to the Court, so vague that it deprives individuals of due process. I see no good reason for the Court to persist in reading the ordinary-case approach into §16(b). The text of §16(b)does not mandate the ordinary-case approach, the concerns that led this Court to adopt it do not apply here, and there are no prudential reasons for retaining it. In my view, we should abandon the categorical approach for §16(b).

At first glance, §16(b) is not clear about the precise question it poses. On the one hand, the statute might refer to the metaphysical "nature" of the offense and ask whether it ordinarily involves a substantial risk of physical force. On the other hand, the statute might refer to the underlying facts of the offense that the offender committed; the words "by its nature," "substantial risk," and "may" would mean only that an offender who engages in risky conduct cannot benefit from the fortuitous fact that physical force was not actually used during his offense.

Although both interpretations are linguistically possible, several factors indicate that the underlying-conduct approach is the better one. To begin, §16(b) asks whether an offense "involves" a substantial risk of force. The word "involves" suggests that the offense must necessarily include a substantial risk of force. That condition is always satisfied if the Government must prove that the alien's underlying conduct involves a substantial risk of force, but it is not always satisfied if the Government need only prove that the "ordinary case" involves such a risk. Tellingly, the other aggravated felonies in the INA that use the word "involves" employ the underlying-conduct approach. See 8 U. S. C. §1101(a)(43)(M)(i) ("an offense that involves fraud or deceit in which the loss to the victim or victims exceeds $10,000"); §1101(h)(3) ("any crime of reckless driving or of driving while intoxicated or under the influence of alcohol or of prohibited substances if such crime involves personal injury to another"). As do the similarly worded provisions of the Comprehensive Crime Control Act of 1984, the bill that contained §16(b).

A comparison of §16(b) and §16(a) further highlights why the former likely adopts an underlying-conduct approach. Section 16(a) covers offenses that have the use, attempted use, or threatened use of physical force "as an element." Because §16(b) covers "other" offenses and is separated from §16(a) by the disjunctive word "or," the natural inference is that §16(b) asks a different question.

In other words, §16(b) must require immigration judges to look beyond the elements of an offense to determine whether it involves a substantial risk of physical force. But if the elements are insufficient, where else should immigration judges look to determine the riskiness of an offense? Two options are possible, only one of which is workable.

The first option is to consult the underlying facts of the alien's crime and then assess its riskiness. This approach would provide a definitive answer in every case. Nothing suggests that Congress imposed a more limited inquiry when it enacted §16(b) in 1984. At the time, Congress had not yet enacted ACCA's residual clause, this Court had not yet created the categorical approach, and this Court had not yet recognized a Sixth Amendment limit on judicial factfinding at sentencing.

The second option is to imagine the "ordinary case" of the alien's crime and then assess the riskiness of that hypothetical offense. But the phrase "ordinary case" does not appear in the statute. And imagining the ordinary case, the Court reminds us, is "hopeless[ly] indetermina[te]," "wholly 'speculative,'" and mere "guesswork." Because courts disfavor interpretations that make a statute impossible to apply, see A. Scalia & B. Garner, Reading Law 63 (2012), this Court should reject the ordinary-case approach for §16(b) and adopt the underlying-facts approach instead.

2

That the categorical approach is not the better reading of §16(b) should not be surprising, since the categorical approach was never really about the best reading of the text. As explained, this Court adopted that approach to avoid a potential Sixth Amendment problem with sentencing judges conducting mini-trials to determine a defendant's past conduct. But even assuming the categorical approach solved this Sixth Amendment problem in criminal cases, no such problem arises in immigration cases."[T]he provisions of the Constitution securing the right of trial by jury have no application" in a removal proceeding. Turner, 194 U. S., at 290. And, in criminal cases, the underlying-conduct approach would be perfectly constitutional if the Government included the defendant's prior conduct in the indictment, tried it to a jury, and proved it beyond a reasonable doubt. See Johnson, 576 U. S., at ___ (ALITO, J., dissenting) (slip op., at 12). Nothing in §16(b) prohibits the Government from proceeding this way, so the plurality is wrong to suggest that the underlying-conduct approach would necessarily "ping-pong us from one constitutional issue to another." Ante, at 14. If constitutional avoidance applies here at all, it requires us to reject the categorical approach for §16(b). According to the Court, the categorical approach is unconstitutionally vague. And, all agree that the underlying-conduct approach would not be. Thus, if the underlying-conduct approach is a "reasonabl[e]" interpretation of §16(b), it is our "plain duty" to adopt it. United States ex rel. Attorney General v. Delaware & Hudson Co., 213 U. S. 366, 407 (1909). And it is reasonable, as explained above.

In Johnson, the Court declined to adopt the underlying-conduct approach for ACCA's residual clause. The Court concluded that the categorical approach was the only reasonable reading of ACCA because the residual clause uses the word "convictions." The Court also stressed the "utter impracticability of requiring a sentencing court to reconstruct, long after the original conviction, the conduct underlying that conviction."

Neither of these arguments is persuasive with respect to the INA. Moreover, this Court has already rejected them. In Nijhawan, this Court unanimously concluded that one of the aggravated felonies in the INA—"an offense that . . . involves fraud or deceit in which the loss to the victim or victims exceeds $10,000," §1101(a)(43)(M)(i)—applies the underlying-conduct approach, not the categorical approach. 557 U. S., at 32. Although the INA also refers to "convict[ions]," §1227(a)(2)(A)(iii), the Court was not swayed by that argument. The word "convict[ion]" means only that the defendant's underlying conduct must "'be tied to the specific counts covered by the conviction,'" not "acquitted or dismissed counts or general conduct."

As for the supposed practical problems with proving an alien's prior conduct, the Court did not find that argument persuasive either. "[T]he 'sole purpose' of the 'aggravated felony' inquiry," the Court explained, "'is to ascertain the nature of a prior conviction; it is not an invitation to relitigate the conviction itself.'" Ibid. And because the INA places the burden on the Government to prove an alien's conduct by clear and convincing evidence, §1229a(c)(3)(A), "uncertainties caused by the passage of time are likely to count in the alien's favor," id., at 42.

There are additional reasons why the practical problems identified in Johnson should not matter for §16(b)—even assuming they should have mattered for ACCA's residual clause. In a removal proceeding, any difficulties with identifying an alien's past conduct will fall on immigration judges, not federal courts. But those judges are already accustomed to finding facts about the conduct underlying an alien's prior convictions, since some of the INA's aggravated felonies employ the underlying-conduct approach. The BIA has instructed immigration judges to determine such conduct based on "any evidence admissible in removal proceedings," not just the elements of the offense or the record of conviction. See Matter of Babaisakov, 24 I. & N. Dec. 306, 307 (2007).

In short, we should not blithely assume that the reasons why this Court adopted the categorical approach for ACCA's residual clause also apply to the INA's list of aggravated felonies.

3

I see no prudential reason for maintaining the categorical approach for §16(b).

Nor should stare decisis prevent us from rejecting the categorical approach for §16(b). This Court has never held that §16(b) incorporates the ordinary-case approach. Although Leocal held that §16(b) incorporates a version of the categorical approach, the Court must not feel bound by that decision, as it largely overrules it today. . . . Instead of adhering to an interpretation that it thinks unconstitutional and then using that interpretation to strike down another statute, the Court should have taken this opportunity to abandon the categorical approach for §16(b) once and for all.

* * *

The Court's decision today is triply flawed. It unnecessarily extends our incorrect decision in Johnson. It uses a constitutional doctrine with dubious origins to invalidate yet another statute (while calling into question countless more). And it does all this in the name of a statutory interpretation that we should have discarded long ago. Because I cannot follow the Court down any of these rabbit holes, I respectfully dissent.

ENFORCEMENT-RELATED EXECUTIVE ORDERS

Executive Order: Border Security and Immigration Enforcement Improvements

Issued on: January 25, 2017

By the authority vested in me as President by the Constitution and the laws of the United States of America, including the Immigration and Nationality Act (8 U.S.C. 1101 et seq.) (INA), the Secure Fence Act of 2006 (Public Law 109-367) (Secure Fence Act), and the Illegal Immigration Reform and Immigrant Responsibility Act of 1996 (Public Law 104-208 Div. C) (IIRIRA), and in order to ensure the safety and territorial integrity of the United States as well as to ensure that the Nation's immigration laws are faithfully executed, I hereby order as follows:

Sec. 1. Purpose. Border security is critically important to the national security of the United States. Aliens who illegally enter the United States without inspection or admission present a significant threat to national security and public safety. Such aliens have not been identified or inspected by Federal immigration officers to determine their admissibility to the United States. The recent surge of illegal immigration at the southern border with Mexico has placed a significant strain on Federal resources and overwhelmed agencies charged with border security and immigration enforcement, as well as the local communities into which many of the aliens are placed.

Transnational criminal organizations operate sophisticated drug- and human-trafficking networks and smuggling operations on both sides of the southern border, contributing to a significant increase in violent crime and United States deaths from dangerous drugs. Among those who illegally enter are those who seek to harm Americans through acts of terror or criminal conduct. Continued illegal immigration presents a clear and present danger to the interests of the United States.

Federal immigration law both imposes the responsibility and provides the means for the Federal Government, in cooperation with border States, to secure the Nation's southern border. Although Federal immigration law provides a robust framework for Federal-State partnership in enforcing our immigration laws – and the Congress has authorized and provided appropriations to secure our borders – the Federal Government has failed to discharge this basic sovereign responsibility.

The purpose of this order is to direct executive departments and agencies (agencies) to deploy all lawful means to secure the Nation's southern border, to prevent further illegal immigration into the United States, and to repatriate illegal aliens swiftly, consistently, and humanely.

Sec. 2. Policy. It is the policy of the executive branch to:

(a) secure the southern border of the United States through the immediate construction of a physical wall on the southern border, monitored and supported by adequate personnel so as to prevent illegal immigration, drug and human trafficking, and acts of terrorism;

(b) detain individuals apprehended on suspicion of violating Federal or State law, including Federal immigration law, pending further proceedings regarding those violations;

(c) expedite determinations of apprehended individuals' claims of eligibility to remain in the United States;

(d) remove promptly those individuals whose legal claims to remain in the United States have been lawfully rejected, after any appropriate civil or criminal sanctions have been imposed;

(e) cooperate fully with States and local law enforcement in enacting Federal-State partnerships to enforce Federal immigration priorities, as well as State monitoring and detention programs that are consistent with Federal law and do not undermine Federal immigration priorities.

Sec. 3. Definitions. (a) "Asylum officer" has the meaning given the term in section 235(b)(1)(E) of the INA (8 U.S.C. 1225(b)(1)).

(b) "Southern border" shall mean the contiguous land border between the United States and Mexico, including all points of entry.

(c) "Border States" shall mean the States of the United States immediately adjacent to the contiguous land border between the United States and Mexico.

(d) Except as otherwise noted, "the Secretary" shall refer to the Secretary of Homeland Security.

(e) "Wall" shall mean a contiguous, physical wall or other similarly secure, contiguous, and impassable physical barrier.

(f) "Executive department" shall have the meaning given in section 101 of title 5, United States Code.

(g) "Regulations" shall mean any and all Federal rules, regulations, and directives lawfully promulgated by agencies.

(h) "Operational control" shall mean the prevention of all unlawful entries into the United States, including entries by terrorists, other unlawful aliens, instruments of terrorism, narcotics, and other contraband.

Sec. 4. Physical Security of the Southern Border of the United States. The Secretary shall immediately take the following steps to obtain complete operational control, as determined by the Secretary, of the southern border:

(a) In accordance with existing law, including the Secure Fence Act and IIRIRA, take all appropriate steps to immediately plan, design, and construct a

238

physical wall along the southern border, using appropriate materials and technology to most effectively achieve complete operational control of the southern border;

(b) Identify and, to the extent permitted by law, allocate all sources of Federal funds for the planning, designing, and constructing of a physical wall along the southern border;

(c) Project and develop long-term funding requirements for the wall, including preparing Congressional budget requests for the current and upcoming fiscal years; and

(d) Produce a comprehensive study of the security of the southern border, to be completed within 180 days of this order, that shall include the current state of southern border security, all geophysical and topographical aspects of the southern border, the availability of Federal and State resources necessary to achieve complete operational control of the southern border, and a strategy to obtain and maintain complete operational control of the southern border.

Sec. 5. Detention Facilities. (a) The Secretary shall take all appropriate action and allocate all legally available resources to immediately construct, operate, control, or establish contracts to construct, operate, or control facilities to detain aliens at or near the land border with Mexico.

(b) The Secretary shall take all appropriate action and allocate all legally available resources to immediately assign asylum officers to immigration detention facilities for the purpose of accepting asylum referrals and conducting credible fear determinations pursuant to section 235(b)(1) of the INA (8 U.S.C. 1225(b)(1)) and applicable regulations and reasonable fear determinations pursuant to applicable regulations.

(c) The Attorney General shall take all appropriate action and allocate all legally available resources to immediately assign immigration judges to immigration detention facilities operated or controlled by the Secretary, or operated or controlled pursuant to contract by the Secretary, for the purpose of conducting proceedings authorized under title 8, chapter 12, subchapter II, United States Code.

Sec. 6. Detention for Illegal Entry. The Secretary shall immediately take all appropriate actions to ensure the detention of aliens apprehended for violations of immigration law pending the outcome of their removal proceedings or their removal from the country to the extent permitted by law. The Secretary shall issue new policy guidance to all Department of Homeland Security personnel regarding the appropriate and consistent use of lawful detention authority under the INA, including the termination of the practice commonly known as "catch and release," whereby aliens are routinely released in the United States shortly after their apprehension for violations of immigration law.

Sec. 7. Return to Territory. The Secretary shall take appropriate action, consistent with the requirements of section 1232 of title 8, United States Code, to ensure that aliens described in section 235(b)(2)(C) of the INA (8 U.S.C. 1225(b)(2)(C)) are returned to the territory from which they came pending a formal removal proceeding.

Sec. 8. Additional Border Patrol Agents. Subject to available appropriations, the Secretary, through the Commissioner of U.S. Customs and Border Protection, shall take all appropriate action to hire 5,000 additional Border Patrol agents, and all appropriate action to ensure that such agents enter on duty and are assigned to duty stations as soon as is practicable.

Sec. 9. Foreign Aid Reporting Requirements. The head of each executive department and agency shall identify and quantify all sources of direct and indirect Federal aid or assistance to the Government of Mexico on an annual basis over the past five years, including all bilateral and multilateral development aid, economic assistance, humanitarian aid, and military aid. Within 30 days of the date of this order, the head of each executive department and agency shall submit this information to the Secretary of State. Within 60 days of the date of this order, the Secretary shall submit to the President a consolidated report reflecting the levels of such aid and assistance that has been provided annually, over each of the past five years.

Sec. 10. Federal-State Agreements. It is the policy of the executive branch to empower State and local law enforcement agencies across the country to perform the functions of an immigration officer in the interior of the United States to the maximum extent permitted by law.

(a) In furtherance of this policy, the Secretary shall immediately take appropriate action to engage with the Governors of the States, as well as local officials, for the purpose of preparing to enter into agreements under section 287(g) of the INA (8 U.S.C. 1357(g)).

(b) To the extent permitted by law, and with the consent of State or local officials, as appropriate, the Secretary shall take appropriate action, through agreements under section 287(g) of the INA, or otherwise, to authorize State and local law enforcement officials, as the Secretary determines are qualified and appropriate, to perform the functions of immigration officers in relation to the investigation, apprehension, or detention of aliens in the United States under the direction and the supervision of the Secretary. Such authorization shall be in addition to, rather than in place of, Federal performance of these duties.

(c) To the extent permitted by law, the Secretary may structure each agreement under section 287(g) of the INA in the manner that provides the most effective model for enforcing Federal immigration laws and obtaining operational control over the border for that jurisdiction.

Sec. 11. Parole, Asylum, and Removal. It is the policy of the executive branch to end the abuse of parole and asylum provisions currently used to prevent the lawful removal of removable aliens.

(a) The Secretary shall immediately take all appropriate action to ensure that the parole and asylum provisions of Federal immigration law are not illegally exploited to prevent the removal of otherwise removable aliens.

(b) The Secretary shall take all appropriate action, including by promulgating any appropriate regulations, to ensure that asylum referrals and credible fear determinations pursuant to section 235(b)(1) of the INA (8 U.S.C. 1125(b)(1)) and 8 CFR 208.30, and reasonable fear determinations pursuant to 8 CFR 208.31, are conducted in a manner consistent with the plain language of those provisions.

(c) Pursuant to section 235(b)(1)(A)(iii)(I) of the INA, the Secretary shall take appropriate action to apply, in his sole and unreviewable discretion, the provisions of section 235(b)(1)(A)(i) and (ii) of the INA to the aliens designated under section 235(b)(1)(A)(iii)(II).

(d) The Secretary shall take appropriate action to ensure that parole authority under section 212(d)(5) of the INA (8 U.S.C. 1182(d)(5)) is exercised only on a case-by-case basis in accordance with the plain language of the statute, and in all circumstances only when an individual demonstrates urgent humanitarian reasons or a significant public benefit derived from such parole.

(e) The Secretary shall take appropriate action to require that all Department of Homeland Security personnel are properly trained on the proper application of section 235 of the William Wilberforce Trafficking Victims Protection Reauthorization Act of 2008 (8 U.S.C. 1232) and section 462(g)(2) of the Homeland Security Act of 2002 (6 U.S.C. 279(g)(2)), to ensure that unaccompanied alien children are properly processed, receive appropriate care and placement while in the custody of the Department of Homeland Security, and, when appropriate, are safely repatriated in accordance with law.

Sec. 12. Authorization to Enter Federal Lands. The Secretary, in conjunction with the Secretary of the Interior and any other heads of agencies as necessary, shall take all appropriate action to:

(a) permit all officers and employees of the United States, as well as all State and local officers as authorized by the Secretary, to have access to all Federal lands as necessary and appropriate to implement this order; and

(b) enable those officers and employees of the United States, as well as all State and local officers as authorized by the Secretary, to perform such actions on Federal lands as the Secretary deems necessary and appropriate to implement this order.

Sec. 13. Priority Enforcement. The Attorney General shall take all appropriate steps to establish prosecution guidelines and allocate appropriate resources to ensure that Federal prosecutors accord a high priority to prosecutions of offenses having a nexus to the southern border.

Sec. 14. Government Transparency. The Secretary shall, on a monthly basis and in a publicly available way, report statistical data on aliens apprehended at or near the southern border using a uniform method of reporting by all Department of Homeland Security components, in a format that is easily understandable by the public.

Sec. 15. Reporting. Except as otherwise provided in this order, the Secretary, within 90 days of the date of this order, and the Attorney General, within 180 days, shall each submit to the President a report on the progress of the directives contained in this order.

Sec. 16. Hiring. The Office of Personnel Management shall take appropriate action as may be necessary to facilitate hiring personnel to implement this order.

Sec. 17. General Provisions. (a) Nothing in this order shall be construed to impair or otherwise affect:

(i) the authority granted by law to an executive department or agency, or the head thereof; or

(ii) the functions of the Director of the Office of Management and Budget relating to budgetary, administrative, or legislative proposals.

(b) This order shall be implemented consistent with applicable law and subject to the availability of appropriations.

(c) This order is not intended to, and does not, create any right or benefit, substantive or procedural, enforceable at law or in equity by any party against the United States, its departments, agencies, or entities, its officers, employees, or agents, or any other person.

DONALD J. TRUMP
THE WHITE HOUSE
January 25, 2017
The White House

. . .

Executive Order: Enhancing Public Safety in the Interior of the United States

By the authority vested in me as President by the Constitution and the laws of the United States of America, including the Immigration and Nationality Act (INA) (8 U.S.C. 1101 et seq.), and in order to ensure the public safety of the American people in communities across the United States as well as to ensure that our Nation's immigration laws are faithfully executed, I hereby declare the policy of the executive branch to be, and order, as follows:

Section 1. Purpose. Interior enforcement of our Nation's immigration laws is critically important to the national security and public safety of the United States. Many aliens who illegally enter the United States and those who overstay or otherwise violate the terms of their visas present a significant threat to national security and public safety. This is particularly so for aliens who engage in criminal conduct in the United States.

Sanctuary jurisdictions across the United States willfully violate Federal law in an attempt to shield aliens from removal from the United States. These jurisdictions have caused immeasurable harm to the American people and to the very fabric of our Republic.

Tens of thousands of removable aliens have been released into communities across the country, solely because their home countries refuse to accept their repatriation. Many of these aliens are criminals who have served time in our Federal, State, and local jails. The presence of such individuals in the United States, and the practices of foreign nations that refuse the repatriation of their nationals, are contrary to the national interest.

Appendix D.   Enforcement-Related Executive Orders

Although Federal immigration law provides a framework for Federal-State partnerships in enforcing our immigration laws to ensure the removal of aliens who have no right to be in the United States, the Federal Government has failed to discharge this basic sovereign responsibility. We cannot faithfully execute the immigration laws of the United States if we exempt classes or categories of removable aliens from potential enforcement. The purpose of this order is to direct executive departments and agencies (agencies) to employ all lawful means to enforce the immigration laws of the United States.

Sec. 2. Policy. It is the policy of the executive branch to:

(a) Ensure the faithful execution of the immigration laws of the United States, including the INA, against all removable aliens, consistent with Article II, Section 3 of the United States Constitution and section 3331 of title 5, United States Code;

(b) Make use of all available systems and resources to ensure the efficient and faithful execution of the immigration laws of the United States;

(c) Ensure that jurisdictions that fail to comply with applicable Federal law do not receive Federal funds, except as mandated by law;

(d) Ensure that aliens ordered removed from the United States are promptly removed; and

(e) Support victims, and the families of victims, of crimes committed by removable aliens.

Sec. 3. Definitions. The terms of this order, where applicable, shall have the meaning provided by section 1101 of title 8, United States Code.

Sec. 4. Enforcement of the Immigration Laws in the Interior of the United States. In furtherance of the policy described in section 2 of this order, I hereby direct agencies to employ all lawful means to ensure the faithful execution of the immigration laws of the United States against all removable aliens.

Sec. 5. Enforcement Priorities. In executing faithfully the immigration laws of the United States, the Secretary of Homeland Security (Secretary) shall prioritize for removal those aliens described by the Congress in sections 212(a)(2), (a)(3), and (a)(6)(C), 235, and 237(a)(2) and (4) of the INA (8 U.S.C. 1182(a)(2), (a)(3), and (a)(6)(C), 1225, and 1227(a)(2) and (4)), as well as removable aliens who:

(a) Have been convicted of any criminal offense;

(b) Have been charged with any criminal offense, where such charge has not been resolved;

(c) Have committed acts that constitute a chargeable criminal offense;

(d) Have engaged in fraud or willful misrepresentation in connection with any official matter or application before a governmental agency;

(e) Have abused any program related to receipt of public benefits;

(f) Are subject to a final order of removal, but who have not complied with their legal obligation to depart the United States; or

(g) In the judgment of an immigration officer, otherwise pose a risk to public safety or national security.

Sec. 6. Civil Fines and Penalties. As soon as practicable, and by no later than one year after the date of this order, the Secretary shall issue guidance and promulgate regulations, where required by law, to ensure the assessment and collection of all fines and penalties that the Secretary is authorized under the law to assess and collect from aliens unlawfully present in the United States and from those who facilitate their presence in the United States.

Sec. 7. Additional Enforcement and Removal Officers. The Secretary, through the Director of U.S. Immigration and Customs Enforcement, shall, to the extent permitted by law and subject to the availability of appropriations, take all appropriate action to hire 10,000 additional immigration officers, who shall complete relevant training and be authorized to perform the law enforcement functions described in section 287 of the INA (8 U.S.C. 1357).

Sec. 8. Federal-State Agreements. It is the policy of the executive branch to empower State and local law enforcement agencies across the country to perform the functions of an immigration officer in the interior of the United States to the maximum extent permitted by law.

(a) In furtherance of this policy, the Secretary shall immediately take appropriate action to engage with the Governors of the States, as well as local officials, for the purpose of preparing to enter into agreements under section 287(g) of the INA (8 U.S.C. 1357(g)).

(b) To the extent permitted by law and with the consent of State or local officials, as appropriate, the Secretary shall take appropriate action, through agreements under section 287(g) of the INA, or otherwise, to authorize State and local law enforcement officials, as the Secretary determines are qualified and appropriate, to perform the functions of immigration officers in relation to the investigation, apprehension, or detention of aliens in the United States under the direction and the supervision of the Secretary. Such authorization shall be in addition to, rather than in place of, Federal performance of these duties.

(c) To the extent permitted by law, the Secretary may structure each agreement under section 287(g) of the INA in a manner that provides the most effective model for enforcing Federal immigration laws for that jurisdiction.

Sec. 9. Sanctuary Jurisdictions. It is the policy of the executive branch to ensure, to the fullest extent of the law, that a State, or a political subdivision of a State, shall comply with 8 U.S.C. 1373.

(a) In furtherance of this policy, the Attorney General and the Secretary, in their discretion and to the extent consistent with law, shall ensure that jurisdictions that willfully refuse to comply with 8 U.S.C. 1373 (sanctuary jurisdictions) are not eligible to receive Federal grants, except as deemed necessary for law enforcement purposes by the Attorney General or the Secretary. The Secretary has the authority to designate, in his discretion and to the extent consistent with law, a jurisdiction as a sanctuary jurisdiction. The Attorney General shall take appropriate enforcement action against any entity that violates 8 U.S.C. 1373, or which has in effect a statute, policy, or practice that prevents or hinders the enforcement of Federal law.

(b) To better inform the public regarding the public safety threats associated with sanctuary jurisdictions, the Secretary shall utilize the Declined Detainer Outcome Report or its equivalent and, on a weekly basis, make public a comprehensive list of criminal actions committed by aliens and any jurisdiction that ignored or otherwise failed to honor any detainers with respect to such aliens.

(c) The Director of the Office of Management and Budget is directed to obtain and provide relevant and responsive information on all Federal grant money that currently is received by any sanctuary jurisdiction.

Sec. 10. Review of Previous Immigration Actions and Policies. (a) The Secretary shall immediately take all appropriate action to terminate the Priority Enforcement Program (PEP) described in the memorandum issued by the Secretary on November 20, 2014, and to reinstitute the immigration program known as "Secure Communities" referenced in that memorandum.

(b) The Secretary shall review agency regulations, policies, and procedures for consistency with this order and, if required, publish for notice and comment proposed regulations rescinding or revising any regulations inconsistent with this order and shall consider whether to withdraw or modify any inconsistent policies and procedures, as appropriate and consistent with the law.

(c) To protect our communities and better facilitate the identification, detention, and removal of criminal aliens within constitutional and statutory parameters, the Secretary shall consolidate and revise any applicable forms to more effectively communicate with recipient law enforcement agencies.

Sec. 11. Department of Justice Prosecutions of Immigration Violators. The Attorney General and the Secretary shall work together to develop and implement a program that ensures that adequate resources are devoted to the prosecution of criminal immigration offenses in the United States, and to develop cooperative strategies to reduce violent crime and the reach of transnational criminal organizations into the United States.

Sec. 12. Recalcitrant Countries. The Secretary of Homeland Security and the Secretary of State shall cooperate to effectively implement the sanctions provided by section 243(d) of the INA (8 U.S.C. 1253(d)), as appropriate. The Secretary of State shall, to the maximum extent permitted by law, ensure that diplomatic efforts and negotiations with foreign states include as a condition precedent the acceptance by those foreign states of their nationals who are subject to removal from the United States.

Sec. 13. Office for Victims of Crimes Committed by Removable Aliens. The Secretary shall direct the Director of U.S. Immigration and Customs Enforcement to take all appropriate and lawful action to establish within U.S. Immigration and Customs Enforcement an office to provide proactive, timely, adequate, and professional services to victims of crimes committed by removable aliens and the family members of such victims. This office shall provide quarterly reports studying the effects of the victimization by criminal aliens present in the United States.

Sec. 14. Privacy Act. Agencies shall, to the extent consistent with applicable law, ensure that their privacy policies exclude persons who are not United States citizens or lawful permanent residents from the protections of the Privacy Act regarding personally identifiable information.

Sec. 15. Reporting. Except as otherwise provided in this order, the Secretary and the Attorney General shall each submit to the President a report on the progress of the directives contained in this order within 90 days of the date of this order and again within 180 days of the date of this order.

Sec. 16. Transparency. To promote the transparency and situational awareness of criminal aliens in the United States, the Secretary and the Attorney General are hereby directed to collect relevant data and provide quarterly reports on the following:

(a) the immigration status of all aliens incarcerated under the supervision of the Federal Bureau of Prisons;

(b) the immigration status of all aliens incarcerated as Federal pretrial detainees under the supervision of the United States Marshals Service; and

(c) the immigration status of all convicted aliens incarcerated in State prisons and local detention centers throughout the United States.

Sec. 17. Personnel Actions. The Office of Personnel Management shall take appropriate and lawful action to facilitate hiring personnel to implement this order.

Sec. 18. General Provisions. (a) Nothing in this order shall be construed to impair or otherwise affect:

(i) the authority granted by law to an executive department or agency, or the head thereof; or

(ii) the functions of the Director of the Office of Management and Budget relating to budgetary, administrative, or legislative proposals.

(b) This order shall be implemented consistent with applicable law and subject to the availability of appropriations.

(c) This order is not intended to, and does not, create any right or benefit, substantive or procedural, enforceable at law or in equity by any party against the United States, its departments, agencies, or entities, its officers, employees, or agents, or any other person.

DONALD J. TRUMP
THE WHITE HOUSE
January 25, 2017
The White House

MS. L.; ET AL., V. U.S. IMMIGRATION AND CUSTOMS ENFORCEMENT ("ICE"); ET AL.

Order Granting Plaintiffs' Motion for Classwide Preliminary Injunction
June 26, 2018

Judge Dana M. Sabraw
U.S. District Court, Southern District of California

Eleven weeks ago, Plaintiffs leveled the serious accusation that our Government was engaged in a widespread practice of separating migrant families, and placing minor children who were separated from their parents in government facilities for "unaccompanied minors." According to Plaintiffs, the practice was applied indiscriminately, and separated even those families with small children and infants—many of whom were seeking asylum. Plaintiffs noted reports that the practice would become national policy. Recent events confirm these allegations. Extraordinary relief is requested, and is warranted under the circumstances.

On May 7, 2018, the Attorney General of the United States announced a "zero tolerance policy," under which all adults entering the United States illegally would be subject to criminal prosecution, and if accompanied by a minor child, the child would be separated from the parent.[1] Over the ensuing weeks, hundreds of migrant children were separated from their parents, sparking international condemnation of the practice. Six days ago on June 20, 2018, the President of the United States signed an Executive Order ("EO") to address the situation and to require preservation of the "family unit" by keeping migrant families together during criminal and immigration proceedings to the extent permitted by law, while also maintaining "rigorous[]" enforcement of immigration laws. See Executive Order, Affording Congress an Opportunity to Address Family Separation § 1, 2018 WL 3046068 (June 20, 2018). The EO did not address reunification of the burgeoning population of over 2,000 children separated from their parents. Public outrage remained at a fever pitch. Three days ago on Saturday, June 23, 2018, the Department of Homeland Security ("DHS") issued a "Fact Sheet" outlining the

---

1. See U.S. Att'y. Gen., Attorney General Sessions Delivers Remarks Discussing the Immigration Enforcement Actions of the Trump Administration (May 7, 2018), https://www.justice.gov/opa/speech/attorney-general-sessions-delivers-remarks-discussing-immigration-enforcement-actions.

government's efforts to "ensure that those adults who are subject to removal are reunited with their children for the purposes of removal."[2]

Plaintiffs assert the EO does not eliminate the need for the requested injunction, and the Fact Sheet does not address the circumstances of this case. Defendants disagree with those assertions, but there is no genuine dispute that the Government was not prepared to accommodate the mass influx of separated children. Measures were not in place to provide for communication between governmental agencies responsible for detaining parents and those responsible for housing children, or to provide for ready communication between separated parents and children. There was no reunification plan in place, and families have been separated for months. Some parents were deported at separate times and from different locations than their children. Migrant families that lawfully entered the United States at a port of entry seeking asylum were separated. And families that were separated due to entering the United States illegally between ports of entry have not been reunited following the parent's completion of criminal proceedings and return to immigration detention.

This Court previously entered an order finding Plaintiffs had stated a legally cognizable claim for violation of their substantive due process rights to family integrity under the Fifth Amendment to the United States Constitution based on their allegations the Government had separated Plaintiffs from their minor children while Plaintiffs were held in immigration detention and without a showing that they were unfit parents or otherwise presented a danger to their children. See Ms. L. v. U.S. Immigration & Customs Enf't, 302 F. Supp. 3d 1149, 2018 WL 2725736, at *7-12 (S.D. Cal. June 6, 2018). A class action has been certified to include similarly situated migrant parents. Plaintiffs now request classwide injunctive relief to prohibit separation of class members from their children in the future absent a finding the parent is unfit or presents a danger to the child, and to require reunification of these families once the parent is returned to immigration custody unless the parent is determined to be unfit or presents a danger to the child.

Plaintiffs have demonstrated a likelihood of success on the merits, irreparable harm, and that the balance of equities and the public interest weigh in their favor, thus warranting issuance of a preliminary injunction. This Order does not implicate the Government's discretionary authority to enforce immigration or other criminal laws, including its decisions to release or detain class members. Rather, the Order addresses only the circumstances under which the Government may separate class members from their children, as well as the reunification of class members who are returned to immigration custody upon completion of any criminal proceedings.

---

2. See U.S. Dep't of Homeland Sec., Fact Sheet: Federal Regulations Protecting the Confidentiality of Asylum Applicants (June 23, 2018), https://www.dhs.gov/news/2018/06/23/fact-sheet-zero-tolerance-prosecution-and-family-reunification.   Case   3:18-cv-00428-DMS-MDD Document 83 Filed 06/26/18 PageID.1725.

Appendix E. Ms. L.; et al., v. U.S. Immigration

I. BACKGROUND

This case started with the filing of a Complaint by Ms. L., a Catholic citizen of the Democratic Republic of the Congo fleeing persecution from her home country because of her religious beliefs. In brief, Ms. L. and her then-six-year-old daughter S.S., lawfully presented themselves at the San Ysidro Port of Entry seeking asylum based on religious persecution. They were initially detained together, but after a few days S.S. was "forcibly separated" from her mother. When S.S. was taken away from her mother, "she was screaming and crying, pleading with guards not to take her away from her mother." Immigration officials claimed they had concerns whether Ms. L. was S.S.'s mother, despite Ms. L.'s protestations to the contrary and S.S.'s behavior. So Ms. L. was placed in immigration custody and scheduled for expedited removal, thus rendering S.S. an "unaccompanied minor" under the Trafficking Victims Protection and Reauthorization Act ("TVPRA"), Pub. L. No. 110-457 (Dec. 23, 2008), and subjecting her to the "care and custody" of the Office of Refugee Resettlement ("ORR").[3] S.S. was placed in a facility in Chicago over a thousand miles away from her mother. Immigration officials later determined Ms. L. had a credible fear of persecution and placed her in removal proceedings, where she could pursue her asylum claim. During this period, Ms. L. was able to speak with her daughter only "approximately 6 times by phone, never by video." Each time they spoke, S.S. "was crying and scared." Ms. L. was "terrified that she would never see her daughter again." After the present lawsuit was filed, Ms. L. was released from ICE detention into the community. The Court ordered the Government to take a DNA saliva sample (or swab), which confirmed that Ms. L. was the mother of S.S. Four days later, Ms. L. and S.S. were reunited after being separated for nearly five months.

In an Amended Complaint filed on March 9, 2018, this case was expanded to include another Plaintiff, Ms. C. She is a citizen of Brazil, and unlike Ms. L., she did not present at a port of entry. Instead, she and her 14-year-old son J. crossed into the United States "between ports of entry," after which they were apprehended by U.S. Border Patrol. Ms. C. explained to the agent that she and her son were seeking asylum, but the Government, as was its right under federal

---

3. The TVPRA provides that "the care and custody of all unaccompanied alien children, including responsibility for their detention, where appropriate, shall be the responsibility of" HHS and its sub-agency, ORR. 8 U.S.C. § 1232(b)(1). An "unaccompanied alien child" ("UAC") is a child under 18 years of age with no lawful immigration status in the United States who has neither a parent nor legal guardian in the United States nor a parent nor legal guardian in the United States "available" to care for them. 6 U.S.C § 279(g)(2). According to the TVPRA, a UAC "may not be placed with a person or entity unless the Secretary of Health and Human Services makes a determination that the proposed custodian is capable of providing for the child's physical and mental well-being. Such determination shall, at a minimum, include verification of the custodian's identity and relationship to the child, if any, as well as an independent finding that the individual has not engaged in any activity that would indicate a potential risk to the child." 8 U.S.C. § 1232(c)(3)(A).

law, charged Ms. C. with entering the country illegally and placed her in criminal custody. This rendered J. an "unaccompanied minor" and he, like S.S., was transferred to the custody of ORR, where he, too, was housed in a facility in Chicago several hundred miles away from his mother. Ms. C. was thereafter convicted of misdemeanor illegal entry and served 25 days in criminal custody. After completing that sentence, Ms. C. was transferred to immigration detention for removal proceedings and consideration of her asylum claim, as she too had passed a credible fear screening. Despite being returned to immigration custody, Ms. C. was not reunited with J. During the five months she was detained, Ms. C. did not see her son, and they spoke on the phone only "a handful of times[.]"Ms. C. was "desperate" to be reunited with her son, worried about him constantly and did not know when she would be able to see him. J. had a difficult time emotionally during the period of separation from his mother. Ms. C. was eventually released from immigration detention on bond, and only recently reunited with J. Their separation lasted more than eight months despite the lack of any allegations or evidence that Ms. C. was unfit or otherwise presented a danger to her son.[4]

Ms. L. and Ms. C. are not the only migrant parents who have been separated from their children at the border. Hundreds of others, who have both lawfully presented at ports of entry (like Ms. L.) and unlawfully crossed into the country (like Ms. C.), have also been separated. Because this practice is affecting large numbers of people, Plaintiffs sought certification of a class consisting of similarly situated individuals. The Court certified that class with minor modifications,[5] and now turns to the important question of whether Plaintiffs are entitled to a classwide preliminary injunction that (1) halts the separation of class members from their children absent a determination that the parent is unfit or presents a danger to the child, and (2) reunites class members who are returned to immigration custody upon completion of any criminal proceedings absent a determination that the parent is unfit or presents a danger to the child.

Since the present motion was filed, several important developments occurred, as previously noted. First, on May 7, 2018, the Government announced its zero tolerance policy for all adult persons crossing the border illegally, which resulted in the separation of hundreds of children who had crossed with their parents. This

---

4. As stated in the Court's Order on Defendants' motion to dismiss, Plaintiffs do not challenge Ms. C.'s initial separation from J. as a result of the criminal charge filed against her. Plaintiffs' only complaint with regard to Ms. C. concerns the Government's failure to reunite her with J. after she was returned to immigration custody.

5. The class is defined to include: "All adult parents who enter the United States at or between designated ports of entry who (1) have been, are, or will be detained in immigration custody by the [DHS], and (2) have a minor child who is or will be separated from them by DHS and detained in ORR custody, ORR foster care, or DHS custody absent a determination that the parent is unfit or presents a danger to the child." (See Order Granting in Part Mot. for Class Cert. at 17.) The class does not include parents with criminal history or communicable disease, or those apprehended in the interior of the country or subject to the EO. (See id. at 4 n.5.)

is what happened with Ms. C., though she crossed prior to the public announcement of the zero tolerance policy.

She is not alone. There are hundreds of similarly situated parents, and there are more than 2,000 children that have now been separated from their parents.

When a parent is charged with a criminal offense, the law ordinarily requires separation of the family. This separation generally occurs regardless of whether the parent is charged with a state or federal offense. The repercussions on the children, however, can vary greatly depending on status. For citizens, there is an established system of social service agencies ready to provide for the care and well-being of the children, if necessary, including child protective services and the foster care system. This is in addition to any family members that may be available to provide shelter for these minor children. Grandparents and siblings are frequently called upon. Non-citizens may not have this kind of support system, such as other family members who can provide shelter for their children in the event the parent is detained at the border. This results in immigrant children going into the custody of the federal government, which is presently not well equipped to handle that important task.

For children placed in federal custody, there are two options. One of those options is ORR, but it was established to address a different problem, namely minor children who were apprehended at the border without their parents, i.e., true "unaccompanied alien children." It was not initially designed to address the problem of migrant children detained with their parents at the border and who were thereafter separated from their parents. The second option is family detention facilities, but the options there are limited. Indeed, at the time of oral argument on this motion, Government counsel represented to the Court that the "total capacity in [family] residential centers" was "less than 2,700." For male heads of households, i.e., fathers traveling with their children, there was only one facility with "86 beds."

The recently issued EO confirms the government is inundated by the influx of children essentially orphaned as a result of family separation. The EO now directs "[h]eads of executive departments and agencies" to make available "any facilities . . . appropriate" for the housing and care of alien families. EO § 3(d). The EO also calls upon the military by directing the Secretary of Defense to make available "any existing" facility and to "construct such facilities[,]" if necessary, id. § 3(c), which is an extraordinary measure. Meanwhile, "tent cities" and other make-shift facilities are springing up. That was the situation into which Plaintiffs, and hundreds of other families that were separated at the border in the past several months, were placed.

This situation has reached a crisis level. The news media is saturated with stories of immigrant families being separated at the border. People are protesting. Elected officials are weighing in. Congress is threatening action. Seventeen states have now filed a complaint against the Federal Government challenging the family separation practice. See State of Washington v. United States, Case No. 18cv0939, United States District Court for the Western District of Washington. And the President has taken action.

Specifically, on June 20, 2018, the President signed the EO referenced above. The EO states it is the Administration's policy "to maintain family unity, including by detaining alien families together where appropriate and consistent with law and available resources."[6] In furtherance of that policy, the EO indicates that parents and children who are apprehended together at the border will be detained together "during the pendency of any criminal improper entry or immigration proceedings" to the extent permitted by law. The language of the EO is not absolute, however, as it states that family unity shall be maintained "where appropriate and consistent with law and available resources[,]"and "to the extent permitted by law and subject to the availability of appropriations[.]"The EO also indicates rigorous enforcement of illegal border crossers will continue. Id. § 1 ("It is the policy of this Administration to rigorously enforce our immigration laws."). And finally, although the Order speaks to a policy of "maintain[ing] family unity," it is silent on the issue of reuniting families that have already been separated or will be separated in the future."

In light of these recent developments, and in particular the EO, the Court held a telephonic status conference with counsel on June 22, 2018. During that conference, the Court inquired about communication between ORR and DHS, and ORR and the Department of Justice ("DOJ"), including the Bureau of Prisons ("BOP"), as it relates to these separated families. Reunification procedures were also discussed, specifically whether there was any affirmative reunification procedure for parents and children after parents were returned to immigration detention following completion of criminal proceedings. Government counsel explained the communication procedures that were in place, and represented, consistent with her earlier representation to the Court, that there was no procedure in place for the reunification of these families.[7]

The day after the status conference, Saturday, June 23, DHS issued the Fact Sheet referenced above. This document focuses on several issues addressed during the status conference, e.g., processes for enhanced communication between separated parents and children, but only "for the purposes of removal." It also addresses coordination between and among three agencies, CBP, ICE, and HHS agency ORR, but again for the purpose of removal. The Fact Sheet does not address reunification for other purposes, such as immigration or asylum

---

6. The Order defines "alien family" as "any person not a citizen or national of the United States who has not been admitted into, or is not authorized to enter or remain in, the United States, who entered this country with an alien child or alien children at or between designated ports of entry and who was detained[.]" Id. § 2(a)(i).

7. The Court: "Is there currently any affirmative reunification process that the government has in place once parent and child are separated? Government counsel: I would say . . . when a parent is released from criminal custody and taken into ICE custody is the practice to reunite them in family detention[?] And at that [previous hearing] I said no, that that was not the practice. I think my answer on that narrow question would be the same." (Rep. Tr. at 29-30, June 22, 2018, ECF No. 77.)

proceedings, which can take months. It also does not mention other vital agencies frequently involved during criminal proceedings: DOJ and BOP.

At the conclusion of the recent status conference, the Court requested supplemental briefing from the parties. Those briefs have now been submitted. After thoroughly considering all of the parties' briefs and the record in this case, and after hearing argument from counsel on these important issues, the Court grants Plaintiffs' motion for a classwide preliminary injunction.

II.   DISCUSSION

Plaintiffs seek classwide preliminary relief that (1) enjoins Defendants' practice of separating class members from their children absent a determination that the parent is unfit or presents a danger to their child, and (2) orders the government to reunite class members with their children when the parent is returned to immigration custody after their criminal proceedings conclude, absent a determination that the parent is unfit or presents a danger to the child. Injunctive relief is "an extraordinary remedy that may only be awarded upon a clear showing that the plaintiff is entitled to such relief." Winter v. Natural Res. Def. Council, Inc., 555 U.S. 7, 22 (2008). To meet that showing, Plaintiffs must demonstrate "'[they are] likely to succeed on the merits, that [they are] likely to suffer irreparable harm in the absence of preliminary relief, that the balance of equities tips in [their] favor, and that an injunction is in the public interest.'" Am. Trucking Ass'ns v. City of Los Angeles, 559 F.3d 1046, 1052 (9th Cir. 2009) (quoting Winter, 555 U.S. at 20).

Before turning to these factors, the Court addresses directly Defendants' argument that an injunction is not necessary here in light of the EO and the recently released Fact Sheet. Although these documents reflect some attempts by the Government to address some of the issues in this case, neither obviates the need for injunctive relief here. As indicated throughout this Order, the EO is subject to various qualifications. For instance, Plaintiffs correctly assert the EO allows the government to separate a migrant parent from his or her child "where there is a concern that detention of an alien child with the child's alien parent would pose a risk to the child's welfare." EO § 3(b) (emphasis added). Objective standards are necessary, not subjective ones, particularly in light of the history of this case. Furthermore, the Fact Sheet focuses on reunification "at time of removal[,]"stating that the parent slated for removal will be matched up with their child at a location in Texas and then removed. It says nothing about reunification during the intervening time between return from criminal proceedings to ICE detention or the time in ICE detention prior to actual removal, which can take months. Indeed, it is undisputed "ICE has no plans or procedures in place to reunify the parent with the child other than arranging for them to be deported together after the parent's immigration case is concluded." Thus, neither of these directives eliminates the need for an injunction in this case. With this finding, the Court now turns to the Winter factors.

A.   Likelihood of Success

"The first factor under Winter is the most important—likely success on the merits." Garcia v. Google, Inc., 786 F.3d 733, 740 (9th Cir. 2015). While Plaintiffs carry the burden of demonstrating likelihood of success, they are not required to prove their case in full at the preliminary injunction stage but only such portions that enable them to obtain the injunctive relief they seek. See Univ. of Texas v. Camenisch, 451 U.S. 390, 395 (1981).

Here, the only claim currently at issue is Plaintiffs' due process claim. Specifically, Plaintiffs contend the Government's practice of separating class members from their children, and failing to reunite those parents who have been separated, without a determination that the parent is unfit or presents a danger to the child violates the parents' substantive due process rights to family integrity under the Fifth Amendment to the United States Constitution. To prevail on this claim, Plaintiffs must show that the Government practice "shocks the conscience." In the Order on Defendants' motion to dismiss, the Court found Plaintiffs had set forth sufficient facts to support that claim. Ms. L., 2018 WL 2725736, at *7-12. The evidence submitted since that time supports that finding, and demonstrates Plaintiffs are likely to succeed on this claim.

As explained in the Court's Order on Defendants' motion to dismiss, the "shocks the conscience" standard is not subject to a rigid list of established elements. See County of Sacramento v. Lewis, 523 U.S. 833, 850 (1998) (stating "[r]ules of due process are not . . . subject to mechanical application in unfamiliar territory.") On the contrary, "an investigation into substantive due process involves an appraisal of the totality of the circumstances rather than a formalistic examination of fixed elements[.]" Armstrong v. Squadrito, 152 F.3d 564, 570 (7th Cir. 1998).

Here, each Plaintiff presents different circumstances, but both were subjected to the same government practice of family separation without a determination that the parent was unfit or presented a danger to the child. Ms. L. was separated from her child without a determination she was unfit or presented a danger to her child, and Ms. C. was not reunited with her child despite the absence of any finding that she was unfit or presented a danger to her child. Outside of the context of this case, namely an international border, Plaintiffs would have a high likelihood of success on a claim premised on such a practice. See D.B. v. Cardall, 826 F.3d 721, 741 (4th Cir. 2016) (citing cases finding due process violation where state action interfered with rights of fit parents); Heartland Academy Community Church v. Waddle, 595 F.3d 798, 808-811 (8th Cir. 2010) (finding removal of children from religious school absent evidence the students were "at immediate risk of child abuse or neglect" was violation of clearly established constitutional right); Brokaw v. Mercer County, 235 F.3d 1000, 1019 (7th Cir. 2000) (citing Croft v. Westmoreland County Children and Youth Services, 103 F.3d 1123, 1126 (3d Cir. 1997) ("courts have recognized that a state has no interest in protecting children from their parents unless it has some definite and articulable evidence giving rise to a reasonable suspicion that a child has been abused or is in imminent danger of abuse.")

The context of this case is different. The Executive Branch, which is tasked with enforcement of the country's criminal and immigration laws, is acting within its powers to detain individuals lawfully entering the United States and to apprehend individuals illegally entering the country. However, as the Court explained in its Order on Defendants' motion to dismiss, the right to family integrity still applies here. The context of the family separation practice at issue here, namely an international border, does not render the practice constitutional, nor does it shield the practice from judicial review.

On the contrary, the context and circumstances in which this practice of family separation were being implemented support a finding that Plaintiffs have a likelihood of success on their due process claim. First, although parents and children may lawfully be separated when the parent is placed in criminal custody, the same general rule does not apply when a parent and child present together lawfully at a port of entry seeking asylum. In that situation, the parent has committed no crime, and absent a finding the parent is unfit or presents a danger to the child, it is unclear why separation of Ms. L. or similarly situated class members would be necessary. Here, many of the family separations have been the result of the Executive Branch's zero tolerance policy, but the record also reflects that the practice of family separation was occurring before the zero tolerance policy was announced, and that practice has resulted in the casual, if not deliberate, separation of families that lawfully present at the port of entry, not just those who cross into the country illegally. Ms. L. is an example of this family separation practice expanding beyond its lawful reach, and she is not alone.

As set out in the Court's prior Order, asylum seekers like Ms. L. and many other class members may be fleeing persecution and are entitled to careful consideration by government officials. Particularly so if they have a credible fear of persecution. We are a country of laws, and of compassion. We have plainly stated our intent to treat refugees with an ordered process, and benevolence, by codifying principles of asylum. See, e.g., The Refugee Act, PL 96-212, 94 Stat. 102 (1980). The Government's treatment of Ms. L. and other similarly situated class members does not meet this standard, and it is unlikely to pass constitutional muster.

Second, the practice of separating these families was implemented without any effective system or procedure for (1) tracking the children after they were separated from their parents, (2) enabling communication between the parents and their children after separation, and (3) reuniting the parents and children after the parents are returned to immigration custody following completion of their criminal sentence. This is a startling reality. The government readily keeps track of personal property of detainees in criminal and immigration proceedings. Money, important documents, and automobiles, to name a few, are routinely catalogued, stored, tracked and produced upon a detainees' release, at all levels — state and federal, citizen and alien. Yet, the government has no system in place to keep track of, provide effective communication with, and promptly produce alien children. The unfortunate reality is that under the present system migrant children are not accounted for with the same efficiency and accuracy as property. Certainly, that cannot satisfy the requirements of due process. See Santosky v. Kramer, 455 U.S. 745, 758-59 (1982) (quoting Lassiter v. Dept. of Soc. Services of Durham County, N.C., 452 U.S. 18, (1981)) (stating it is "'plain beyond the need for multiple citation' that a natural parent's 'desire for and right to the companionship, care, custody, and management of his or her children' is an interest far more precious than any property right.") (internal quotation marks omitted).

The lack of effective methods for communication between parents and children who have been separated has also had a profoundly negative effect on the parents' criminal and immigration proceedings, as well as the childrens' immigration proceedings. See United States v. Dominguez-Portillo, No:EP-17-MJ-4409-MAT, 2018 WL 315759, at *1-2 (W.D. Tex. Jan. 5, 2018) (explaining that criminally charged defendants "had not received any paperwork or information concerning the whereabouts or well-being of" their children). In effect, these parents have been left "in a vacuum, without knowledge of the well-being and location of their children, to say nothing of the immigration proceedings in which those minor children find themselves." This situation may result in a number of different scenarios, all of which are negative — some profoundly so. For example, "[i]f parent and child are asserting or intending to assert an asylum claim, that child may be navigating those legal waters without the benefit of communication with and assistance from her parent; that defendant, too, must make a decision on his criminal case with total uncertainty about this issue." Furthermore, " a defendant facing certain deportation would be unlikely to know whether he might be deported before, simultaneous to, or after their child, or whether they would have the opportunity to even discuss their deportations[.]" Id. Indeed, some parents have already been deported without their children, who remain in government facilities in the United States.

The absence of established procedures for dealing with families that have been separated at the border, and the effects of that void on the families involved, is borne out in the cases of Plaintiffs here. Ms. L. was separated from her child when immigration officials claimed they could not verify she was S.S.'s mother, and detained her for expedited removal proceedings. That rendered S.S. "unaccompanied" under the TVPRA and subject to immediate transfer to ORR, which accepted responsibility for S.S. There was no further communication between the agencies, ICE and ORR. The filing of the present lawsuit prompted release and reunification of Ms. L. and her daughter, a process that took close to five months and court involvement. Ms. C. completed her criminal sentence in 25 days, but it took nearly eight months to be reunited with her son. She, too, had to file suit to regain custody of her son from ORR.

These situations confirm what the Government has already stated: it is not affirmatively reuniting parents like Plaintiffs and their fellow class members for purposes other than removal. Outside of deportation, the onus is on the parents, who, for the most part, are themselves in either criminal or immigration proceedings, to contact ORR or otherwise search for their children and make application for reunification under the TVPRA. However, this reunification procedure was not designed to deal with the present circumstances. Rather, "ORR's reunification process was designed to address the situation of children who come to the border or are apprehended outside the company of a parent or legal guardian." Placing the burden on the parents to find and request reunification with their children under the circumstances presented here is backwards. When children are separated from their parents under these circumstances, the Government has an affirmative obligation to track and promptly reunify these family members.

This practice of separating class members from their minor children, and failing to reunify class members with those children, without any showing the parent is unfit or presents a danger to the child is sufficient to find Plaintiffs have a likelihood of success on their due process claim. When combined with the manner in which that practice is being implemented, e.g., the lack of any effective procedures or protocols for notifying the parents about their childrens' whereabouts or ensuring communication between the parents and children, and the use of the children as tools in the parents' criminal and immigration proceedings, a finding of likelihood of success is assured. A practice of this sort implemented in this way is likely to be "so egregious, so outrageous, that it may fairly be said to shock the contemporary conscience," Lewis, 523 U.S. at 847 n.8, interferes with rights "'implicit in the concept of ordered liberty[,]'" Rochin v. Cal., 342 U.S. 165, 169 (1952) (quoting Palko v. State of Conn., 302 U.S. 319, 325 (1937)), and is so "'brutal' and 'offensive' that it [does] not comport with traditional ideas of fair play and decency." Breithaupt v. Abram, 352 U.S. 432, 435 (1957).

For all of these reasons, the Court finds there is a likelihood of success on Plaintiffs' due process claim.

B.   Irreparable Injury

Turning to the next factor, Plaintiffs must show they are "'likely to suffer irreparable harm in the absence of preliminary relief.'" Hernandez v. Sessions, 872 F.3d 976, 994 (9th Cir. 2017) (quoting Winter, 555 U.S. at 20). "'It is well established that the deprivation of constitutional rights unquestionably constitutes irreparable injury.'" Id. (quoting Melendres v. Arpaio, 695 F.3d 990, 1002 (9th Cir. 2012) (internal quotation marks omitted). As explained, Plaintiffs have demonstrated the likelihood of a deprivation of their constitutional rights, and thus they have satisfied this factor.

The injury in this case, however, deserves special mention. That injury is the separation of a parent from his or her child, which the Ninth Circuit has repeatedly found constitutes irreparable harm. See Leiva–Perez v. Holder, 640 F.3d 962, 969–70 (9th Cir. 2011); Washington v. Trump, 847 F.3d 1151, 1169 (9th Cir. 2017) (identifying "separated families" as an irreparable harm).

Furthermore, the record in this case reflects that the separations at issue have been agonizing for the parents who have endured them. One of those parents, Mr. U., an asylum seeker from Kyrgyzstan, submitted a declaration in this case in which he stated that after he was told he was going to be separated from his son he "felt as though [he] was having a heart attack." (Reply in Supp. of Mot. for Class Cert., Ex. 21 ¶ 4.) Another asylum-seeking parent from El Salvador who was separated from her two sons writes,

> The separation from my sons has been incredibly hard, because I have never been away from them before. I do not want my children to think that I abandoned them. [My children] are so attached to me. [One of my children] used to sleep in bed with me every night while [my other child] slept in his own bed in the same room. . . . It hurts me to think how anxious and distressed they must be without me.

(Reply in Supp. of Mot. for Class Cert., Ex. 24 ¶ 9.) And another asylum-seeking parent from Honduras described having to place her crying 18-month old son in a car seat in a government vehicle, not being able to comfort him, and her crying as the officers "took [her] son away." (Reply in Supp. of Mot. for Class Cert., Ex. 25 ¶ 7.) There has even been a report that one father committed suicide in custody after being separated from his wife and three-year-old child. See Molly Hennessy-Fiske, Honduran Migrant Who Was Separated From Family is Found Dead in Texas Jail in an Apparent Suicide, L.A. TIMES (June 9, 2018, 5:35 PM), http://www.latimes.com/nation/la-na-border-patrol-suicide-20180609-story.html.

The parents, however, are not the only ones suffering from the separations. One of the amici in this case, Children's Defense Fund, states,

> there is ample evidence that separating children from their mothers or fathers leads to serious, negative consequences to children's health and development. Forced separation disrupts the parent-child relationship and puts children at increased risk for both physical and mental illness. . . . And the psychological distress, anxiety, and depression associated with separation from a parent would follow the children well after the immediate period of separation—even after eventual reunification with a parent or other family.

(ECF No. 17-11 at 3.) Other evidence before the Court reflects that "separating children from parents is a highly destabilizing, traumatic experience that has long term consequences on child well-being, safety, and development." (ECF No. 17-13 at 2.) That evidence reflects:

> Separation from family leaves children more vulnerable to exploitation and abuse, no matter what the care setting. In addition, traumatic separation from parents creates toxic stress in children and adolescents that can profoundly impact their development. Strong scientific evidence shows that toxic stress disrupts the development of brain architecture and other organ systems, and increases the risk for stress-related disease and cognitive impairment well into adult years. Studies have shown that children who experience such traumatic events can suffer from symptoms of anxiety and post-traumatic stress disorder, have poorer behavioral and educational outcomes, and experience higher rates of poverty and food insecurity.

(ECF No. 17-13 at 2.) And Martin Guggenheim, the Fiorello LaGuardia Professor of Clinical Law at New York University School of Law and Founding Member of the Center for Family Representation, states:

> Children are at risk of suffering great emotional harm when they are removed from their loved ones. And children who have traveled from afar and made their way to this country to seek asylum are especially at risk of suffering irreversible psychological harm when wrested from the custody of the parent or caregiver with whom they traveled to the United States.

(Mem. in Supp. of Classwide Prelim. Inj., Ex. 17 ¶ 16.) All of this evidence, combined with the constitutional violation alleged here, conclusively shows that Plaintiffs and the class members are likely to suffer irreparable injury if a preliminary injunction does not issue.

C.   Balance of Equities

Turning to the next factor, "[t]o obtain a preliminary injunction, a plaintiff must also demonstrate that 'the balance of equities tips in his favor.'" Hernandez, 872 F.3d at 995 (quoting Winter, 555 U.S. at 20). As with irreparable injury, when a plaintiff establishes "a likelihood that Defendants' policy violates the U.S. Constitution, Plaintiffs have also established that both the public interest and the balance of the equities favor a preliminary injunction." Arizona Dream Act Coalition v. Brewer, 757 F.3d 1053, 1069 (9th Cir. 2014).

Plaintiffs here assert the balance of equities weighs in favor of an injunction in this case. Specifically, Plaintiffs argue Defendants would not suffer any hardship if the preliminary injunction is issued because the Government "cannot suffer harm from an injunction that merely ends an unlawful practice[.]" Rodriguez v. Robbins, 715 F.3d 1127, 1145 (9th Cir. 2013); see also Arizona Dream Act Coalition, 757 F.3d at 1069 (quoting Melendres v. Arpaio, 695 F.3d 990, 1002 (9th Cir. 2012)) (stating balance of equities favors "'prevent[ing] the violation of a party's constitutional rights.'"). When the absence of harm to the Government is weighed against the harms to Plaintiffs set out above, Plaintiffs argue this factor weighs in their favor. The Court agrees.

The primary harm Defendants assert here is the possibility that an injunction would have a negative impact on their ability to enforce the criminal and immigration laws. However, the injunction here—preventing the separation of parents from their children and ordering the reunification of parents and children that have been separated—would do nothing of the sort. The Government would remain free to enforce its criminal and immigration laws, and to exercise its discretion in matters of release and detention consistent with law. See EO §§ 1, 3(a) & (e) (discussing Flores v. Sessions, CV 85-4544); see also Comm. of Cent. Am. Refugees v. I.N.S., 795 F.2d 1434, 1439-40 (9th Cir. 1986) (stating "prudential considerations preclude[] interference with the Attorney General's [exercise of] discretion" in selecting the detention facilities where aliens are to be detained). It would just have to do so in a way that preserves the class members' constitutional rights to family association and integrity. See Rodriguez, 715 F.3d at 1146 ("While ICE is entitled to carry out its duty to enforce the mandates of Congress, it must do so in a manner consistent with our constitutional values.") Thus, this factor also weighs in favor of issuing the injunction.

D.   Public Interest

The final factor for consideration is the public interest. See Hernandez, 872 F.3d at 996 (quoting Stormans, Inc. v. Selecky, 586 F.3d 1109, 1139 (9th Cir. 2009)) ("When, as here, 'the impact of an injunction reaches beyond the parties, carrying with it a potential for public consequences, the public interest will be relevant to whether the district court grants the preliminary injunction.'") To obtain the requested relief, "Plaintiffs must demonstrate that the public interest favors granting the injunction 'in light of [its] likely consequences,' i.e., 'consequences [that are not] too remote, insubstantial, or speculative and [are] supported by evidence.'" Id. (quoting Stormans, 586 F.3d at 1139). "'Generally, public interest concerns are implicated when a constitutional right has been violated, because all citizens have a stake in upholding the Constitution.'" Id. (quoting Preminger v. Principi, 422 F.3d 815, 826 (9th Cir. 2005)).

This case involves two important public interests: the interest in enforcing the country's criminal and immigration laws and the constitutional liberty interest "of parents in the care, custody, and control of their children[,]" which "is perhaps the oldest of the fundamental liberty interests recognized by" the Supreme Court. Troxel v. Granville, 530 U.S. 57, 65 (2000). Both of these interests are valid and important, and both can be served by the issuance of an injunction in this case.

As stated, the public's interest in enforcing the criminal and immigration laws of this country would be unaffected by issuance of the requested injunction. The Executive Branch is free to prosecute illegal border crossers and institute immigration proceedings against aliens, and would remain free to do so if an injunction were issued. Plaintiffs do not seek to enjoin the Executive Branch from carrying out its duties in that regard.

What Plaintiffs do seek by way of the requested injunction is to uphold their rights to family integrity and association while their immigration proceedings are underway. This right, specifically, the relationship between parent and child, is "constitutionally protected," Quilloin v. Walcott, 434 U.S. 246, 255 (1978), and "well established." Rosenbaum v. Washoe Cty., 663 F.3d 1071, 1079 (9th Cir. 2011). The public interest in upholding and protecting that right in the circumstances presented here would be served by issuance of the requested injunction. See Arizona Dream Act Coalition, 757 F.3d at 1069 (quoting Valle del Sol Inc.

v. Whiting, 732 F.3d 1006, 1029 (9th Cir. 2013) ("'[I]t is clear that it would not be equitable or in the public's interest to allow the state . . . to violate the requirements of federal law, especially when there are no adequate remedies available.'") Accordingly, this factor, too, weighs in favor of issuing the injunction.

III.   CONCLUSION

The unfolding events—the zero tolerance policy, EO and DHS Fact Sheet— serve to corroborate Plaintiffs' allegations. The facts set forth before the Court portray reactive governance—responses to address a chaotic circumstance of the Government's own making. They belie measured and ordered governance, which is central to the concept of due process enshrined in our Constitution. This is particularly so in the treatment of migrants, many of whom are asylum seekers and small children. The extraordinary remedy of classwide preliminary injunction is warranted based on the evidence before the Court. For the reasons set out above, the Court hereby GRANTS Plaintiffs' motion for classwide preliminary injunction, and finds and orders as follows:

(1)   Defendants, and their officers, agents, servants, employees, attorneys, and all those who are in active concert or participation with them, are preliminarily enjoined from detaining Class Members in DHS custody without and apart from their minor children, absent a determination that the parent is unfit or presents a danger to the child, unless the parent affirmatively, knowingly, and voluntarily declines to be reunited with the child in DHS custody.

(2)   If Defendants choose to release Class Members from DHS custody, Defendants, and their officers, agents, servants, employees and attorneys, and all those who are in active concert or participation with them, are preliminary enjoined from continuing to detain the minor children of the Class Members and must release the minor child to the custody of the Class Member, unless there is a determination that the parent is unfit or presents a danger to the child, or the parent affirmatively, knowingly, and voluntarily declines to be reunited with the child.

(3)   Unless there is a determination that the parent is unfit or presents a danger to the child, or the parent affirmatively, knowingly, and voluntarily declines to be reunited with the child:

(a)   Defendants must reunify all Class Members with their minor children who are under the age of five (5) within fourteen (14) days of the entry of this Order; and

(b)   Defendants must reunify all Class Members with their minor children age five (5) and over within thirty (30) days of the entry of this Order.

(4)   Defendants must immediately take all steps necessary to facilitate regular communication between Class Members and their children who remain in ORR custody, ORR foster care, or DHS custody. Within ten (10) days, Defendants must provide parents telephonic contact with their children if the parent is not already in contact with his or her child.

(5)   Defendants must immediately take all steps necessary to facilitate regular communication between and among all executive agencies responsible for the custody, detention or shelter of Class Members and the custody and care of their children, including at least ICE, CBP, BOP, and ORR, regarding the location and well-being of the Class Members' children.

(6)   Defendants, and their officers, agents, servants, employees, attorneys, and all those who are in active concert or participation with them, are preliminarily enjoined from removing any Class Members without their child, unless the Class Member affirmatively, knowingly, and voluntarily declines to be reunited with the child prior to the Class Member's deportation, or there is a determination that the parent is unfit or presents a danger to the child.

(7)   This Court retains jurisdiction to entertain such further proceedings and to enter such further orders as may be necessary or appropriate to implement and enforce the provisions of this Order and Preliminary Injunction.

A status conference will be held on July 6, 2018, at 12:00 noon, to discuss all necessary matters. A notice of teleconference information sheet will be provided in a separate order.

IT IS SO ORDERED.

COUNTY OF SANTA CLARA V. TRUMP

Order Granting Motion for Summary Judgment
November 20, 2017

Judge William H. Orrick
U.S. District Court, Northern District of California
On April 25, 2017, I entered a preliminary injunction against Section 9(a) of Executive Order 13768, "Enhancing Public Safety in the Interior of the United States,", 82 Fed. Reg. 8799 (Jan. 25, 2017) (the "Executive Order"). Preliminary Injunction Order ("PI Order"). I concluded that the County of Santa Clara and the City and County of San Francisco had pre-enforcement standing to protect hundreds of millions of dollars of federal grants from the unconstitutionally broad sweep of the Executive Order. The federal government argued for the first time at the hearing for the preliminary injunction that the Executive Order was meant to be far more narrow than I interpreted it, a mere directive to the Department of Homeland Security ("DHS") and the Department of Justice ("DOJ") that does not seek to place any new conditions on federal funds. I concluded that this interpretation was not legally plausible in light of the Executive Order's plain language, as confirmed by the administration's many statements indicating the Executive Order's expansive scope.

A month later, the Attorney General issued a two page memorandum memorializing the DOJ's interpretation (the "AG Memorandum") and asked me to reconsider the injunction. Because the AG's Memorandum does not amend the Executive Order, is not binding on the Executive Branch and suggests an implausible interpretation of Section 9(a), I denied the federal government's motion on July 20, 2017.

Now on summary judgment, the parties have shown that there are no material facts in dispute concerning the Executive Order. This Order plows no new ground: for the reasons summarized below, and as further described in my earlier Orders, I GRANT the Counties' motions for summary judgment on the Executive Order and permanently enjoin Section 9(a).

SUMMARY

The Executive Order, in addition to outlining a number of immigration enforcement policies, purports to "[e]nsure that jurisdictions that fail to comply with applicable Federal law do not receive Federal funds, except as mandated by law" and to establish a procedure to make "sanctuary jurisdictions" ineligible to receive federal grants. In two related actions, the County of Santa Clara and the City and County of San Francisco challenge Section 9 of the Executive Order as facially unconstitutional and have brought motions seeking summary judgment. San Francisco also seeks a declaration that its laws comply with Section 1373.

The Counties argue that Section 9(a) violates the separation of powers doctrine enshrined in the Constitution because it improperly seeks to wield congressional spending powers. It is so overbroad and coercive that even if the President had spending powers, the Executive Order would clearly exceed them and violate the Tenth Amendment's prohibition against commandeering local jurisdictions. It is so vague and standardless that it violates the Fifth Amendment's Due Process Clause and is void for vagueness. And because it seeks to deprive local jurisdictions of congressionally allocated funds without any notice or opportunity to be heard, it violates the procedural due process requirements of the Fifth Amendment.

The federal government responds that the Counties' cannot demonstrate that Section 9 of the Executive Order is invalid under all circumstances, which the federal government contends is the proper standard for a facial challenge. It also claims that the grant eligibility provision in Section 9(a) is consistent with the Constitution's separation of powers; that it is a valid exercise of the Spending Power because it is not overly coercive, does not force the Counties to take unconstitutional actions to receive the funds, and the funds bear a relationship to immigration; that the AG Memorandum clarifies the meaning of Section 9(a), eliminating its vagueness (and alternatively, the Counties' vagueness challenge impermissibly relies on speculation); and, finally, in light of the AG Memorandum, Section 9(a) does not apply to funding in which the County might have a constitutionally protectable interest (and alternatively that the federal government will apply the applicable procedures).

Section 9(a), by its plain language, attempts to reach all federal grants, not merely the three grants listed in the AG's Memorandum. The rest of the Executive Order is broader still, addressing all federal funding. And if there was doubt about the scope of the Executive Order, the President and Attorney General erased it with their public comments. The President has called it "a weapon" to use against jurisdictions that disagree with his preferred policies of immigration enforcement, and his press secretary reiterated that the President intends to ensure that "counties and other institutions that remain sanctuary cites don't get federal government funding in compliance with the executive order." The Attorney General has warned that jurisdictions that do not comply with Section 1373 would suffer "withholding grants, termination of grants, and disbarment or ineligibility for future grants," and the "claw back" of any funds previously awarded. The AG Memorandum not only provides an implausible interpretation of Section 9 (a) but is functionally an "illusory promise" because it does not amend Section 9(a) and does not bind the Executive branch. It does not change the plain meaning of the Executive Order.

The Constitution vests the spending powers in Congress, not the President, so the Executive Order cannot constitutionally place new conditions on federal funds. Further, the Tenth Amendment requires that conditions on federal funds be unambiguous and timely made; that they bear some relation to the funds at issue; and that they not be unduly coercive. Federal funding that bears no meaningful relationship to immigration enforcement cannot be threatened merely because a jurisdiction chooses an immigration enforcement strategy of which the President disapproves. Because the Executive Order violates the separation of powers doctrine and deprives the Counties of their Tenth and Fifth Amendment rights, I GRANT the Counties' motions for summary judgment and permanently enjoin the defunding and enforcement provisions of Section 9(a).

BACKGROUND

I.   THE EXECUTIVE ORDER

On January 25, 2017, President Donald J. Trump issued Executive Order 13768, "Enhancing Public Safety in the Interior of the United States." In outlining the Executive Order's purpose, Section 1 reads, in part, "Sanctuary jurisdictions across the United States willfully violate Federal law in an attempt to shield aliens from removal from the United States." EO § 1. Section 2 states that the policy of the executive branch is to "[e]nsure that jurisdictions that fail to comply with applicable Federal law do not receive Federal funds, except as mandated by law." Id. § 2(c).

Section 9, titled "Sanctuary Jurisdictions," lays out this policy in more detail. It reads:

> Sec. 9. Sanctuary Jurisdictions. It is the policy of the executive branch to ensure, to the fullest extent of the law, that a State, or a political subdivision of a State, shall comply with 8 U.S.C. 1373.

(a) In furtherance of this policy, the Attorney General and the Secretary, in their discretion and to the extent consistent with law, shall ensure that jurisdictions that willfully refuse to comply with 8 U.S.C. 1373 (sanctuary jurisdictions) are not eligible to receive Federal grants, except as deemed necessary for law enforcement purposes by the Attorney General or the Secretary. The Secretary has the authority to designate, in his discretion and to the extent consistent with law, a jurisdiction as a sanctuary jurisdiction. The Attorney General shall take appropriate enforcement action against any entity that violates 8 U.S.C. 1373, or which has in effect a statute, policy, or practice that prevents or hinders the enforcement of Federal law.

(b) To better inform the public regarding the public safety threats associated with sanctuary jurisdictions, the Secretary shall utilize the Declined Detainer Outcome Report or its equivalent and, on a weekly basis, make public a comprehensive list of criminal actions committed by aliens and any jurisdiction that ignored or otherwise failed to honor any detainers with respect to such aliens.

(c) The Director of the Office of Management and Budget is directed to obtain and provide relevant and responsive information on all Federal grant money that currently is received by any sanctuary jurisdiction.

Id. § 9.

Section 3 of the Executive Order, titled "Definitions," incorporates the definitions listed in 8 U.S.C. § 1101. Id. § 3. Section 1101 does not define "sanctuary jurisdiction." The term is not defined anywhere in the Executive Order. Similarly, neither section 1101 nor the Executive Order defines what it means for a jurisdiction to "willfully refuse to comply" with Section 1373 or for a policy to "prevent[] or hinder[] the enforcement of Federal law." Id. § 9(a).

II.   SECTION 1373

Section 1373, to which Section 9 refers, prohibits local governments from restricting government officials or entities from communicating immigration status information to ICE. It states in relevant part:

(a) In General. Notwithstanding any other provision of Federal, State, or local law, a Federal, State, or local government entity or official may not prohibit, or in any way restrict, any government entity or official from sending to, or receiving from, the Immigration and Naturalization Service information regarding the citizenship or immigration status, lawful or unlawful, of any individual.

(b) Additional Authority of Government Entities. Notwithstanding any other provision of Federal, State, or local law, no person or agency may prohibit, or in any way restrict, a Federal, State, or local government entity from doing any of the following with respect to information regarding the immigration status, lawful or unlawful, of any individual:

> (1) Sending such information to, or requesting or receiving such information from, the Service.
>
> (2) Maintaining such information.
>
> (3) Exchanging such information with any other Federal, State, or local government entity.

8 U.S.C. 1373.

In July, 2016, the U.S. Department of Justice issued guidance linking two federal grant programs, the State Criminal Alien Assistance Program ("SCAAP") and Edward Byrne Memorial Justice Assistance Grant ("JAG"), to compliance with Section 1373.3 This guidance states that all applicants for these two grant programs are required to "assure and certify compliance with all applicable federal statutes, including Section 1373, as well as all applicable federal regulations, policies, guidelines, and requirements." Id. The DOJ has indicated that the Community Oriented Policing Services Grant ("COPS") is also conditioned on compliance with Section 1373.

III. THE AG MEMORANDUM

On May 22, 2017, Attorney General Sessions issued the AG Memorandum, putting forward the DOJ's "conclusive" interpretation of the Executive Order. The AG Memorandum states that the Executive Order does not "purport to expand the existing statutory or constitutional authority of the Attorney General and the Secretary of Homeland Security in any respect" and instead instructs those officials to take action "to the extent consistent with the law." It also states that the defunding provision in section 9(a) will be applied "solely to federal grants administered by [DOJ] or [DHS]" and to grants that require the applicant to "certify . . . compliance with federal law, including 8 U.S.C. section 1373, as a condition for receiving an award." The AG Memorandum also states that DHS and DOJ may only impose these conditions pursuant to "existing statutory or constitutional authority," and only where "grantees will receive notice of their obligation to comply with section 1373."

The AG Memorandum purports to clarify the scope of the Executive Order to a more narrow interpretation than what its plain meaning allows. To fix the constitutional problems I have identified, the Executive Order itself would need to be amended. I have concluded that the AG Memorandum amounts to "nothing more than an illusory promise to enforce the Executive Order narrowly."

IV. CIVIL DETAINER REQUESTS

An ICE civil detainer request asks a local law enforcement agency to continue to hold an inmate who is in local jail because of actual or suspected violations of state criminal laws for up to 48 hours after his or her scheduled release so that ICE can determine if it wants to take that individual into custody. See 8 C.F.R. § 287.7. ICE civil detainer requests are voluntary and local governments are not required to honor them. See 8 C.F.R. § 287.7(a); Galarza v. Szalczyk, 745 F.3d 634, 643 (3d Cir. 2014) ("[S]ettled constitutional law clearly establishes that [immigration detainers] must be deemed requests" because any other interpretation would render them unconstitutional under the Tenth Amendment).

Several courts have held that it is a violation of the Fourth Amendment for local jurisdictions to hold suspected or actual removable aliens subject to civil detainer requests because those requests are often not supported by an individualized determination of probable cause that a crime has been committed. See Morales v. Chadbourne, 793 F.3d 208, 215-217 (1st Cir. 2015); Miranda-Olivares v. Clackamas Cty., No. 3:12-cv-02317-ST, 2014 WL 1414305, at *9-11 (D. Or. Apr. 11, 2014). ICE does not reimburse local jurisdictions for the cost of detaining individuals in response to a civil detainer request and does not indemnify local jurisdictions for potential liability they could face for related Fourth Amendment violations. See 8 C.F.R. § 287.7(e).

V.   THE COUNTIES' POLICIES

Santa Clara's Policies

A.

Santa Clara asserts that its local policies and practices with regard to federal immigration enforcement are at odds with the Executive Order's provisions regarding Section 1373. In 2010, the Santa Clara County Board of Supervisors adopted a Resolution prohibiting Santa Clara employees from using County resources to transmit any information to ICE that was collected in the course of providing critical services or benefits. The Resolution also prohibits employees from initiating an inquiry or enforcement action based solely on the individual's actual or suspected immigration status, national origin, race or ethnicity, or English-speaking ability, or from using County resources to pursue an individual solely because of an actual or suspected violation of immigration law.

Santa Clara also asserts that its policies with regard to ICE civil detainer requests are inconsistent with the Executive Order and the President's stated immigration enforcement agenda. Prior to late 2011, Santa Clara responded to and honored ICE civil detainer requests, housing an average of 135 additional inmates each day at a daily cost of approximately $159 per inmate. When the County raised concerns about the costs associated with complying with detainer requests and potential civil liability, ICE confirmed that it would not reimburse the County or indemnify it for the associated costs and liabilities.

Santa Clara subsequently convened a task force and adopted a new policy where the County agreed to honor requests for individuals with serious or violent felony convictions, but only if ICE would reimburse the County for the cost of holding those individuals. ICE has never agreed to reimburse the County for any costs, so since November 2011 the County has declined to honor all ICE detainer requests.

Appendix F.   County of Santa Clara v. Trump

San Francisco's Policies

B.

San Francisco's sanctuary city policies are contained in Chapters 12H and 12I of its Administrative Code. See S.F. Admin Code § 12. The stated purpose of these laws is "to foster respect and trust between law enforcement and residents, to protect limited local resources, to encourage cooperation between residents and City officials, including especially law enforcement and public health officers and employees, and to ensure community security, and due process for all." S.F. Admin Code § 12I.1.

As relevant to Section 1373, Chapter 12H prohibits San Francisco departments, agencies, commissions, officers, and employees from using San Francisco funds or resources to assist in enforcing federal immigration law or gathering or disseminating information regarding an individual's release status, or other confidential identifying information (which as defined does not include immigration status), unless such assistance is required by federal or state law. Id. § 12H.2. Although Chapter 12H previously prohibited city employees from sharing information regarding individuals' immigration status, the San Francisco Board of Supervisors removed this restriction in July 2016 due to concerns that the provision violated Section 1373.

With regard to civil detainer requests, Chapter 12I prohibits San Francisco law enforcement from detaining an individual, otherwise eligible for release from custody, solely on the basis of a civil immigration detainer request. It also prohibits local law enforcement from providing ICE with advanced notice that an individual will be released from custody, unless the individual meets certain criteria. Chapter 12I.3.(e) provides that a "[l]aw enforcement official shall not arrest or detain an individual, or provide any individual's personal information to a federal immigration officer, on the basis of an administrative warrant, prior deportation order, or other civil immigration document based solely on alleged violations of the civil provisions of immigration laws." San Francisco explains that it adopted these policies due to concerns that holding people in response to civil detainers would violate the Fourth Amendment and require it to dedicate scarce law enforcement personnel and resources to holding these individuals.

VI.   THE COUNTIES' FEDERAL FUNDING

Santa Clara's Federal Funding

A.

In the 2015-2016 fiscal year, Santa Clara received approximately $1.7 billion in federal and federally dependent funds, making up roughly 35% of the County's total revenues. This figure includes federal funds provided through entitlement programs.

Most of the County's federal funds are used to provide essential services to its residents. In support of its motion, the County includes a number of declarations outlining how a loss of any substantial amount of federal funding would force it to make substantial cut backs to safety-net programs and essential services and would require it to lay off thousands of employees. It highlights that the County's Valley Medical Center, the only public safety-net healthcare provider in the County, relies on $1 billion in federal funds each year, which covers up to 70% of its total annual costs. A loss of all federal funds would shut down Valley Medical Center and cut off the only healthcare option for thousands of poor, elderly, and vulnerable people in the County. It further highlights that Santa Clara's Social Services Agency, which provides various services to vulnerable residents, including child welfare and protection, aid to needy families, and support for disabled children, adults and the elderly, receives roughly 40% of its budget, $300 million, from federal funds. The County's Public Health Department receives 40% of its budget and $38 million in federal funds. And the County's Office of Emergency Services, whose job is to prepare for and respond to disasters such as earthquakes and terrorism, receives more than two-thirds of its budget from federal funds.

In the 2014-2015 fiscal year, the County received over $565 million in non-entitlement federal grants. This represents approximately 11% of the County's budget.

San Francisco's Federal Funding

B.

San Francisco's yearly budget is approximately $9.6 billion; it receives approximately $1.2 billion of this from the federal government. San Francisco uses these federal funds to provide vital services such as medical care, social services, and meals to vulnerable residents, to maintain and upgrade roads and public transportation, and to make needed seismic upgrades. Losing all, or a substantial amount, of federal funds would have significant effects on core San Francisco programs. Federal funds make up 30% of the budget for San Francisco's Department of Emergency Management, 33% of the budget for San Francisco's Human Services Agency, and 40% of the budget for San Francisco's Department of Public Health.

Approximately 20% of the federal funds, or $240 million, are from federal grants. San Francisco also receives $800 million each year in federal multi-year grants, primarily for public infrastructure projects.

San Francisco must adopt a balanced budget for each fiscal year beginning on July 1. Under local law, the Mayor must submit a balanced budget to the Board of Supervisors by June 1 and make fundamental budget decisions by May 15, including whether to create a budget reserve to account for the potential loss of significant funds. Any money placed in the budget reserve would not be available to be used for other programs or services in the coming fiscal year.

DISCUSSION

I.   JUSTICIABILITY

The federal government raises three primary arguments against the justiciability of the Counties' claims. First, it asserts that the Counties have not established a concrete risk of losing any funds under Section 9(a). Second, it argues that the Counties cannot establish the "concrete" injury necessary for standing nor "concrete" impact necessary for ripeness because neither the President nor the Secretary of DHS has disagreed with the "plan" set forth by the Attorney General in the AG Memorandum. Lastly, the federal government argues that because the Executive Order is merely a "internal directive," it does not affect the Counties.

I address its arguments in turn, repeating my previous conclusions. All of the Counties' claims are justiciable.

The Counties Establish a Concrete Risk of Losing Funds

A.

The federal government repeatedly indicated its intent to enforce the Executive Order in its public statements and through its actions. Although the defunding provision was not enforced against any jurisdiction prior to the nationwide injunction, the President and other members of the administration have made numerous statements reaffirming the federal government's intent to enforce the Executive Order and to use the threat of withholding federal funds as a tool to coerce states and local jurisdictions to change their policies.

For example, on February 5, 2017, after signing the Executive Order, President Trump confirmed that he was willing and able to use "defunding" as a "weapon" so that sanctuary cities would change their policies. Attorney General Sessions confirmed the federal government's intent to enforce the defunding provisions, stating that if jurisdictions do not comply with Section 1373, such violations would result in "withholding grants, termination of grants, and disbarment or ineligibility for future grants," and that the federal government would seek to "claw back any funds awarded to a jurisdiction that willfully violates 1373."

The statements of the President and the Attorney General repeatedly indicated an intent to defund sanctuary jurisdictions in compliance with the Executive Order. Though such explicit statements have been scant since I entered the preliminary injunction, the Counties' concerns that the federal government will enforce the defunding provision are well supported by the federal government's public statements and actions, all of which are consistent with enforcing the Executive Order.

In addition to demonstrating that the federal government is likely to enforce the Executive Order, the Counties have shown that the federal government is particularly likely to target them and the funds on which they rely. In the February 5, 2017 interview, President Trump specifically threatened to defund California, stating: "I'm very much opposed to sanctuary cities. They breed crime. There's a lot of problems. If we have to we'll defund, we give tremendous amounts of money to California . . . California in many ways is out of control." The Counties have established that they both receive large percentages of their federal funding through the State of California and that they would suffer injury if California was "defunded." ICE has identified California, Santa Clara County, and San Francisco as jurisdictions with policies that "Restrict Cooperation with ICE" and has identified Santa Clara County Main Jail and San Francisco County Jail as two of eleven detention centers with the "highest volume of detainers issued" that "do not comply with detainers on a routine basis."

The President and the Attorney General have also repeatedly held up San Francisco as an example of how sanctuary policies threaten public safety. In an op-ed recently published in the San Francisco Chronicle, the Attorney General wrote that "Kathryn Steinle might be alive today if she had not lived in a 'sanctuary city'" and implored "San Francisco and other cities to re-evaluate these policies." In his statements to federal, state, and local law enforcement on July 12, 2017, Attorney General Sessions referenced the tragic death of Ms. Steinle and noted that her killer "admitted that one reason he was in San Francisco that day was that he knew the city had these policies in place". These statements indicate not only the belief that San Francisco is a "sanctuary jurisdiction" but that its policies are particularly dangerous and in need of change. They also reveal a choice by the administration to hold up San Francisco as an exemplar of a sanctuary jurisdiction.

The federal government's specific criticisms of San Francisco, Santa Clara, and California support a well-founded fear that San Francisco and Santa Clara will face enforcement directly under the Executive Order, or could be subject to defunding indirectly through enforcement against California. San Francisco and Santa Clara have shown that their current practices and policies are targeted by the Executive Order. They have demonstrated that the federal government has repeatedly indicated its intent to enforce it. And they have established that the federal government has specifically highlighted Santa Clara and San Francisco as jurisdictions with sanctuary policies. On these facts, Santa Clara and San Francisco have demonstrated that the "threat of enforcement [is] credible, not simply imaginary or speculative." Id. (internal quotation marks omitted). Because the enforcement of Section 9(a) involves defunding, this establishes the Counties' concrete risk of losing funds.

The Counties Show Concrete Injury and Concrete Impact

B.

The Counties assert that the Executive Order threatens to penalize them for failing to comply with Section 1373 and for failing to honor detainer requests by withholding all federal funds, or at least all federal grants. Section 9(a) does not threaten all federal funding, but it does include all federal grants, which make up a significant part of the Counties' budgets. This threatened injury meets Article III's standing requirements. A "loss of funds promised under federal law [] satisfies Article III's standing requirement." Organized Village of Kake v. U.S. Dep't of Agric., 795 F.3d 956, 965 (9th Cir. 2015).

The Counties explained that the need to mitigate a potential sudden loss of federal funds wreaked havoc with their budgeting processes prior to issuance of the preliminary injunction. They could not make informed decisions about whether to keep spending federal funds on needed services for which they may not be reimbursed; they were forced to make contingency plans to deal with a potential loss of funds, including placing funds in a budget reserve in lieu of spending that money on needed programs; and the obligation to mitigate potential harm to their residents and drastic cuts to services could ultimately compel them to change their local policies to comply with what they believe to be an unconstitutional Executive Order. The potential loss of all federal grants creates a contingent liability large enough to have real and concrete impacts on the Counties' ability to budget and plan for the future. As discussed in more detail below, the Counties demonstrated that they are suffering a present "injury [] inflicted by the mere existence and threatened enforcement of the [Executive Order]." Village of Euclid, 272 U.S. at 385. Along with the threatened loss of funds, this may also establish Article III standing.

A sudden loss of grant funding would have another effect. The Counties receive large portions of their federal grants through reimbursement structures; the Counties first spend their own money on particular services and then receive reimbursements from the federal government based on the actual services provided. Because these funds are spent on an ongoing basis, at all times the Counties are expecting, and relying on, millions of dollars in federal reimbursements for services already provided. A sudden cut to funding, including a cut to these reimbursements, could place them immediately in significant debt. A sudden and unanticipated cut mid-fiscal year would substantially increase the injury to the Counties by forcing them to make even more drastic cuts to absorb the loss of funds during a truncated period in order to stay on budget.

San Francisco explains that a mid-year loss of only $120 million in federal funding would: require the City to make significant cuts to critical services and would result in reductions in the numbers of first responders, such as police officers, firefighters, and paramedics; require severe cuts to the City's MUNI transportation system; threaten the Mayor's program to end chronic veterans' homelessness by 2018; and likely require cuts to social services, such as senior meals, safety net services for low-income children, and domestic violence prevention services. Because federal grants support key services, San Francisco asserts that, without clarity about the funds the Executive Order could withhold or claw back, it would have needed to allocate millions of dollars to a budget reserve on May 15, 2017 to prepare for the potential loss of significant funds during the 2017 fiscal year.

Any funds placed in a reserve fund would not be available to fund other City programs and services for the 2017 fiscal year, which would have resulted in a dollar-for-dollar reduction in services the City is able to provide its residents.

Santa Clara asserts that the budgetary uncertainty put it in an "untenable position." It explained that Santa Clara's budget for the fiscal year is in place and was developed based on careful weighing of various factors, including anticipated revenues, specific service needs, salary and benefits for the County's 19,000 employees, and the County's fiscal priorities. Because Santa Clara operates federally funded programs on a daily basis, and incurs costs in anticipation that it will be reimbursed, its ability to provide these services depends on the County having some confidence that it will continue to receive the federal reimbursements and funds on which it depends. With the Executive Order's unclear and broad language threatening a significant cut to funding, the County did not know "whether to (1) continue incurring hundreds of millions of dollars in costs that may never be reimbursed by the federal government, (2) discontinue basic safety-net services delivered to its most vulnerable residents, or (3) in an attempt to avoid either of these outcomes, be effectively conscripted into using local law enforcement and other resources to assist the federal government in its immigration enforcement efforts."

The potential loss of funds also impacts the Counties' potential borrowing power and financial strength; San Francisco noted that it had received inquiries from credit rating agencies about the Executive Order and its impact on San Francisco's finances. This budget uncertainty is not abstract. It has caused the Counties real and tangible harms. They have adequately demonstrated that budgetary uncertainty of the type threatened by the Executive Order constitutes a sufficiently concrete injury and demonstrates a sufficiently concrete impact for purposes of justiciability.

The Executive Order is Not an Internal Directive

C.

The federal government argues that the Executive Order does not change the law, but merely directs the Attorney General and Secretary to enforce existing law. But the Executive Order is not readily susceptible to the federal government's narrow interpretation. Indeed, "[t]o read [the Executive Order] as the federal government desires requires rewriting, not just reinterpretation." U.S. v. Stevens, 559 U.S. 460, 481 (2010).

The federal government attempts to read out all of Section 9(a)'s unconstitutional directives to render it an ominous, misleading, and ultimately toothless threat. It urges that all it does is direct the Attorney General and Secretary to enforce existing grant conditions "consistent with law." But in reality, the defunding provision instructs the Attorney General and the Secretary to do something that only Congress has the authority to do – place new conditions on federal funds. If Section 9(a) does not direct the Attorney General and Secretary to place new conditions on federal funds, then it only authorizes them to do something they already have the power to do, which is to enforce existing grant requirements; effectively, the federal government argues that Section 9(a) is "valid" and does not raise constitutional issues as long as it does nothing at all. But a construction so narrow that it renders a legal action legally meaningless cannot possibly be reasonable and is clearly inconsistent with the Executive Order's broad intent.

The federal government's construction requires a complete rewriting of the Executive Order's language and does not retain any of Section 9(a)'s legal effect. The Executive Order, as written, is not merely an internal directive but an order intended to have the full force of the law.

II.   CONSTITUTIONALITY OF THE EXECUTIVE ORDER

The Executive Order Violates the Separation of Powers

A.

The Counties argue that the Executive Order is unconstitutional because it seeks to wield powers that belong exclusively to Congress, the spending powers. The federal government contends that (i) the grant eligibility provision in Section 9(a) is consistent with separation of powers; (ii) authority to impose at least some conditions is inherent in the statutory authority to administer a grant program; and (iii) the Counties have failed to establish that the Executive Order would be unconstitutional in all its applications.

The parties disagree about the standard for a facial challenge. Relying on United States v. Salerno, 481 U.S. 739, 745 (1987), the federal government argues that the Counties must demonstrate that Section 9(a) is invalid under all circumstances. Santa Clara asserts, and I agree, that a proper facial challenge can be brought when the challenged law cannot be narrowly construed by the courts or narrowly interpreted as to avoid constitutional questions. Jackson v. City & Cty. Of San Francisco, 746 F.3d 953, 963 (9th Cir. 2014). I have found that the Executive Order cannot be narrowly interpreted or construed to avoid constitutional questions, and the federal government makes no argument regarding the separation of powers principles other than its misguided assertion regarding the standard for a facial challenge. The Executive Order violates the Constitution's separation of powers principles.

The constitutional principle at issue is pretty basic. Article I of the Constitution grants Congress the federal spending powers. See U.S. Const. art. I, § 8, cl. 1. "Incident to this power, Congress may attach conditions on the receipt of federal funds, and has repeatedly employed the power 'to further broad policy objectives by conditioning receipt of federal moneys upon compliance by the recipient with federal statutory and administrative directives.'" South Dakota v. Dole, 483 U.S. 203, 206 (1987) (citing Fullilove v. Klutznick, 448 U.S. 448, 474

(1980) (emphasis added). While the President may veto a Congressional enactment under the Presentment Clause, he must "either 'approve all the parts of a Bill, or reject it in total.'" Clinton v. City of New York, 524 U.S. 417, 438 (1998) (quoting 33 Writings of George Washington 96 (J. Fitzpatrick ed., 1940)). He cannot "repeal[] or amend[] parts of duly enacted statues" after they become law. Id. at 439.

This is true even if Congress has attempted to expressly delegate such power to the President. Id. In City of New York, the Supreme Court concluded that the Line Item Veto Act, which sought to grant the President the power to cancel particular direct spending and tax benefit provisions in bills, was unconstitutional because it ran afoul of the " 'finely wrought' procedures commanded by the Constitution" for enacting laws. Id. at 448 (quoting INS v. Chadha, 462 U.S. 919, 951 (1983)). While Congress can delegate some discretion to the President to decide how to spend appropriated funds, any delegation and discretion is cabined by these constitutional boundaries.

After a bill becomes law, the President is required to "take Care that the Law be faithfully executed." See U.S. Const. art. II, § 3, cl. 5. Where Congress has failed to give the President discretion in allocating funds, the President has no constitutional authority to withhold such funds and violates his obligation to faithfully execute the laws duly enacted by Congress if he does so. See City of New York, 524 U.S. at 439; U.S. Const. art. I, § 8, cl. 1. Further, "[w]hen the President takes measures incompatible with the expressed or implied will of Congress, his power is at its lowest ebb." Youngstown Sheet & Tube Co. v. Sawyer, 343 U.S. 579, 637 (1952) (Jackson, J., concurring). Congress has intentionally limited the ability of the President to withhold or "impound" appropriated funds and has provided that the President may only do so after following particular procedures and after receiving Congress's express permission. See Impoundment Control Act of 1974, 2 U.S.C. §§ 683 et seq.

The Executive Order runs afoul of this fundamental constitutional structure. The President does not have the power to place conditions on federal funds and, obviously, cannot delegate this power. But that is what Section 9(a) purports to do, to give the Attorney General and the Secretary the power to place a new condition on federal funds (compliance with Section 1373) not authorized by Congress.

Section 9(a) is particularly problematic because Congress has repeatedly declined to broadly condition federal funds or grants on compliance with Section 1373 or other federal immigration laws as the Executive Order purports to do. See, e.g., Ending Sanctuary Cities Act of 2016, H.R. 6252, 114th Cong. (2016); Stop Dangerous Sanctuary Cities Act, S. 3100, 114th Cong. (2016); Stop Dangerous Sanctuary Cities Act, H.R. 5654, 114th Cong. (2016); Stop Sanctuary Policies and Protect Americans Act, S. 2146, 114th Cong. (2016). This puts the President's power "at its lowest ebb." Youngstown, 343 U.S. at 637. The Executive Order's attempt to place new conditions on federal funds is an improper attempt to wield Congress's exclusive spending power and is a violation of the Constitution's separation of powers principles.

Appendix F.   County of Santa Clara v. Trump

The Counties' Spending Clause Claims

B.

The Counties also argue that, even if the President had the spending power, the Executive Order would be unconstitutional under the Tenth Amendment because it exceeds those powers. Relying largely on the language in the AG Memorandum, the federal government counters that: (i) the Counties do not demonstrate that Section 9(a) is clearly coercive; (ii) Section 9(a) does not induce the Counties to violate any applicable constitutional or statutory limitation; (iii) the AG Memorandum eliminated the possibility of Section 9(a) being applied in arenas unrelated to immigration; and (iv) the AG Memorandum clarifies how the provisions of Section 9(a) will be applied. As I explained in the Order Denying Reconsideration, the AG Memorandum does not resolve the Executive Order's constitutional issues or alter the constitutional analysis, and there is no need to discuss further those latter two arguments.

Regarding the first two arguments, Congress has significant authority to encourage policy through its spending power. The Supreme Court, however, has articulated a number of limitations to the conditions Congress can place on federal funds. The Executive Order likely violates at least three of these restrictions: (1) conditions must be unambiguous and cannot be imposed after funds have already been accepted; (2) there must be a nexus between the federal funds at issue and the federal program's purpose; and (3) the financial inducement cannot be coercive.

1. Unambiguous Requirement

When Congress places conditions on federal funds, "it must do so unambiguously" so that state and local jurisdictions contemplating whether to accept such funds can "exercise their choice knowingly, cognizant of the consequences of their participation." Dole, 483 U.S. at 203 (internal quotation marks omitted). Because states must opt-in to a federal program willingly, fully aware of the associated conditions, Congress cannot implement new conditions after-the-fact. See Nat'l Fed. of Indep. Bus. v. Sebelius ("NFIB"), 132 S. Ct. 2566, 2602-04 (2012). "The legitimacy of Congress's exercise of the spending power thus rests on whether the state voluntarily and knowingly accepts the terms of the contract" at the time Congress offers the money. Id. at 2602.

The Executive Order purports retroactively to condition all "federal grants" on compliance with Section 1373. As this condition was not an unambiguous condition that the states and local jurisdictions voluntarily and knowingly accepted at the time Congress appropriated these funds, it cannot be imposed now by the Executive Order. Moreover, the Executive Order's language refers to all federal grants but the DOJ says it only applies to three grants issued through the Departments of Justice and Homeland Security. If the funds at stake are not clear, the Counties cannot voluntarily and knowingly choose to accept the conditions on such funds.

277

Finally, as discussed below in Section II.D., the Executive Order's vague language does not make clear what conduct it proscribes or give jurisdictions a reasonable opportunity to avoid its penalties. The unclear and untimely conditions in the Executive Order fail the "unambiguous" restriction because the Executive Order does not make clear to states and local governments what funds are at issue and what conditions apply to those funds, making it impossible for them to "voluntarily and knowingly accept[] the terms of the contract." NFIB, 132 S. Ct. at 2602.

2. Nexus Requirement

The conditions placed on congressional spending must have some nexus with the purpose of the implicated funds. "Congress may condition grants under the spending power only in ways reasonably related to the purpose of the federal program." Dole, 483 U.S. at 213. This means that funds conditioned on compliance with Section 1373 must have some nexus to immigration enforcement.

The Executive Order's attempt to condition all federal grants on compliance with Section 1373 clearly runs afoul of the nexus requirement: there is no nexus between Section 1373 and most categories of federal funding, such as funding related to Medicare, Medicaid, transportation, child welfare services, immunization and vaccination programs, and emergency preparedness. The Executive Order inverts the nexus requirement, directing the Attorney General and Secretary to cut off all federal grants to "sanctuary jurisdictions" but giving them discretion to allow "sanctuary jurisdictions" to receive grants "deemed necessary for law enforcement purposes." EO § 9(a). As the subset of grants "deemed necessary for law enforcement purposes" likely includes any federal funds related to immigration enforcement, the Executive Order expressly targets for defunding grants with no nexus to immigration enforcement at all. This is the precise opposite of what the nexus test requires.

3. Not Coercive Requirement

Finally, Congress cannot use the spending power in a way that compels local jurisdictions to adopt certain policies. Congress cannot offer "financial inducement . . . so coercive as to pass the point at which pressure turns to compulsion." Dole, 483 U.S. at 211 (internal quotation marks omitted). Legislation that "coerces a State to adopt a federal regulatory system as its own" "runs contrary to our system of federalism." NFIB, 132 S. Ct. at 2602. States must have a "legitimate choice whether to accept the federal conditions in exchange for federal funds." Id. at 2602-03.

In NFIB, the Supreme Court concluded that the Affordable Care Act's threat of denying Medicaid funds, which constituted over 10 percent of the State's overall budget, was unconstitutionally coercive and represented a "gun to the head." Id. at 2604. The Executive Order threatens to deny sanctuary jurisdictions all federal grants, hundreds of millions of dollars on which the Counties rely. The threat is unconstitutionally coercive.

Appendix F.   County of Santa Clara v. Trump

The Counties' Tenth Amendment Claim

C.

The Counties argue that Section 9(a) violates the Tenth Amendment because it attempts to conscript states and local jurisdictions into carrying out federal immigration law. The federal government does not specifically address the constitutional argument. Instead, it asserts that in order to successfully bring a facial challenge, San Francisco must demonstrate that the "appropriate enforcement action" provision of Section 9(a) would violate the Tenth Amendment in all of its applications. As previously discussed, this argument misinterprets the facial challenge standard.

"The Federal government may not compel the States to enact or administer a federal regulatory program." New York, 505 U.S. at 188. "The Federal government may neither issue directives requiring the States to address particular problems, nor command the States' officers, or those of their political subdivisions, to administer or enforce a federal regulatory program." Printz v. United States, 521 U.S. 898, 935 (1997). "That is true whether Congress directly commands a State to regulate or indirectly coerces a State to adopt a federal regulatory system as its own." NFIB, 132 S. Ct. at 2602.

The Counties have demonstrated that under their reasonable interpretation, the Executive Order equates "sanctuary jurisdictions" with "any jurisdiction that ignored or otherwise failed to honor any detainers" and therefore places such jurisdictions at risk of losing all federal grants. See EO § 9(b). The Counties have shown that losing all of their federal grant funding would have significant effects on their ability to provide services to their residents and that they may have no legitimate choice but to accept the federal government's conditions in exchange for those funds.

To the extent the Executive Order seeks to condition all federal grants on honoring civil detainer requests, it is likely unconstitutional under the Tenth Amendment because it seeks to compel the states and local jurisdictions to enforce a federal regulatory program through coercion. It directs the Attorney General to "take appropriate enforcement action against any entity that violates 8 U.S.C. 1373, or which has in effect a statute, policy, or practice that prevents or hinders the enforcement of Federal law." EO § 9(a). Although the Executive Order provides no further clarification on what this "enforcement" might entail or what policies might "hinder[] the enforcement of Federal law," Attorney General Sessions, who is tasked with implementing this provision, has equated failure to honor civil detainer requests with policies that "frustrate th[e] enforcement of immigration laws." See Sessions Press Conference at 2. Given the Attorney General's apparent interpretation of Section 1373, the Executive Order threatens "enforcement action" against any jurisdiction that refuses to comply with detainer requests or otherwise fails to enforce federal immigration law. While this threat of "enforcement" is left vague and unexplained, "enforcement" by its own definition means to "compel[] compliance." See BLACK'S LAW DICTIONARY 645 (10th ed. 2014) (defining "enforcement" as "The act or process of compelling compliance with a law, mandate, command, decree, or agreement."). By seeking to compel states and local jurisdictions to honor civil detainer requests by threatening enforcement action, the Executive Order violates the Tenth Amendment's provisions against conscription.

The Supreme Court has repeatedly held that, "The Federal government cannot compel the States to enact or administer a federal regulatory program." New York v. United States, 505 U.S. 144, 188 (1992). The federal government cannot command them to adopt certain policies, id. at 188, command them to carry out federal programs, Printz, 521 U.S. at 935, or otherwise to "coerce them into adopting a federal regulatory system as their own," NFIB, 132 S. Ct. at 2602. The Executive Order uses coercive means in an attempt to force states and local jurisdictions to honor civil detainer requests, which are voluntary "requests" precisely because the federal government cannot command states to comply with them under the Tenth Amendment. The Executive Order attempts to use coercive methods to circumvent the Tenth Amendment's direct prohibition against conscription. While the federal government may incentivize states to adopt federal programs voluntarily, it cannot use means that are so coercive as to compel their compliance. The Executive Order's threat to pull all federal grants from jurisdictions that refuse to honor detainer requests or to bring "enforcement action" against them violates the Tenth Amendment's prohibitions against commandeering.

Santa Clara's Fifth Amendment Vagueness Claim

D.

The Counties assert that the Executive Order is unconstitutionally vague in violation of the Fifth Amendment's Due Process Clause. The federal government responds, first, that the Executive Order is an internal directive that does not have a direct effect on Santa Clara and so Santa Clara needs no notice. This argument holds no weight; as discussed before, the Executive Order is not merely an internal directive. Next, it argues that the AG Memorandum "authoritatively clarifies" the terms and makes it clear which federal grants will be affected by the Executive Order. As previously explained, the AG Memorandum is not authoritative and does not amend the Executive Order or bind the rest of the Executive Branch, and it does not affect the constitutional analysis.

A law is unconstitutionally vague and void under the Fifth Amendment if it fails to make clear what conduct it prohibits and if it fails to lay out clear standards for enforcement. See Gaynard v. City of Rockford, 408 U.S. 104, 108 (1972). To satisfy due process, courts insist that laws (1) "give the person of ordinary intelligence a reasonable opportunity to know what is prohibited, so that he may act accordingly" and (2) "provide explicit standards for those who apply them." Id. The Executive Order does not meet either of these requirements.

Appendix F.   County of Santa Clara v. Trump

The Executive Order does not make clear what conduct might subject a state or local jurisdiction to defunding or enforcement action, making it impossible for jurisdictions to determine how to modify their conduct, if at all, to avoid the Executive Order's penalties. The Executive Order directs the Attorney General and Secretary to ensure that jurisdictions that "willfully refuse to comply" with Section 1373, "sanctuary jurisdictions," are not eligible to receive federal grants. Past DOJ guidance and various court cases interpreting Section 1373 have not reached consistent conclusions as to what Section 1373 requires. In the face of conflicting guidance, with no clear standard from the federal government, jurisdictions do not know how to avoid the Executive Order's defunding penalty.

Further, because the Executive Order does not clearly define "sanctuary jurisdictions," the conduct that will subject a jurisdiction to defunding under the Executive Order is not fully outlined. In addition, the Executive Order directs the Attorney General to take "appropriate enforcement action" against any jurisdiction that willfully refuses to comply with Section 1373 or otherwise has a policy or practice that "hinders the enforcement of Federal law." This provision vastly expands the scope of the Executive Order. What does it mean to "hinder" the enforcement of federal law? What federal law is at issue: immigration laws? All federal laws? The Executive Order offers no clarification. Although the AG Memorandum purports to clarify these op en questions, it cannot "authoritatively" do so because it does not carry the force of law. It cannot address these constitutional failings of the Executive Order.

The Executive Order also fails to provide clear standards to the Secretary and the Attorney General to prevent "arbitrary and discriminatory enforcement." Id. The Executive Order gives the Secretary discretion to designate jurisdictions as "sanctuary jurisdictions" to the extent consistent with law. But there are no laws, besides the Executive Order, outlining what a sanctuary jurisdiction is, leaving the Secretary with unfettered discretion and the Executive Order's vague language to make "sanctuary jurisdiction" designations. Similarly, the Executive Order directs the Attorney General to take "appropriate enforcement action" against any jurisdiction that "hinders the enforcement of Federal law." This expansive, standardless language creates huge potential for arbitrary and discriminatory enforcement, leaving the Attorney General to figure out what "appropriate enforcement action" might entail and what policies and practices might "hinder[] the enforcement of Federal law." This language is "so standardless that it authorizes or encourages seriously discriminatory enforcement." United States v. Williams, 553 U.S. 285, 304 (2008).

The Executive Order gives the Counties no clear guidance on how to comply with its provisions or what penalties will result from non-compliance, and its standardless guidance and enforcement provisions are also likely to result in arbitrary and discriminatory enforcement. It does not "give the person of ordinary intelligence a reasonable opportunity to know what is prohibited, so that he may act accordingly." Gaynard, 408 U.S. at 108. Section 9(a) is void for vagueness under the Fifth Amendment.

Santa Clara's Fifth Amendment Procedural Due Process Claim

E.

The Counties assert that the Executive Order fails to provide them with procedural due process in violation of the Fifth Amendment. Again relying on the AG Memorandum, the federal government argues that Section 9(a) does not apply to funding "in which the County might have a constitutionally protectable property interest." SC Oppo. at 19.

To have a legitimate property interest, a person "must have more than a unilateral expectation of it. He must, instead, have a legitimate claim of entitlement to it." Bd. of Regents v. Roth, 408 U.S. 564, 577 (1972). A state or local government has a legitimate claim of entitlement to congressionally appropriated funds, which are akin to funds owed on a contract. See NFIB, 132 S. Ct. at 2602 ("The legitimacy of Congress' power to legislate under the spending power [] rests on whether the State voluntarily and knowingly accepts the terms of the 'contract.' "). The Counties have a legitimate property interest in federal funds that Congress has already appropriated and that the Counties have accepted.

The Executive Order purports to make the Counties ineligible to receive these funds through a discretionary and undefined process. The Executive Order directs the Attorney General and Secretary to designate various states and local jurisdictions as "sanctuary jurisdictions," ensure that such jurisdictions are "not eligible" to receive federal grants, and "take enforcement action" against them. EO § 9 (a). It does not direct the Attorney General or Secretary to provide "sanctuary jurisdictions" with any notice of an unfavorable designation or impending cut to funding. And it does not set up any administrative or judicial procedure for states and local jurisdictions to be heard, to challenge enforcement action, or to appeal any action taken against them under the Executive Order. This complete lack of process violates the Fifth Amendment's due process requirements. Matthew v. Eldridge, 424 U.S. 319, 349 (1976) ("The essence of due process is the requirement that a person in jeopardy of serious loss be given notice of the case against him and opportunity to meet it.") (internal alterations and quotations omitted).

The Counties have demonstrated that the Executive Order has caused and will cause them constitutional injuries by violating the separation of powers doctrine and depriving them of their Tenth and Fifth Amendment rights. Accordingly, the Counties' motions for summary judgment are GRANTED with respect to Section 9(a) of the Executive Order.

* * *

CONCLUSION

The Counties have demonstrated that the Executive Order has caused and will cause them constitutional injuries by violating the separation of powers doctrine and depriving them of their Tenth and Fifth Amendment rights. Accordingly, the Counties' motions for summary judgment are GRANTED regarding Section 9(a). The defendants are permanently enjoined from enforcing Section 9(a) of the Executive Order against jurisdictions they deem as sanctuary jurisdictions. Because Section 9(a) is unconstitutional on its face, and not simply in its application to the plaintiffs here, a nationwide injunction against the defendants other than President Trump is appropriate. See California v. Yamasaki, 442 U.S. 682, 702 (1979)("[T]he scope of injunctive relief is dictated by the extent of the violation established, not by the geographical extent of the plaintiff."); Washington v. Trump, 847 F.3d 1151, 1161-67 (9th Cir. 2017) (affirming nationwide injunction against executive travel ban order).

IT IS SO ORDERED.
Dated: November 20, 2017
William H. Orrick
United States District Judge

BARBOSA V. BARR

Case No. 15-72092, 9th Cir., March 5, 2019

Before: Susan P. Graber and Marsha S. Berzon, Circuit Judges, and John R. Tunheim,* Chief District Judge.

Opinion by Judge Graber; Concurrence by Judge Berzon

GRABER, Circuit Judge:

Petitioner Pedro Aguirre Barbosa, a Mexican citizen, was convicted of robbery in the third degree in violation of Oregon Revised Statutes section 164.395. An immigration judge ("IJ") denied relief from removal, and the Board of Immigration Appeals ("BIA") dismissed Petitioner's appeal. As relevant here, the BIA held that section 164.395 categorically constitutes a crime involving moral turpitude ("CIMT") and that Petitioner had failed to prove membership in a "particular social group" for the purpose of establishing refugee status.

We hold that section 164.395 is not categorically a CIMT, but we agree that Petitioner did not demonstrate membership in a "particular social group." Accordingly, we grant the petition for review in part, deny it in part, and remand to the BIA for further proceedings consistent with this decision.

Sometime between 1997 and 1999, Petitioner entered the United States. In 2008, he was charged with, and pleaded no contest to, a violation of Oregon Revised Statutes section 164.395, which provides:

(1) A person commits the crime of robbery in the third degree if in the course of committing or attempting to commit theft or unauthorized use of a vehicle as defined in ORS 164.135[1] the person uses or threatens the immediate use of physical force upon another person with the intent of:

   (a) Preventing or overcoming resistance to the taking of the property or to retention thereof immediately after the taking; or

   (b) Compelling the owner of such property or another person to deliver the property or to engage in other conduct which might aid in the commission of the theft or unauthorized use of a vehicle.

(2) Robbery in the third degree is a Class C felony.

---

1. Oregon Revised Statutes section 164.135 defines unauthorized use of a vehicle.

In 2010, the government served Petitioner with a notice to appear. Petitioner conceded removability and applied for cancellation of removal, withholding of removal, and other forms of relief.

An IJ denied all of Petitioner's claims. The BIA affirmed the IJ's decision. The BIA held, among other things, that section 164.395 constitutes a categorical CIMT and that Petitioner is therefore statutorily ineligible for cancellation of removal under 8 U.S.C. § 1229b. Additionally, the BIA held that Petitioner failed to establish membership in a "particular social group," so he was not entitled to withholding of removal under 8 U.S.C. § 1231(b)(3)(A). Petitioner then filed this timely petition for review.

A.   Section 164.395 and Crimes Involving Moral Turpitude

To determine whether section 164.395 is a CIMT, we follow the three-step process mandated by Descamps v. United States, 570 U.S. 254 (2013):

At the first step, we compare the elements of the state offense to the elements of the generic offense defined by federal law. If this "categorical approach" reveals that the elements of the state crime are the same as or narrower than the elements of the federal offense, then the state crime is a categorical match and every conviction under that statute qualifies as [a CIMT]. When a statute is "overbroad," meaning that it criminalizes conduct that goes beyond the elements of the federal offense, we turn to step two: determining whether the statute is "divisible" or "indivisible." If the statute is indivisible, "our inquiry ends, because a conviction under an indivisible, overbroad statute can never serve as a predicate offense." Only when a statute is overbroad and divisible do we turn to step three—the "modified categorical approach." At this step, we may examine certain documents from the defendant's record of conviction to determine what elements of the divisible statute he was convicted of violating. Almanza-Arenas v. Lynch, 815 F.3d 469, 475 (9th Cir. 2016) (en banc) (quoting Lopez-Valencia v. Lynch, 798 F.3d 863, 867–68 (9th Cir. 2015)).

1. Step One: Categorical Approach

To determine whether a state criminal statute is categorically a CIMT, we use a two-step process. Castrijon- Garcia v. Holder, 704 F.3d 1205, 1208 (9th Cir. 2013). First, we "identify the elements of the statute of conviction." Id. Because "the BIA has no special expertise by virtue of its statutory responsibilities in construing state or federal criminal statutes," we review this step de novo. Id. (internal quotation marks and brackets omitted). Second, we "compare the elements of the statute of conviction to the generic definition of a [CIMT] and decide whether the conviction meets that definition." Id. "The BIA's conclusion that a particular crime does or does not involve moral turpitude is subject to different standards of review depending on whether the BIA issues or relies on a published decision in coming to its conclusion." Nunez v. Holder, 594 F.3d 1124, 1129 (9th Cir. 2010). Here, the BIA neither issued nor relied on its own published decision. Therefore, "we defer to its conclusion to the extent that it has the 'power to persuade.'" Id. (quoting Marmolejo-Campos v. Holder, 558 F.3d 903, 909 (9th Cir. 2009) (en banc)).

The question at this step is "not whether some of the conduct prohibited by the statute is morally turpitudinous, but rather whether all of the conduct prohibited by the statute is morally turpitudinous." Morales-Garcia v. Holder, 567 F.3d 1058, 1062 (9th Cir. 2009) (internal quotation marks and brackets omitted). The Immigration and Nationality Act ("INA") does not define the term "moral turpitude" or detail particular crimes involving moral turpitude. Mendoza v. Holder, 623 F.3d 1299, 1302 (9th Cir. 2010). We have noted that "'moral turpitude' is perhaps the quintessential example of an ambiguous phrase." Marmolejo-Campos, 558 F.3d at 909. Despite that ambiguity, there is agreement that "moral turpitude" generally inheres in offenses involving fraud or those that are inherently "base, vile, or depraved—if they offend society's most fundamental values, or shock society's conscience." Mendoza, 623 F.3d at 1302; see, e.g., In re Flores, 17 I. & N. Dec. 225, 227–28 (B.I.A. 1980). "These two categories, however, are not exhaustive." Rivera v. Lynch, 816 F.3d 1064, 1074 (9th Cir. 2016) (providing common law perjury as an example of a CIMT that "does not fit neatly into the two-part framework").

"Absent consistent or logical rules to follow as we determine whether a crime (other than one involving fraud) involves moral turpitude, our most useful guidance often comes from comparing the crime with others that we have previously deemed morally turpitudinous." Nunez, 594 F.3d at 1131. When analyzing robbery offenses, we have compared robbery offenses to theft offenses, many of which involve moral turpitude. See Mendoza, 623 F.3d at 1303–04 ("The BIA's determination that robbery is a CIMT is also a logical outgrowth of its holding that theft offenses are CIMTs."). Here, the BIA held that section 164.395 "describes an offense that is committed by a defendant who employs the use or threatened use of physical force with the intent to commit the theft or unauthorized use of a vehicle." The decision cites Mendoza, 623 F.3d at 1303–04, which analogized robbery to theft and applied that comparison to hold that California's robbery statute is categorically a CIMT.

But Oregon Revised Statutes section 164.395 is materially broader than the California robbery statute at issue in Mendoza. Specifically, section 164.395 encompasses the unauthorized use of a vehicle, which does not include as an essential element an intent to deprive the owner of his or her property permanently. See State v. Pusztai, 348 P.3d 241, 243–44 (Or. Ct. App. 2015) (holding that unauthorized use of a vehicle under section 164.135 requires knowing use of the vehicle but does not require an intent to deprive the owner of the vehicle permanently). Under longstanding BIA precedent, "a theft offense [was] not categorically a crime of moral turpitude if the statute of conviction is broad enough to criminalize a taking with intent to deprive the owner of his property only temporarily." Almanza-Arenas, 815 F.3d at 476 (quoting Castillo-Cruz v. Holder, 581 F.3d 1154, 1159 (9th Cir. 2009)).

We recognize that the BIA recently adopted a more expansive standard for determining whether a theft offense constitutes a CIMT. See In re Diaz-Lizarraga, 26 I. & N. Dec. 847, 854–55 (B.I.A. 2016). Because Petitioner received his notice to appear before the BIA changed its interpretation, the new standard does not apply retroactively to his case. See Garcia-Martinez v. Sessions, 886 F.3d 1291, 1296 (9th Cir. 2018). Accordingly, under the theft framework for a CIMT applicable to Petitioner, section 164.395 is not a categorical CIMT.[2]

Robbery includes the additional factor of actual or threatened violence. State v. Hamilton, 233 P.3d 432, 436 (Or. 2010). But it is clear that a conviction under section 164.395 requires only minimal physical force. See, e.g., State v. Johnson, 168 P.3d 312, 314–15 (Or. Ct. App. 2007) (holding that sufficient evidence supported a conviction under section 164.395 even though the victim only "felt that she was losing her purse"). "Non-fraudulent CIMTs almost always involve an intent to harm someone, " Mtoched v. Lynch, 786 F.3d 1210, 1216 (9th Cir. 2015) (internal quotation marks omitted), or an "intent to injure, actual injury, or a protected class of victim," Turijan v. Holder, 744 F.3d 617, 619 (9th Cir. 2014); Castrijon-Garcia, 704 F.3d at 1213. Because section 164.395 requires only minimal physical force, the statute does not meet the level of force required to be a CIMT. Therefore, we hold that, although robbery under section 164.395 involves a taking of property and the threatened or actual use of force, the minimal force required for conviction is insufficient to label the crime a CIMT.

2. *Step Two: Divisibility*

After determining that section 164.395 is not categorically a CIMT, we ordinarily proceed to step two, that is, deciding whether the statute is divisible or indivisible. Almanza- Arenas, 815 F.3d at 476–77. The government argues that we should remand this case to the BIA to address the question of divisibility. We disagree. "We owe no deference to the decision of the BIA on [divisibility] and there is no reason to remand for the BIA to decide the issue of divisibility in the first instance." Sandoval v. Sessions, 866 F.3d 986, 993 (9th Cir. 2017).

On the merits of the divisibility inquiry, the government did not argue to us that section 164.395 is divisible. We therefore deem the issue waived. See Rizk v.

---

2. By contrast, permanent deprivation is not a required element when considering whether a theft offense is an aggravated felony under INA § 101(a)(43)(G). Ngaeth v. Mukasey, 545 F.3d 796, 800–01 (9th Cir. 2008) (per curiam).

Holder, 629 F.3d 1083, 1091 n.3 (9th Cir. 2011) (holding that issues not raised in the opening brief are waived).

Having held that Petitioner's conviction is not for a CIMT, we remand this matter to the BIA to consider on the merits Petitioner's request for cancellation of removal.

B.   "Particular Social Group" Determination

[This portion of the opinion is omitted from the excerpt.]

Petition GRANTED in part and DENIED in part; REMANDED with instructions. Costs on appeal awarded to Petitioner.

BERZON, Circuit Judge, concurring:

I concur in the majority opinion in full. I write separately to join the chorus of voices calling for renewed consideration as to whether the phrase "crime involving moral turpitude" is unconstitutionally vague.

As Judge Fletcher recently noted, "[d]espite many years of trying, courts and administrators have not been able to establish coherent criteria" for determining whether an offense constitutes a crime involving moral turpitude. Islas- Veloz v. Whitaker, 914 F.3d 1249, 1258 (9th Cir. 2019) (Fletcher, J., concurring). Earlier, I made a similar observation myself. See Marmolejo-Campos v. Holder, 558 F.3d 903, 922 (9th Cir. 2009) (en banc) (Berzon, J., dissenting) ("[I]t is hard to say that any articulable principle distinguishes the offenses that are CIMTs from those that are not.").

Judge Fletcher and I are not the first to make these observations, and I am confident that we will not be the last. See, e.g., Arias v. Lynch, 834 F.3d 823, 830 (7th Cir. 2016) Posner, J., concurring) ("It is preposterous that that stale, antiquated, and, worse, meaningless phrase should continue to be a part of American law."); Marciano v. INS, 450 F.2d 1022, 1026 n.1 (8th Cir. 1971) (Eisele, J., dissenting) ("[T]hat the phrase 'crime involving moral turpitude' is unconstitutionally vague and violates the due process clause . . . seems manifest by the variety and inconsistency of the various opinions attempting to deal with the phrase."); Jordan v. De George, 341 U.S. 223, 232 (1951) (Jackson, J., dissenting) ("[T]he phrase 'crime involving moral turpitude' . . . has no sufficiently definite meaning to be a constitutional standard for deportation."); see also Jennifer Lee Koh, Crimmigration and the Void for Vagueness Doctrine, 2016 Wis. L. Rev. 1127, 1177–79; Lindsay M. Kornegay & Evan Tsen Lee, Why Deporting Immigrants for "Crimes Involving Moral Turpitude" Is Now Unconstitutional, 13 Duke J. Const. L. & Pub. Pol'y 47, 48–49 (2017).

The Supreme Court has recognized that "the failure of 'persistent efforts . . . to establish a standard' can provide evidence of vagueness." Johnson v. United States, 135 S. Ct. 2551, 2558 (2015) (quoting United States v. L. Cohen Grocery Co., 255 U.S. 81, 91 (1921)). This case provides yet another example. Under longstanding Board of Immigration Appeals (BIA) precedent, a theft statute does not constitute a crime involving moral turpitude if the statute criminalizes temporary takings. See, e.g., Matter of H-, 2 I. & N. Dec. 864, 865 (B.I.A. 1947); see also Almanza-Arenas v. Lynch, 815 F.3d 469, 476 (9th Cir. 2016) (en banc). The primary opinion holds that, because third-degree robbery under section 164.395 of the Oregon Revised Statutes covers temporary takings, it does not constitute a conviction for a crime involving moral turpitude. But an immigrant who faces deportation today may well face a different result; in 2016, the BIA departed from this decades-old interpretation. See Matter of Diaz-Lizarraga, 26 I. & N. Dec. 847, 855 (B.I.A. 2016); see also Garcia-Martinez v. Sessions, 886 F.3d 1291, 1296 (9th Cir. 2018).

Recognizing that "'moral turpitude' is perhaps the quintessential example of an ambiguous phrase," we have attempted to resolve these cases on a case-by-case basis. Marmolejo-Campos, 558 F.3d at 909. "Absent consistent or logical rules to follow as we determine whether a crime . . . involves moral turpitude, our most useful guidance often comes from comparing the crime with others that we have previously deemed morally turpitudinous." Nunez v. Holder, 594 F.3d 1124, 1131 (9th Cir. 2010). This approach has been, as Judge Fletcher stated, a "failed enterprise." Islas-Veloz, 914 F.3d at 1261 (Fletcher, J., concurring). We should instead recognize that, "[a]bsent consistent or logical rules," Nunez, 594 F.3d at 1131, the phrase "crime involving moral turpitude" is unconstitutionally vague.

I recognize that history is not on our side. The term "crime involving moral turpitude" has persisted in our immigration law since 1891, and in our common law tradition for nearly a century longer. See Julia Ann Simon-Kerr, Moral Turpitude, 2012 Utah L. Rev. 1001, 1010, 1039. Indeed, in holding in 1951 that the term was not void for vagueness, the Supreme Court thought it "significant that the phrase has been part of the immigration laws for more than sixty years." De George, 341 U.S. at 229; see also Martinez-de Ryan v. Whitaker, 909 F.3d 247, 252 (9th Cir. 2018). Committed to the principle of stare decisis, we judges are loath to upset long-settled doctrine. As the Supreme Court has recognized, however, "stare decisis does not matter for its own sake. It matters because it 'promotes the evenhanded, predictable, and consistent development of legal principles.'" Johnson, 135 S. Ct. at 2563 (quoting Payne v. Tennessee, 501 U.S. 808, 827 (1991)).

In Johnson, the Court recognized that "[d]ecisions under the residual clause have proved to be anything but evenhanded, predictable, or consistent." Id. The same is true of our tortured attempts to find logical consistency in the term "moral turpitude." Especially given the revitalization of the void-for-vagueness doctrine in Johnson and Sessions v. Dimaya, 138 S. Ct. 1204 (2018), the time is ripe for reconsideration of this issue.